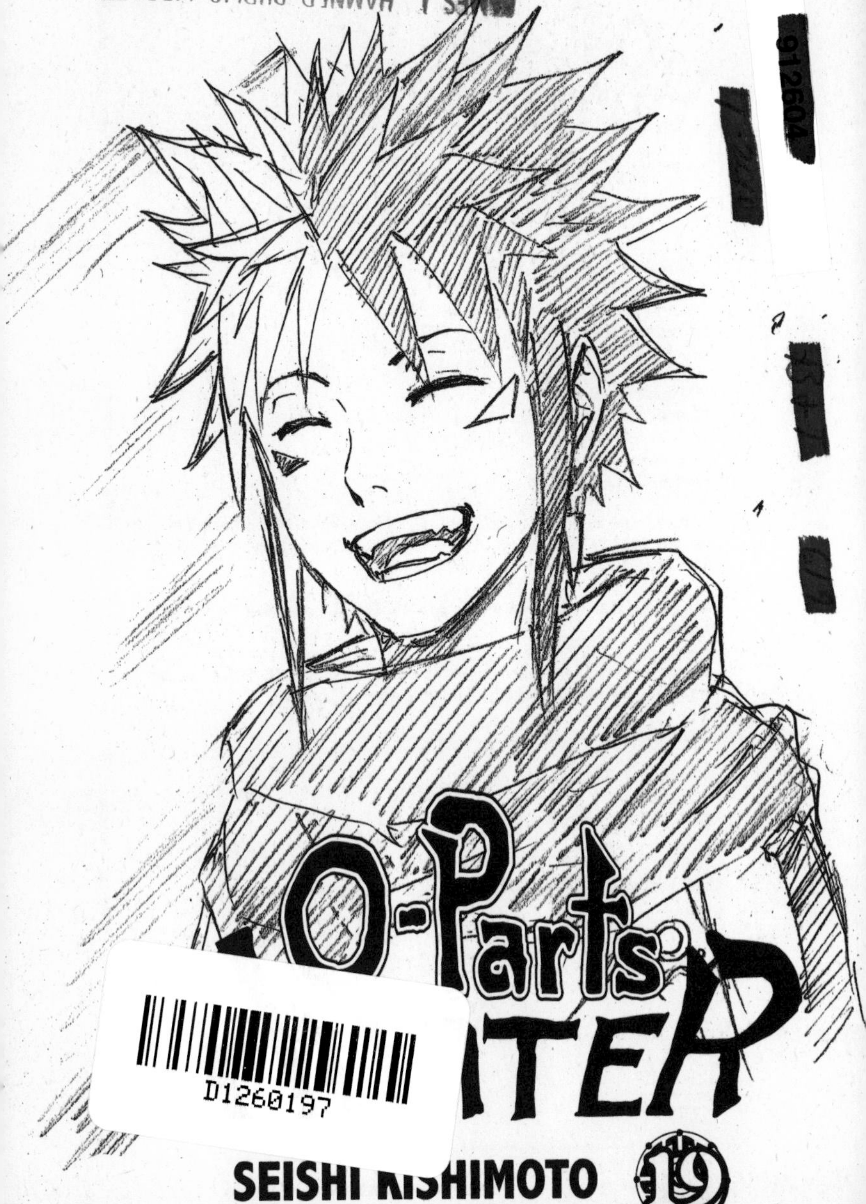
O-Parts
TER

SEISHI KISHIMOTO

19

O-Parts Hunter™ 19

VIZ Media Edition
STORY AND ART BY SEISHI KISHIMOTO

English Adaptation/David R. Valois
Translation/Tetsuichiro Miyaki
Touch-up Art & Lettering/HudsonYards
Design/Andrea Rice
Editor/Gary Leach

VP, Production/Alvin Lu
VP, Publishing Licensing/Rika Inouye
VP, Sales & Product Marketing/Gonzalo Ferreyra
VP, Creative/Linda Espinosa
Publisher/Hyoe Narita

Printed in the U.S.A.

Published by VIZ Media, LLC
P.O. Box 77010
San Francisco, CA 94107

10 9 8 7 6 5 4 3 2 1
First printing, December 2009

www.viz.com

RATED T+ FOR OLDER TEEN

PARENTAL ADVISORY
O-PARTS HUNTER is rated T+ for Older Teen and is recommended for ages 16 and up. This volume contains realistic and fantasy violence and adult situations.

ratings.viz.com

SEISHI KISHIMOTO

Thank you very much for showing your support over the course of this series. This is the last you'll see of that demon, but just in case, let me drive all the evil spirits away from you. Yeeeeeaaargh!

CHARACTERS of O-Parts HUNTER

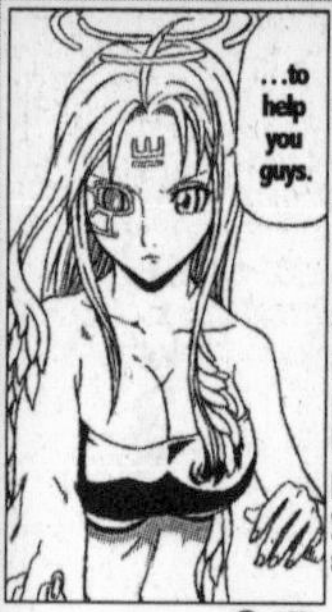
...to help you guys.

Having gotten close to her true Angel form, she is now able to wield Sandalphon's powers, but her true powers are yet to be seen...

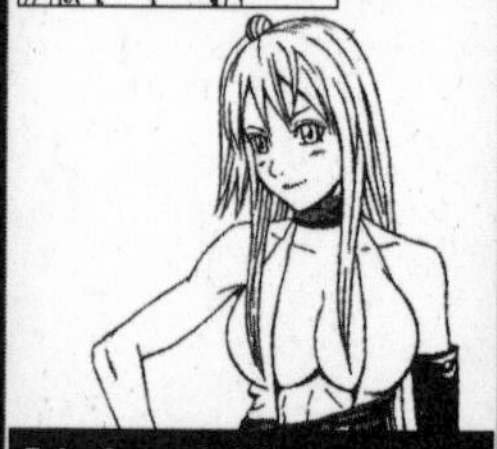

Ruby Crescent: A treasure hunter in search of the Legendary O-Part and her missing father. Rescued from Stea HQ, she turns out to be a Recipe for the Kabbalah. Jio brings her back into this world.

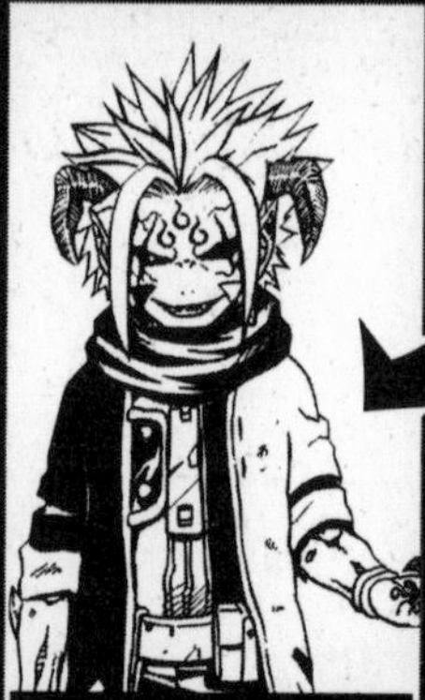

Satan: An alternate personality that exists inside Jio's body. The ultimate weapon of the Kabbalah who holds earth-shattering powers.

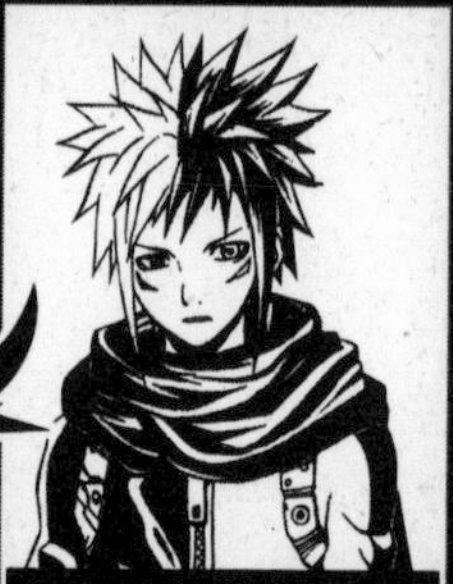

Jio Freed: A wild O.P.T. boy whose dream is world domination. He has been emotionally hurt from his experiences in the past but has become strong after meeting Ruby. Ever since the Rock Bird incident, he has had Ruby's soul inside him.

Jio's Friends

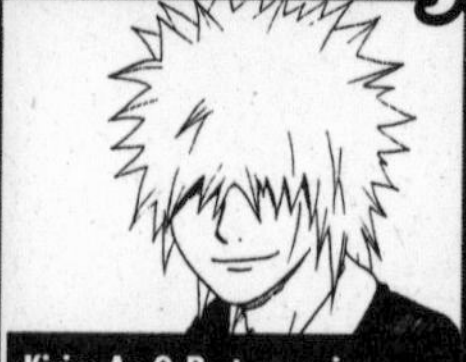

Kirin: An O-Part appraiser and a master of dodging attacks. He trained Jio and Ball into strong O.P.T.s.

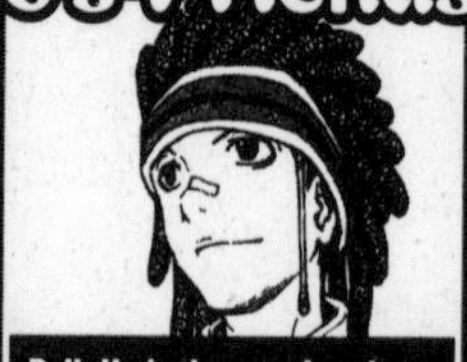

Ball: He is the mood-maker of the group and the kind of person who cares about his friends.

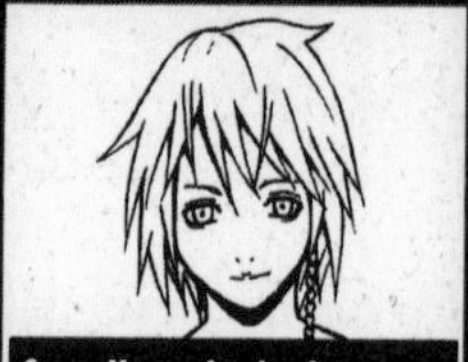

Cross: He used to be the Commander in Chief of the Stea Government's battleship. He and Jio have become good friends.

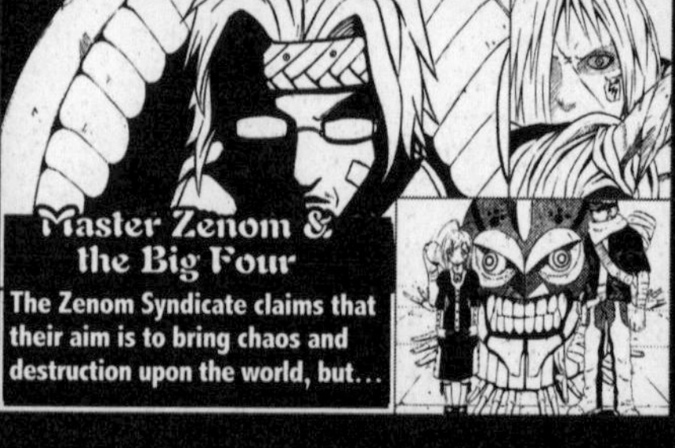

Master Zenom & the Big Four

The Zenom Syndicate claims that their aim is to bring chaos and destruction upon the world, but...

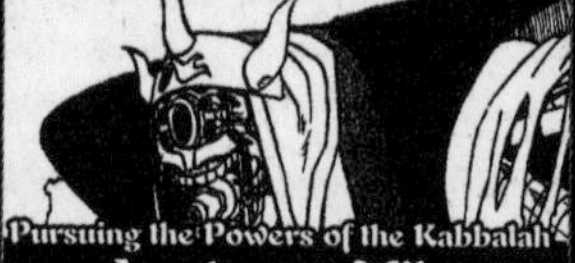

Pursuing the Powers of the Kabbalah

Amaterasu Miko

The leader of the Stea Government and the person who turned it into a huge military machine. She now controls Shin.

KABBALAH

the keyword of 666

A legacy left by the Ancient Race who are said to have come from the Blue Planet. The Kabbalah is the Ultimate Memorization Weapon, which absorbs every kind of "information" that makes up this world, and evolves along with the passing of time! It consists of two counterparts, the Formal Kabbalah and the Reverse Kabbalah.

10i
Nahema
(Materialism)
9i
Lilith
(Instability)
7i
Baal
(Lust)
8i
Adramelech
(Avarice)
6i
Belphegor
(Odious-
ness)
4i
Astaroth
(Apathy)
5i
Asmodeus
(Cruelty)
2i
Beelzebub
(Stupidity)
3i
Lucifuge
(Rejection)
1i
Satan
(Atheism)

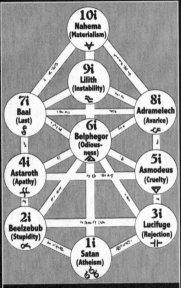

Reverse Kabbalah

The symbol of destruction with the names of the powerful archdemons listed on the sephirot from one to ten.

1
Metatron
(Crown)
3
Zaphkiel
(Understand-
ing)
2
Raziel
(Wisdom)
5
Samael
(Might)
4
Zadkiel
(Benevo-
lence)
6
Michael
(Beauty)
8
Raphael
(Splendor)
7
Haniel
(Victory)
9
Gabriel
(Foundation)
10
Sandalphon
(Kingdom)

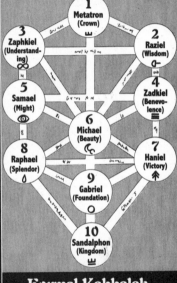

Formal Kabbalah

The symbol of creation with the names of the great archangels listed on the sephirot from one to ten.

STORY

Ascald: a world where people fight amongst themselves to get their hands on mystical objects left behind by an ancient civilization…the O-Parts.

In that world, a monster that strikes fear into the hearts of the strongest of men is rumored to exist. Those who have seen the monster all tell of the same thing–that the number of the beast, 666, is engraved on its forehead.

***

Miko has taken over Shin and has arrived at the headquarters of the Zenom Syndicate to acquire the Reverse Kabbalah. Jio and his friends, after defeating the Zenom Big Four, reach the throne room of Master Zenom, who has been awaiting their arrival. The final battle is imminent, with the fate of the entire world in the balance!

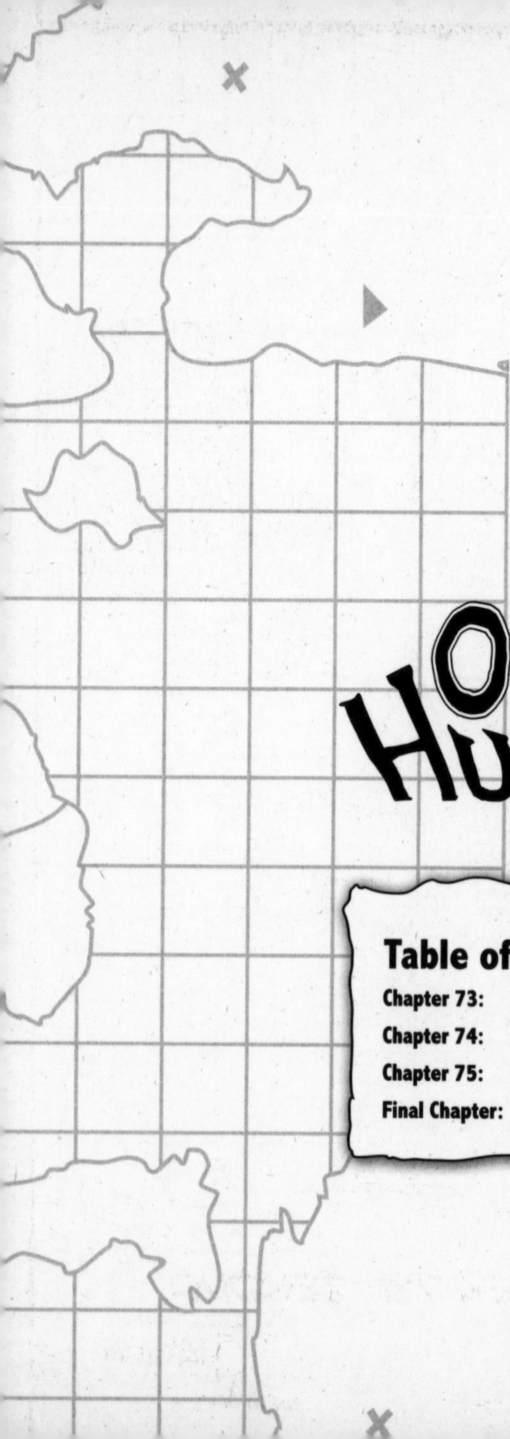

O-Parts Hunter

19

Table of Contents

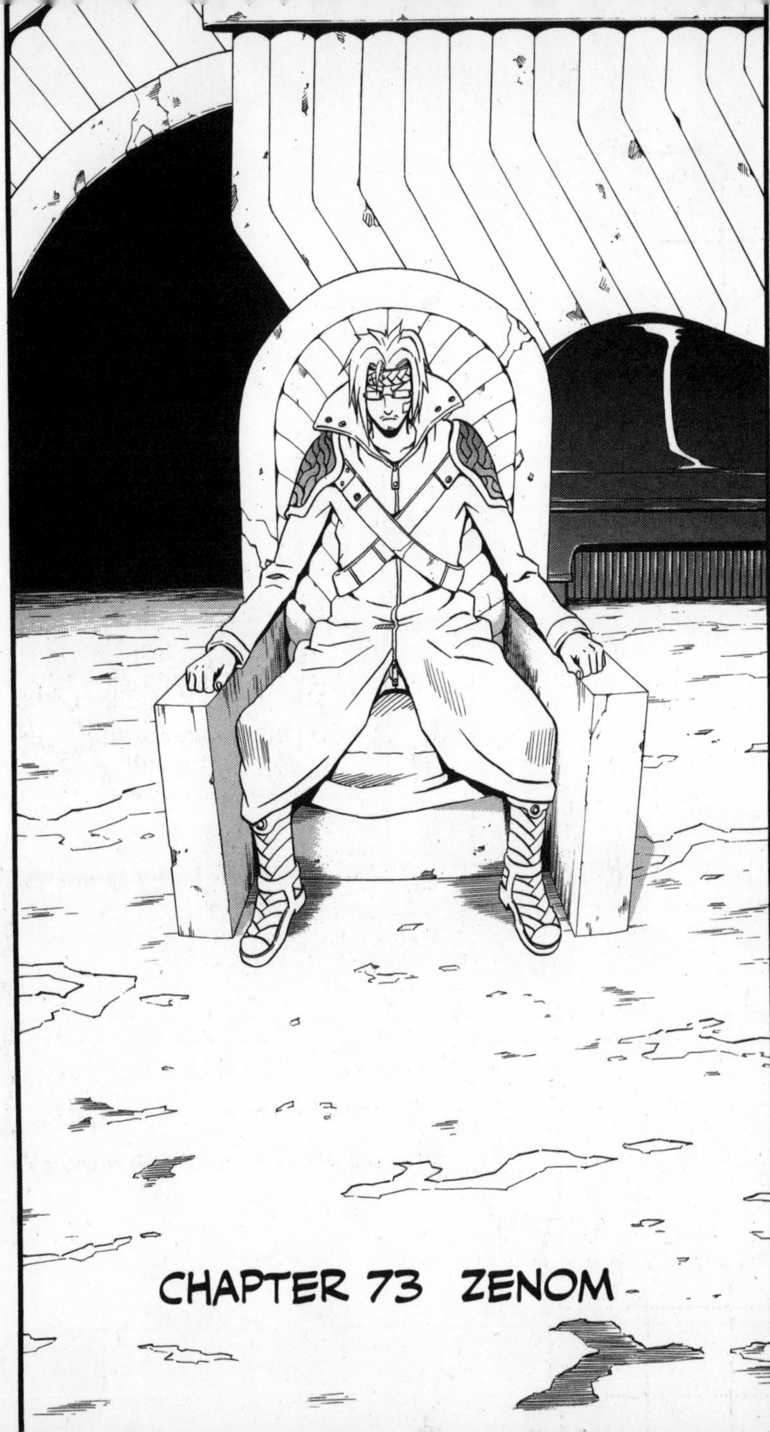
CHAPTER 73 ZENOM

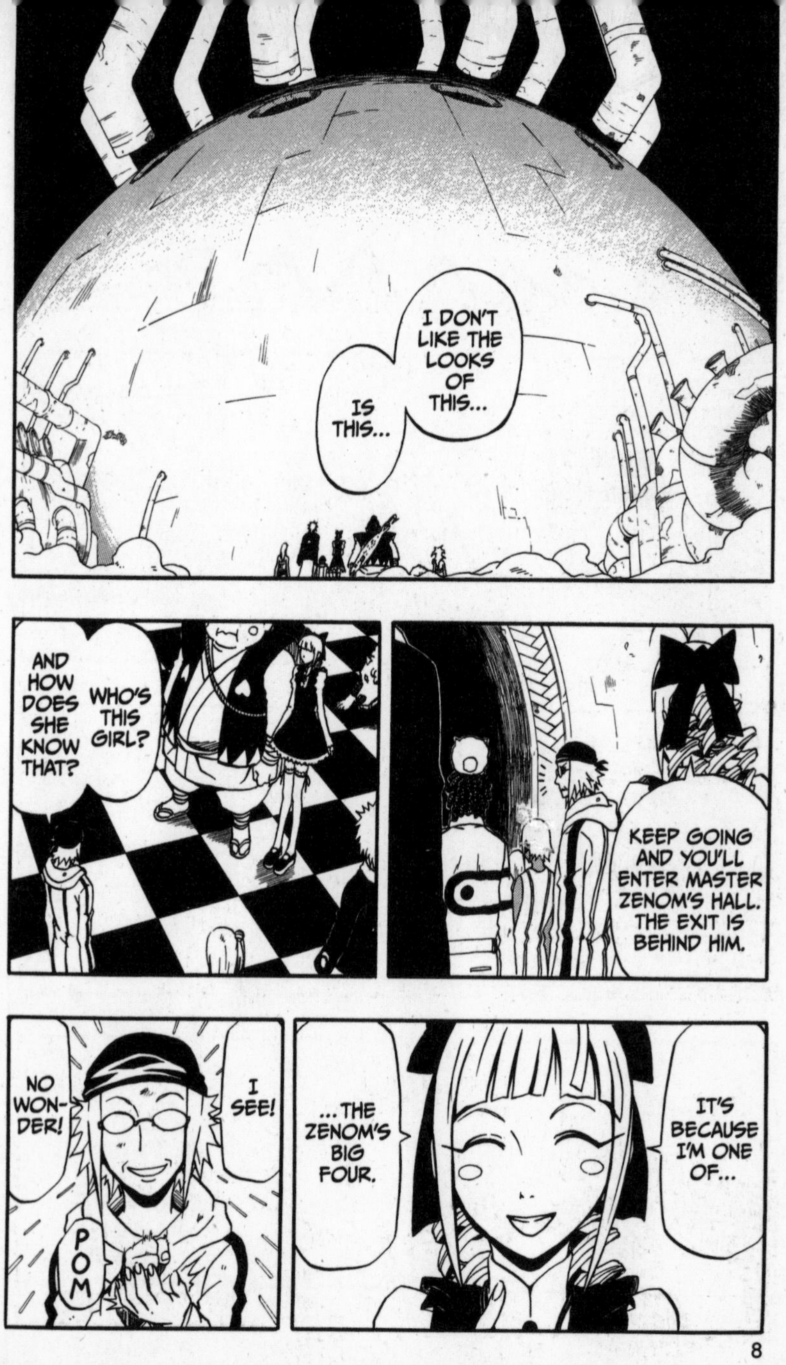
I DON'T LIKE THE LOOKS OF THIS...
IS THIS...
KEEP GOING AND YOU'LL ENTER MASTER ZENOM'S HALL. THE EXIT IS BEHIND HIM.
WHO'S THIS GIRL?
AND HOW DOES SHE KNOW THAT?
IT'S BECAUSE I'M ONE OF...
...THE ZENOM'S BIG FOUR.
I SEE!
NO WONDER!
POM

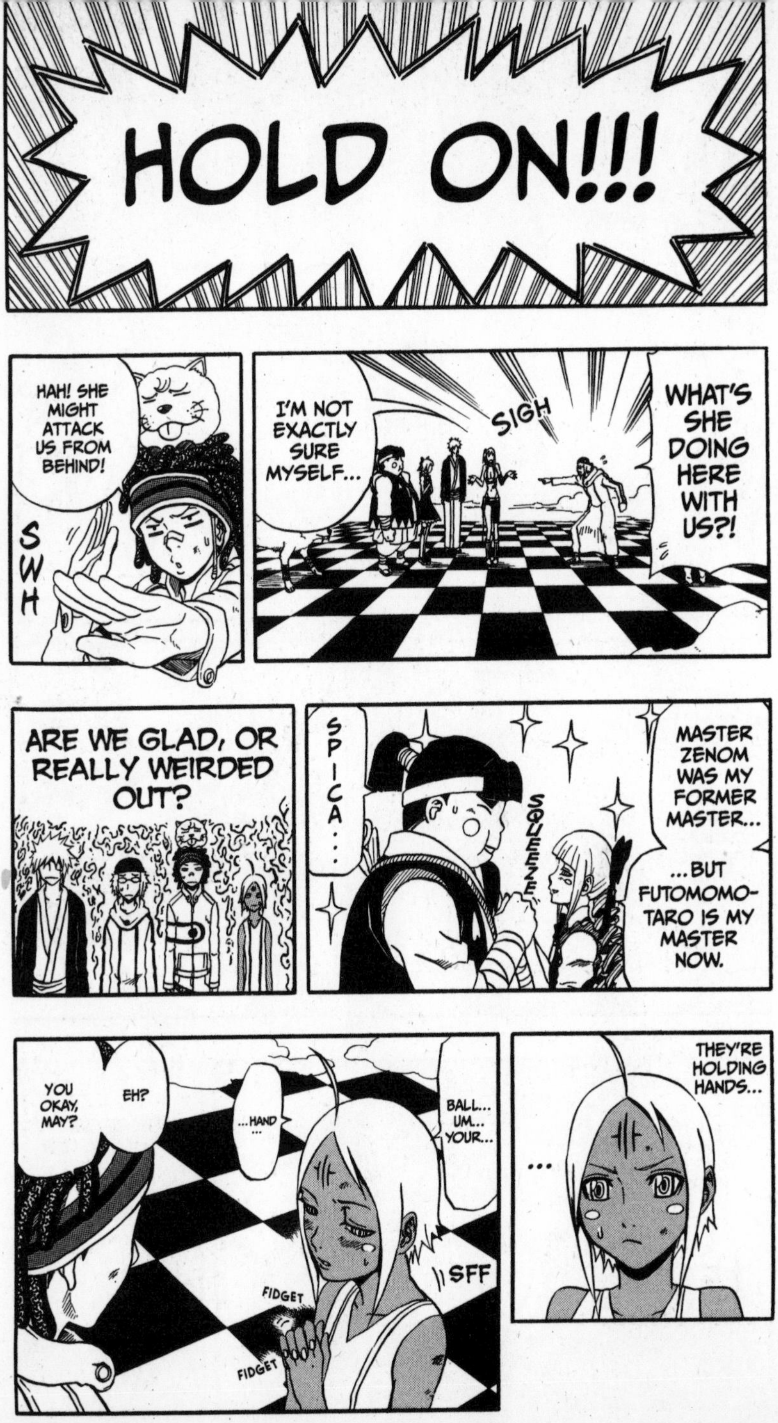
HOLD ON!!!
WHAT'S SHE DOING HERE WITH US?!
SIGH
I'M NOT EXACTLY SURE MYSELF...
HAH! SHE MIGHT ATTACK US FROM BEHIND!
SWH
MASTER ZENOM WAS MY FORMER MASTER...
...BUT FUTOMOMO-TARO IS MY MASTER NOW.
SQUEEZE
SPICA...
ARE WE GLAD, OR REALLY WEIRDED OUT?
THEY'RE HOLDING HANDS...
...
BALL... UM... YOUR...
...HAND...
SFF
EH?
YOU OKAY, MAY?
FIDGET
FIDGET

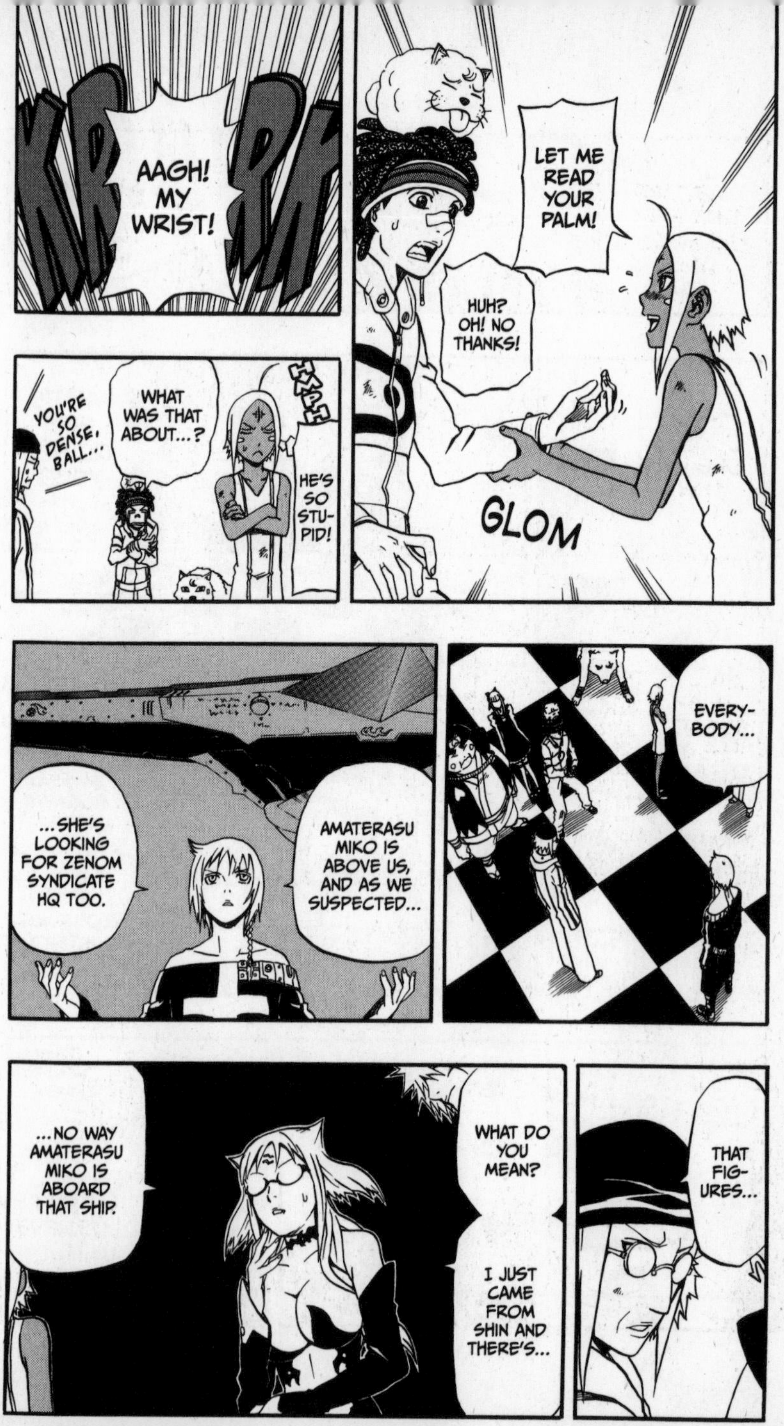
LET ME READ YOUR PALM!
HUH? OH! NO THANKS!
GLOM
AAGH! MY WRIST!
HE'S SO STUPID!
WHAT WAS THAT ABOUT...?
YOU'RE SO DENSE, BALL...
EVERY-BODY...
AMATERASU MIKO IS ABOVE US, AND AS WE SUSPECTED...
...SHE'S LOOKING FOR ZENOM SYNDICATE HQ TOO.
THAT FIG-URES...
WHAT DO YOU MEAN?
I JUST CAME FROM SHIN AND THERE'S...
...NO WAY AMATERASU MIKO IS ABOARD THAT SHIP.

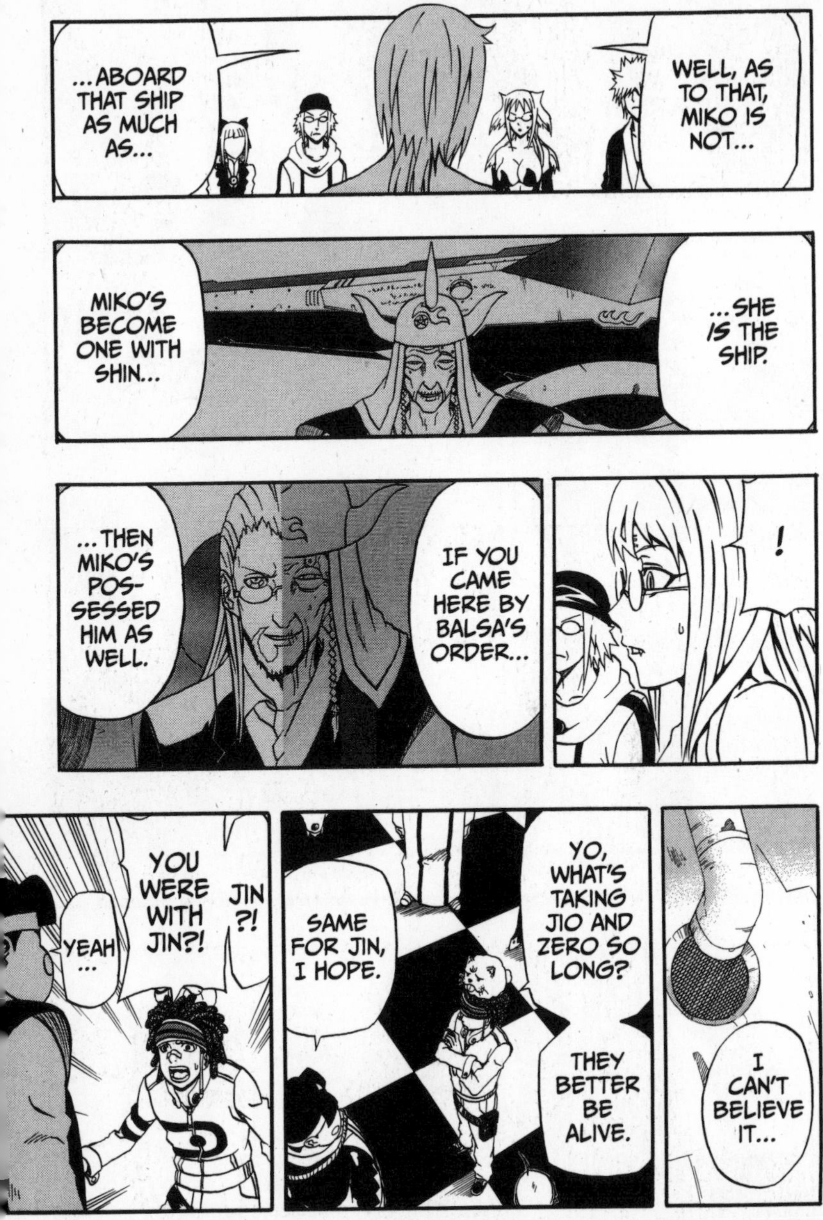
WELL, AS TO THAT, MIKO IS NOT...
...ABOARD THAT SHIP AS MUCH AS...
...SHE IS THE SHIP.
MIKO'S BECOME ONE WITH SHIN...
!
IF YOU CAME HERE BY BALSA'S ORDER...
...THEN MIKO'S POS-SESSED HIM AS WELL.
I CAN'T BELIEVE IT...
YO, WHAT'S TAKING JIO AND ZERO SO LONG?
THEY BETTER BE ALIVE.
SAME FOR JIN, I HOPE.
JIN ?!
YOU WERE WITH JIN?!
YEAH ...

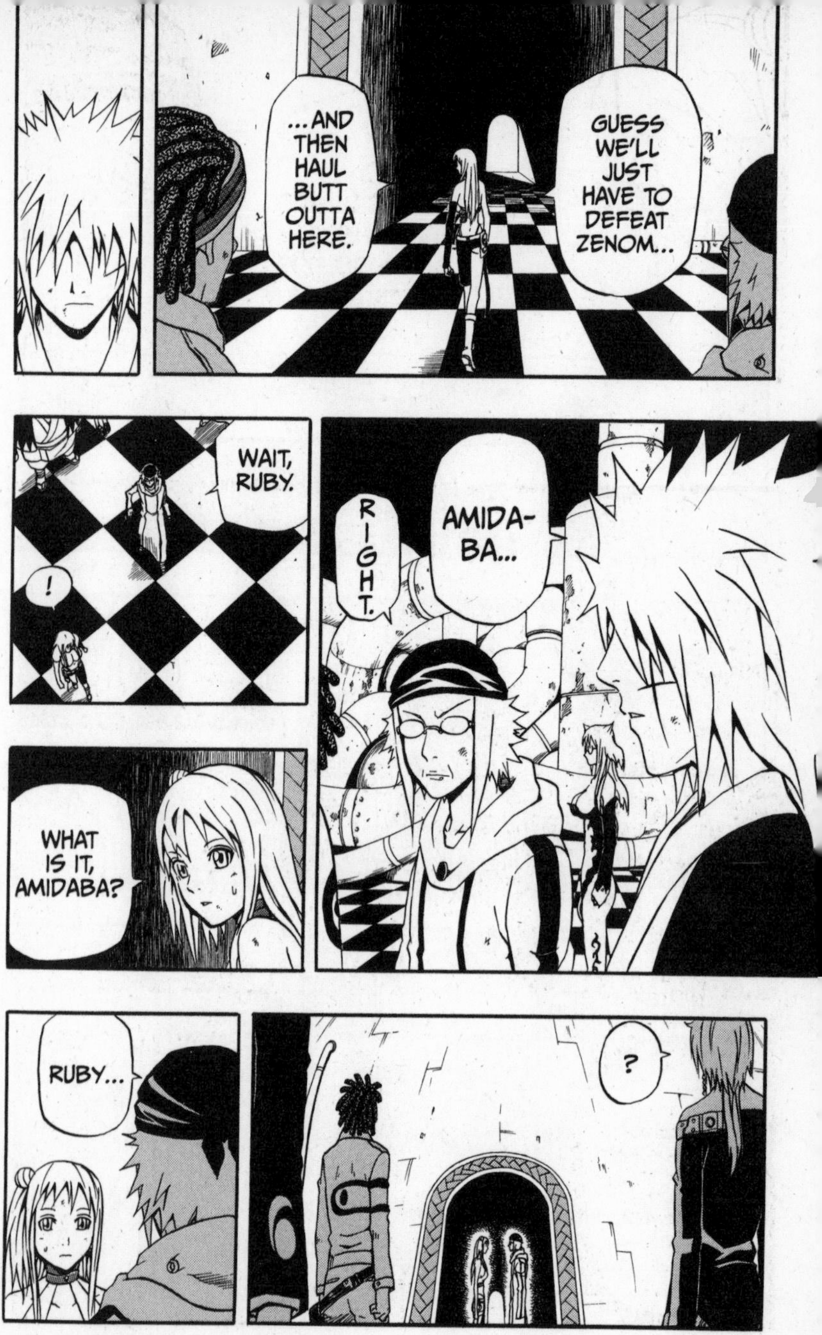
GUESS WE'LL JUST HAVE TO DEFEAT ZENOM...
...AND THEN HAUL BUTT OUTTA HERE.
AMIDA-BA...
RIGHT.
WAIT, RUBY.
!
WHAT IS IT, AMIDABA?
?
RUBY...

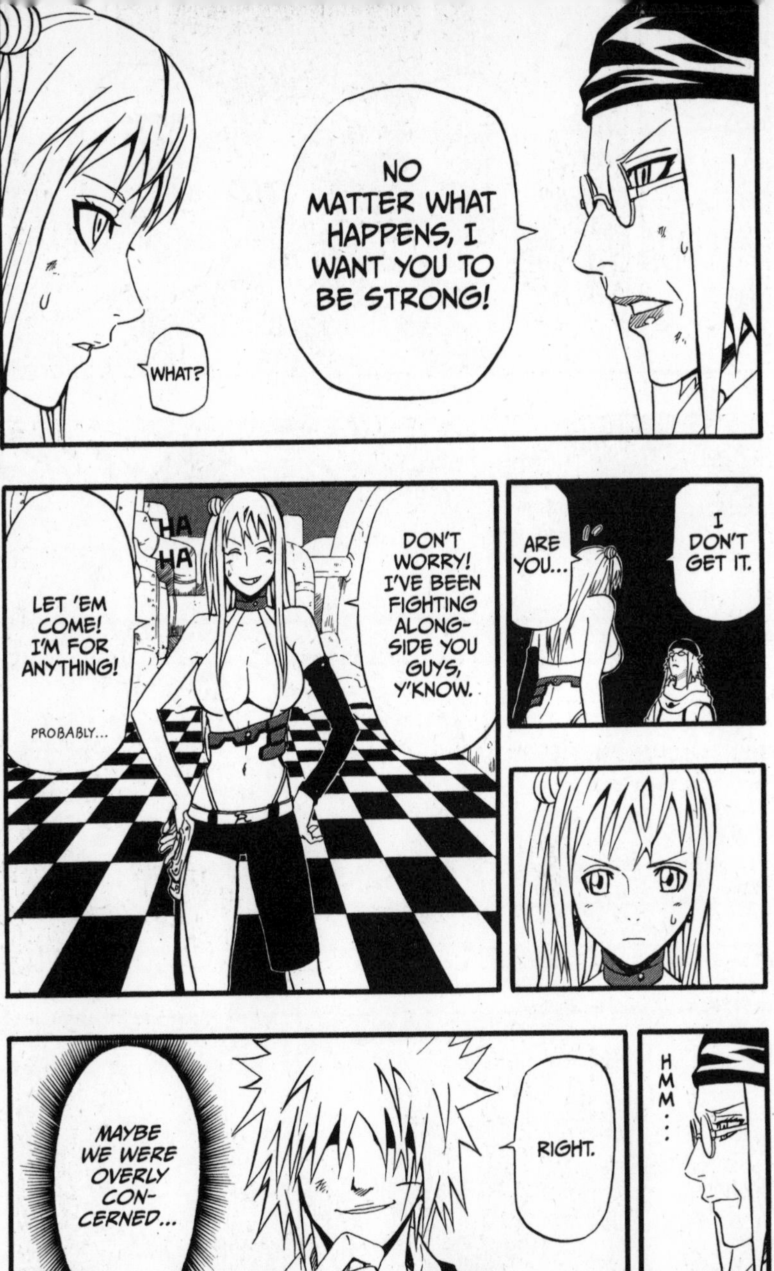
NO MATTER WHAT HAPPENS, I WANT YOU TO BE STRONG!
WHAT?
I DON'T GET IT.
ARE YOU...
DON'T WORRY! I'VE BEEN FIGHTING ALONG-SIDE YOU GUYS, Y'KNOW.
HA HA
LET 'EM COME! I'M FOR ANYTHING!
PROBABLY...
HMM...
RIGHT.
MAYBE WE WERE OVERLY CON-CERNED...

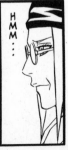

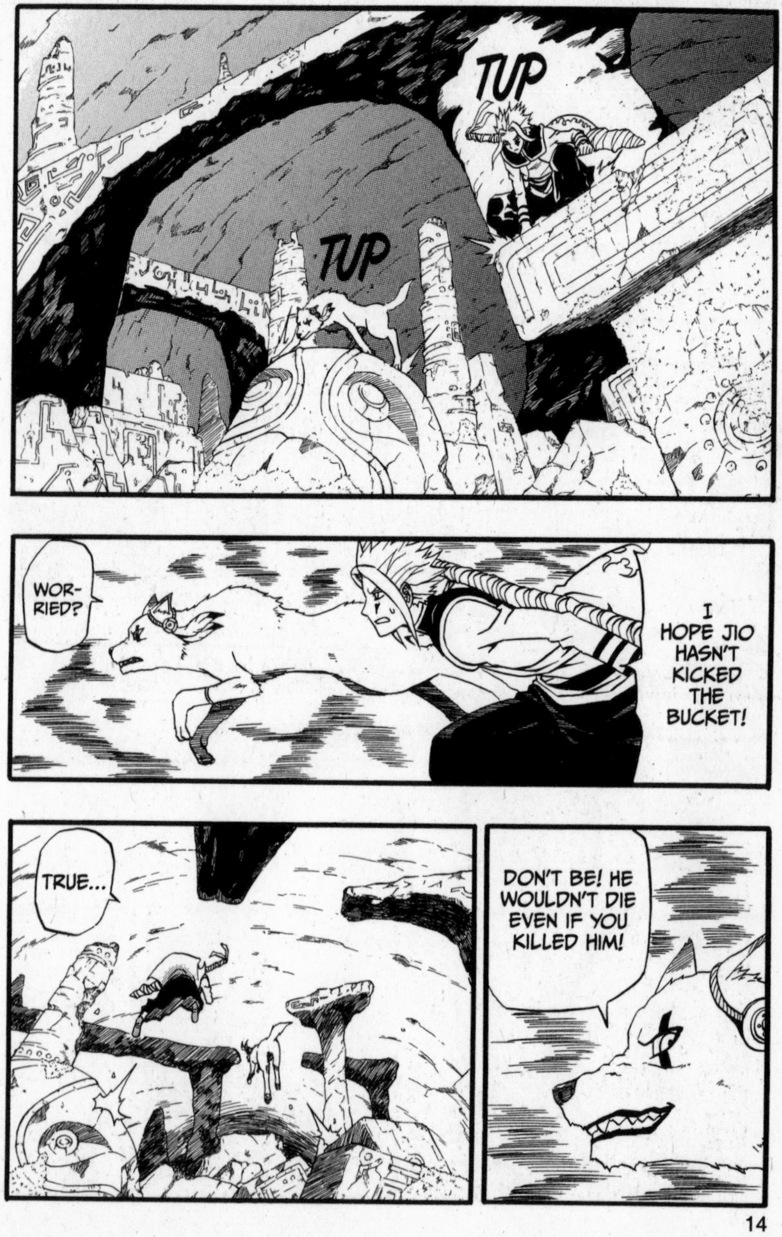
TUP
TUP
I HOPE JIO HASN'T KICKED THE BUCKET!
WOR-RIED?
DON'T BE! HE WOULDN'T DIE EVEN IF YOU KILLED HIM!
TRUE...

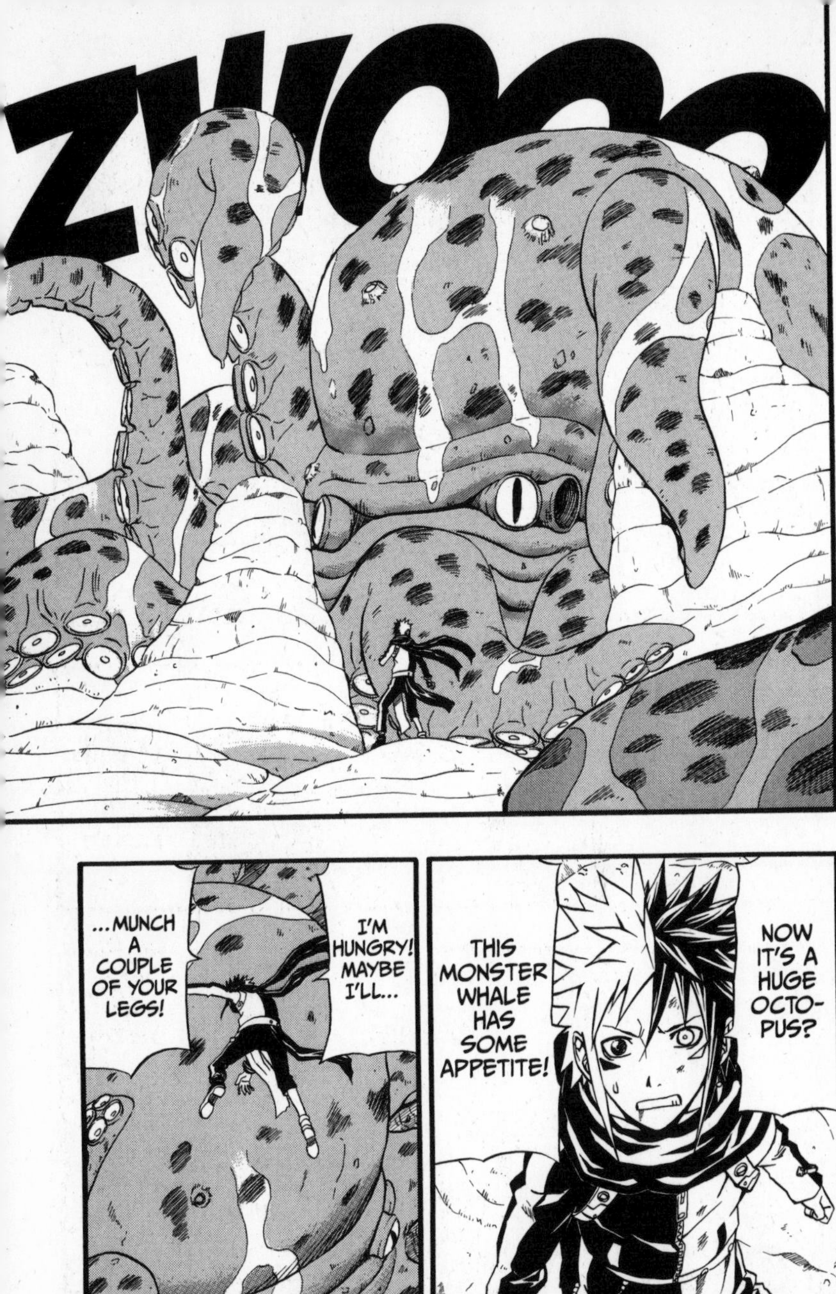
ZWOOO
NOW IT'S A HUGE OCTO-PUS?
THIS MONSTER WHALE HAS SOME APPETITE!
I'M HUNGRY! MAYBE I'LL...
...MUNCH A COUPLE OF YOUR LEGS!

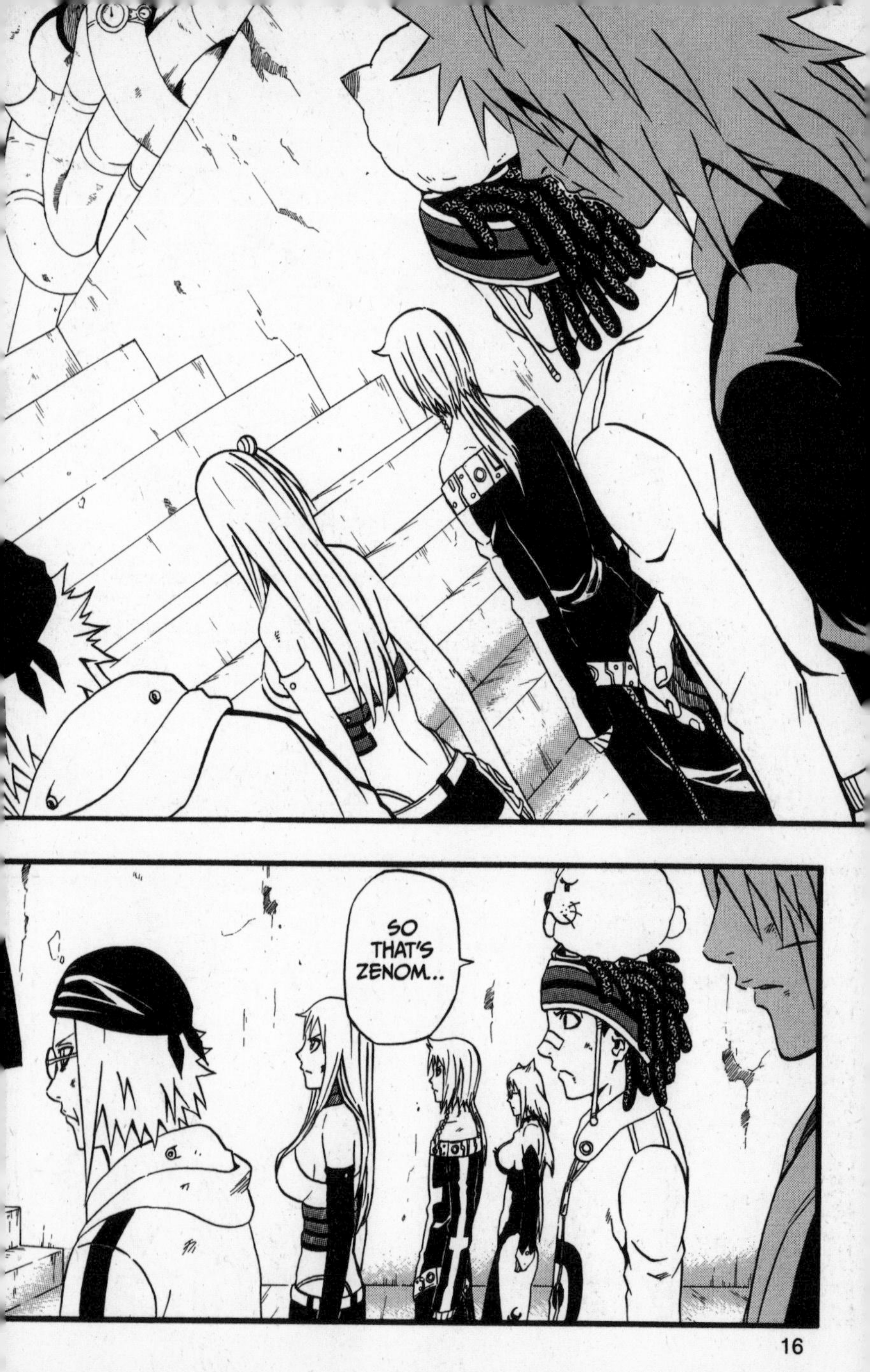
SO THAT'S ZENOM...

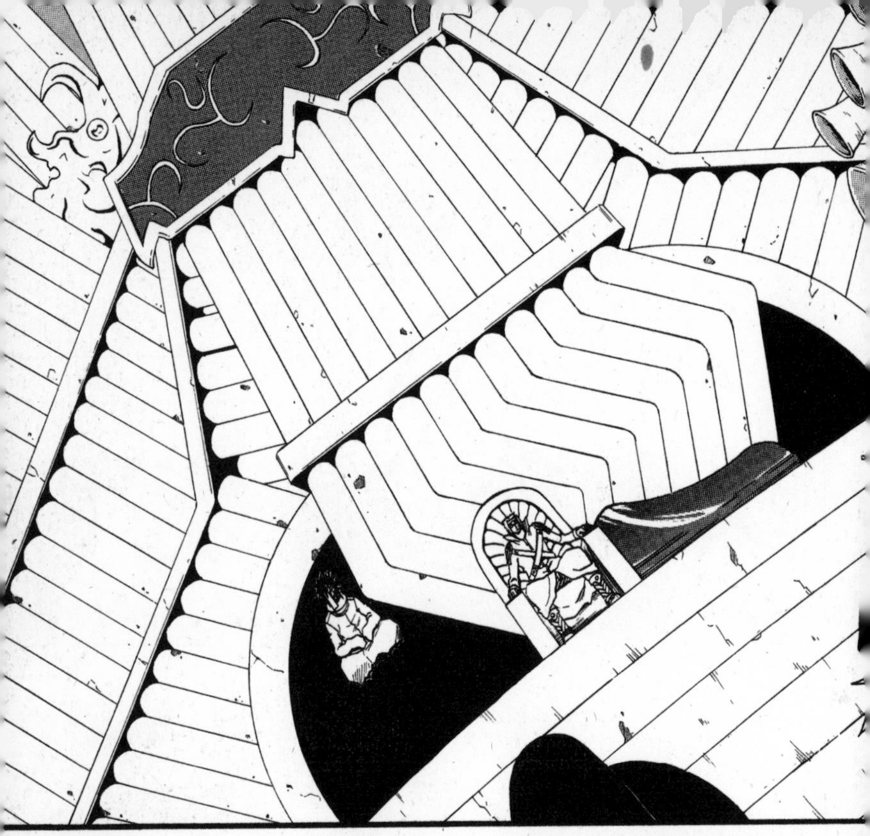

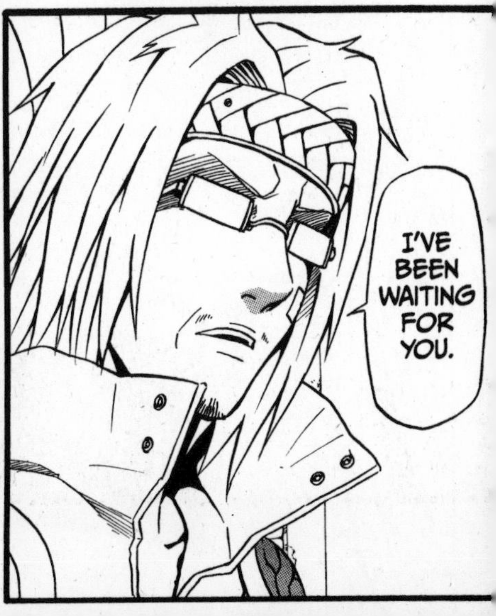
I'VE BEEN WAITING FOR YOU.

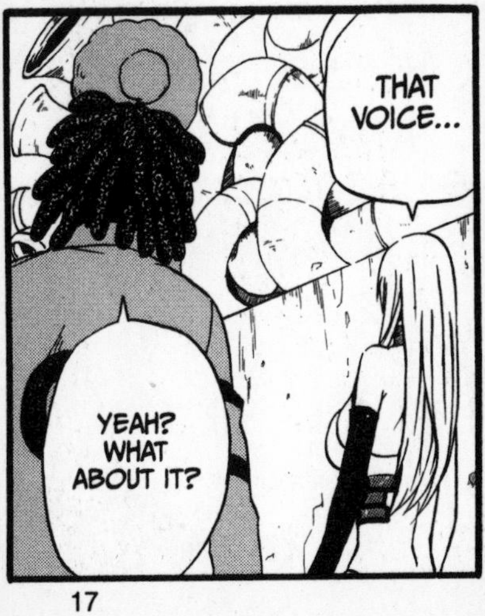
THAT VOICE...
YEAH? WHAT ABOUT IT?

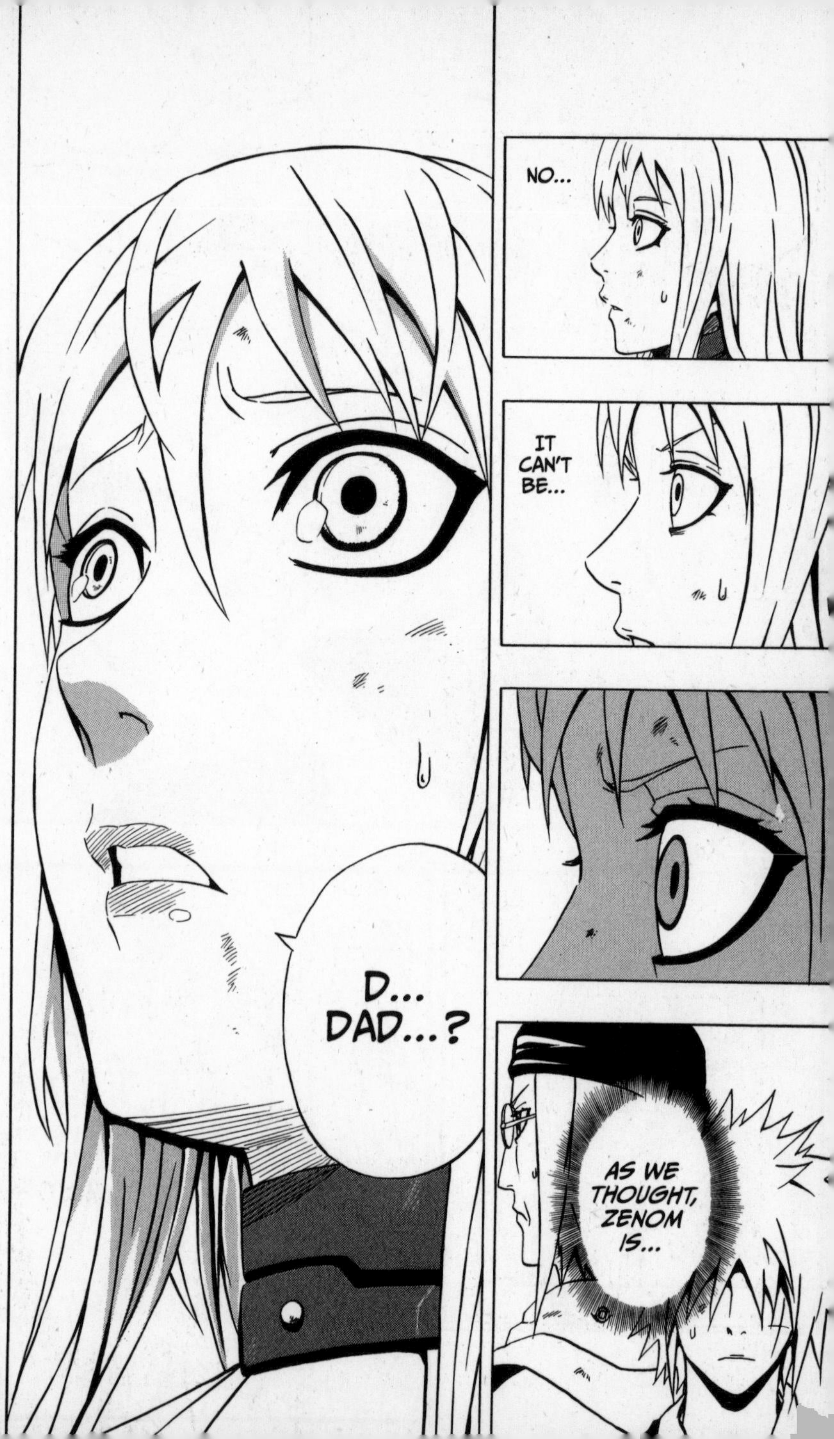
NO...
IT CAN'T BE...
AS WE THOUGHT, ZENOM IS...
D... DAD...?

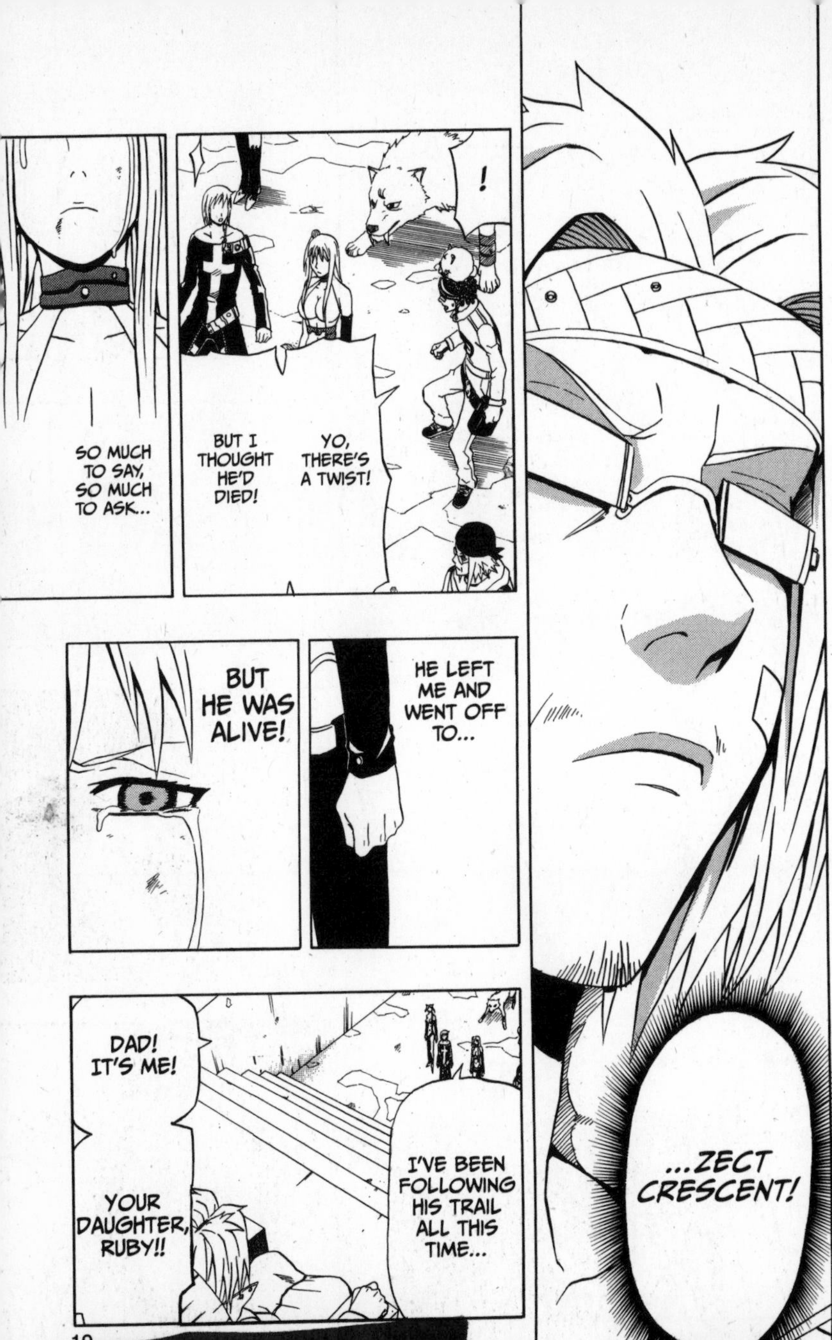
...ZECT CRESCENT!
YO, THERE'S A TWIST!
BUT I THOUGHT HE'D DIED!
SO MUCH TO SAY, SO MUCH TO ASK...
HE LEFT ME AND WENT OFF TO...
BUT HE WAS ALIVE!
I'VE BEEN FOLLOWING HIS TRAIL ALL THIS TIME...
DAD! IT'S ME!
YOUR DAUGHTER, RUBY!!

[redacted]

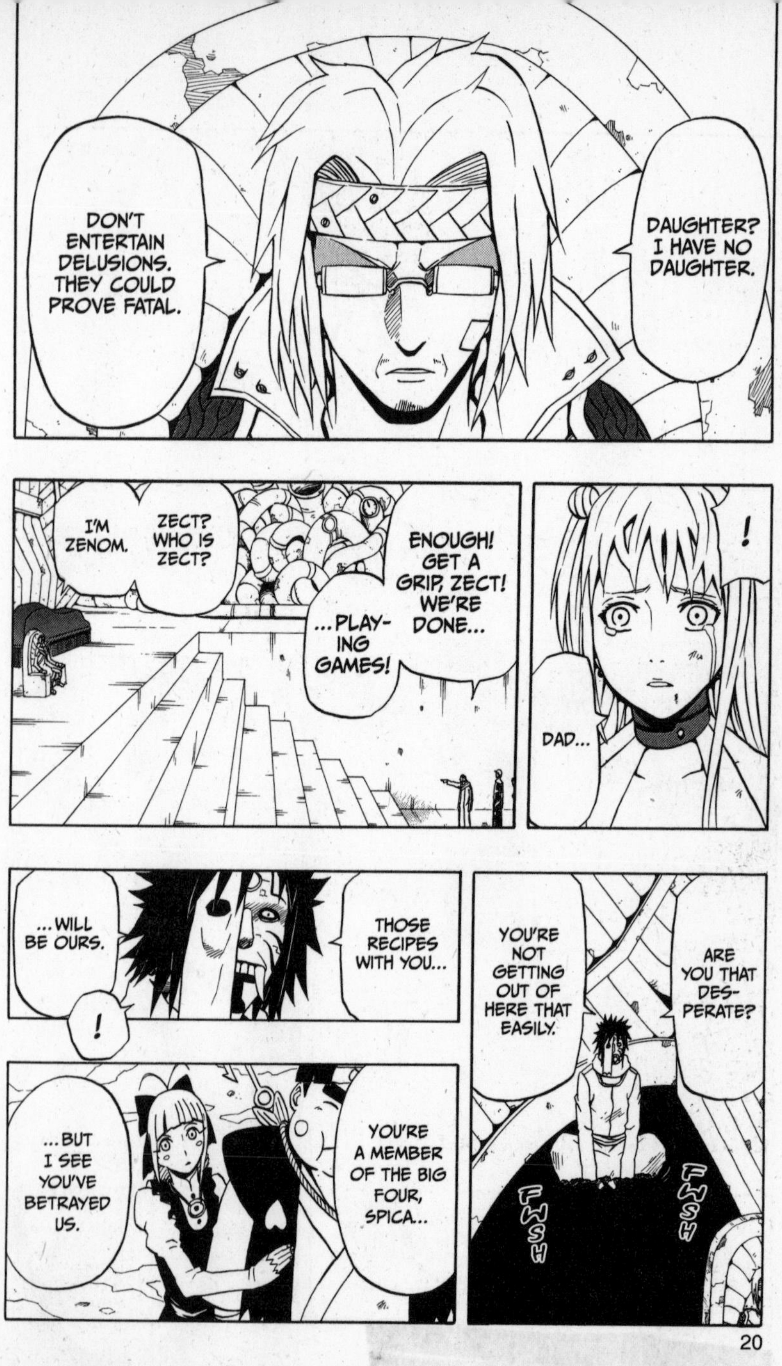
DAUGHTER? I HAVE NO DAUGHTER.
DON'T ENTERTAIN DELUSIONS. THEY COULD PROVE FATAL.
!
DAD...
ENOUGH! GET A GRIP, ZECT! WE'RE DONE...
...PLAY-ING GAMES!
ZECT? WHO IS ZECT?
I'M ZENOM.
ARE YOU THAT DES-PERATE?
YOU'RE NOT GETTING OUT OF HERE THAT EASILY.
FWSH
FWSH
THOSE RECIPES WITH YOU...
...WILL BE OURS.
!
YOU'RE A MEMBER OF THE BIG FOUR, SPICA...
...BUT I SEE YOU'VE BETRAYED US.

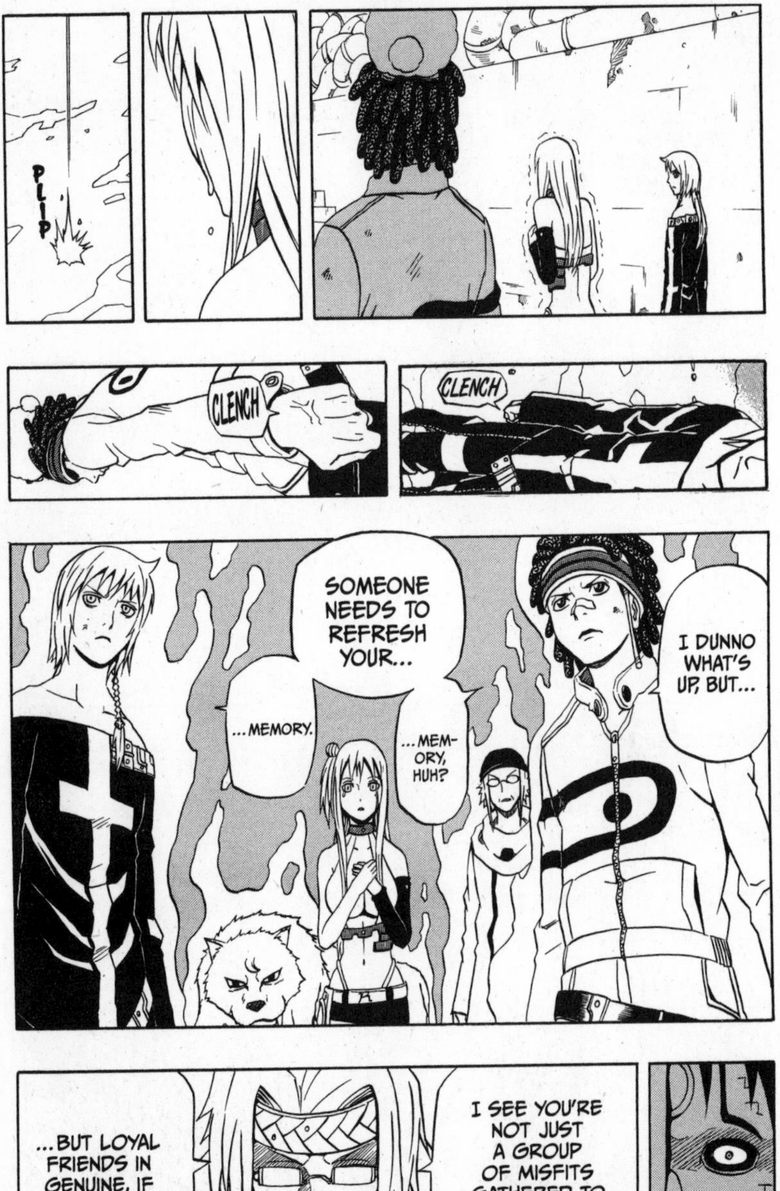
PLIP
CLENCH
CLENCH
I DUNNO WHAT'S UP, BUT...
SOMEONE NEEDS TO REFRESH YOUR...
...MEMORY.
...MEM-ORY, HUH?
I SEE YOU'RE NOT JUST A GROUP OF MISFITS GATHERED TO ACHIEVE SOME COMMON GOAL...
...BUT LOYAL FRIENDS IN GENUINE, IF HAPHAZARD, UNITY.

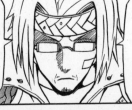

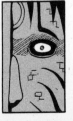

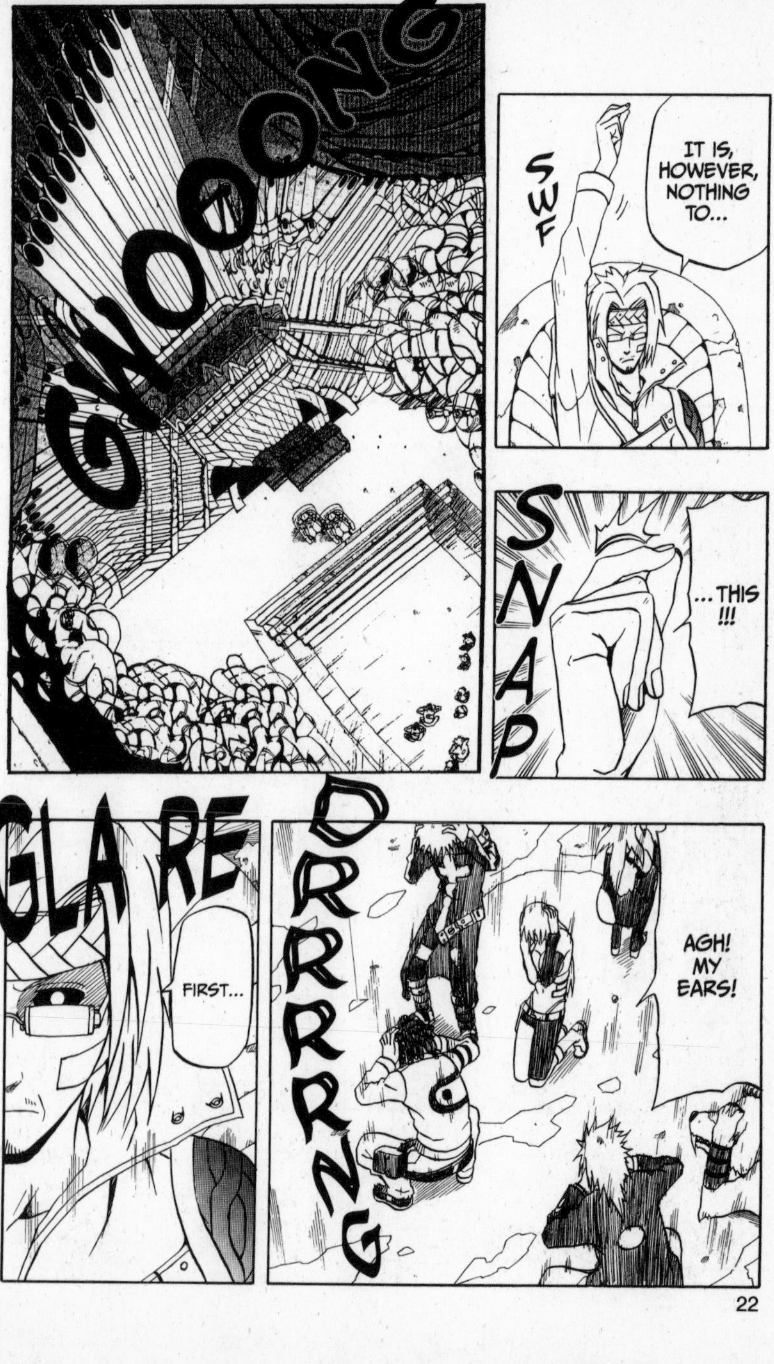
SWF
IT IS, HOWEVER, NOTHING TO...
SNAP
...THIS !!!
GWOOONG
DRRRRNG
AGH! MY EARS!
GLARE
FIRST...

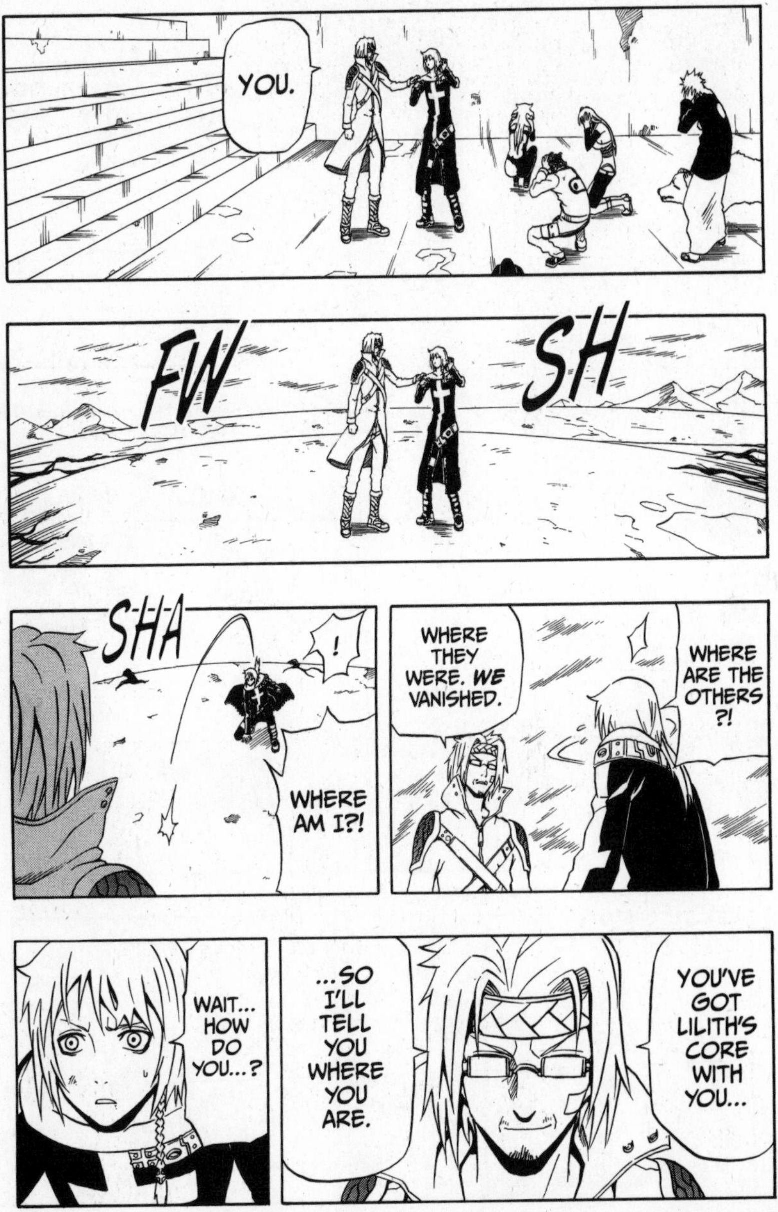
YOU.
SH
FW
WHERE ARE THE OTHERS?!
WHERE THEY WERE. *WE* VANISHED.
!
SHA
WHERE AM I?!
YOU'VE GOT LILITH'S CORE WITH YOU...
...SO I'LL TELL YOU WHERE YOU ARE.
WAIT... HOW DO YOU...?

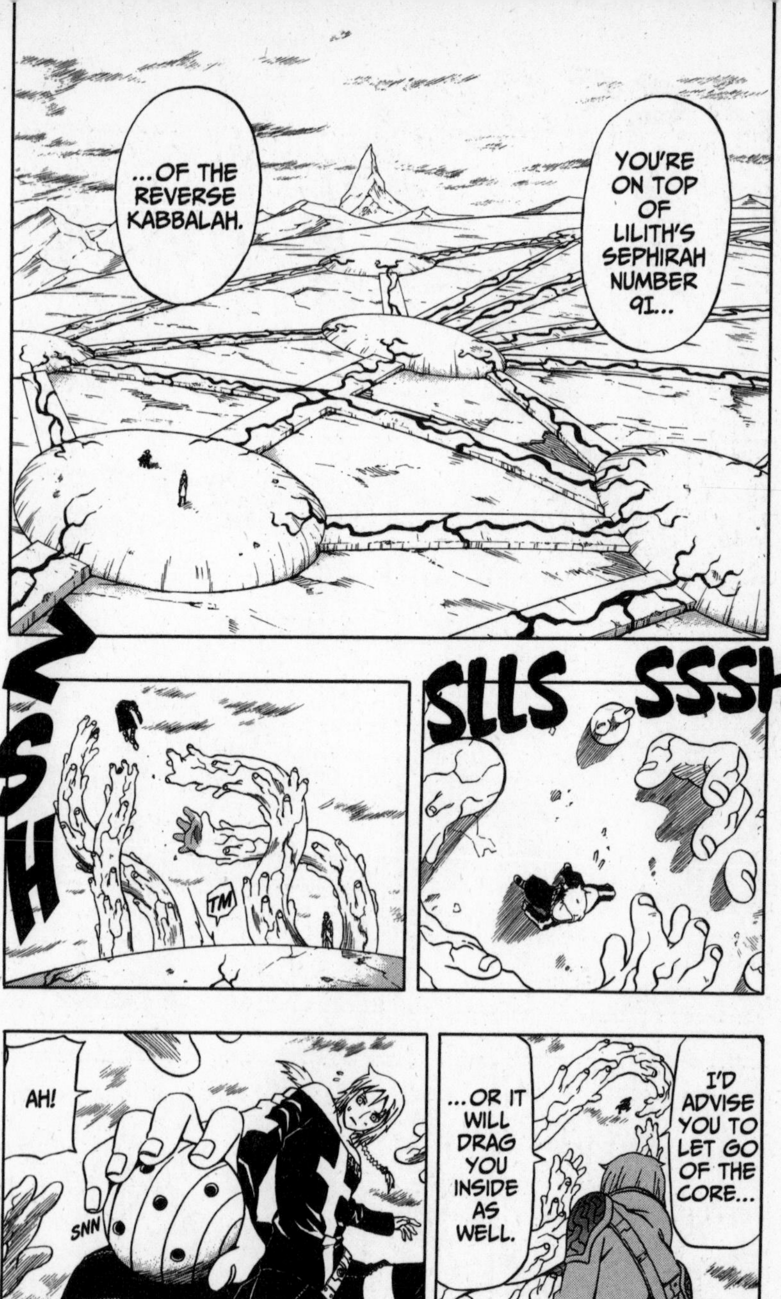
YOU'RE ON TOP OF LILITH'S SEPHIRAH NUMBER 91...
...OF THE REVERSE KABBALAH.
SLLS SSSH
ZSSH
TM
I'D ADVISE YOU TO LET GO OF THE CORE...
...OR IT WILL DRAG YOU INSIDE AS WELL.
AH!
SNN

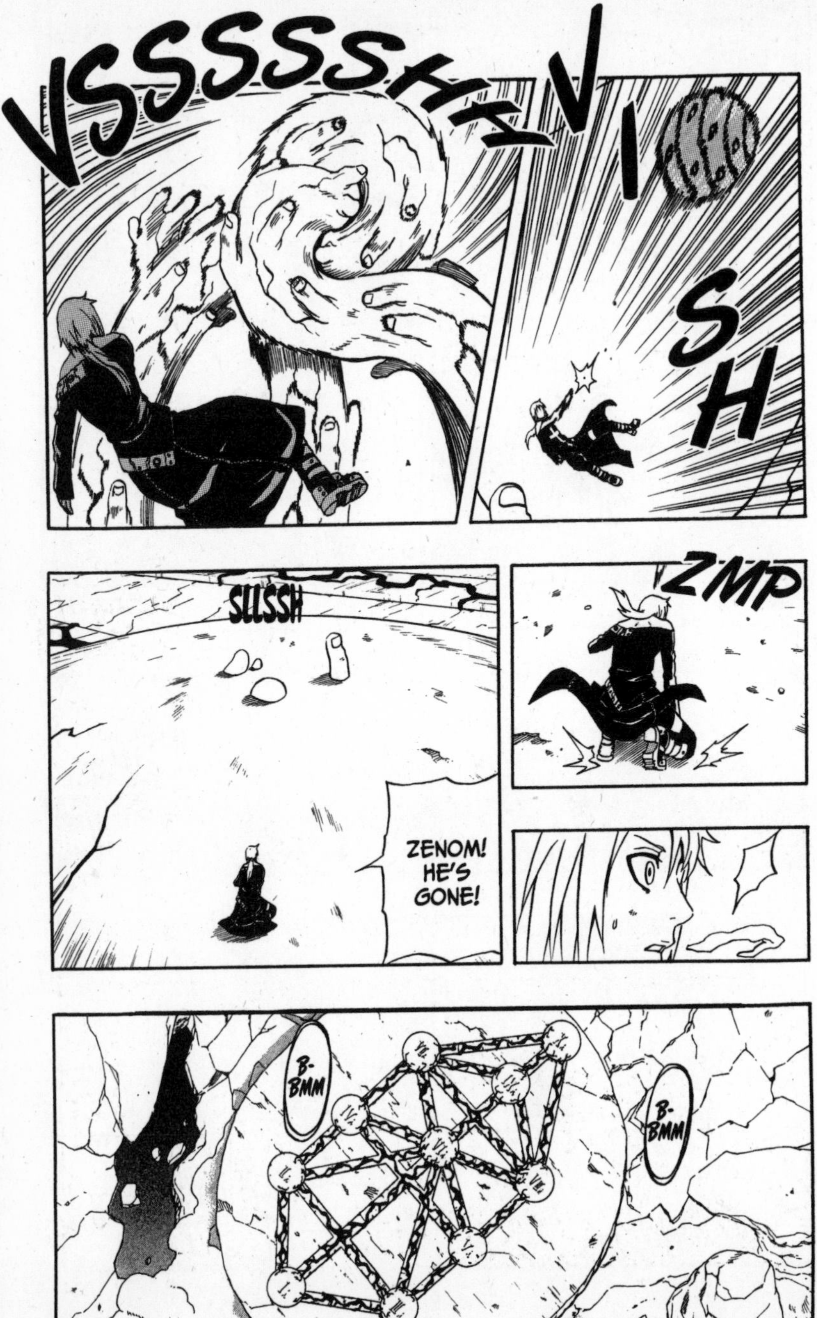
VISH
VSSSSSHH
ZMP
SLISSH
ZENOM! HE'S GONE!
B-BMM
B-BMM
B-

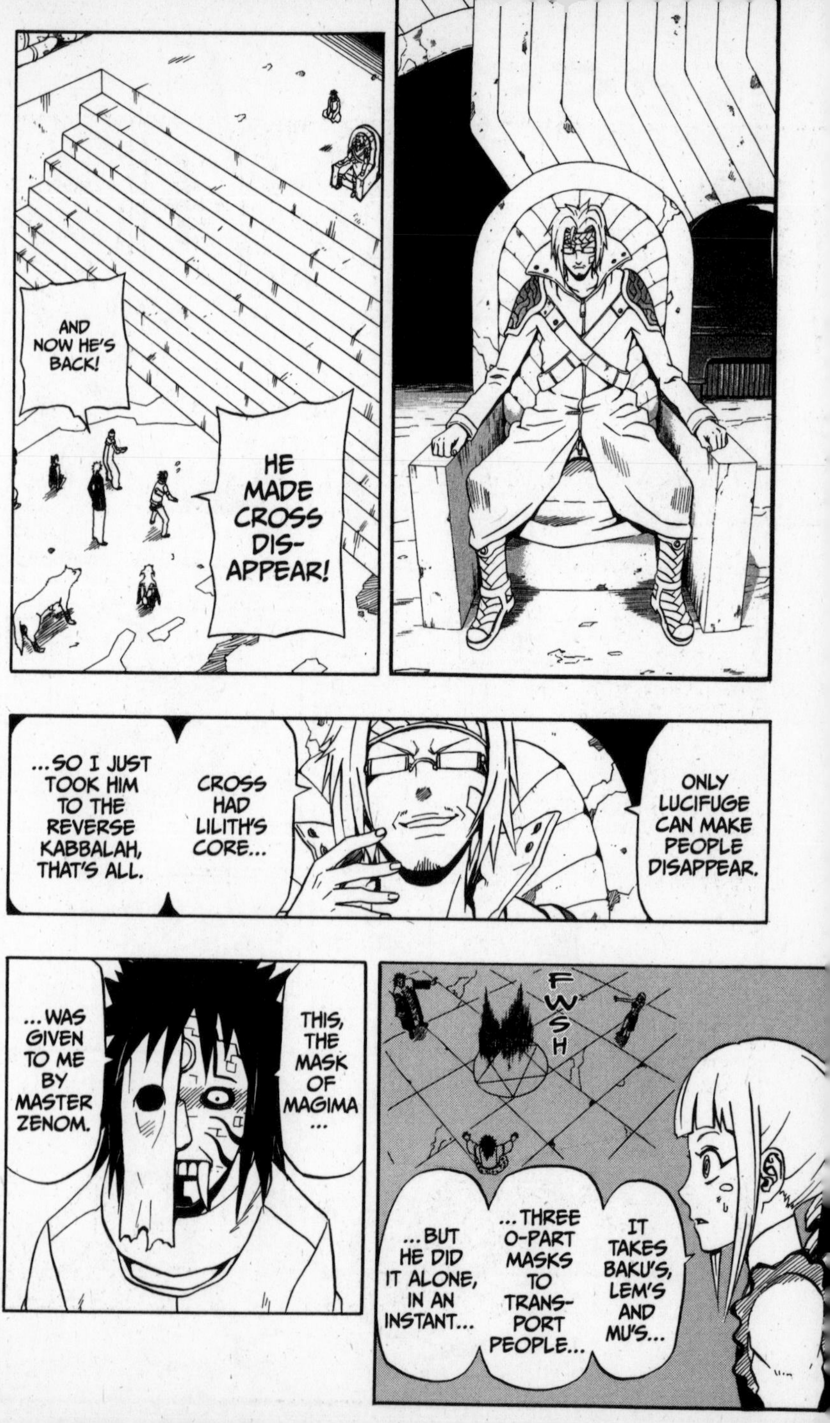
AND NOW HE'S BACK!
HE MADE CROSS DIS-APPEAR!
ONLY LUCIFUGE CAN MAKE PEOPLE DISAPPEAR.
CROSS HAD LILITH'S CORE...
...SO I JUST TOOK HIM TO THE REVERSE KABBALAH, THAT'S ALL.
FWSH
IT TAKES BAKU'S, LEM'S AND MU'S...
...THREE O-PART MASKS TO TRANS-PORT PEOPLE...
...BUT HE DID IT ALONE, IN AN INSTANT...
THIS, THE MASK OF MAGIMA...
...WAS GIVEN TO ME BY MASTER ZENOM.

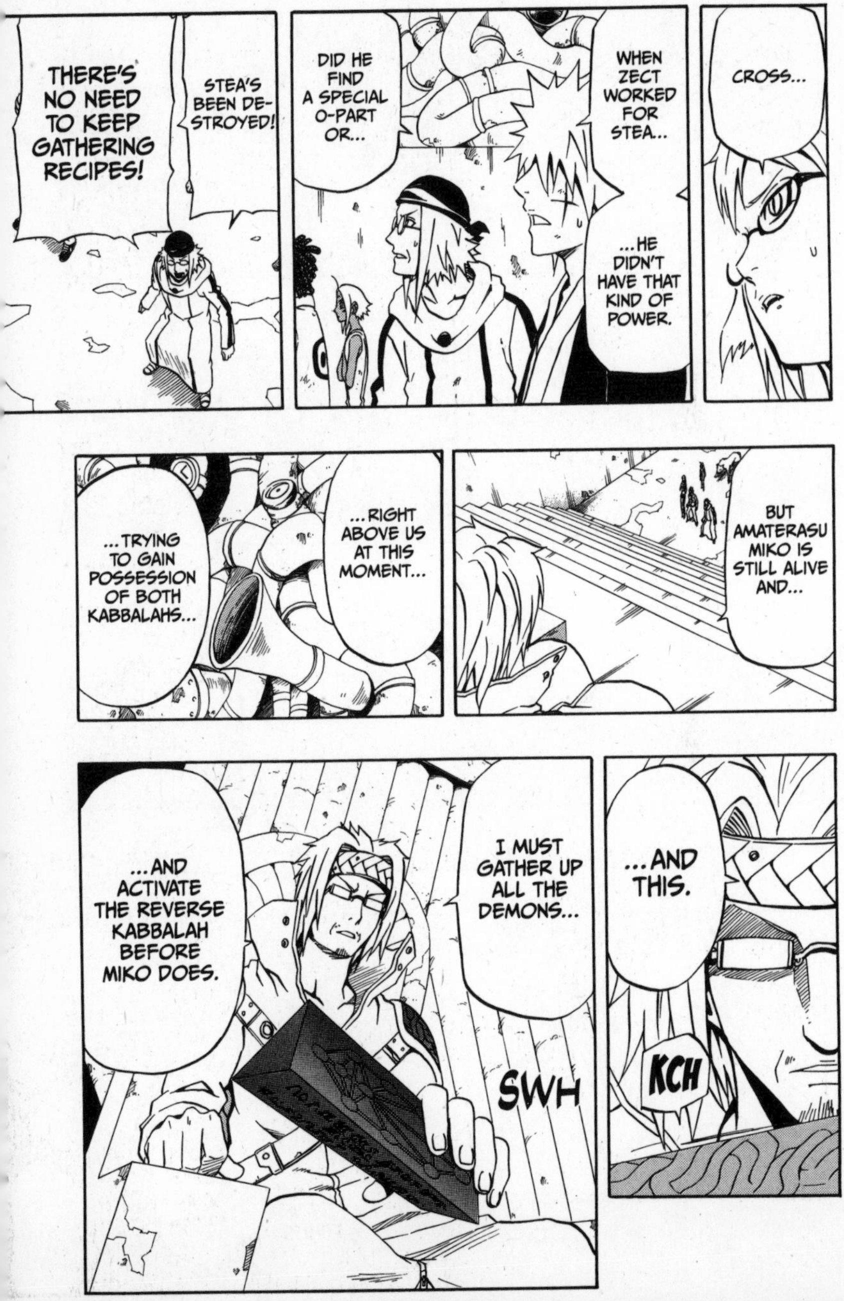
CROSS...
WHEN ZECT WORKED FOR STEA...
...HE DIDN'T HAVE THAT KIND OF POWER.
DID HE FIND A SPECIAL O-PART OR...
STEA'S BEEN DE-STROYED!
THERE'S NO NEED TO KEEP GATHERING RECIPES!
BUT AMATERASU MIKO IS STILL ALIVE AND...
...RIGHT ABOVE US AT THIS MOMENT...
...TRYING TO GAIN POSSESSION OF BOTH KABBALAHS...
...AND THIS.
KCH
I MUST GATHER UP ALL THE DEMONS...
...AND ACTIVATE THE REVERSE KABBALAH BEFORE MIKO DOES.
SWH

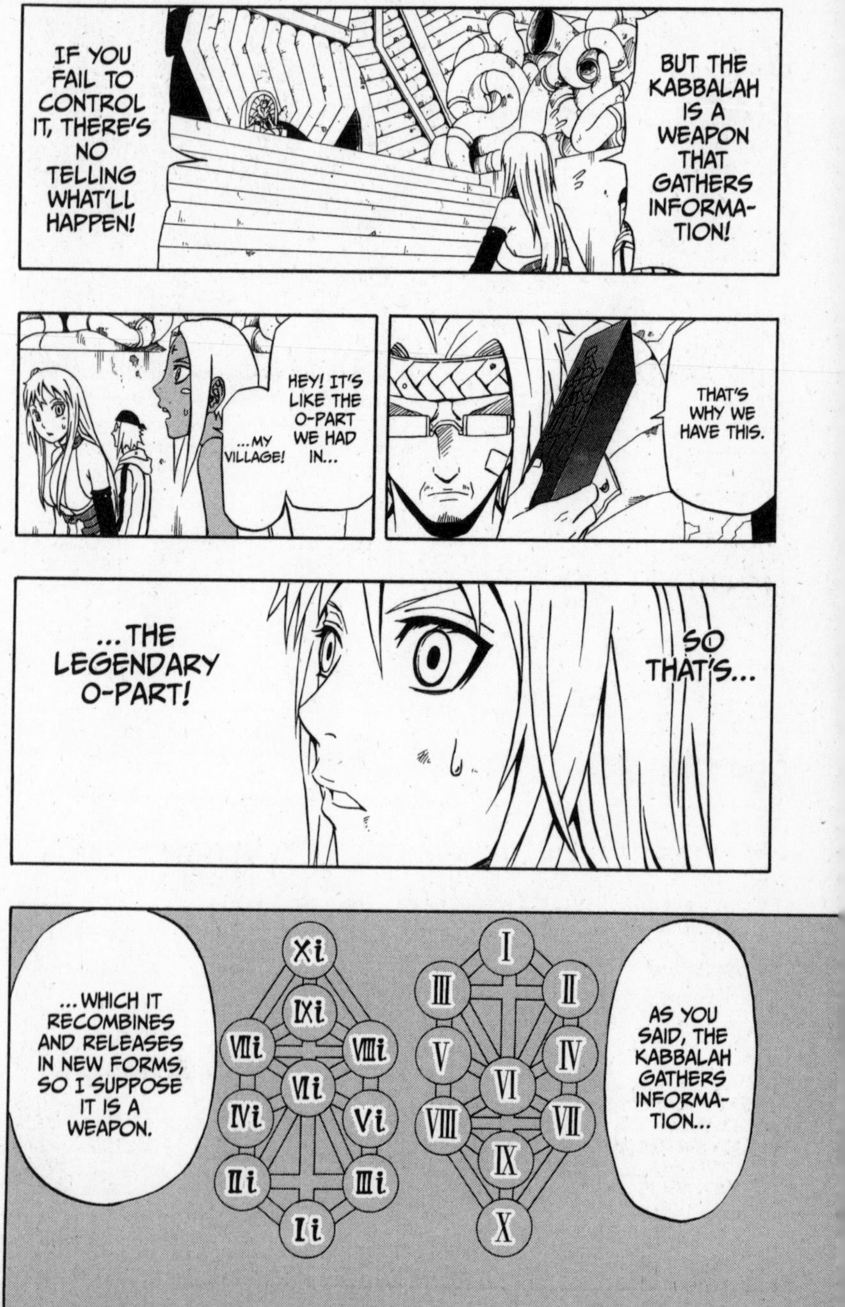
BUT THE KABBALAH IS A WEAPON THAT GATHERS INFORMATION!
IF YOU FAIL TO CONTROL IT, THERE'S NO TELLING WHAT'LL HAPPEN!
THAT'S WHY WE HAVE THIS.
HEY! IT'S LIKE THE O-PART WE HAD IN...
...MY VILLAGE!
SO THAT'S...
...THE LEGENDARY O-PART!
AS YOU SAID, THE KABBALAH GATHERS INFORMATION...
I II III IV V VI VII VIII IX X
Xi IXi VIIIi VIIi VIi Vi IVi IIIi IIi Ii
...WHICH IT RECOMBINES AND RELEASES IN NEW FORMS, SO I SUPPOSE IT IS A WEAPON.

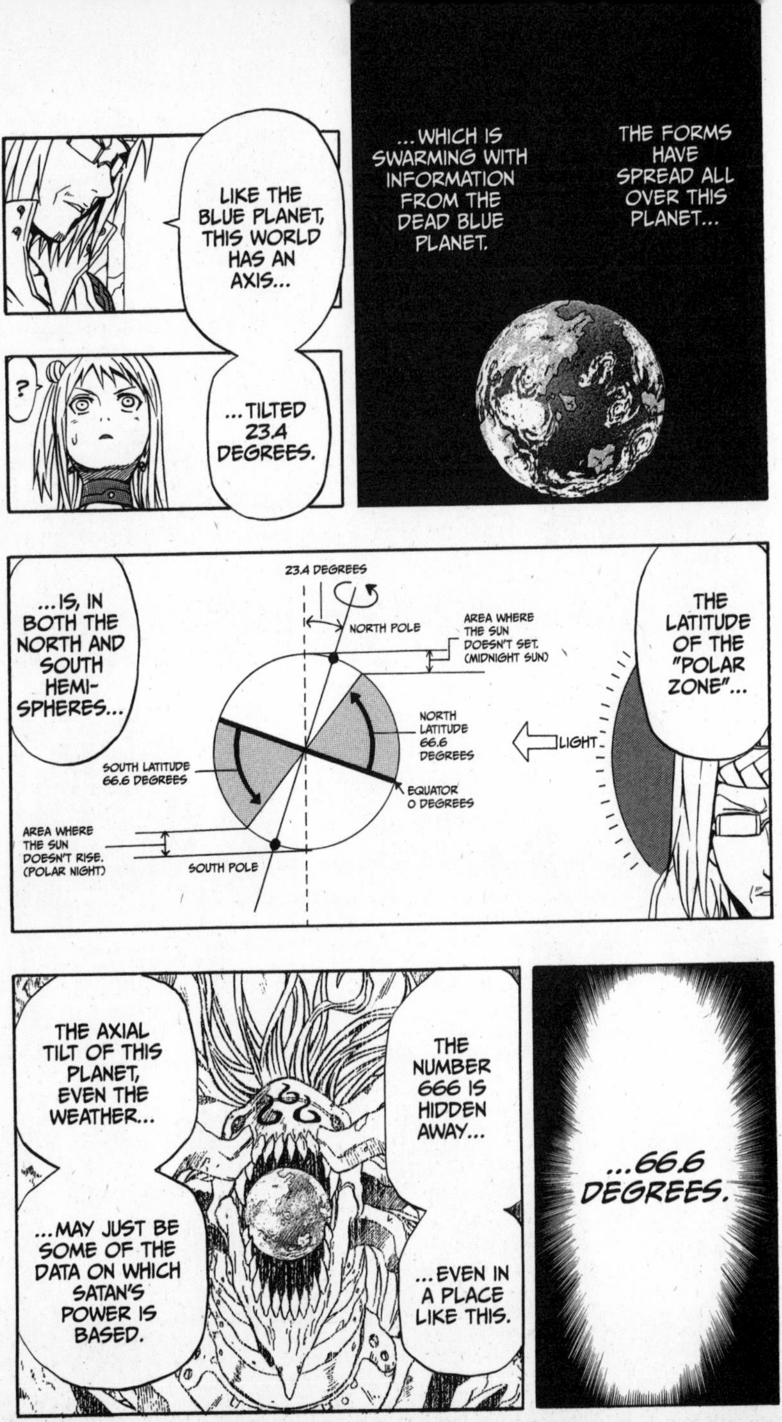
THE FORMS HAVE SPREAD ALL OVER THIS PLANET...
...WHICH IS SWARMING WITH INFORMATION FROM THE DEAD BLUE PLANET.
LIKE THE BLUE PLANET, THIS WORLD HAS AN AXIS...
?
...TILTED 23.4 DEGREES.
THE LATITUDE OF THE "POLAR ZONE"...
LIGHT
23.4 DEGREES
NORTH POLE
AREA WHERE THE SUN DOESN'T SET. (MIDNIGHT SUN)
NORTH LATITUDE 66.6 DEGREES
EQUATOR 0 DEGREES
SOUTH LATITUDE 66.6 DEGREES
AREA WHERE THE SUN DOESN'T RISE. (POLAR NIGHT)
SOUTH POLE
...IS, IN BOTH THE NORTH AND SOUTH HEMI-SPHERES...
...66.6 DEGREES.
THE NUMBER 666 IS HIDDEN AWAY...
...EVEN IN A PLACE LIKE THIS.
THE AXIAL TILT OF THIS PLANET, EVEN THE WEATHER...
...MAY JUST BE SOME OF THE DATA ON WHICH SATAN'S POWER IS BASED.

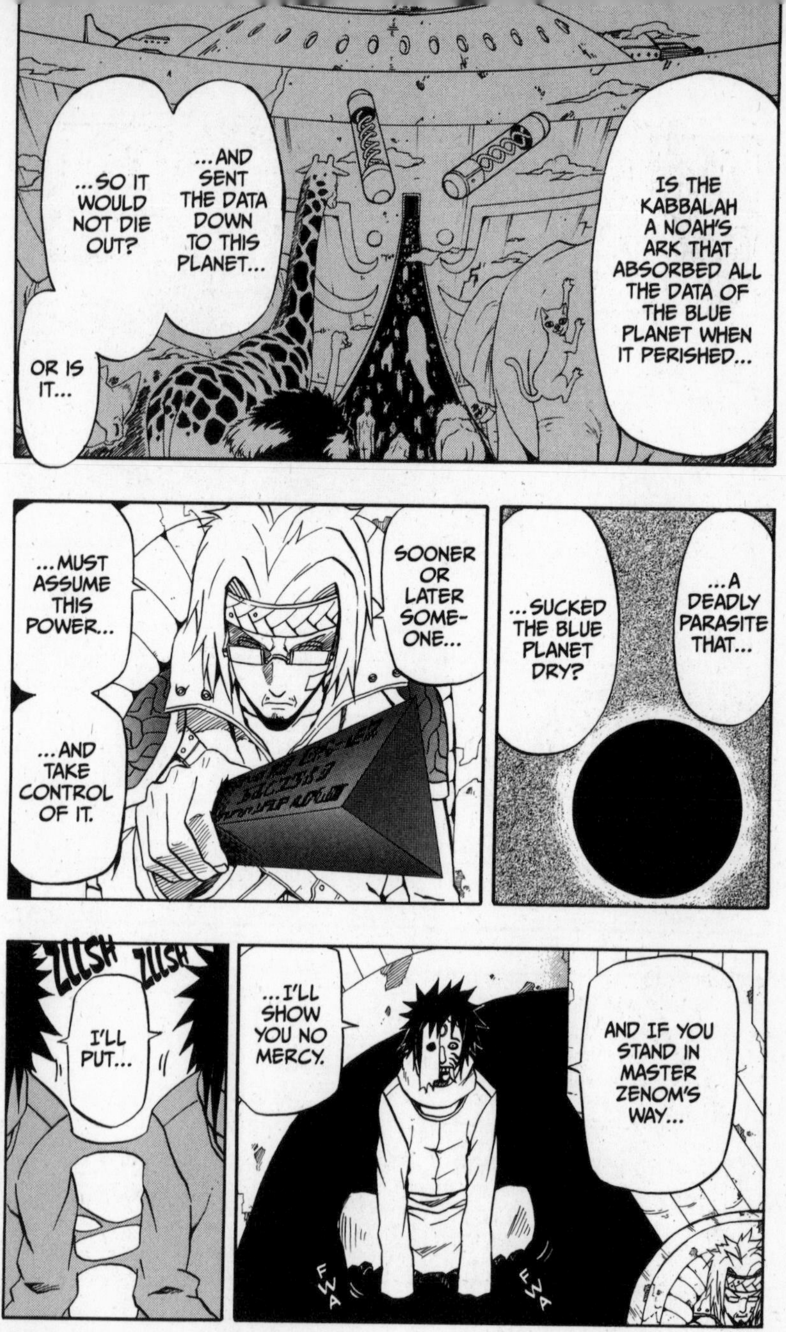
IS THE KABBALAH A NOAH'S ARK THAT ABSORBED ALL THE DATA OF THE BLUE PLANET WHEN IT PERISHED...
...AND SENT THE DATA DOWN TO THIS PLANET...
...SO IT WOULD NOT DIE OUT?
OR IS IT...
...A DEADLY PARASITE THAT...
...SUCKED THE BLUE PLANET DRY?
SOONER OR LATER SOME-ONE...
...MUST ASSUME THIS POWER...
...AND TAKE CONTROL OF IT.
AND IF YOU STAND IN MASTER ZENOM'S WAY...
...I'LL SHOW YOU NO MERCY.
FWA
FWA
ZLLSH
ZLLSH
I'LL PUT...

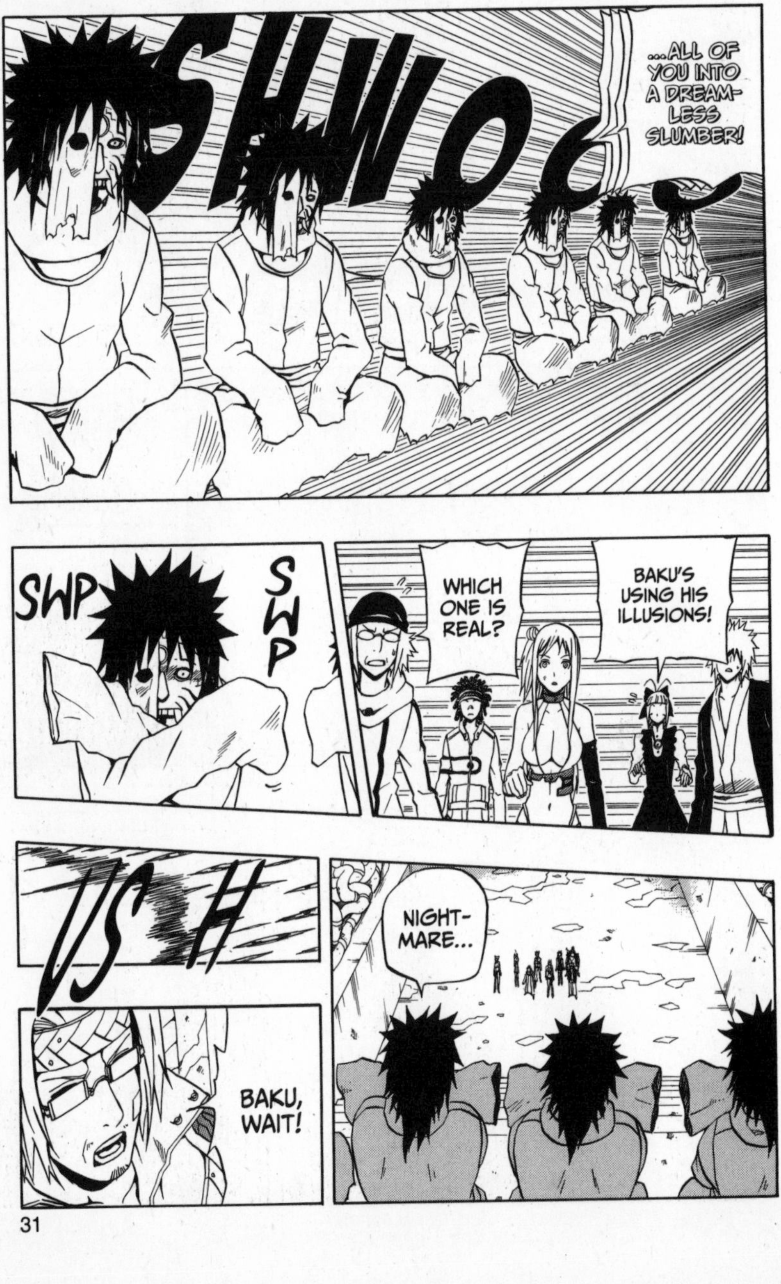
...ALL OF YOU INTO A DREAM-LESS SLUMBER!
SHWOO
BAKU'S USING HIS ILLUSIONS!
WHICH ONE IS REAL?
SWP
SWP
NIGHT-MARE...
VSH
BAKU, WAIT!

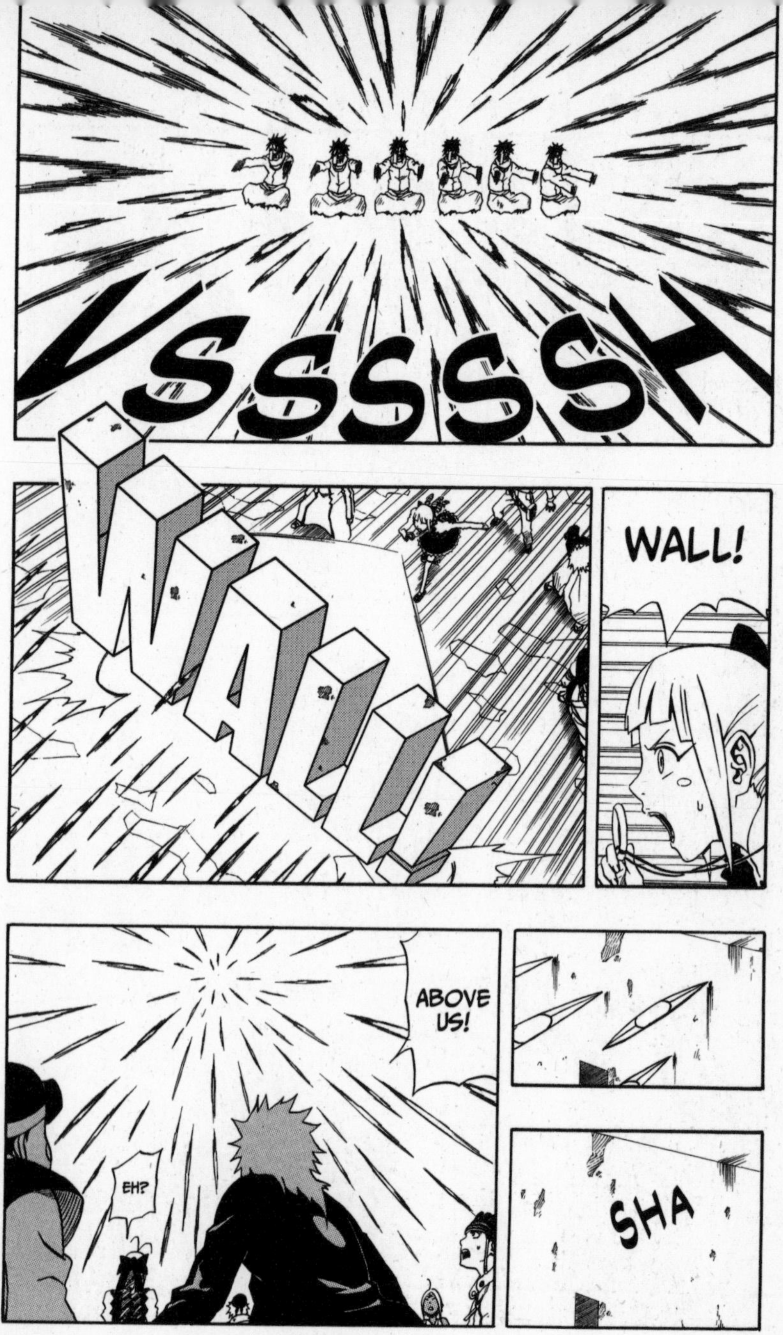
VSSSSSH
WALL!
WALL
SHA
ABOVE US!
EH?

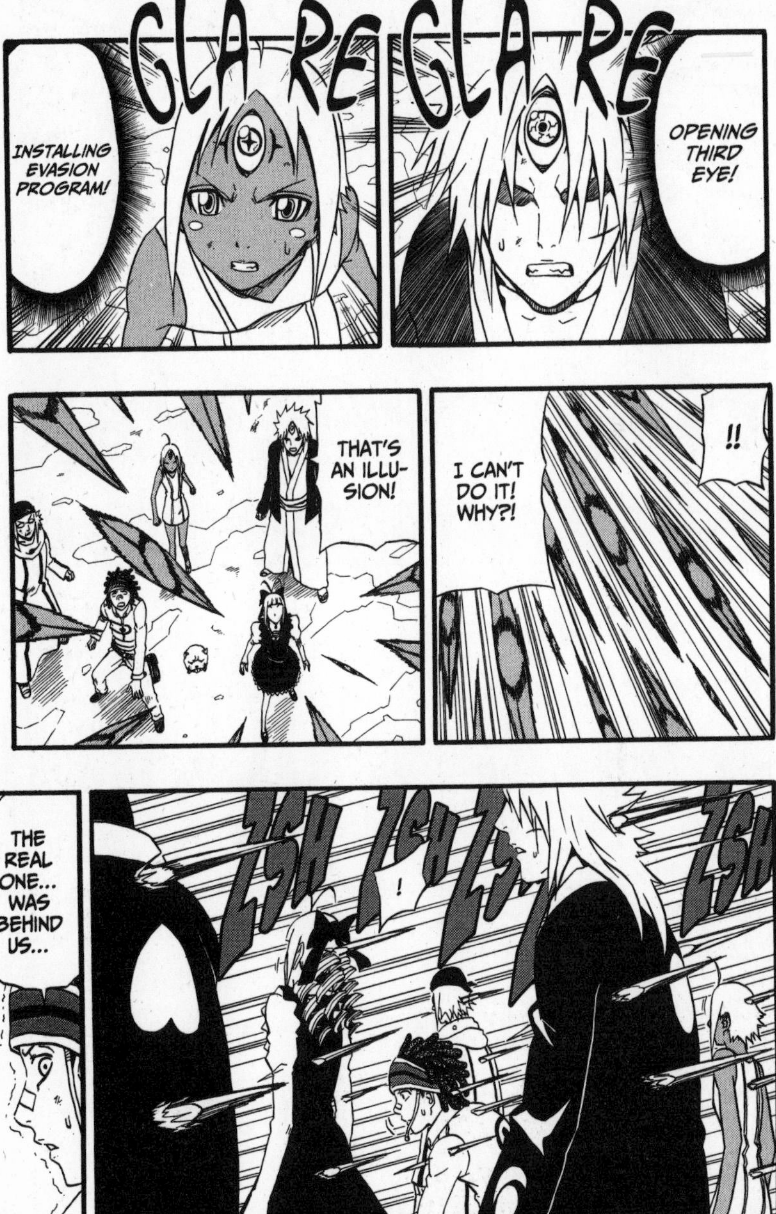
GLA RE GLA RE
OPENING THIRD EYE!
INSTALLING EVASION PROGRAM!
!!
I CAN'T DO IT! WHY?!
THAT'S AN ILLU-SION!
ZSH ZSH ZSH ZSH
!
THE REAL ONE... WAS BEHIND US...

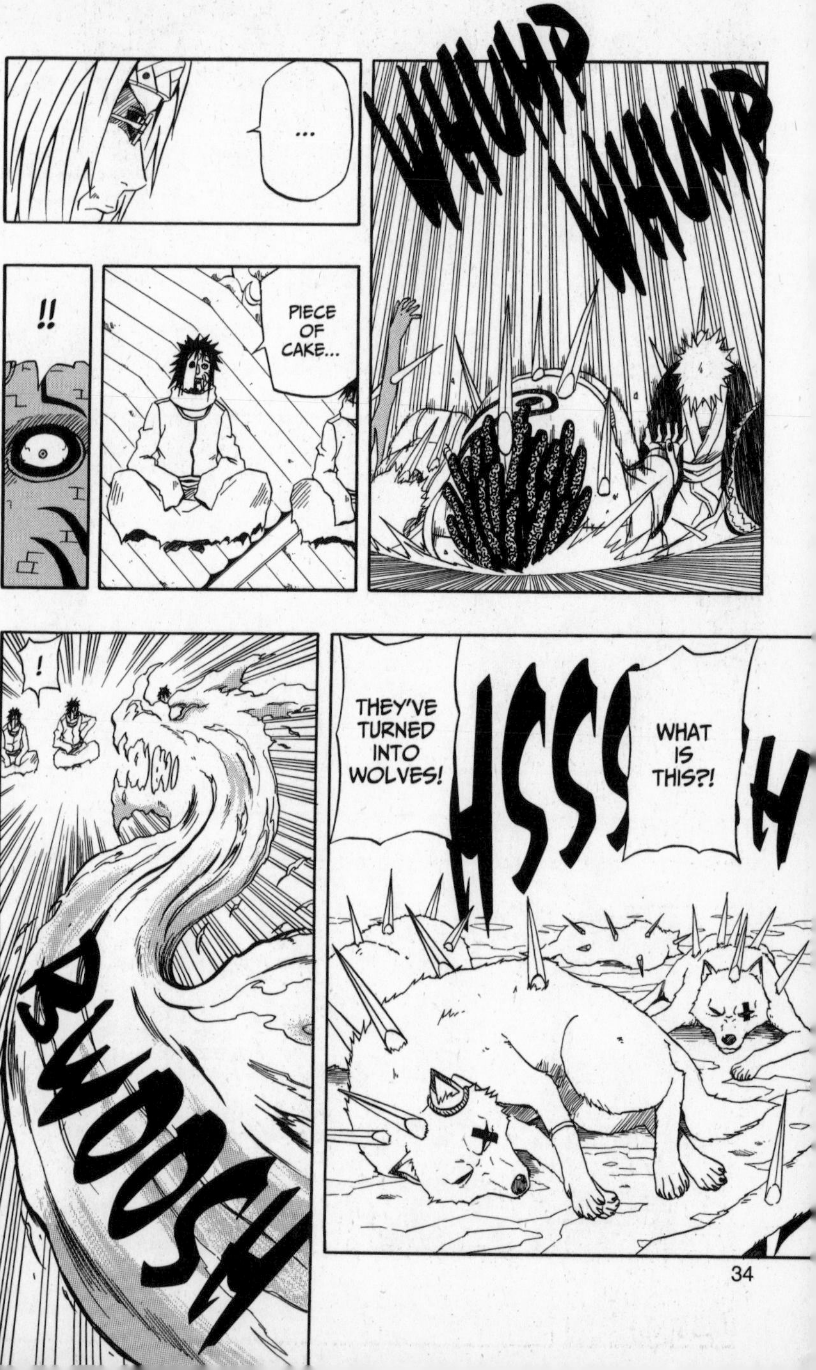
WHUMP
WHUMP
...
PIECE OF CAKE...
!!
WHAT IS THIS?!
THEY'VE TURNED INTO WOLVES!
HSSSH
!
BWOOSH

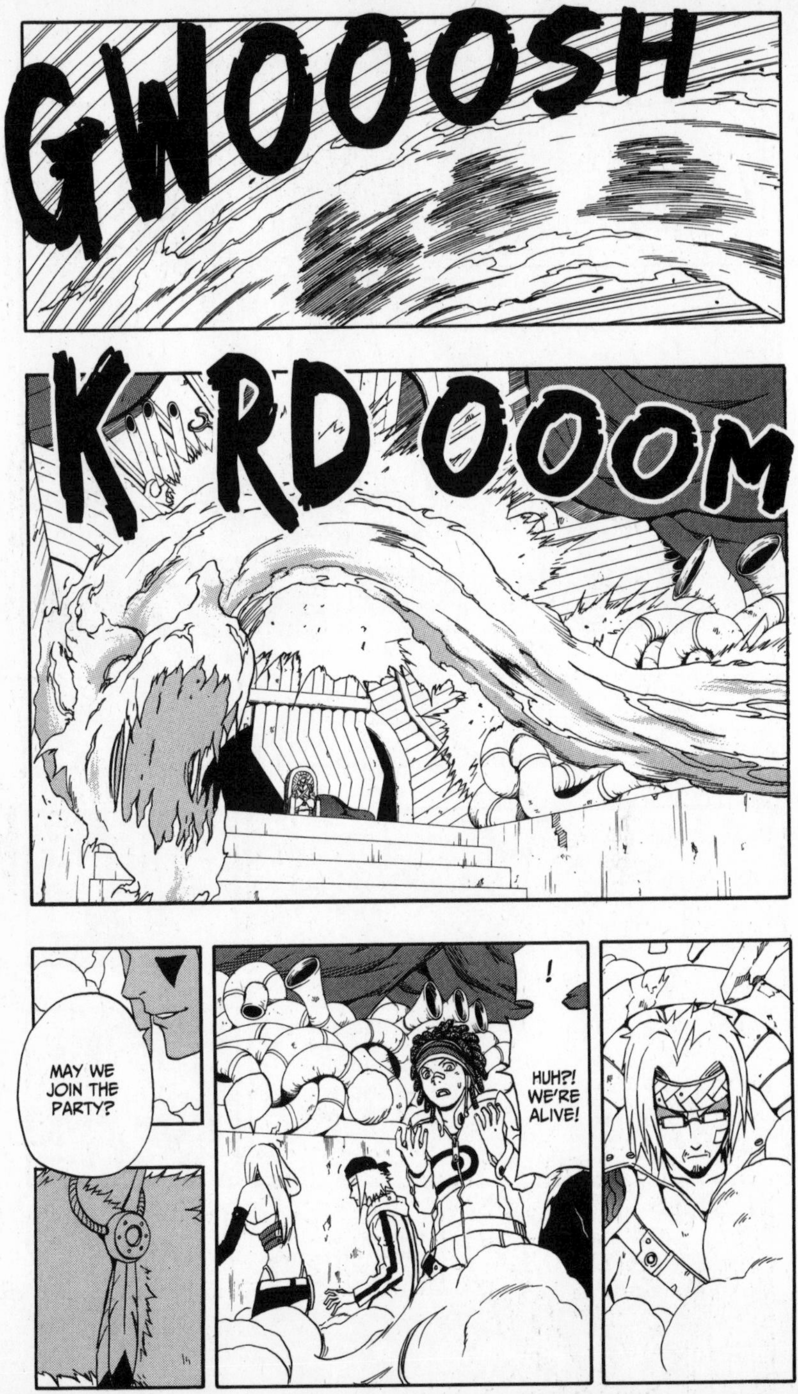
GWOOOSH
KRDOOOM
!
HUH?! WE'RE ALIVE!
MAY WE JOIN THE PARTY?

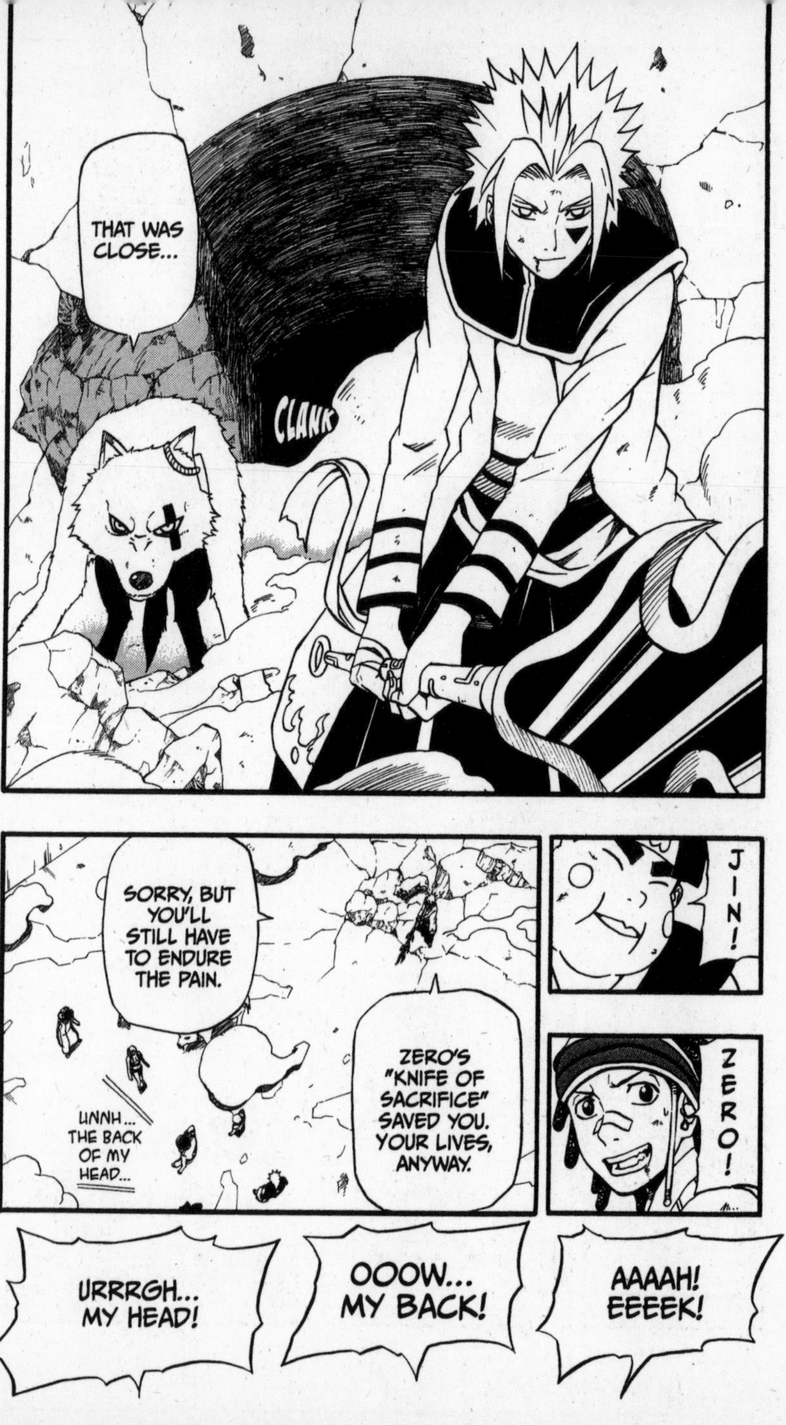
THAT WAS CLOSE...
CLANK
JIN!
ZERO!
ZERO'S "KNIFE OF SACRIFICE" SAVED YOU. YOUR LIVES, ANYWAY.
SORRY, BUT YOU'LL STILL HAVE TO ENDURE THE PAIN.
UNNH... THE BACK OF MY HEAD...
AAAAH! EEEEK!
OOOW... MY BACK!
URRRGH... MY HEAD!

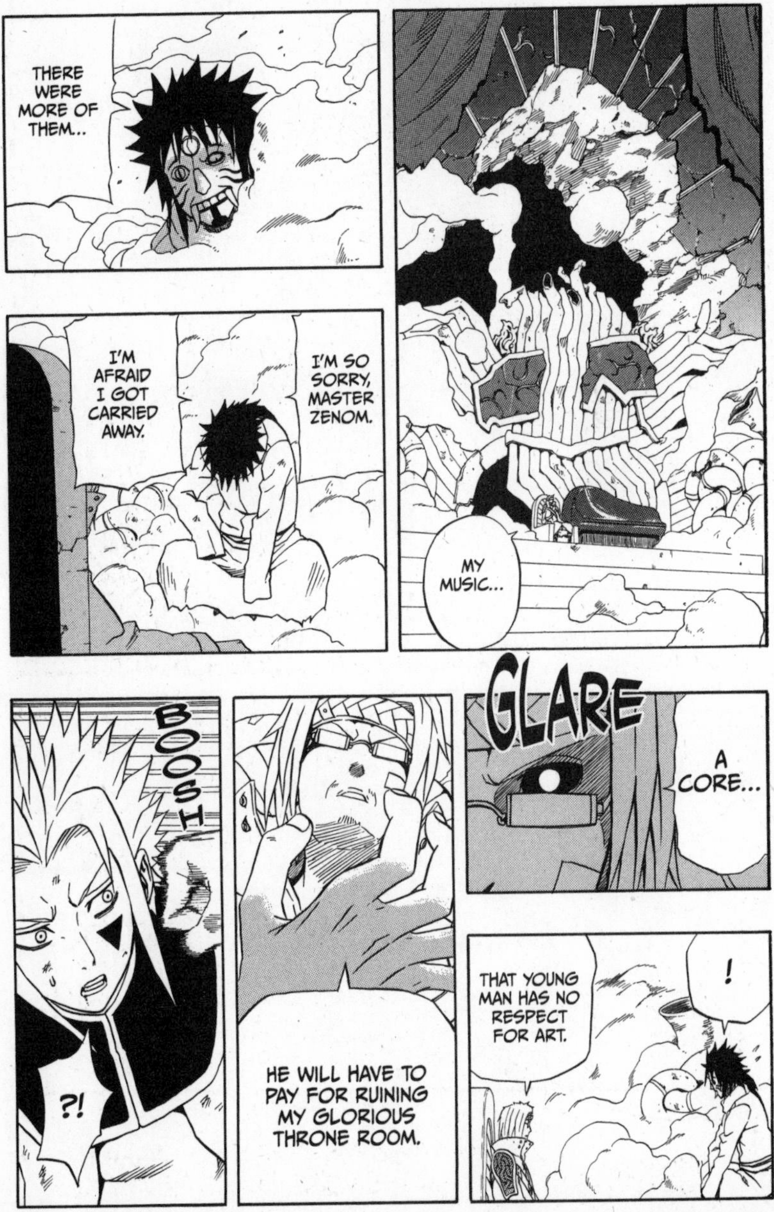
MY MUSIC...
THERE WERE MORE OF THEM...
I'M SO SORRY, MASTER ZENOM.
I'M AFRAID I GOT CARRIED AWAY.
GLARE
A CORE...
!
THAT YOUNG MAN HAS NO RESPECT FOR ART.
HE WILL HAVE TO PAY FOR RUINING MY GLORIOUS THRONE ROOM.
BOOSH
?!

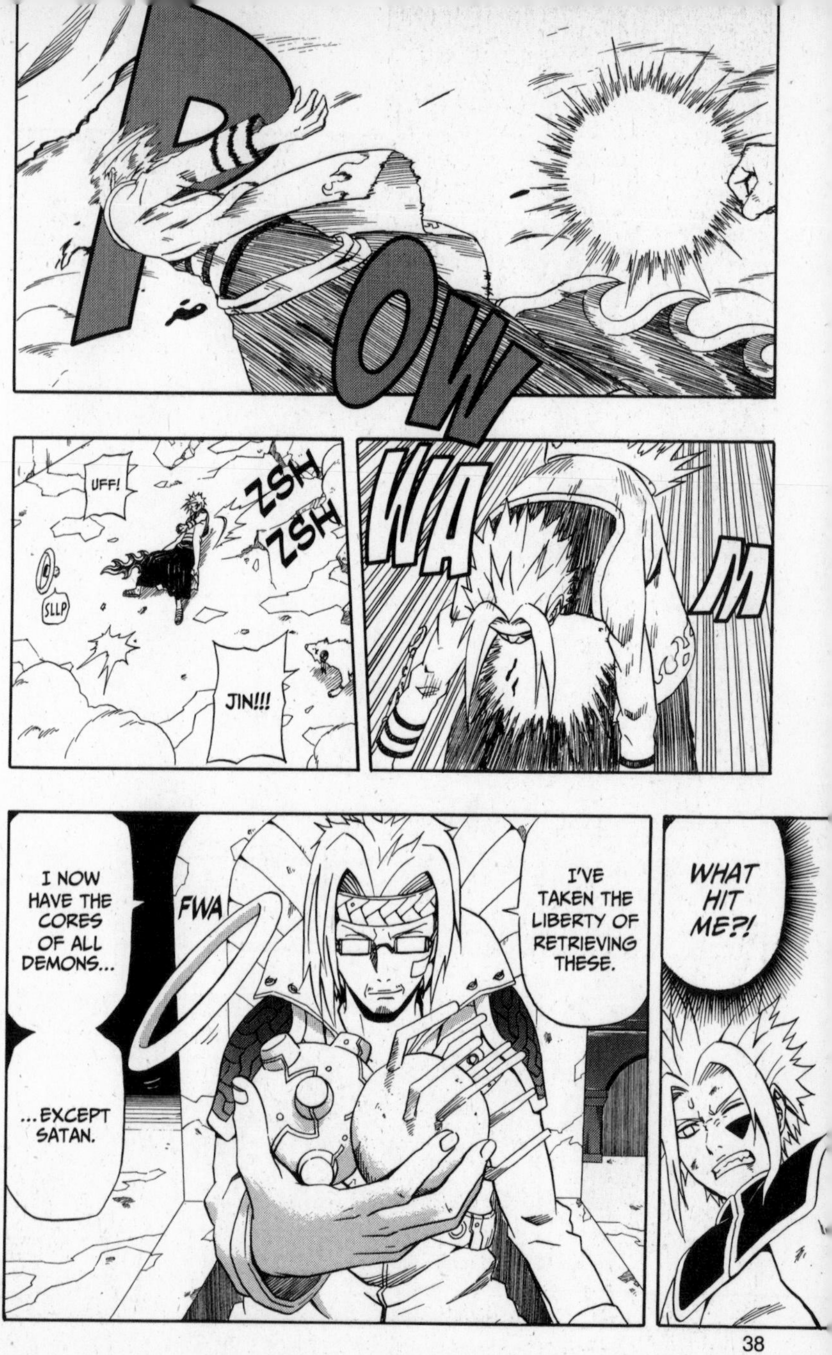
POW
WAM
ZSH
ZSH
UFF!
SLLP
JIN!!!
WHAT HIT ME?!
I'VE TAKEN THE LIBERTY OF RETRIEVING THESE.
FWA
I NOW HAVE THE CORES OF ALL DEMONS...
...EXCEPT SATAN.

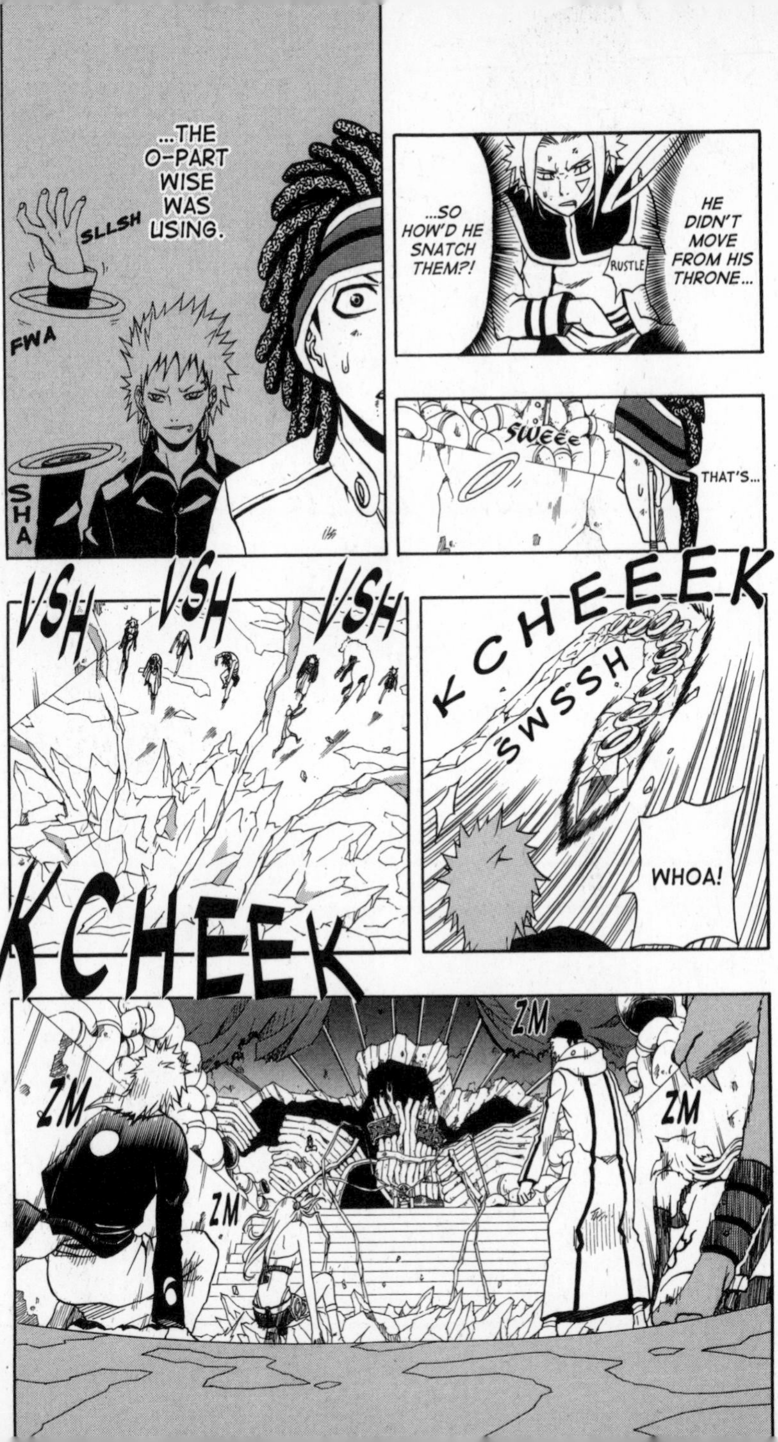
HE DIDN'T MOVE FROM HIS THRONE...
RUSTLE
...SO HOW'D HE SNATCH THEM?!
SWEEE
THAT'S...
...THE O-PART WISE WAS USING.
SLLSH
FWA
SHA
KCHEEEK
SWSSH
WHOA!
VSH
VSH
VSH
KCHEEK
ZM
ZM
ZM
ZM

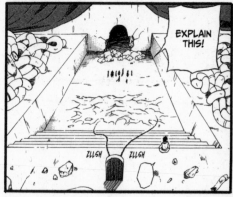

SHURI'S O-PART!
EXPLAIN THIS!
ZLLSH
ZLLSH
MOST OF THE O-PARTS USED BY ZENOM O.P.T.S...
...WERE PRESENTED TO THEM BY MASTER ZENOM.
IN SHORT, HE CREATED THEM!
SWSH
I HAVE INSIDE ME THE POWER OF DEMON NUMBER 61, BELPHEGOR...
SWSH
...THE LORD OF INVENTION AND DISCOVERY.
!

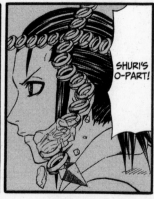

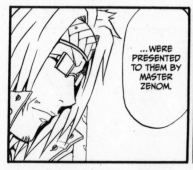

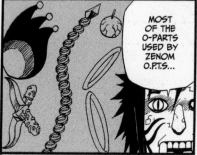

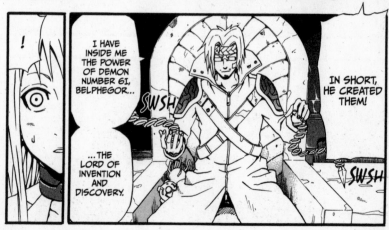

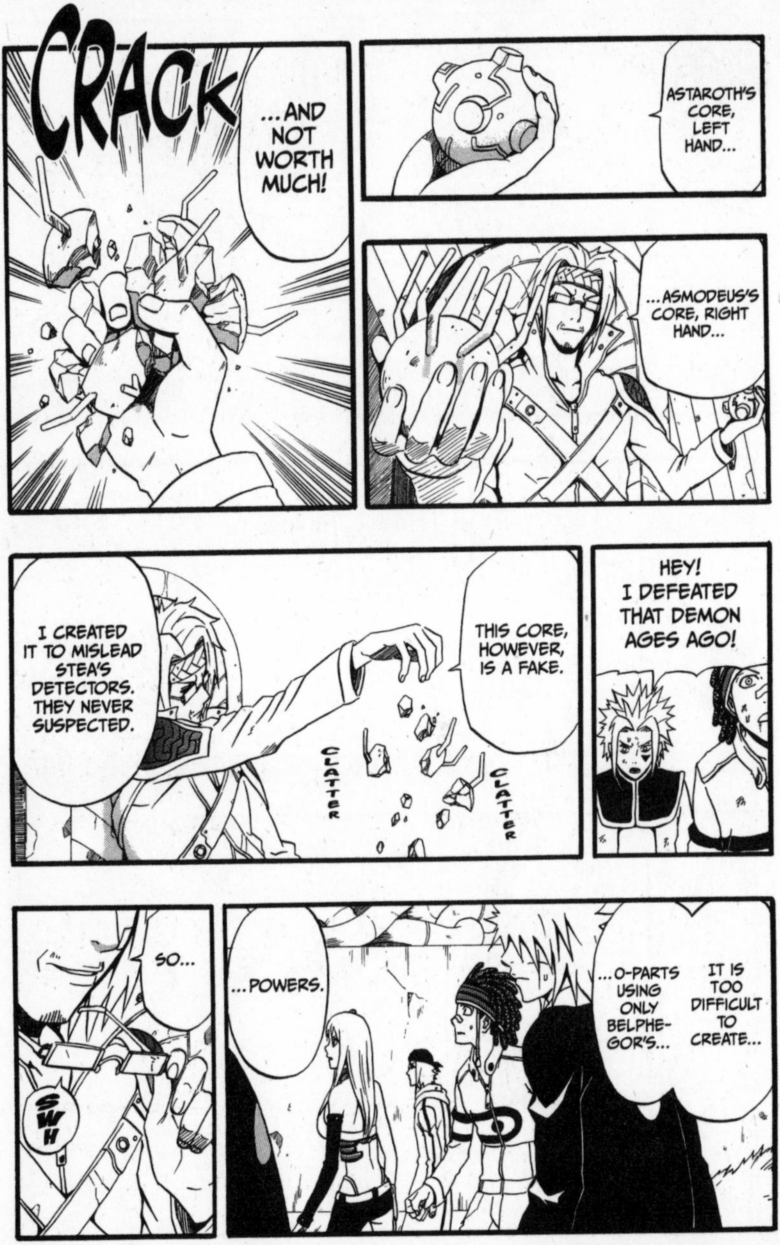
ASTAROTH'S CORE, LEFT HAND...
...ASMODEUS'S CORE, RIGHT HAND...
CRACK
...AND NOT WORTH MUCH!
HEY! I DEFEATED THAT DEMON AGES AGO!
THIS CORE, HOWEVER, IS A FAKE.
I CREATED IT TO MISLEAD STEA'S DETECTORS. THEY NEVER SUSPECTED.
CLATTER
CLATTER
IT IS TOO DIFFICULT TO CREATE...
...O-PARTS USING ONLY BELPHEGOR'S...
...POWERS.
SO...
SWH

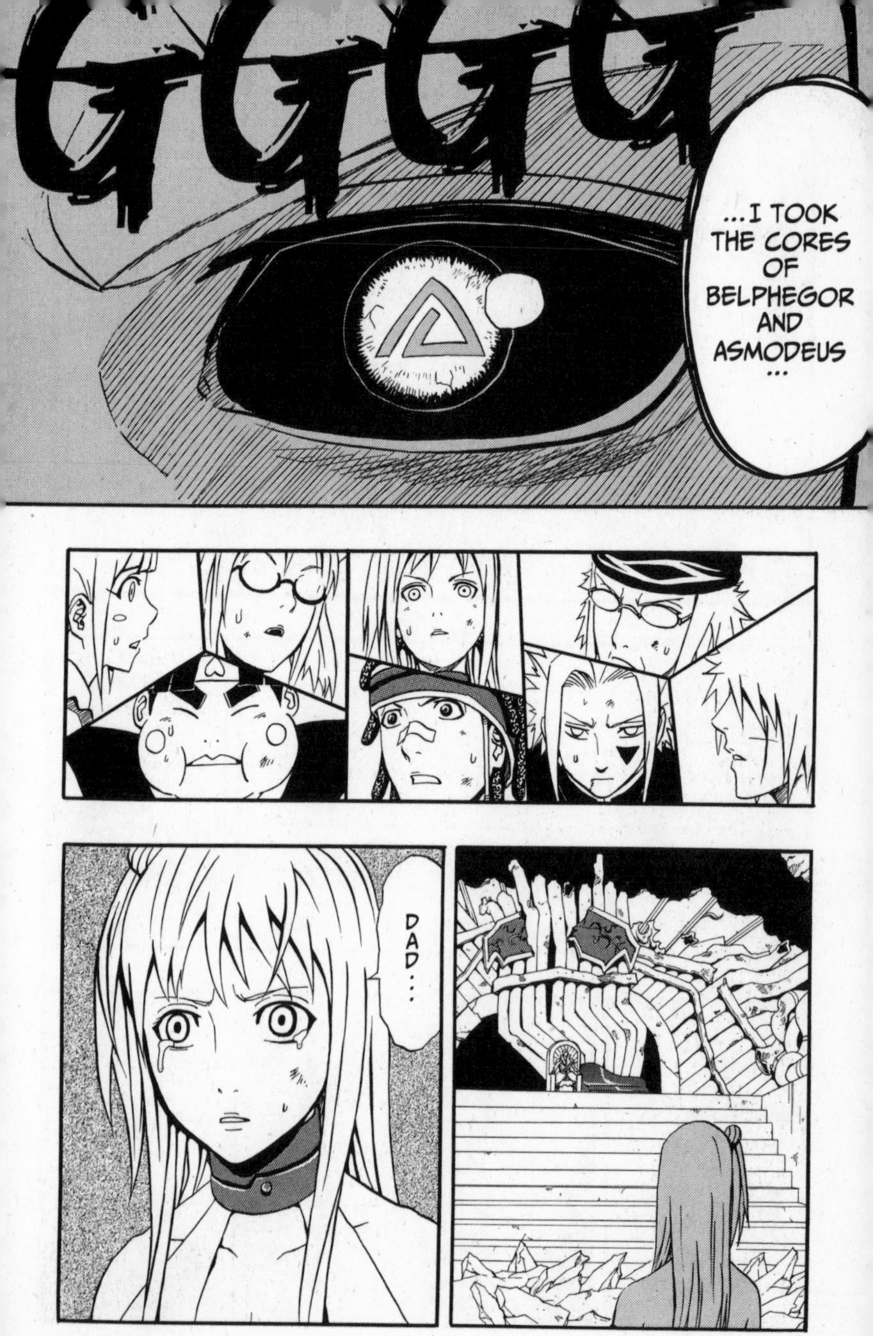
GGGG
...I TOOK THE CORES OF BELPHEGOR AND ASMODEUS ...
DAD...

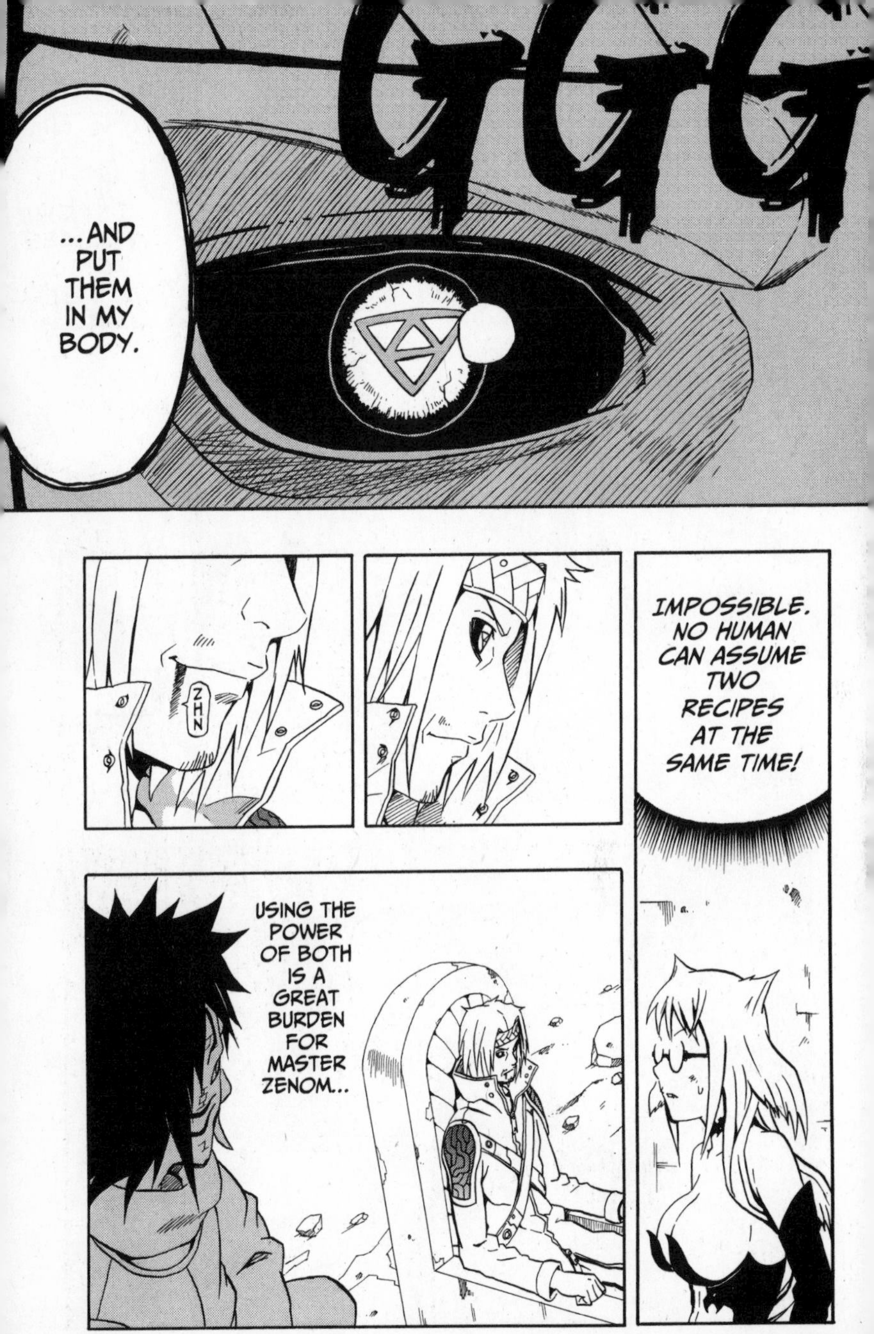
...AND PUT THEM IN MY BODY.
IMPOSSIBLE. NO HUMAN CAN ASSUME TWO RECIPES AT THE SAME TIME!
ZHN
USING THE POWER OF BOTH IS A GREAT BURDEN FOR MASTER ZENOM...

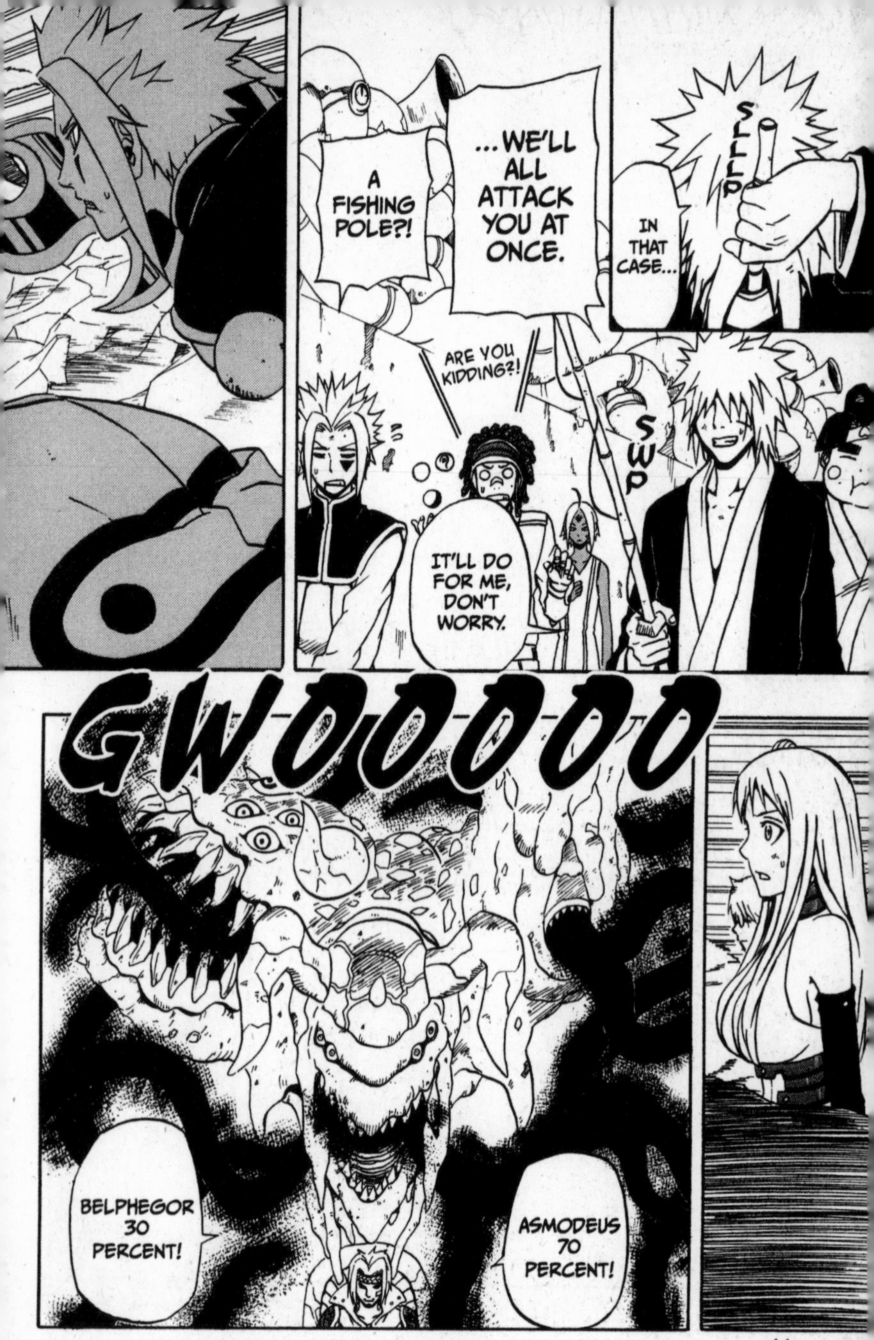
SLLLP
IN THAT CASE...
...WE'LL ALL ATTACK YOU AT ONCE.
A FISHING POLE?!
SWP
ARE YOU KIDDING?!
IT'LL DO FOR ME, DON'T WORRY.
GWOOOOOO
ASMODEUS 70 PERCENT!
BELPHEGOR 30 PERCENT!

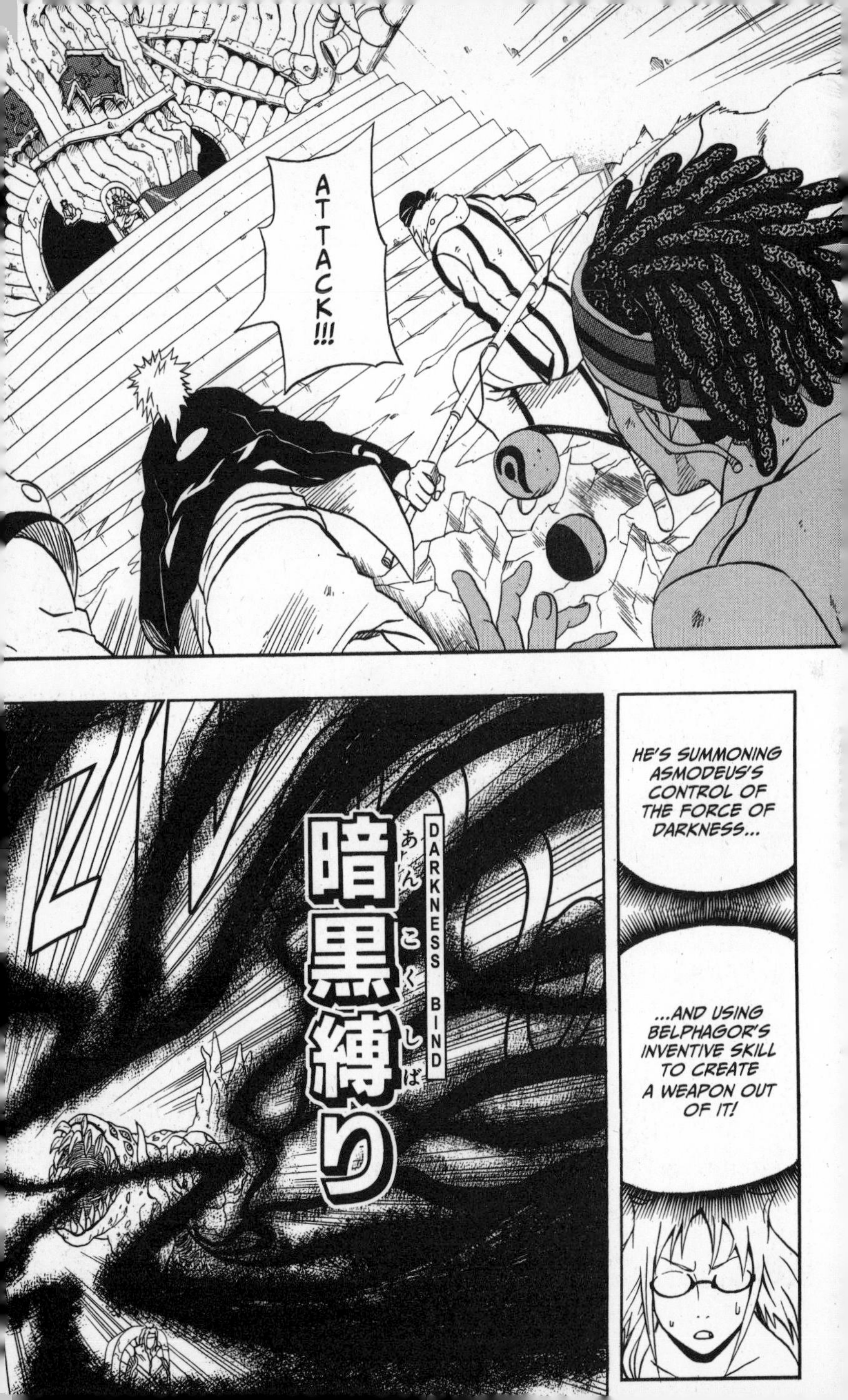
ATTACK!!!
HE'S SUMMONING ASMODEUS'S CONTROL OF THE FORCE OF DARKNESS...
...AND USING BELPHAGOR'S INVENTIVE SKILL TO CREATE A WEAPON OUT OF IT!
暗黒縛り
あんこくしば
DARKNESS BIND

SWIP

SWIP

VISH

OUR
ATTACKS
HAVE NO
EFFECT
ON IT!

!

SWIP

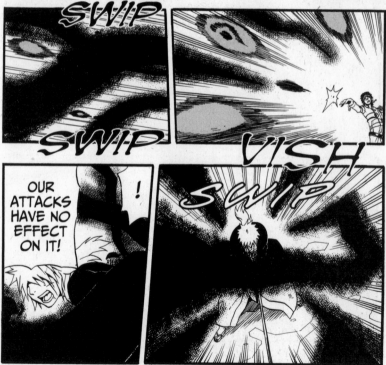

46

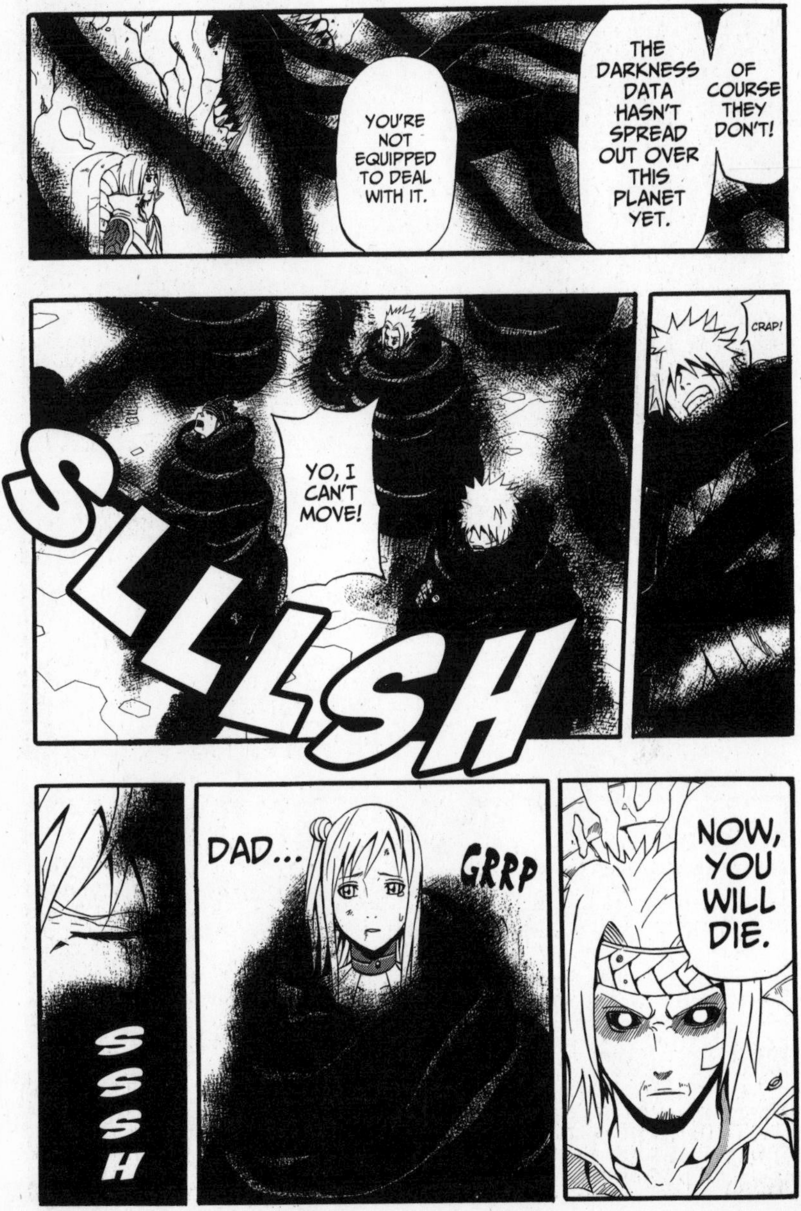
OF COURSE THEY DON'T!
THE DARKNESS DATA HASN'T SPREAD OUT OVER THIS PLANET YET.
YOU'RE NOT EQUIPPED TO DEAL WITH IT.
CRAP!
YO, I CAN'T MOVE!
SLLSH
NOW, YOU WILL DIE.
GRRP
DAD...
SSSH

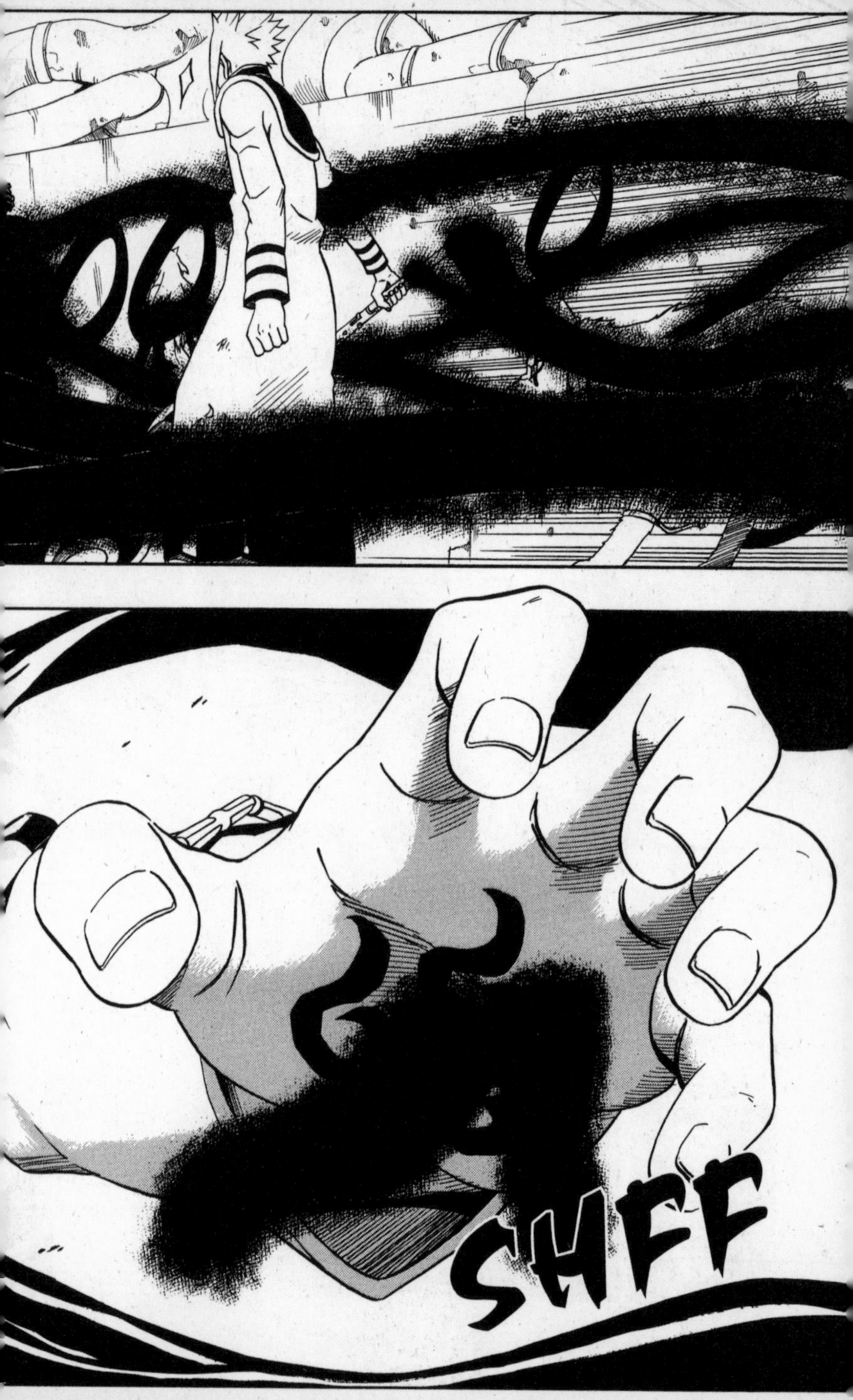
SHFF

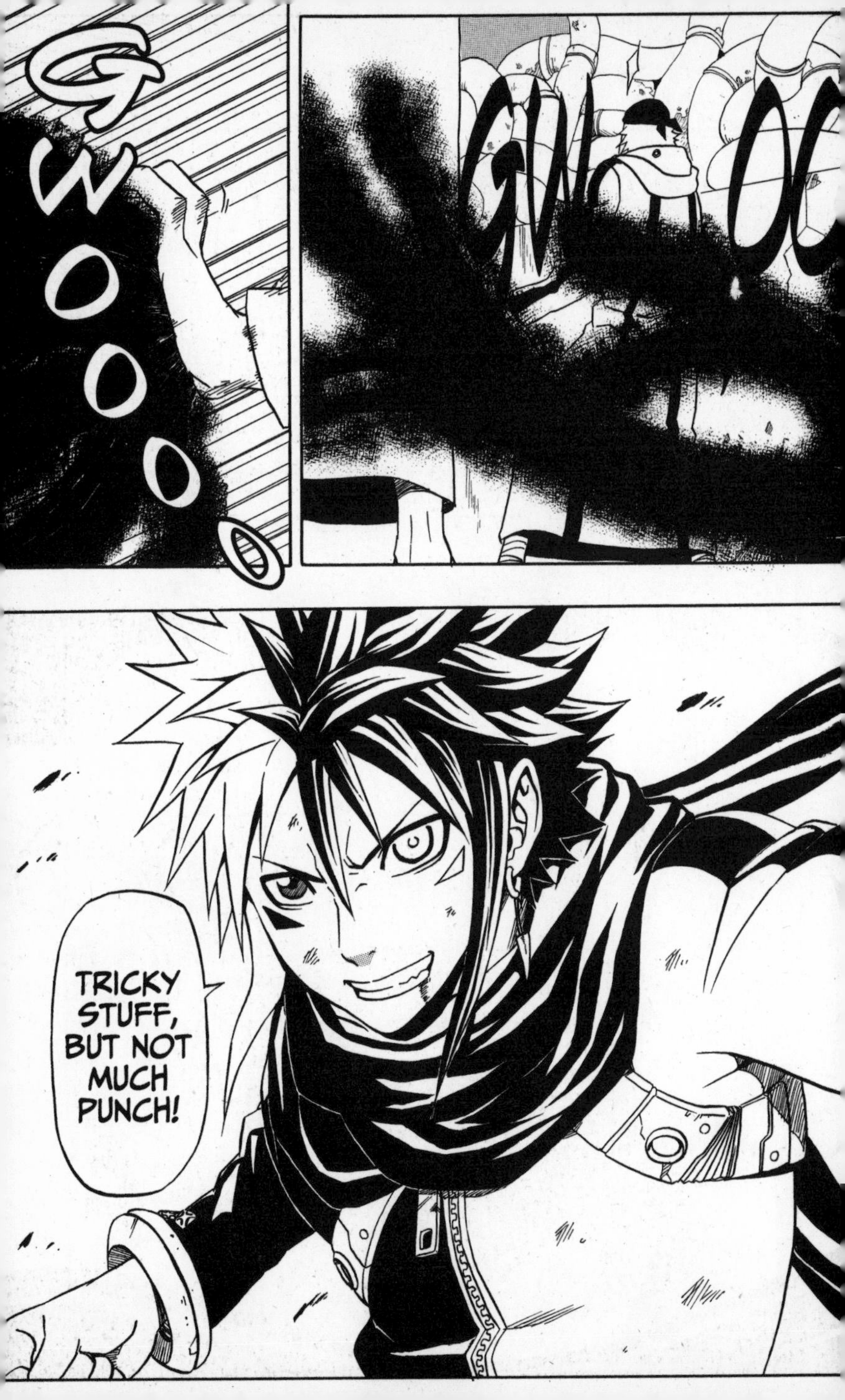
GWOO
GWOOOO
TRICKY STUFF, BUT NOT MUCH PUNCH!

J-O!

NICE SAVE TOO!

'BOUT TIME YOU GOT HERE, DUDE!

J-O...

!

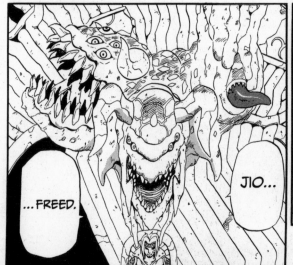

...FREED.

J-O...

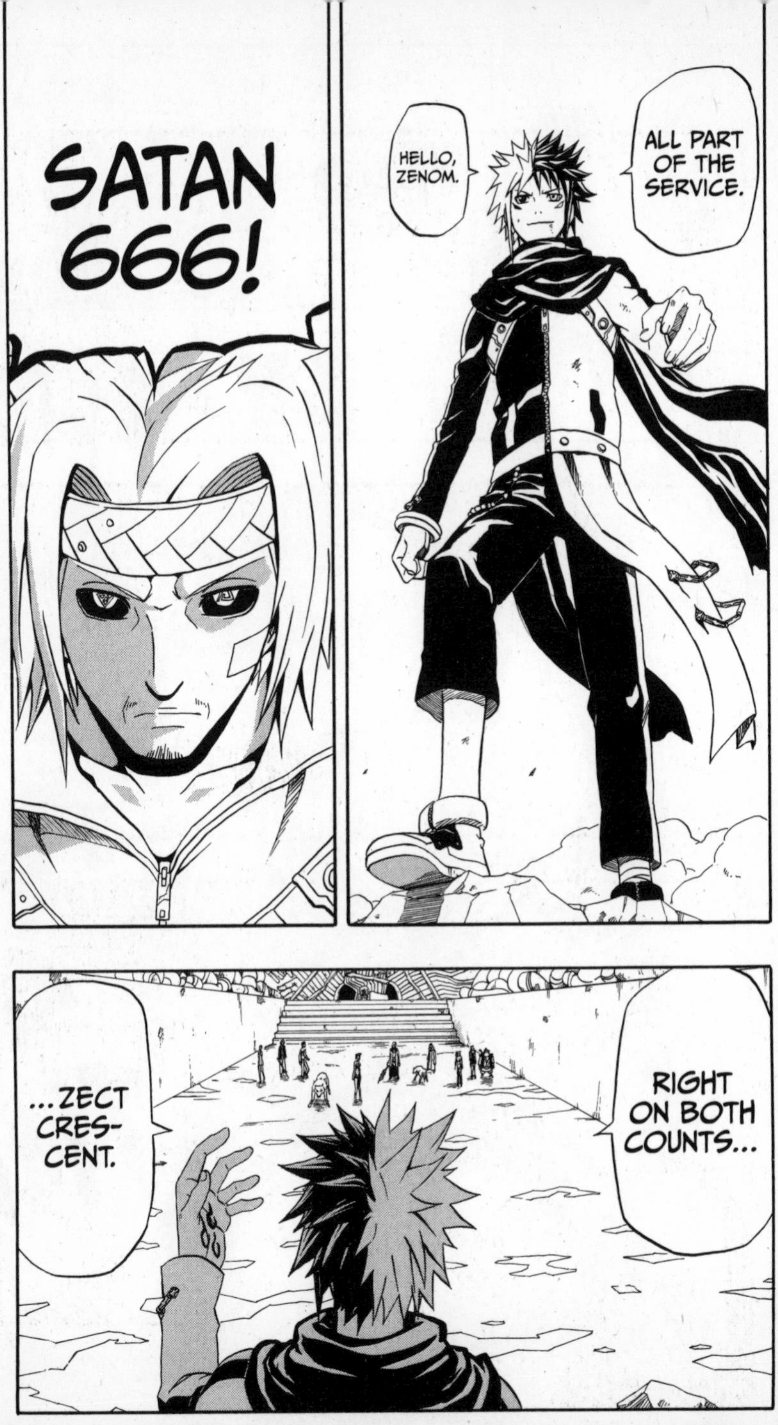
ALL PART OF THE SERVICE.
HELLO, ZENOM.
SATAN 666!
...ZECT CRES-CENT.
RIGHT ON BOTH COUNTS...

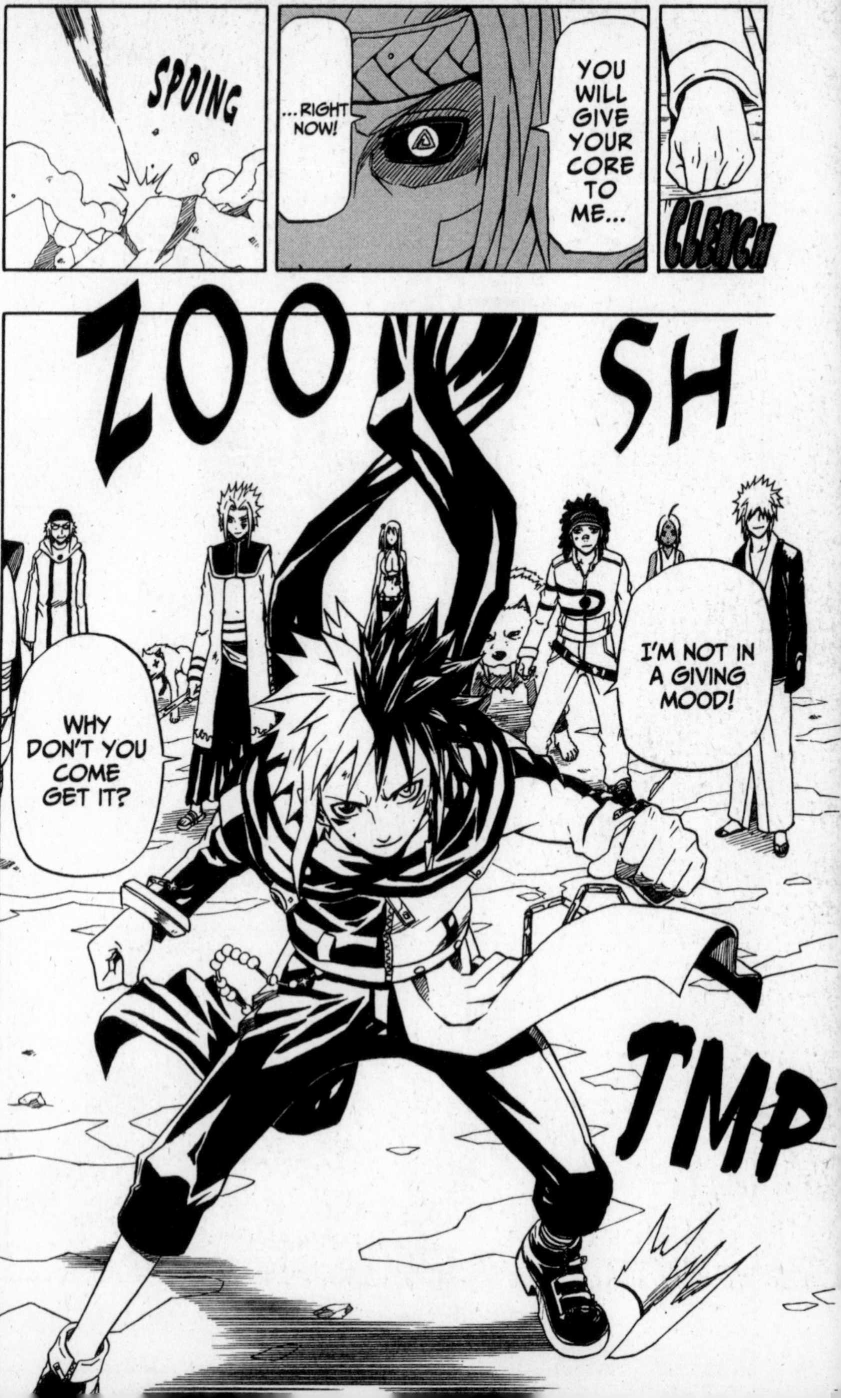
CLENCH
YOU WILL GIVE YOUR CORE TO ME...
...RIGHT NOW!
SPOING
ZOOSH
I'M NOT IN A GIVING MOOD!
WHY DON'T YOU COME GET IT?
TMP

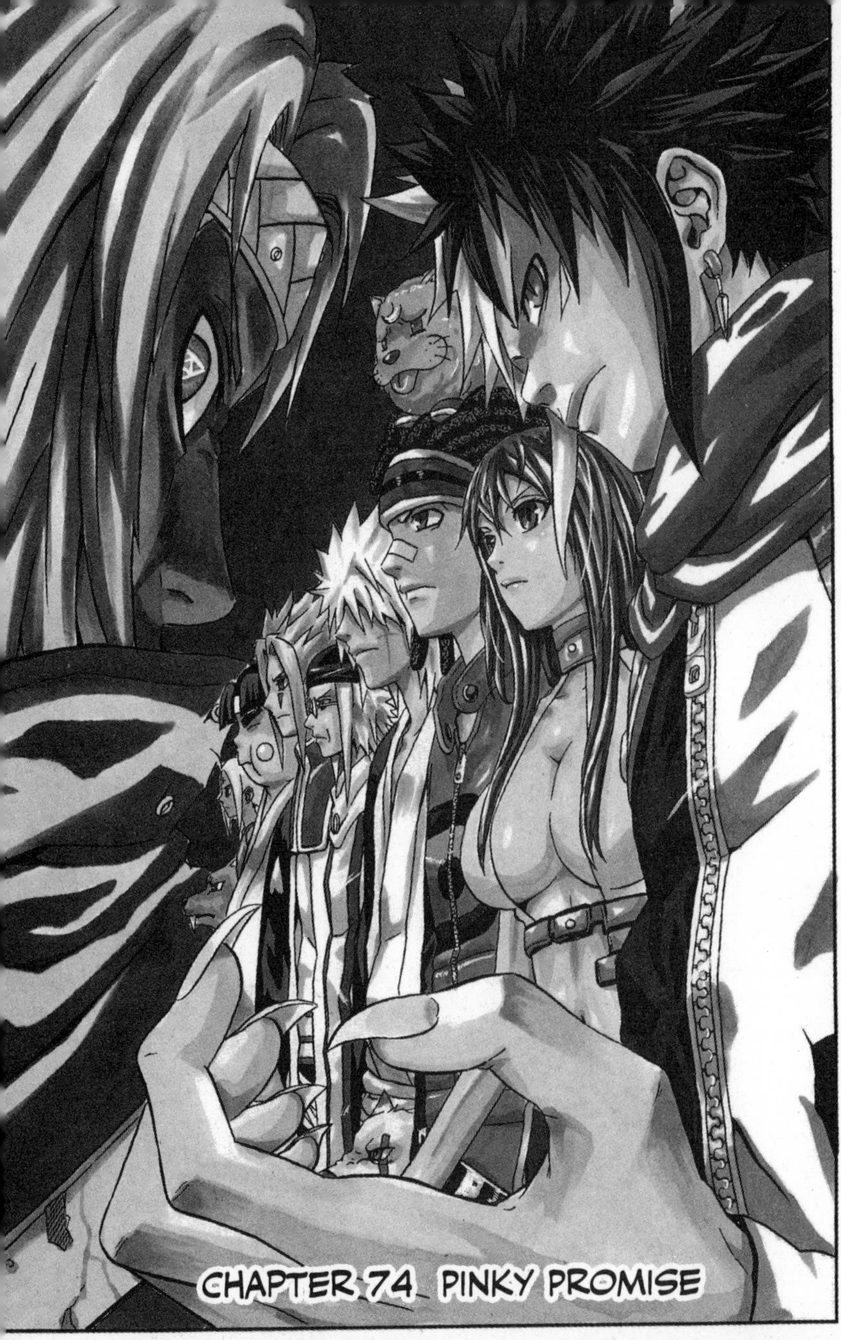
CHAPTER 74 PINKY PROMISE

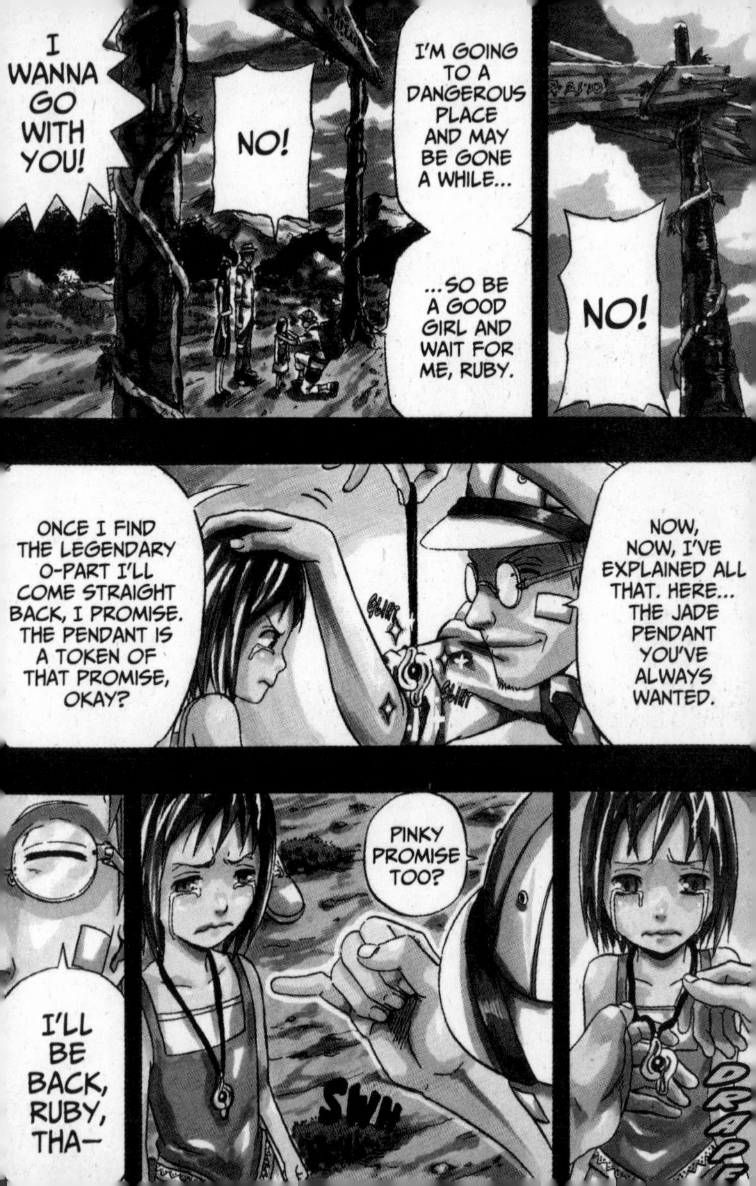
NO!
I'M GOING TO A DANGEROUS PLACE AND MAY BE GONE A WHILE...
...SO BE A GOOD GIRL AND WAIT FOR ME, RUBY.
NO!
I WANNA GO WITH YOU!
NOW, NOW, I'VE EXPLAINED ALL THAT. HERE... THE JADE PENDANT YOU'VE ALWAYS WANTED.
GLINT
GLINT
ONCE I FIND THE LEGENDARY O-PART I'LL COME STRAIGHT BACK, I PROMISE. THE PENDANT IS A TOKEN OF THAT PROMISE, OKAY?
DRAPE
PINKY PROMISE TOO?
SWN
I'LL BE BACK, RUBY, THA—

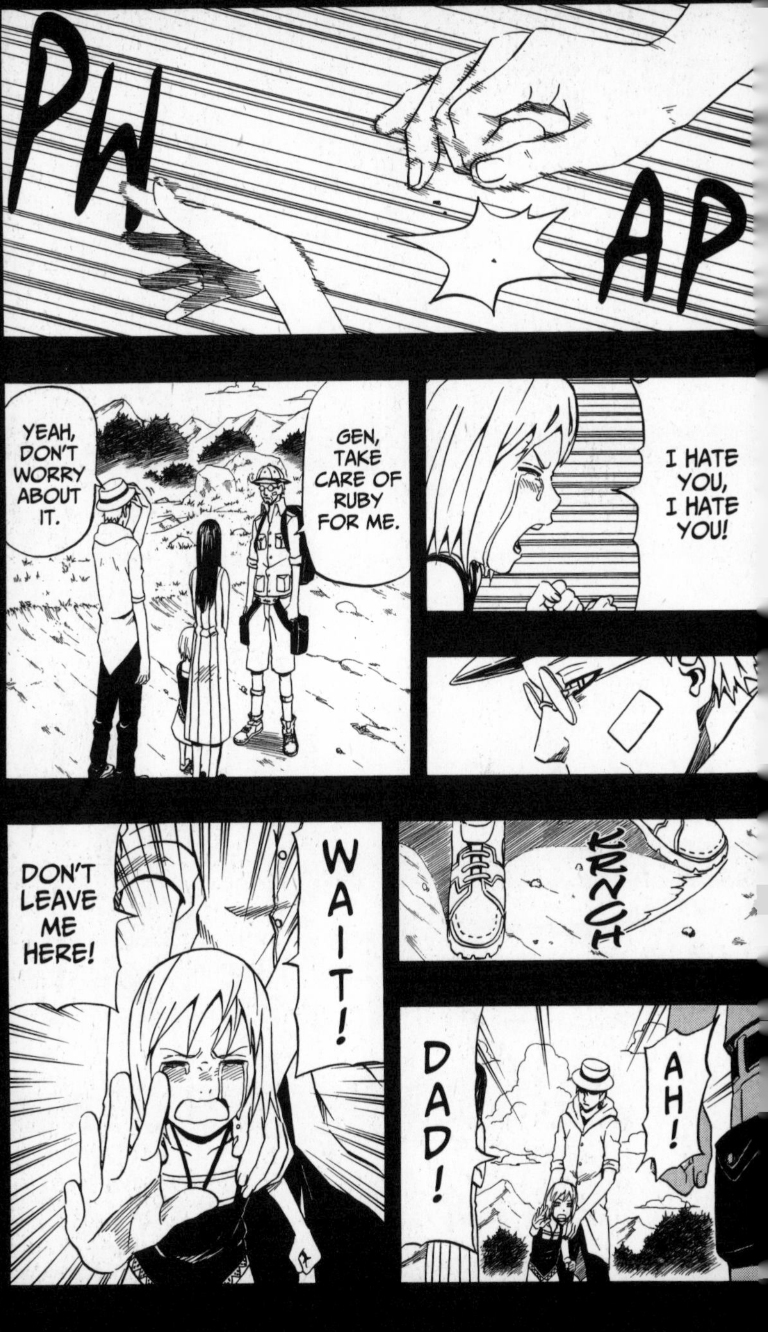
PHWAP
I HATE YOU, I HATE YOU!
GEN, TAKE CARE OF RUBY FOR ME.
YEAH, DON'T WORRY ABOUT IT.
KRNCH
AH!
DAD!
WAIT!
DON'T LEAVE ME HERE!

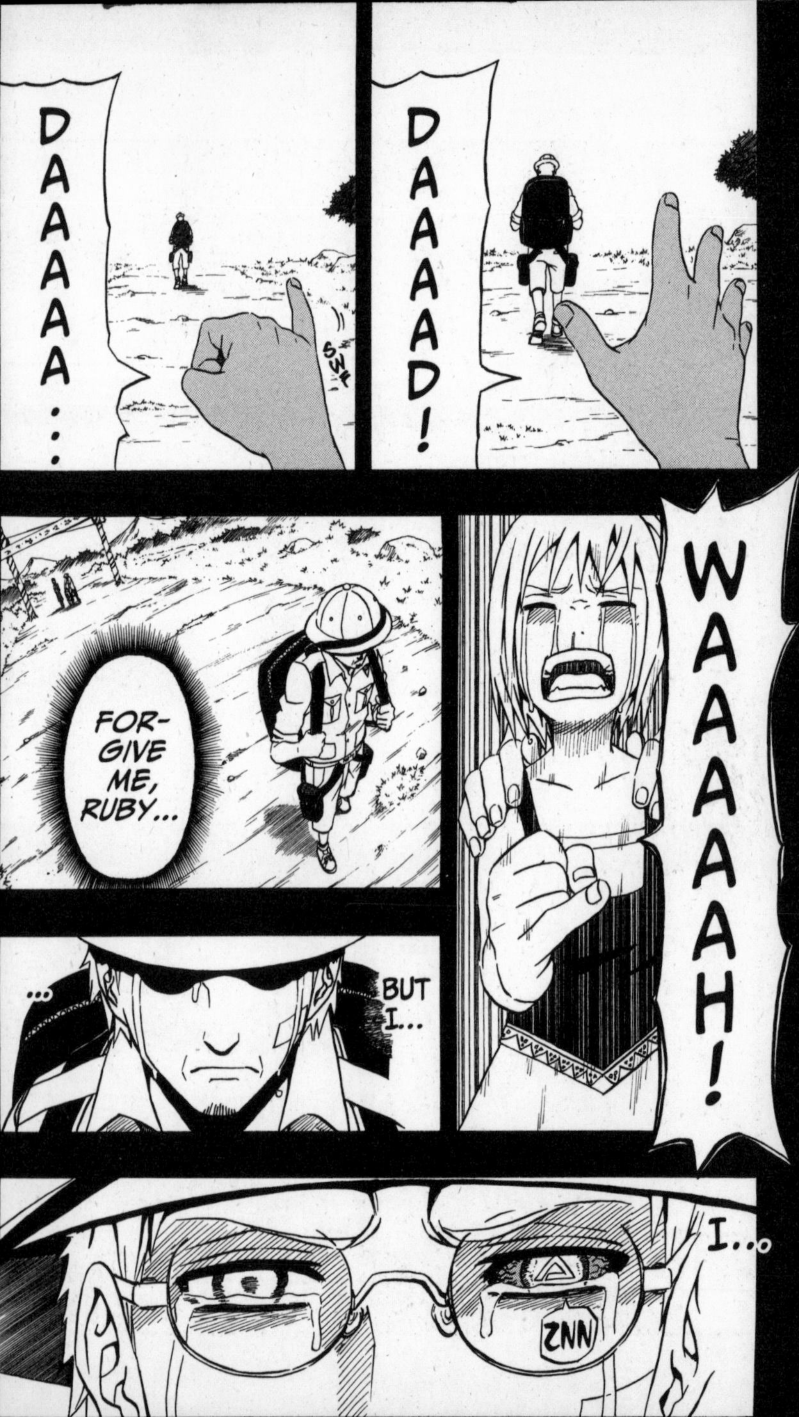
DAAAAAD!
DAAAAAA...
SWF
WAAAAAH!
FOR-GIVE ME, RUBY...
BUT I...
...
I...
ZNN

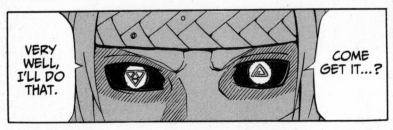

VERY WELL, I'LL DO THAT.

COME GET IT...?

SATAN...

LET'S GET ONE THING STRAIGHT...

WHOA!

YOU'RE TALKING TO JIO FREED, FULL STOP...

...END OF STORY, GOT IT?

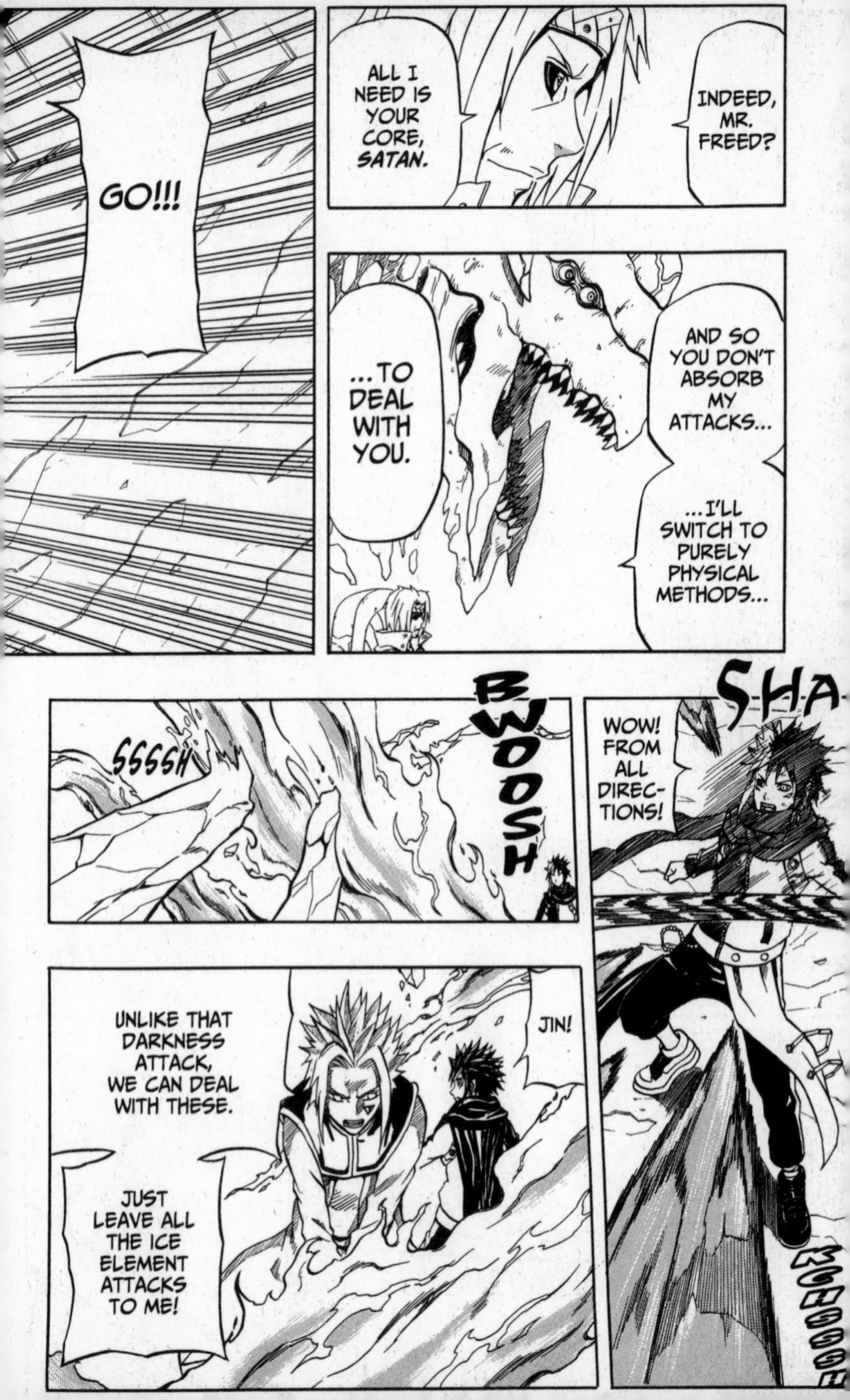
INDEED, MR. FREED?
ALL I NEED IS YOUR CORE, SATAN.
AND SO YOU DON'T ABSORB MY ATTACKS...
...I'LL SWITCH TO PURELY PHYSICAL METHODS...
...TO DEAL WITH YOU.
GO!!!
SHA
WOW! FROM ALL DIRECTIONS!
KSHSSSH
BWOOSH
SSSSH
JIN!
UNLIKE THAT DARKNESS ATTACK, WE CAN DEAL WITH THESE.
JUST LEAVE ALL THE ICE ELEMENT ATTACKS TO ME!

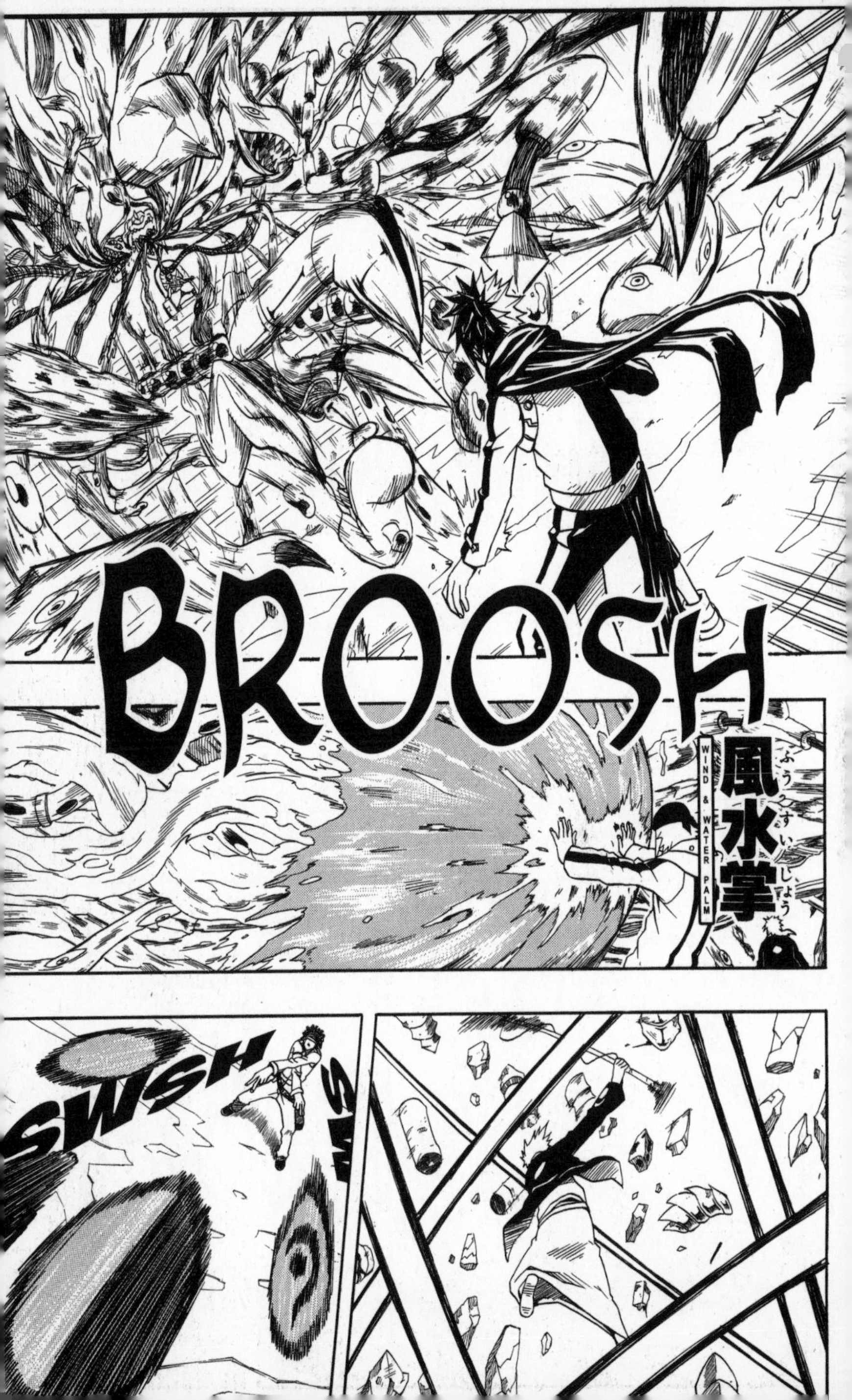
BROOSH
風水掌
ふうすいしょう
WIND & WATER PALM
SWSH
SWSH

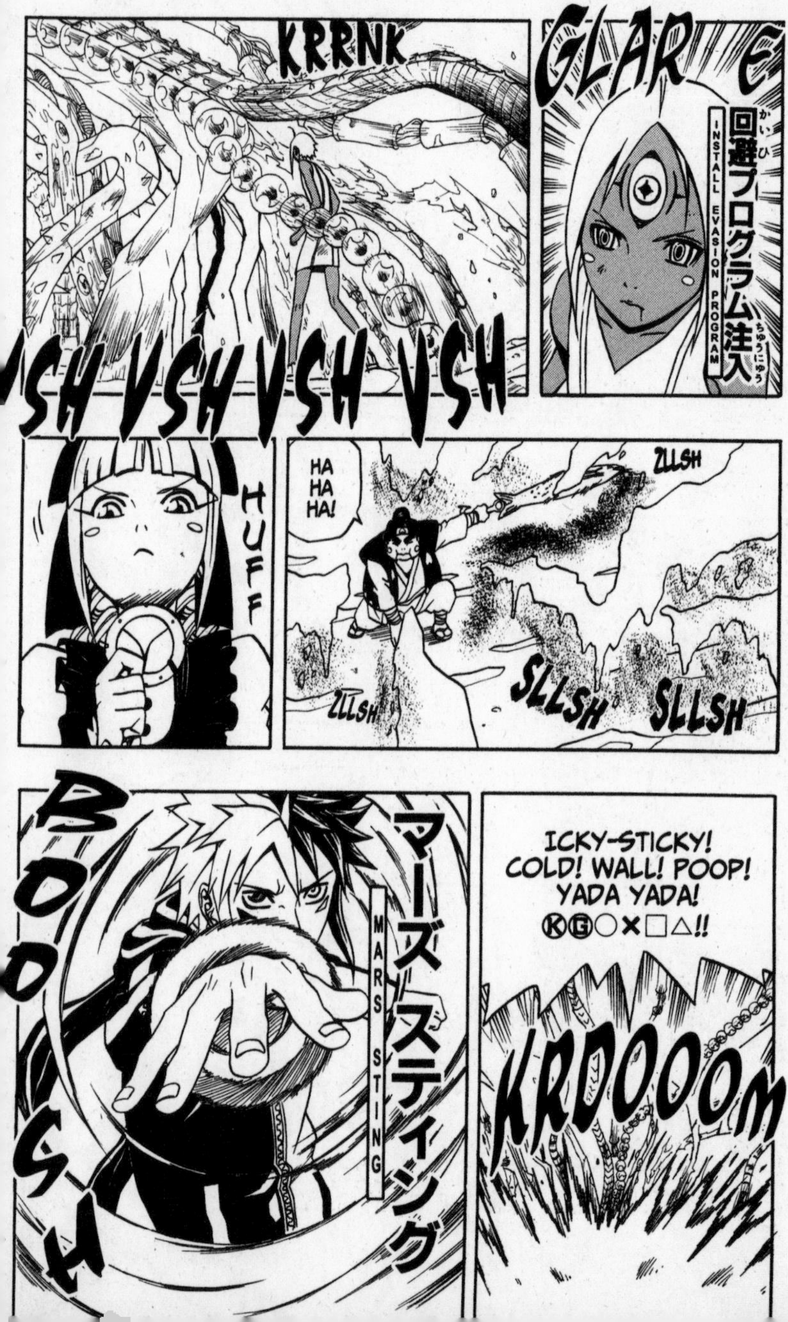
GLARE
回避プログラム注入
かいひ
ちゅうにゅう
INSTALL EVASION PROGRAM
KRRNK
VSH VSH VSH VSH
HA HA HA!
ZLLSH
SLLSH
SLLSH
ZLLSH
HUFF
ICKY-STICKY! COLD! WALL! POOP! YADA YADA! ⓀⒼ○×□△!!
KRDOOOM
マーズスティング
MARS STING
BOOSH

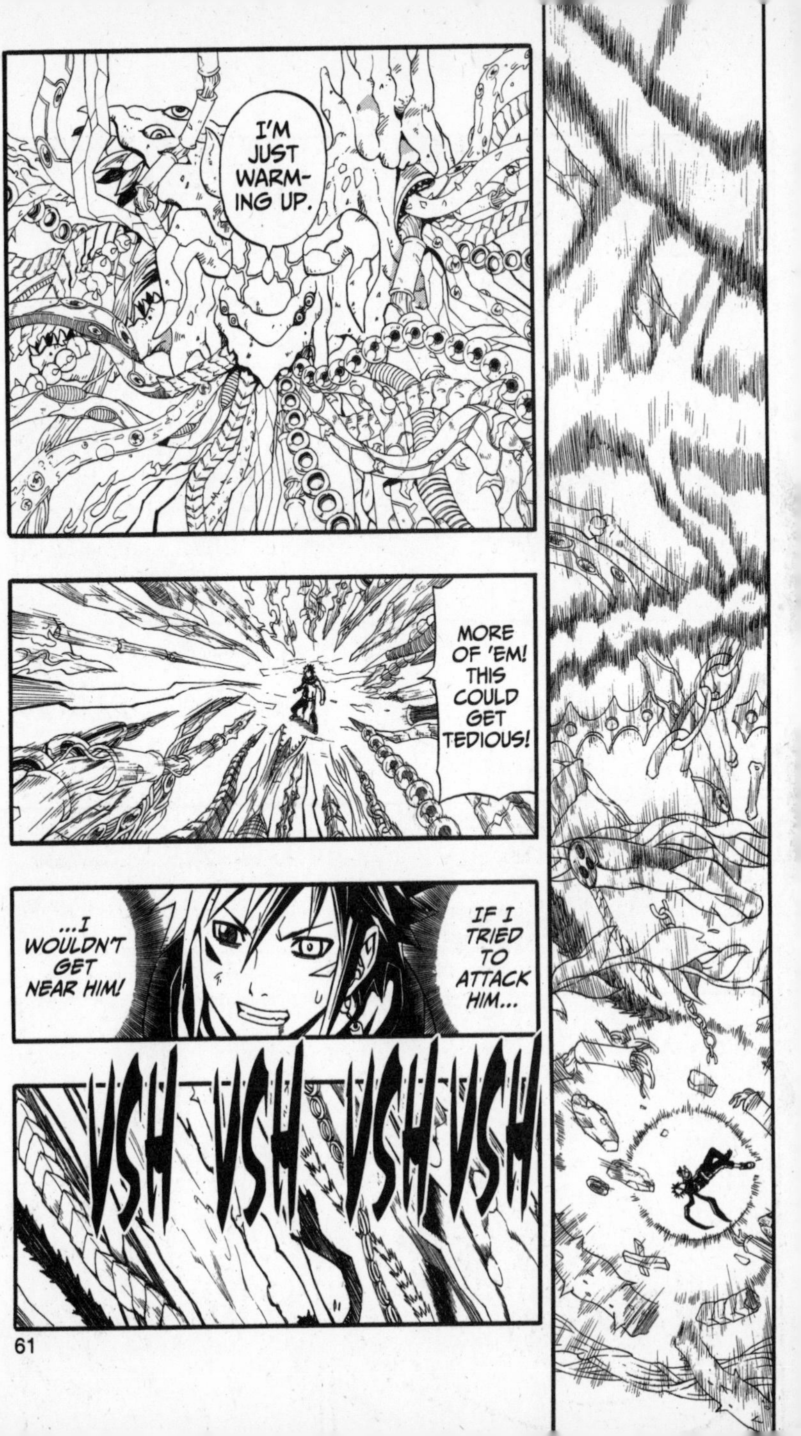
I'M JUST WARMING-UP.
MORE OF 'EM! THIS COULD GET TEDIOUS!
IF I TRIED TO ATTACK HIM...
...I WOULDN'T GET NEAR HIM!
VSH VSH VSH VSH

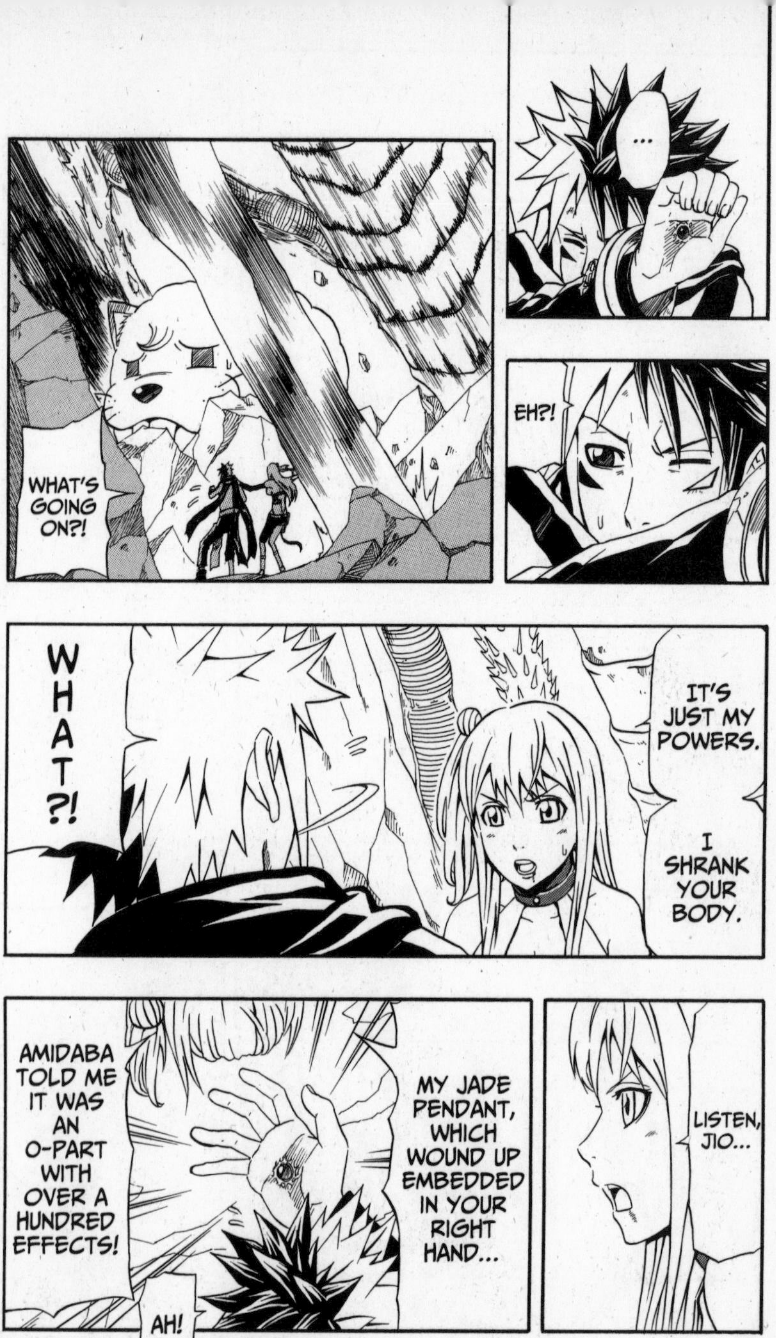
...
EH?!
WHAT'S GOING ON?!
IT'S JUST MY POWERS.
I SHRANK YOUR BODY.
WHAT?!
LISTEN, JIO...
MY JADE PENDANT, WHICH WOUND UP EMBEDDED IN YOUR RIGHT HAND...
AMIDABA TOLD ME IT WAS AN O-PART WITH OVER A HUNDRED EFFECTS!
AH!

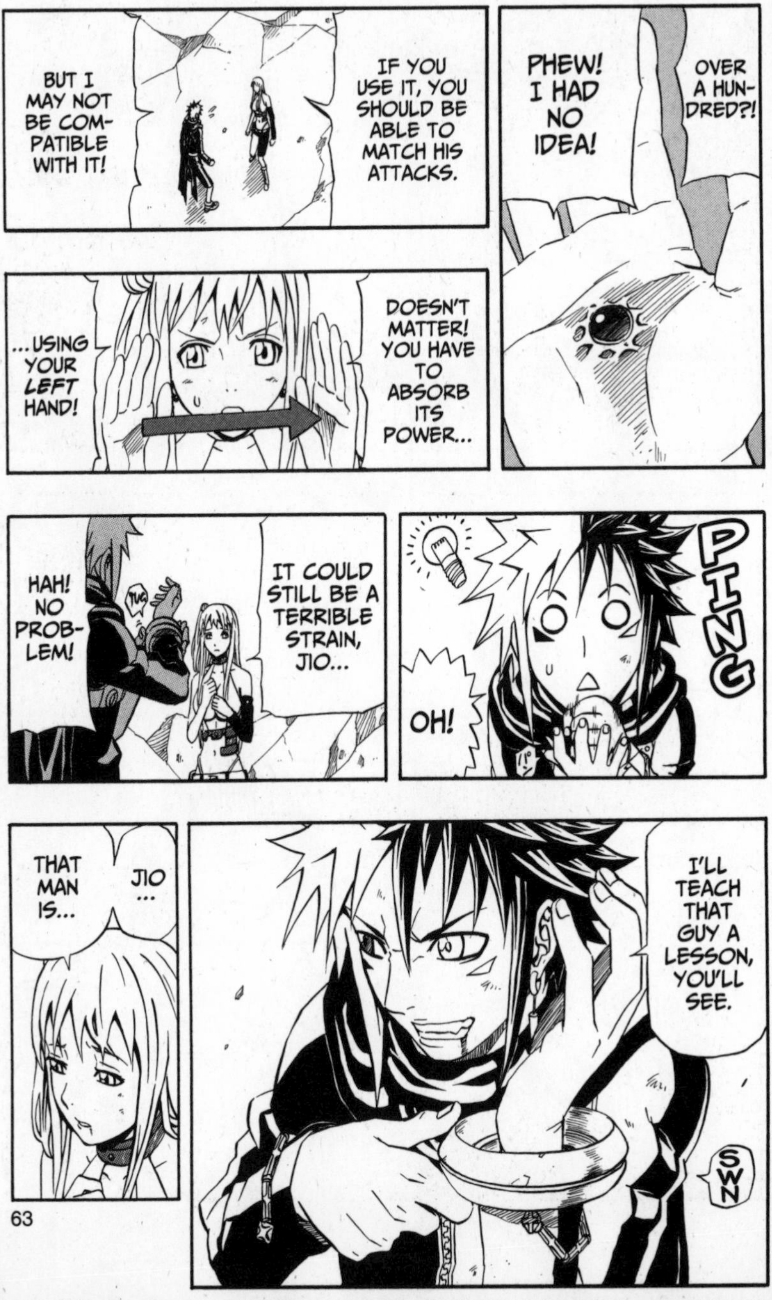
OVER A HUNDRED?!
PHEW! I HAD NO IDEA!
IF YOU USE IT, YOU SHOULD BE ABLE TO MATCH HIS ATTACKS.
BUT I MAY NOT BE COMPATIBLE WITH IT!
DOESN'T MATTER! YOU HAVE TO ABSORB ITS POWER...
...USING YOUR LEFT HAND!
PING
OH!
IT COULD STILL BE A TERRIBLE STRAIN, JIO...
TUG
HAH! NO PROBLEM!
I'LL TEACH THAT GUY A LESSON, YOU'LL SEE.
SWN
JIO...
THAT MAN IS...

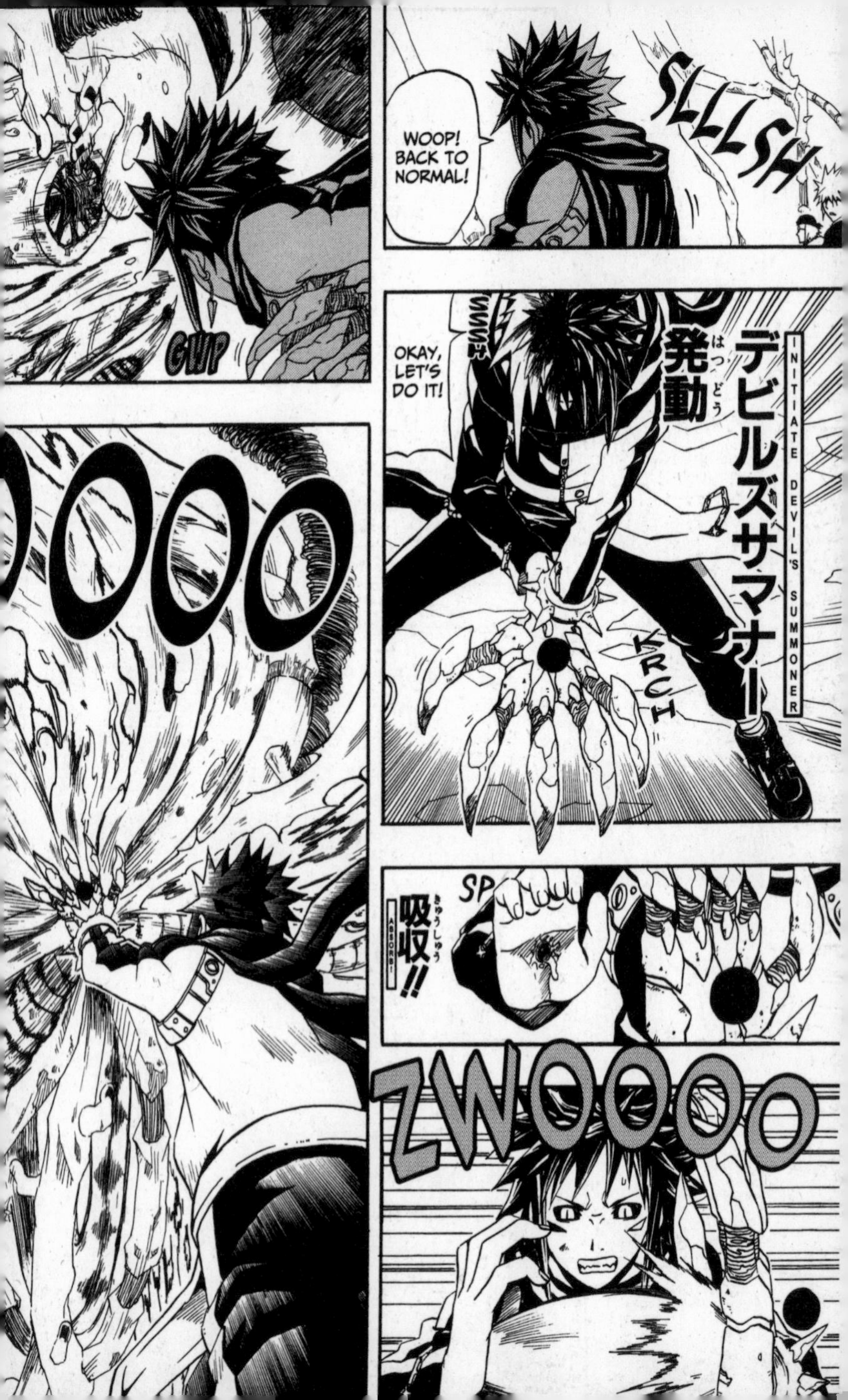

SLLSH
WOOP! BACK TO NORMAL!
GWIP
デビルズサマナー発動
INITIATE DEVIL'S SUMMONER
OKAY, LET'S DO IT!
KRCH
SP
吸収!!
ABSORB!
ZWOOOO
OOOOO

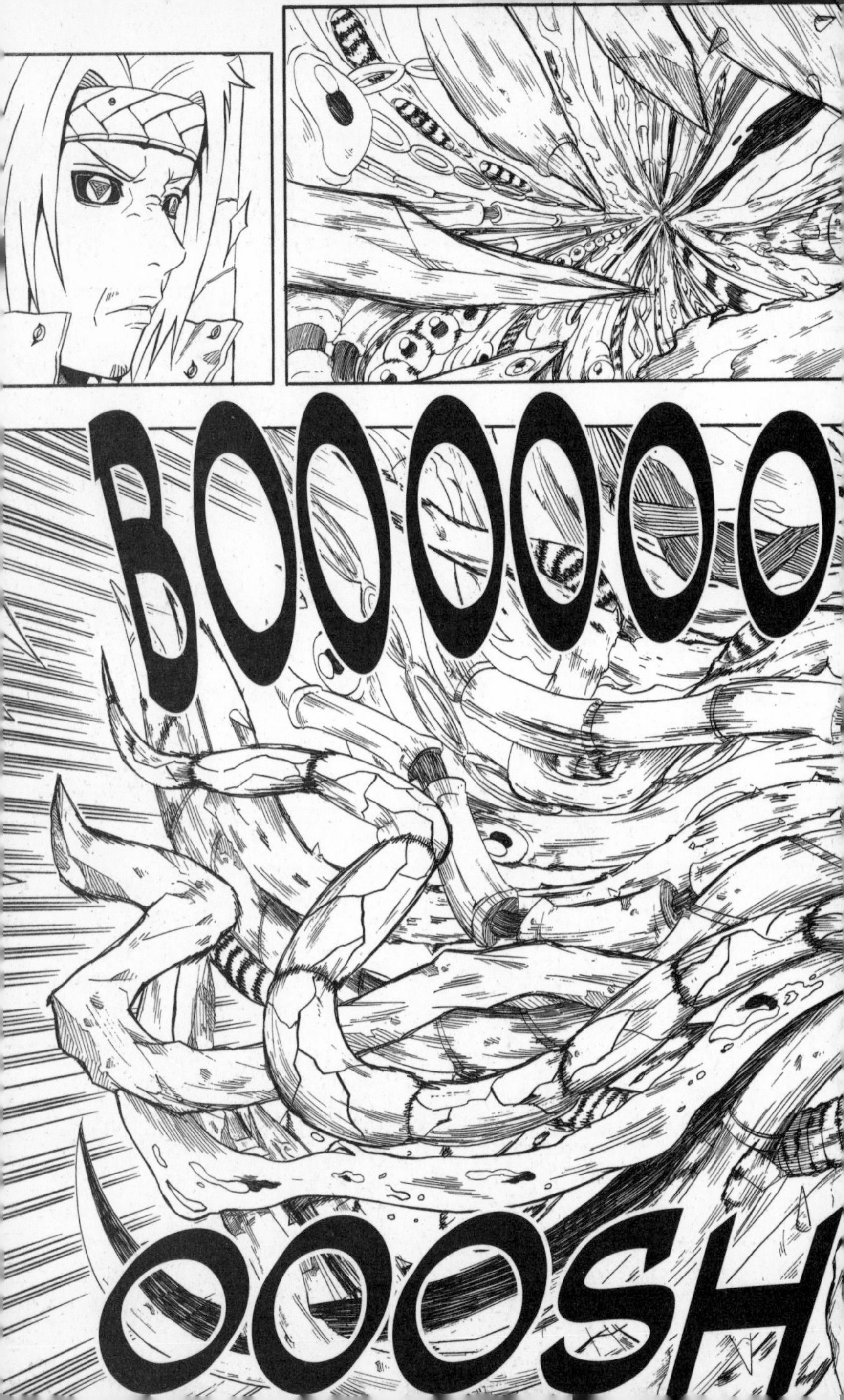
BOOOOOO
OOOSH

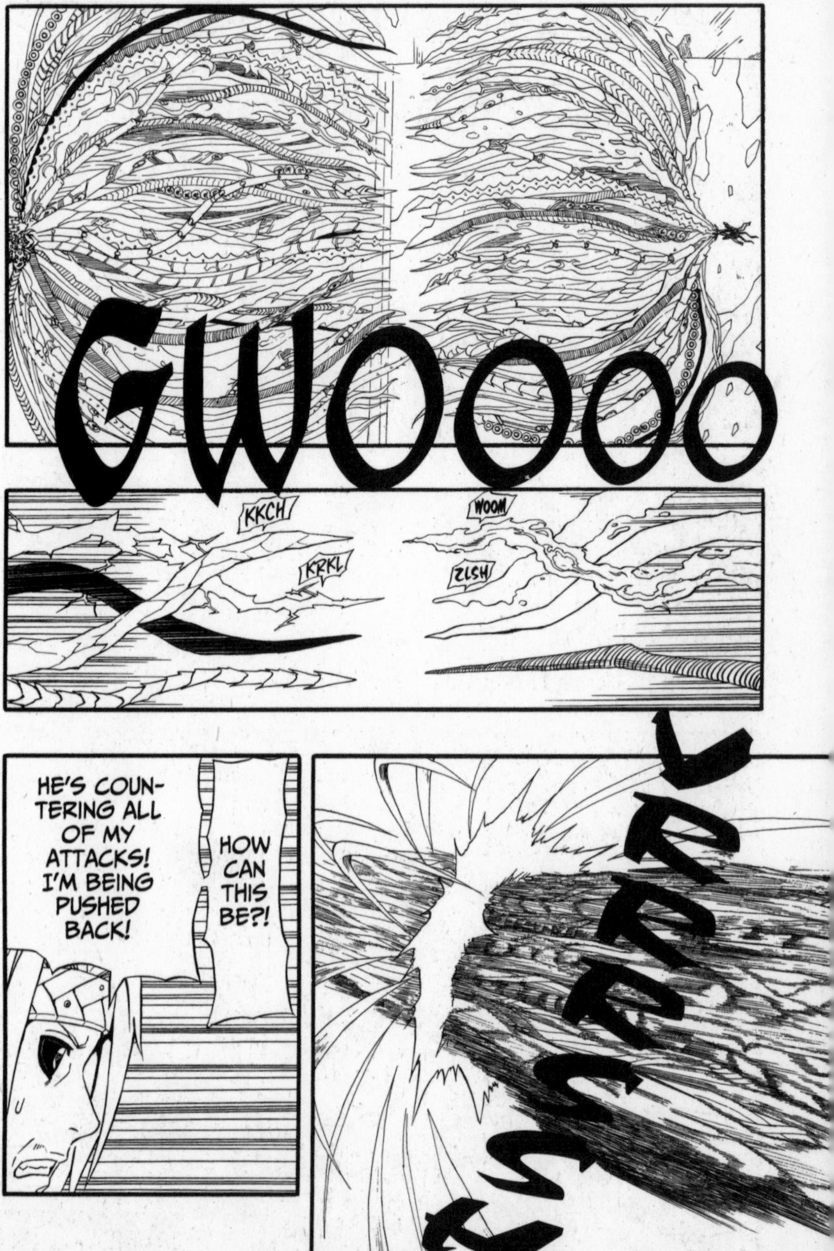
GWOOOO
WOOM
ZLSH
KKCH
KRKL
HOW CAN THIS BE?!
HE'S COUNTERING ALL OF MY ATTACKS! I'M BEING PUSHED BACK!

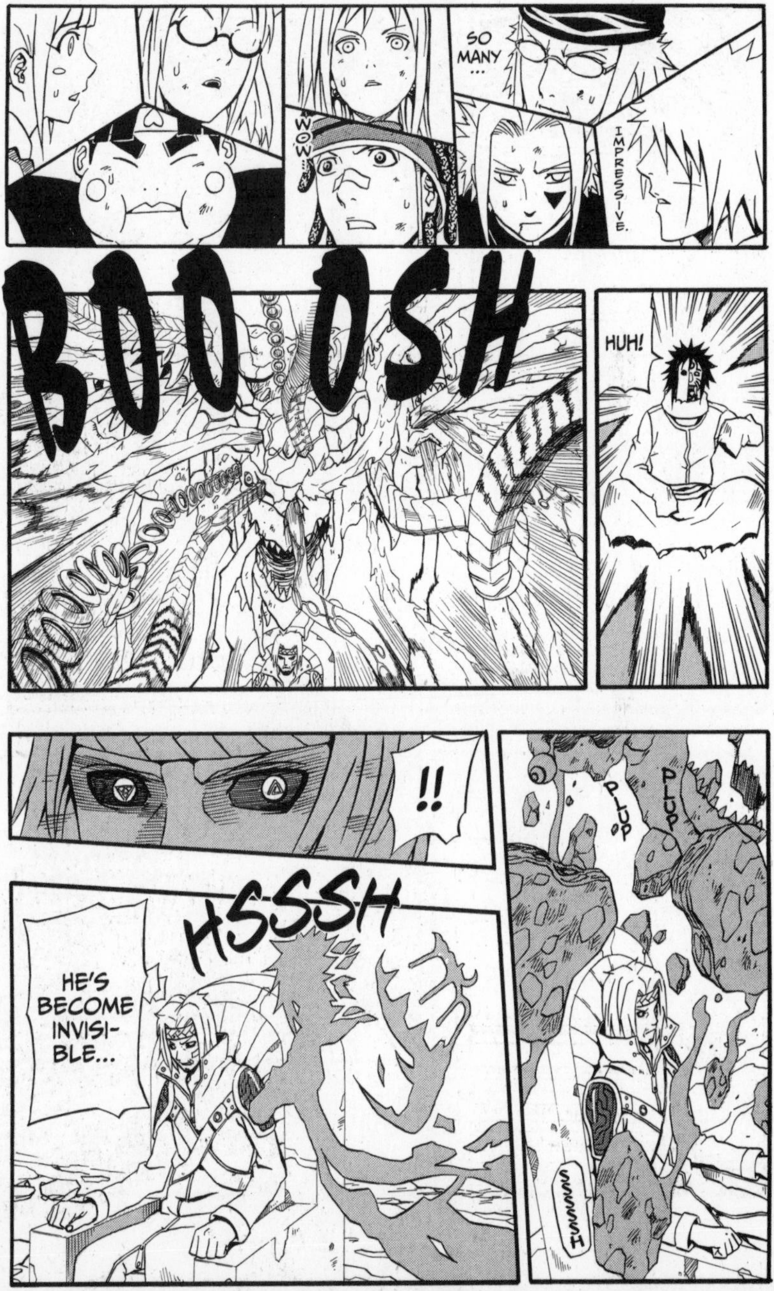
SO MANY ...
IMPRESSIVE.
WOW...
HUH!
BOOOSH
PLUP
PLUP
SSSSSH
!!
HSSSH
HE'S BECOME INVISIBLE...

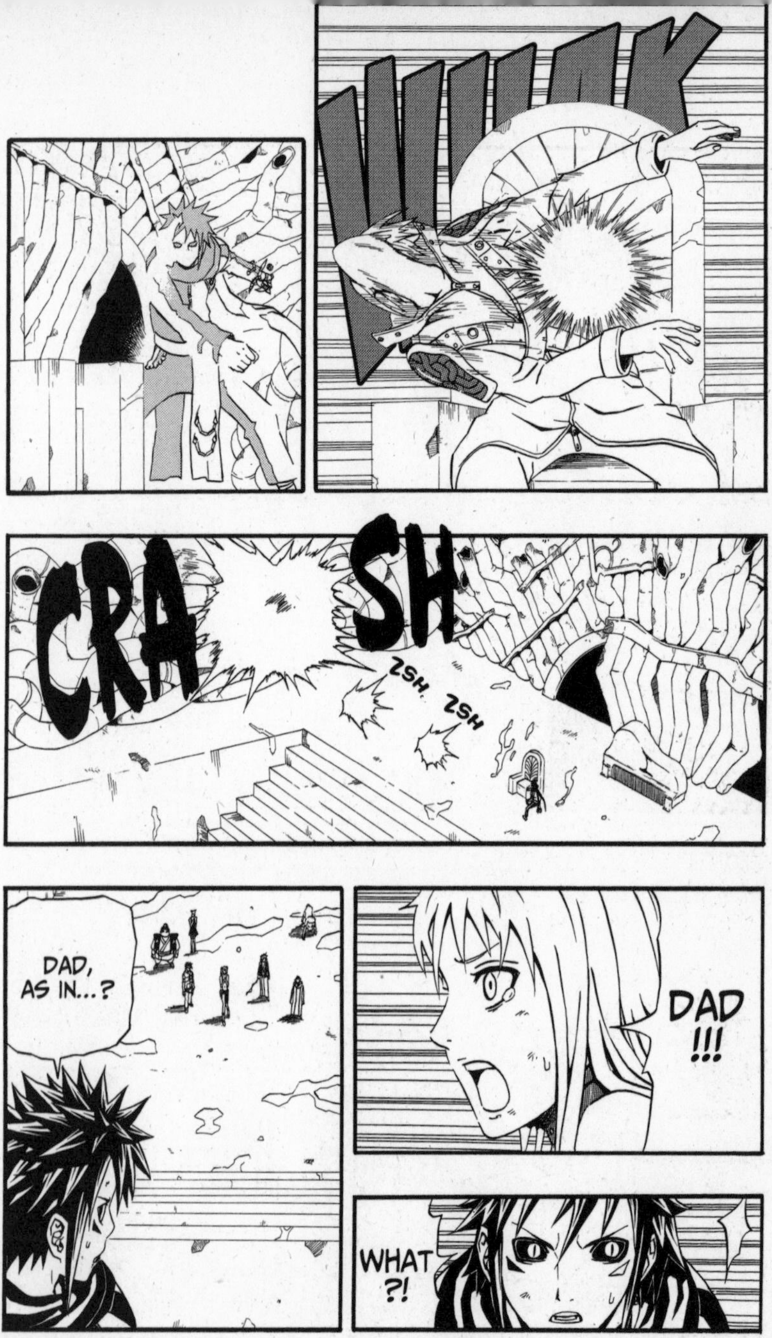
WHAK
CRASH
ZSH
ZSH
DAD !!!
WHAT ?!
DAD, AS IN...?

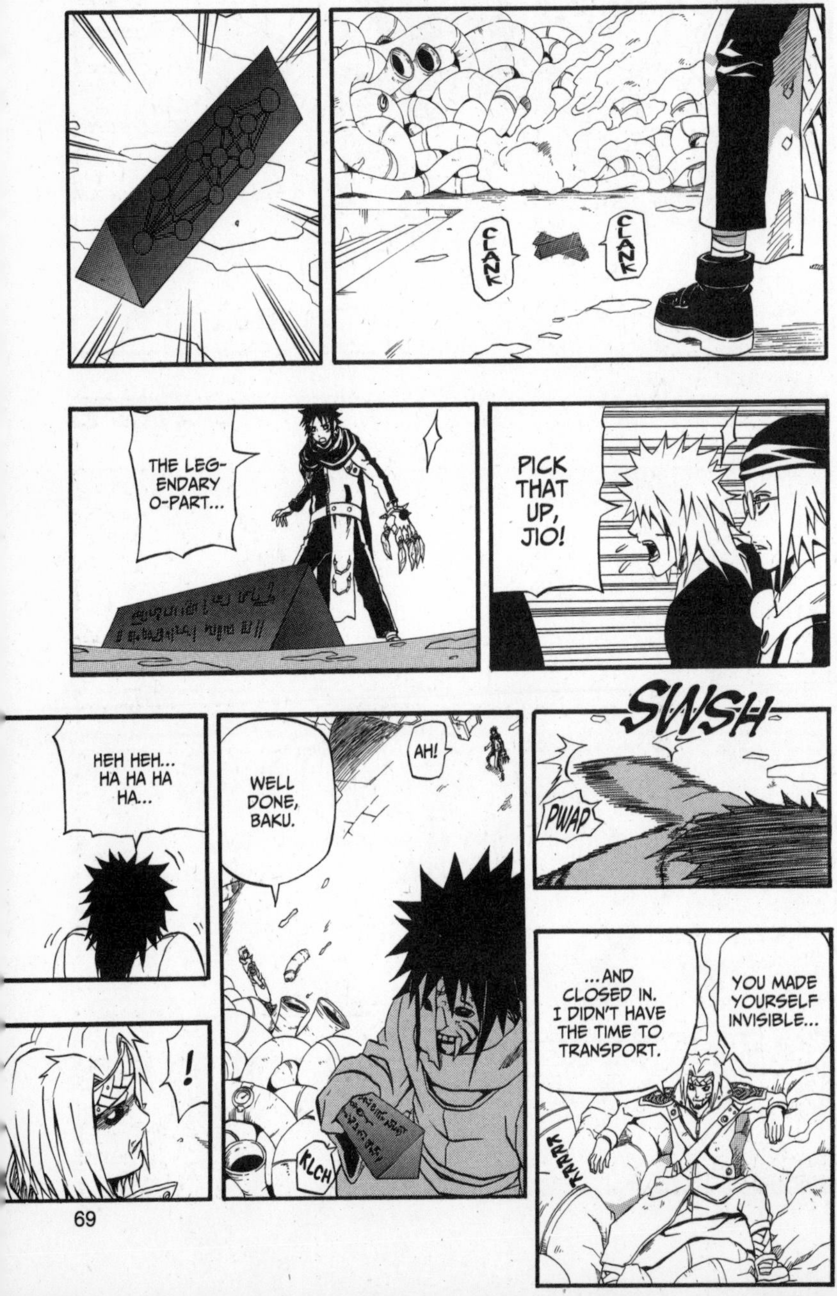

CLANK
CLANK
PICK THAT UP, JIO!
THE LEG-ENDARY O-PART...
SWSH
PWAP
YOU MADE YOURSELF INVISIBLE...
...AND CLOSED IN. I DIDN'T HAVE THE TIME TO TRANSPORT.
KRRRK
AH!
WELL DONE, BAKU.
KLCH
HEH HEH... HA HA HA HA...
!

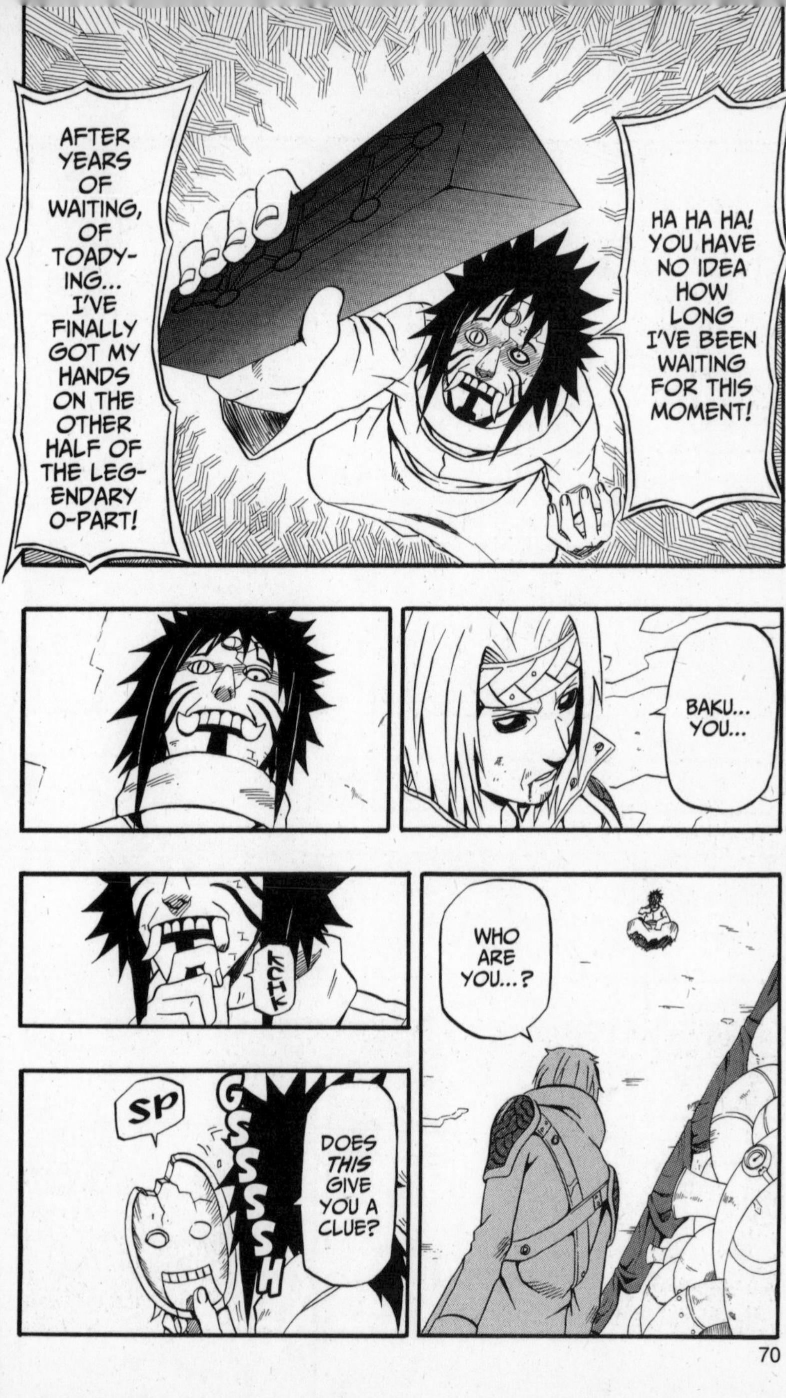
HA HA HA! YOU HAVE NO IDEA HOW LONG I'VE BEEN WAITING FOR THIS MOMENT!
AFTER YEARS OF WAITING, OF TOADY-ING... I'VE FINALLY GOT MY HANDS ON THE OTHER HALF OF THE LEG-ENDARY O-PART!
BAKU... YOU...
WHO ARE YOU...?
KCHK
DOES THIS GIVE YOU A CLUE?
GSSSSH
SP

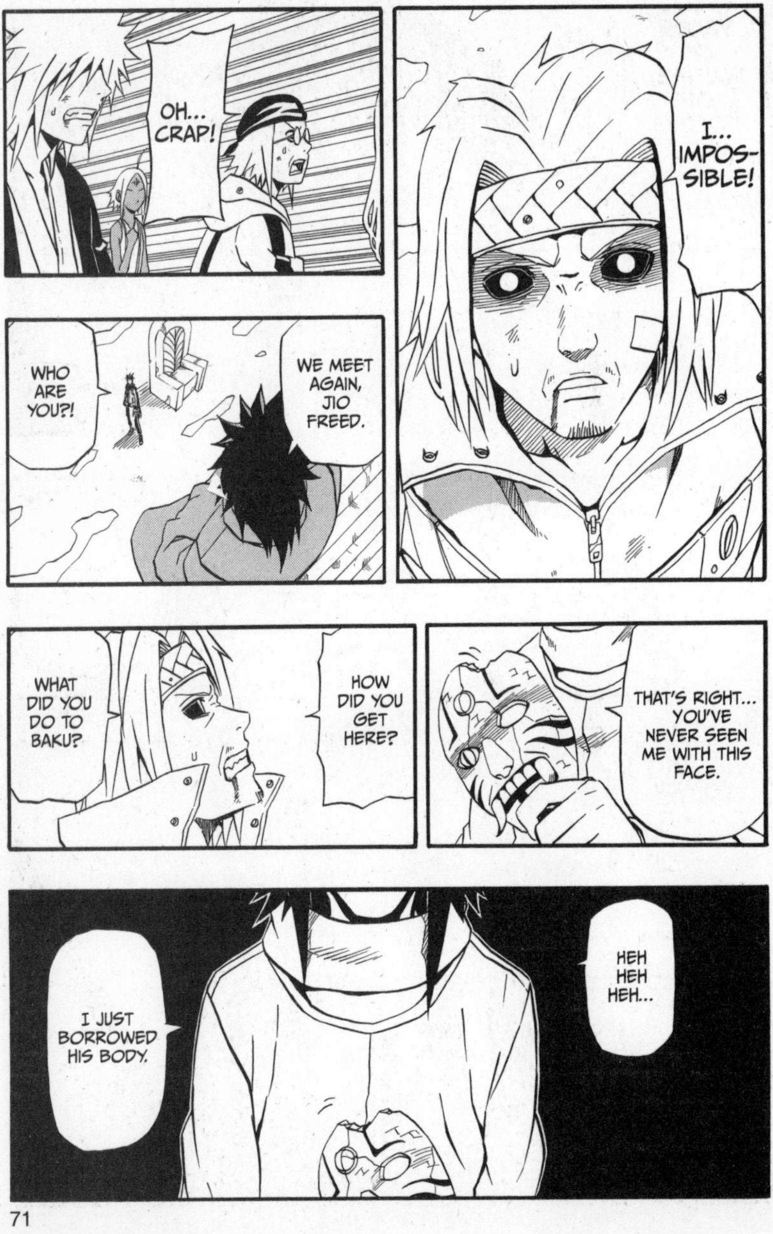
I... IMPOS-SIBLE!
OH... CRAP!
WE MEET AGAIN, JIO FREED.
WHO ARE YOU?!
THAT'S RIGHT... YOU'VE NEVER SEEN ME WITH THIS FACE.
HOW DID YOU GET HERE?
WHAT DID YOU DO TO BAKU?
HEH HEH HEH...
I JUST BORROWED HIS BODY.

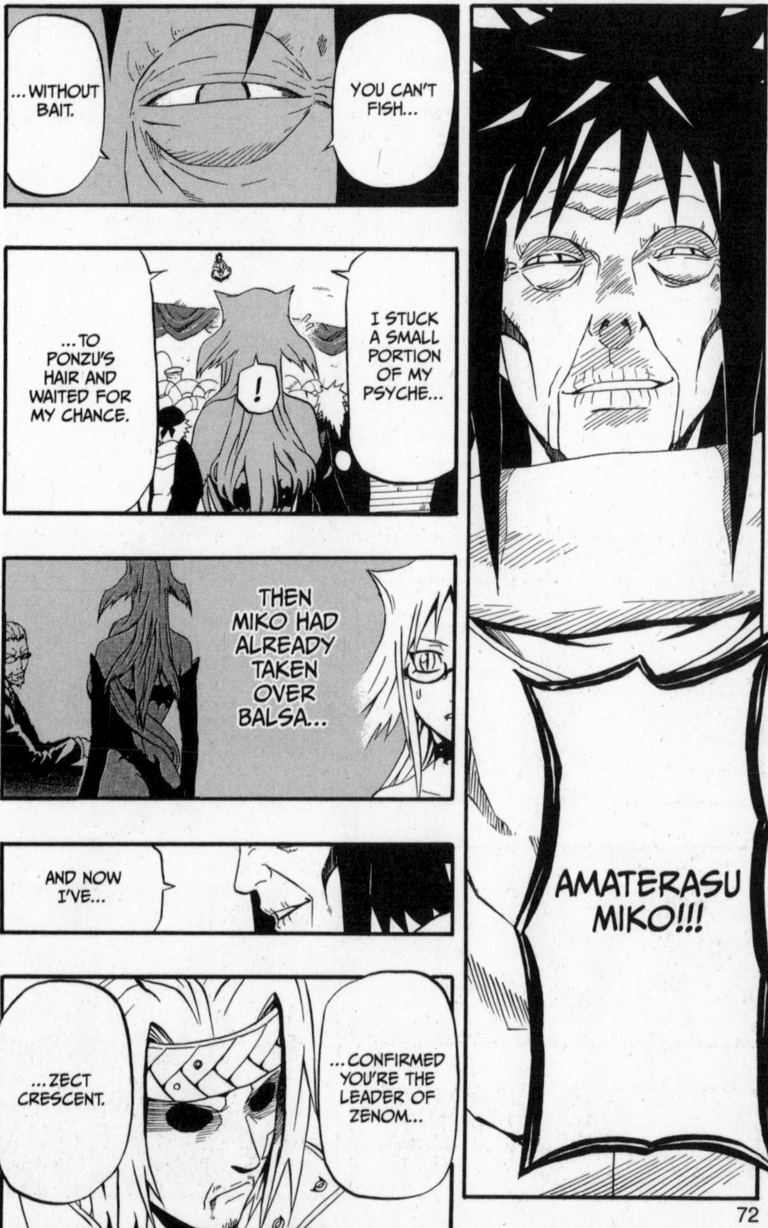

AMATERASU MIKO!!!
YOU CAN'T FISH...
...WITHOUT BAIT.
I STUCK A SMALL PORTION OF MY PSYCHE...
!
...TO PONZU'S HAIR AND WAITED FOR MY CHANCE.
THEN MIKO HAD ALREADY TAKEN OVER BALSA...
AND NOW I'VE...
...CONFIRMED YOU'RE THE LEADER OF ZENOM...
...ZECT CRESCENT.

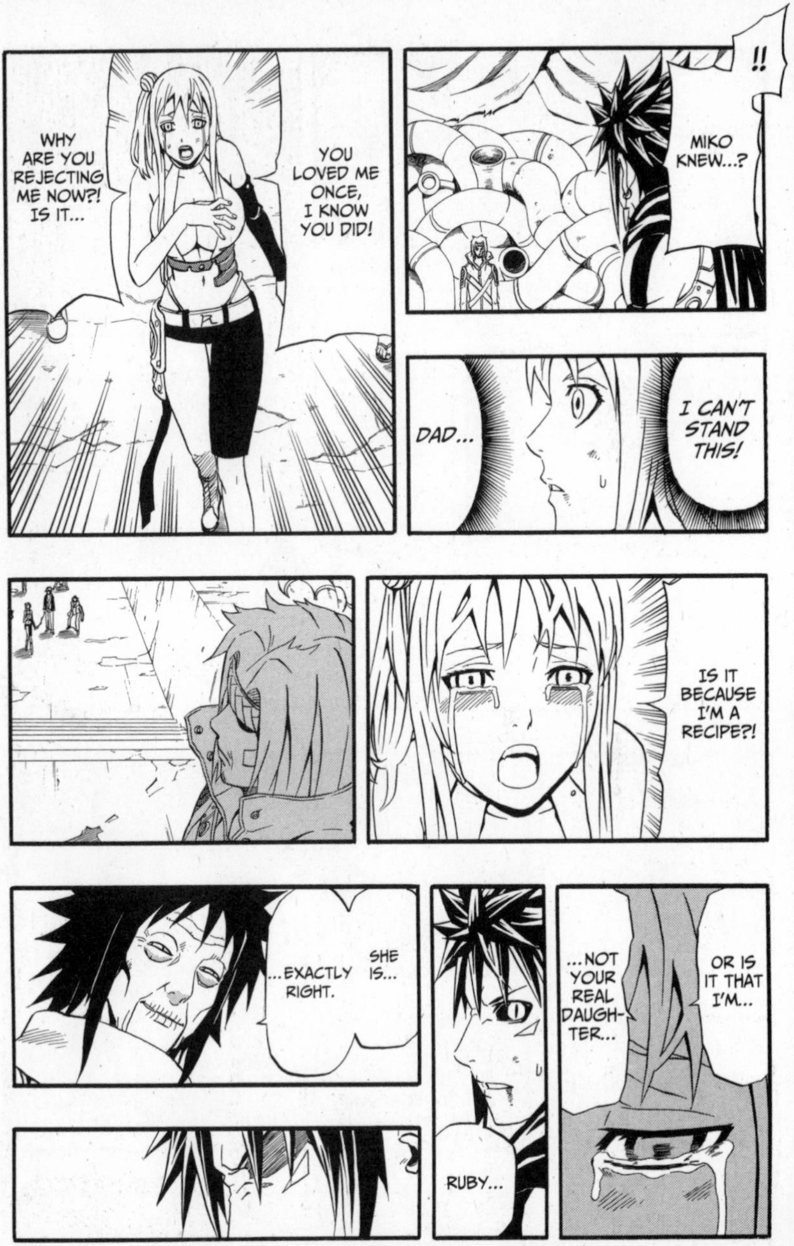
!!
MIKO KNEW...?
I CAN'T STAND THIS!
DAD...
YOU LOVED ME ONCE, I KNOW YOU DID!
WHY ARE YOU REJECTING ME NOW?! IS IT...
IS IT BECAUSE I'M A RECIPE?!
OR IS IT THAT I'M...
...NOT YOUR REAL DAUGHTER...
RUBY...
SHE IS...
...EXACTLY RIGHT.

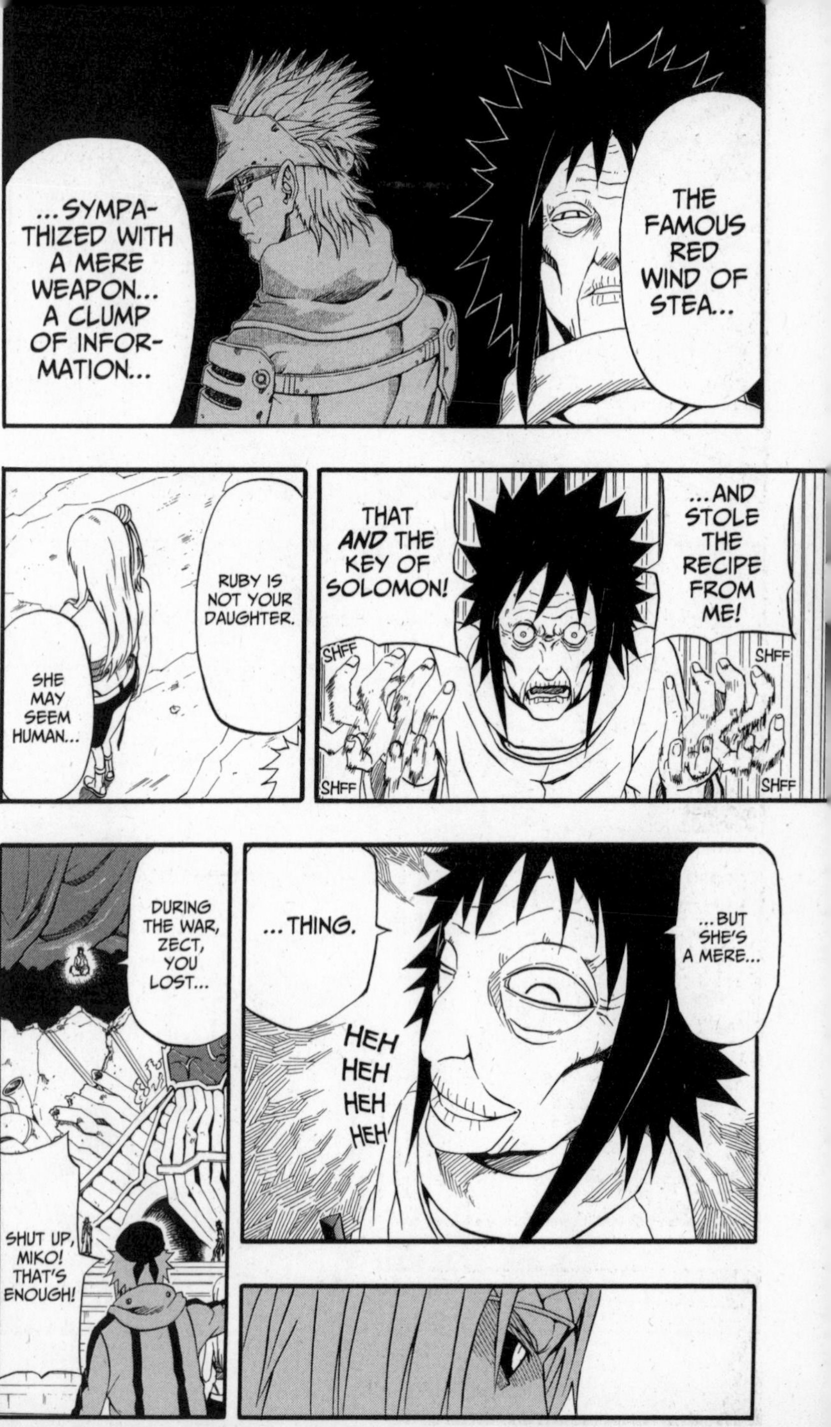
THE FAMOUS RED WIND OF STEA...
...SYMPATHIZED WITH A MERE WEAPON... A CLUMP OF INFORMATION...
...AND STOLE THE RECIPE FROM ME!
THAT *AND* THE KEY OF SOLOMON!
SHFF
SHFF
SHFF
SHFF
RUBY IS NOT YOUR DAUGHTER.
SHE MAY SEEM HUMAN...
...BUT SHE'S A MERE...
HEH HEH HEH HEH
...THING.
DURING THE WAR, ZECT, YOU LOST...
SHUT UP, MIKO! THAT'S ENOUGH!

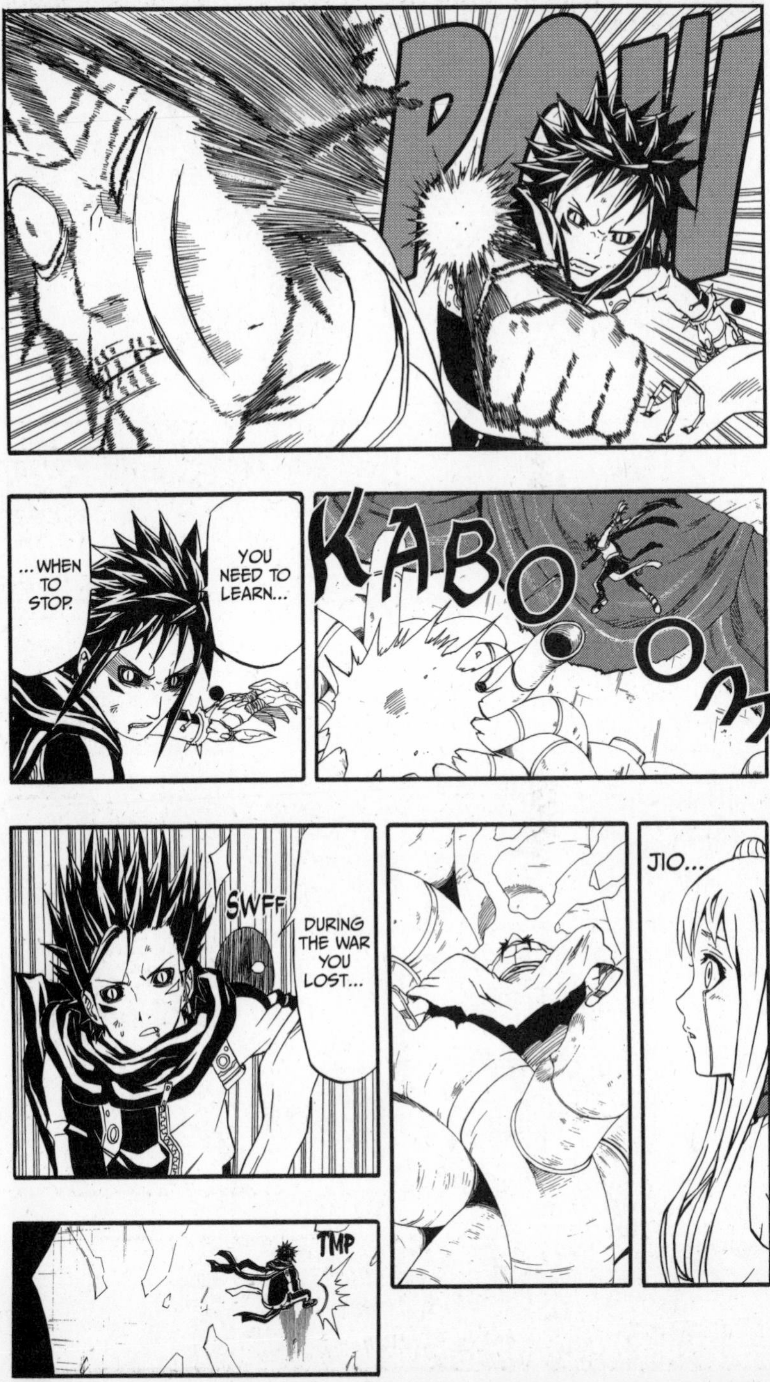
POW
KABOOOM
YOU NEED TO LEARN...
...WHEN TO STOP.
JIO...
DURING THE WAR YOU LOST...
SWFF
TMP

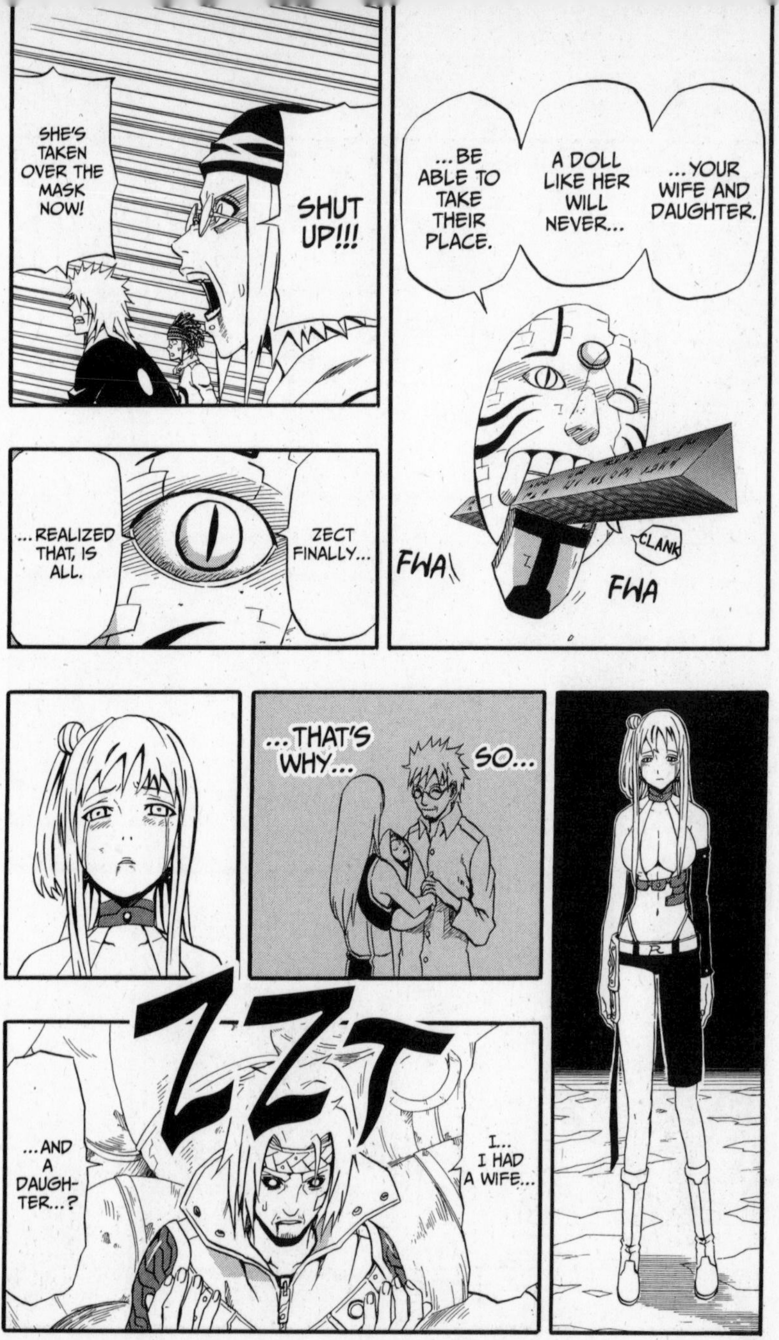
...YOUR WIFE AND DAUGHTER.
A DOLL LIKE HER WILL NEVER...
...BE ABLE TO TAKE THEIR PLACE.
CLANK
FWA
FWA
SHUT UP!!!
SHE'S TAKEN OVER THE MASK NOW!
ZECT FINALLY...
...REALIZED THAT, IS ALL.
SO...
...THAT'S WHY...
ZZT
I... I HAD A WIFE...
...AND A DAUGH-TER...?

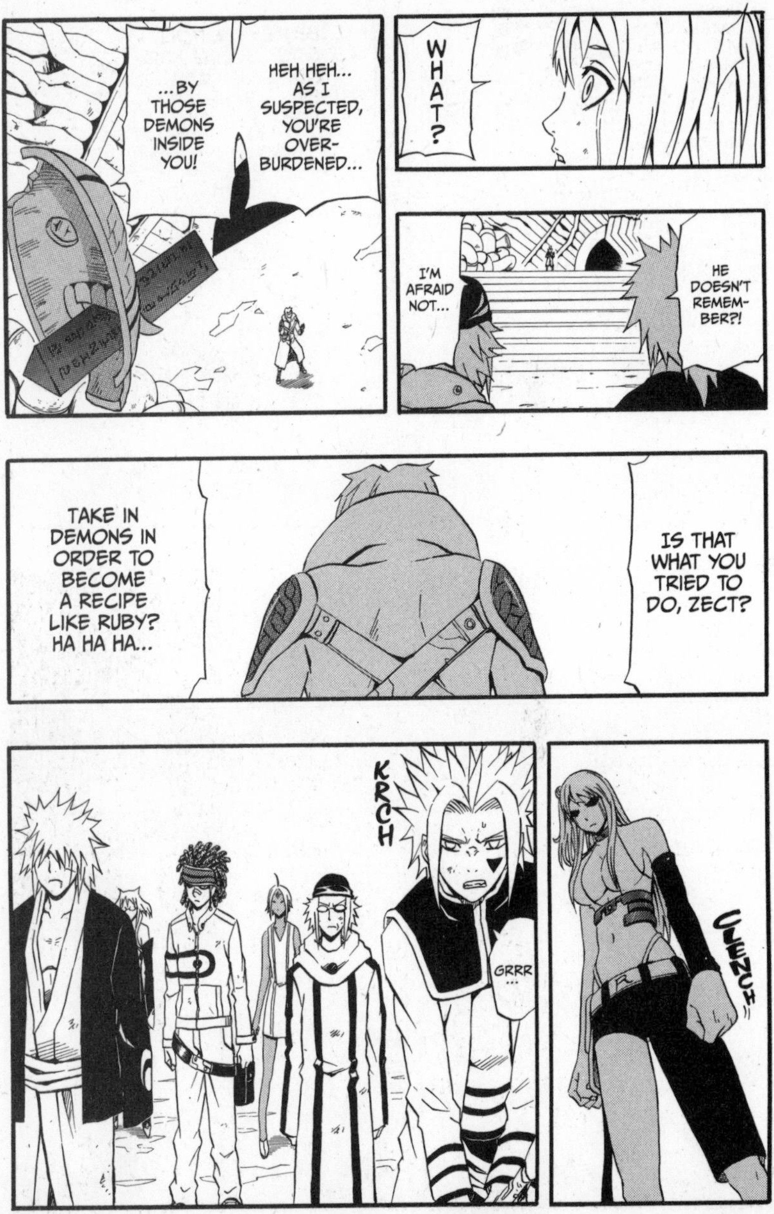
WHAT?
HE DOESN'T REMEMBER?!
I'M AFRAID NOT...
HEH HEH... AS I SUSPECTED, YOU'RE OVER-BURDENED...
...BY THOSE DEMONS INSIDE YOU!
IS THAT WHAT YOU TRIED TO DO, ZECT?
TAKE IN DEMONS IN ORDER TO BECOME A RECIPE LIKE RUBY? HA HA HA...
CLENCH
KRCH
GRRR...

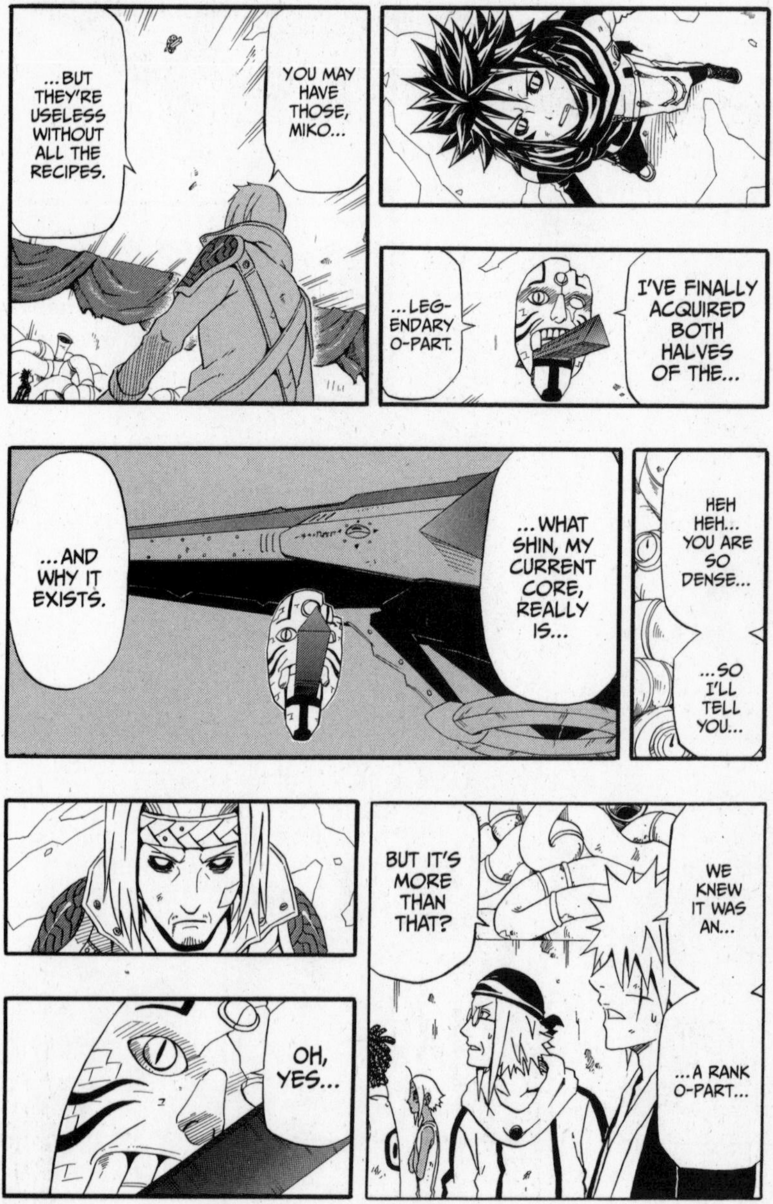
I'VE FINALLY ACQUIRED BOTH HALVES OF THE...
...LEG-ENDARY O-PART.
YOU MAY HAVE THOSE, MIKO...
...BUT THEY'RE USELESS WITHOUT ALL THE RECIPES.
HEH HEH... YOU ARE SO DENSE...
...SO I'LL TELL YOU...
...WHAT SHIN, MY CURRENT CORE, REALLY IS...
...AND WHY IT EXISTS.
WE KNEW IT WAS AN...
...A RANK O-PART...
BUT IT'S MORE THAN THAT?
OH, YES...

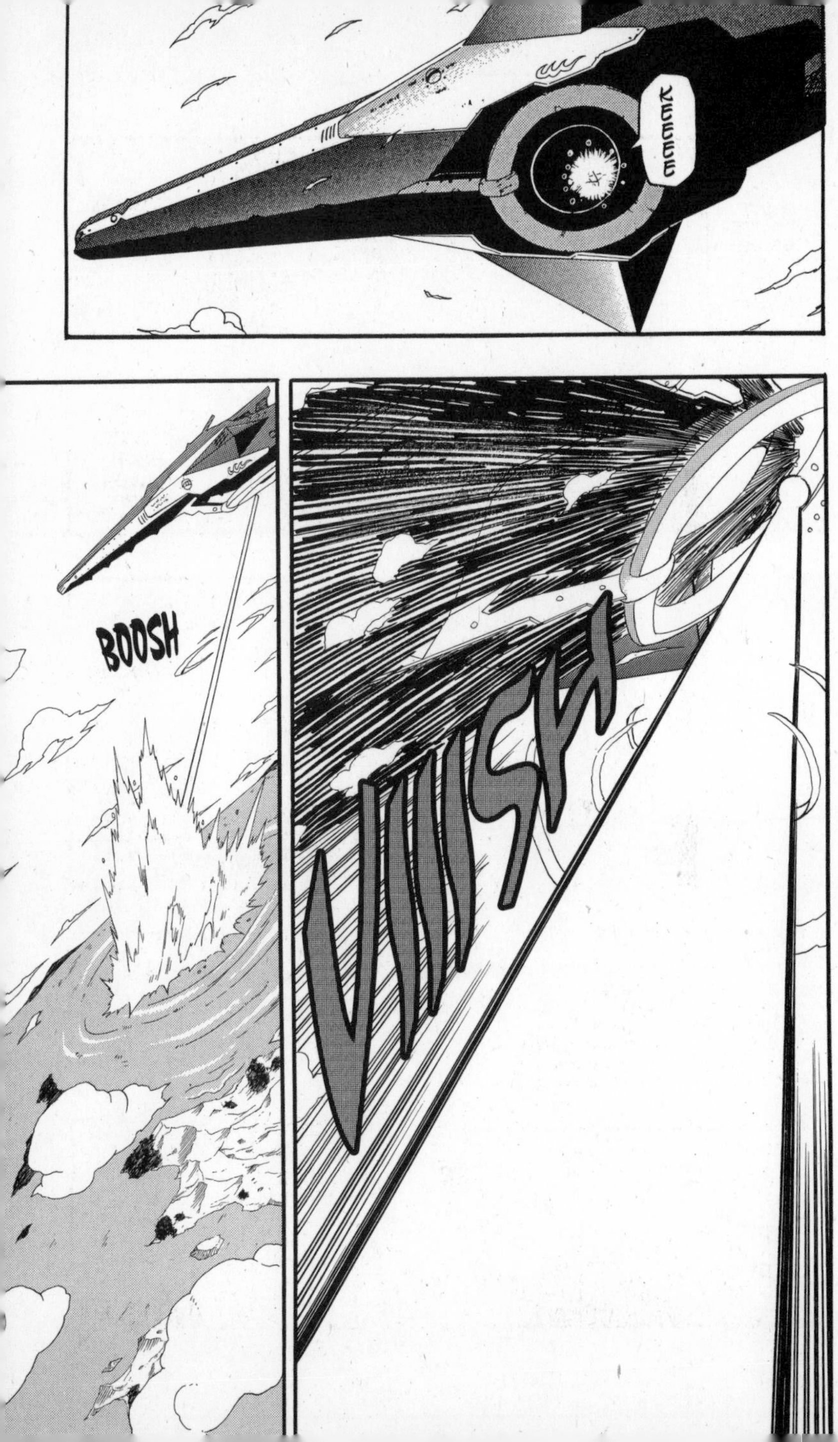
KEEEEEE
BOOSH

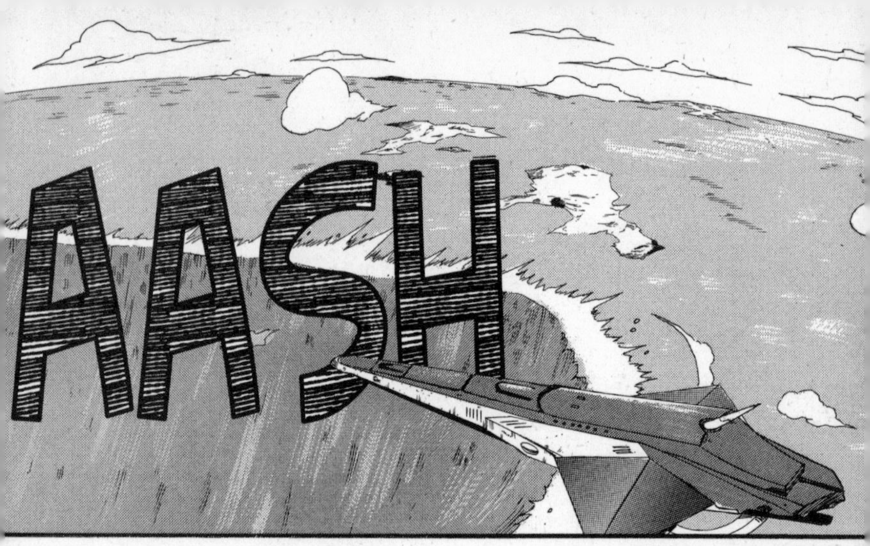
AASH
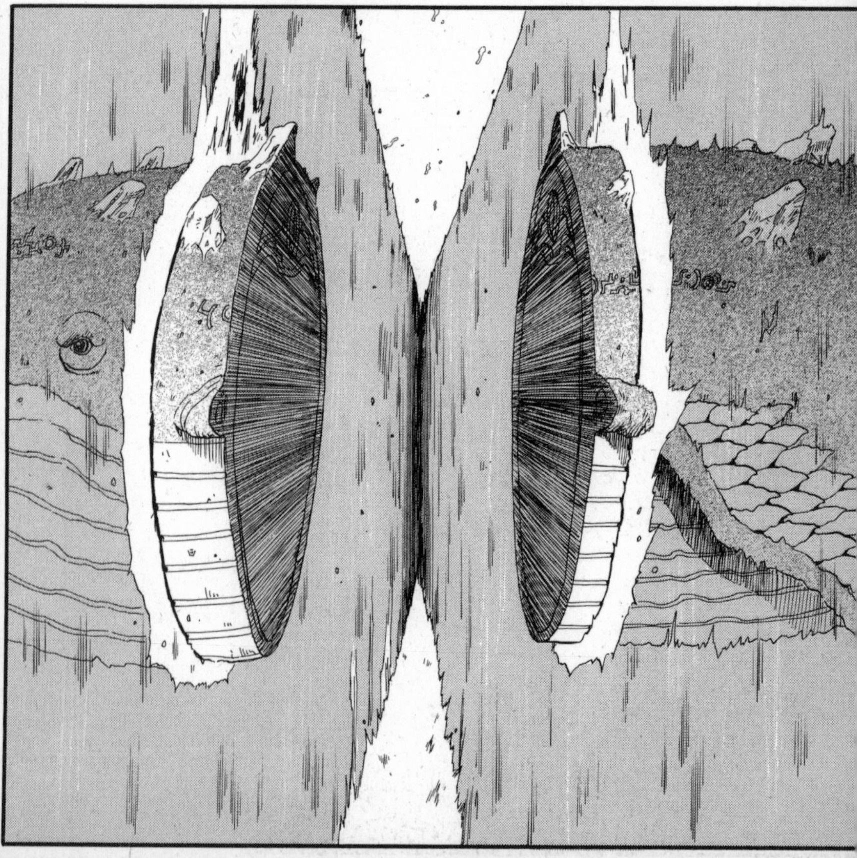

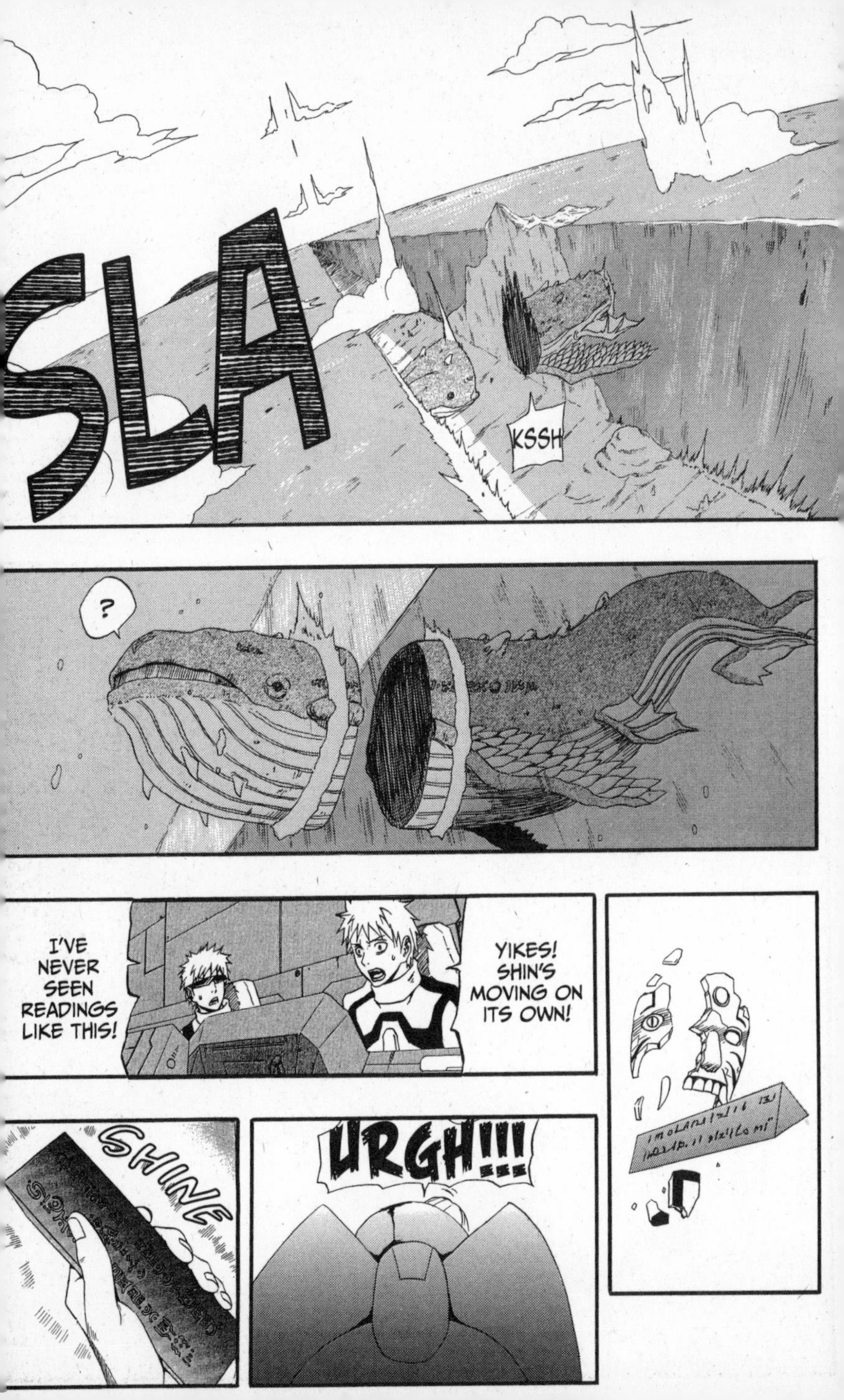

SLA
KSSH
?
YIKES! SHIN'S MOVING ON ITS OWN!
I'VE NEVER SEEN READINGS LIKE THIS!
URGH!!!
SHINE

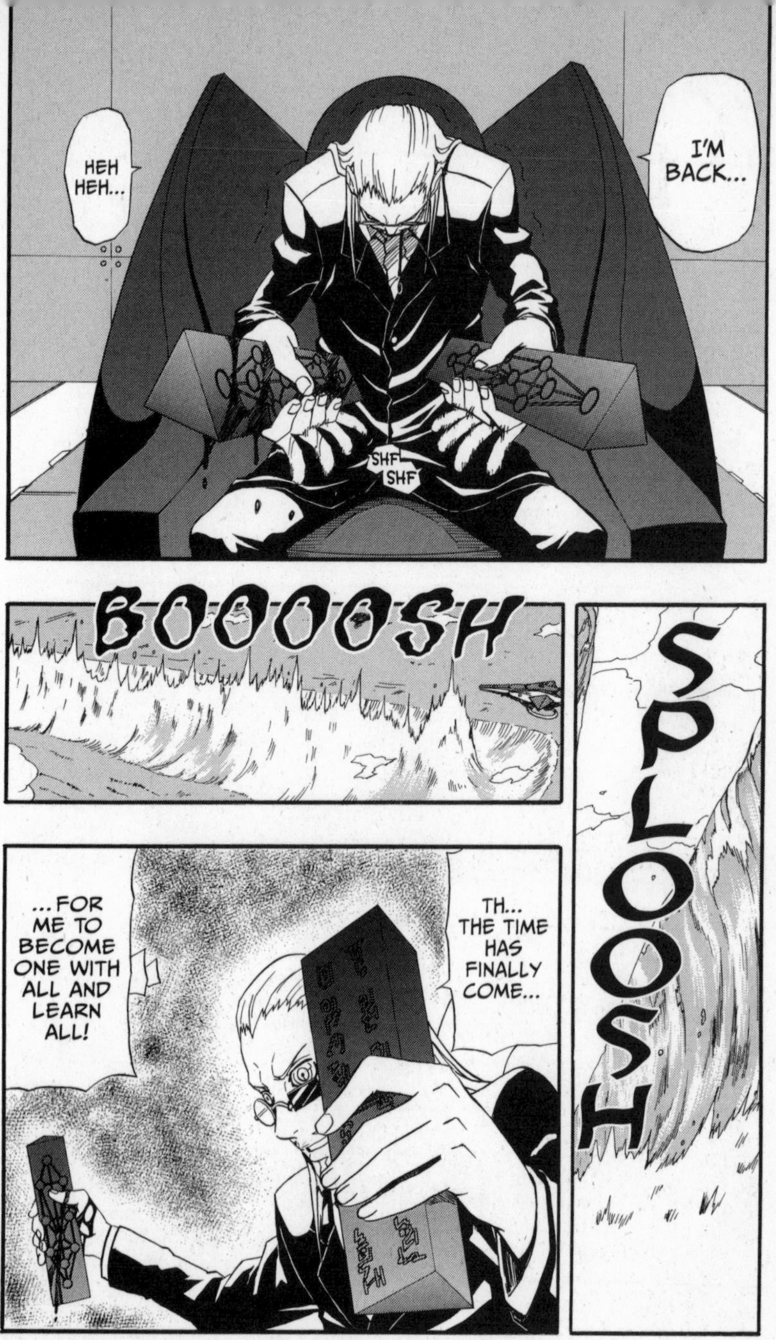
I'M BACK...
HEH HEH...
SHF SHF
SPLOOSH
BOOOOSH
TH... THE TIME HAS FINALLY COME...
...FOR ME TO BECOME ONE WITH ALL AND LEARN ALL!

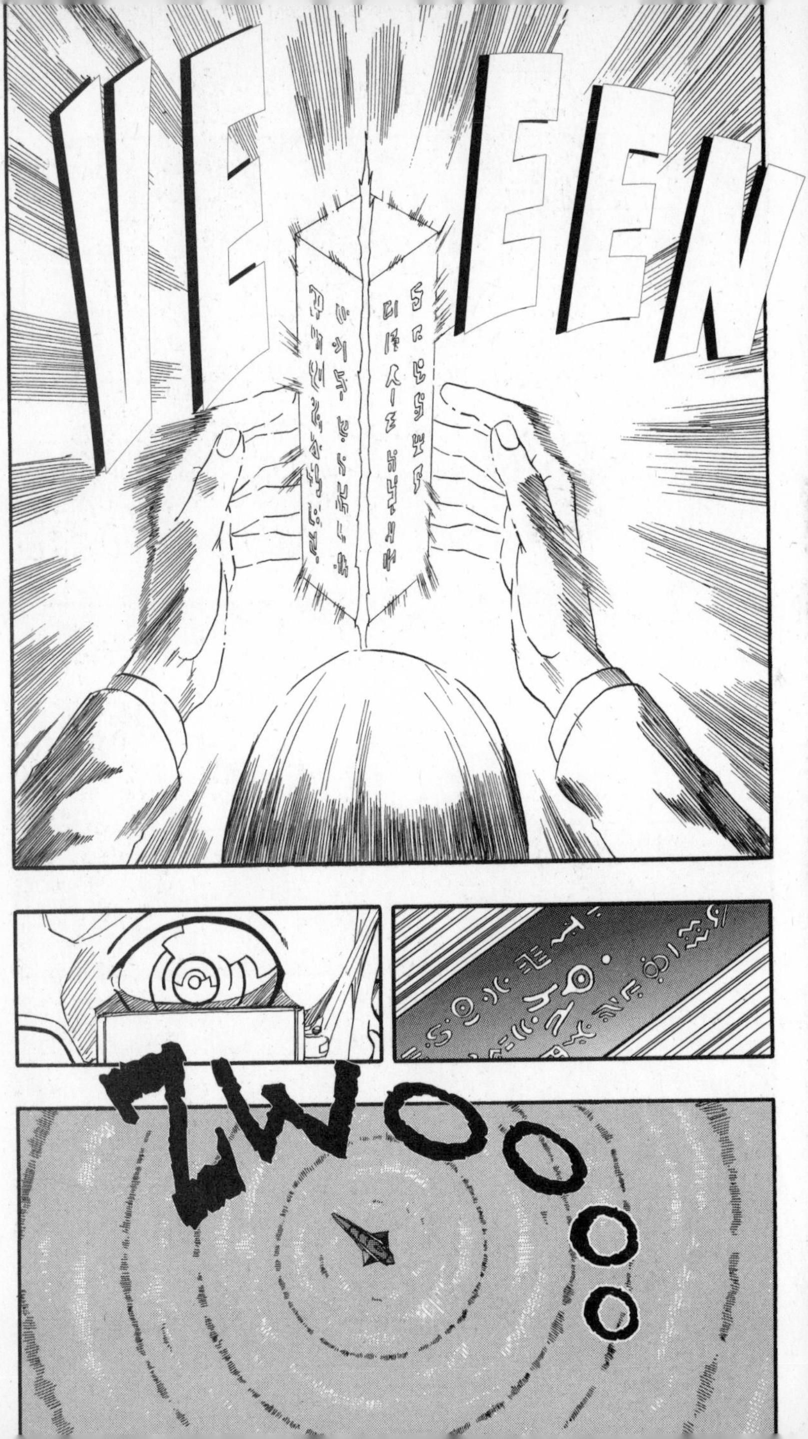
VEEEN
ZWOOOO

STEA NORTH POLE BRANCH OFFICE
FWOOOO
B-BMM
B-BMM
B-BMM
FOR-MAL KAB-BALAH
KRRK
GGGG
FWU SH

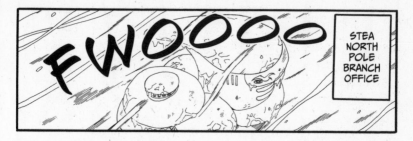

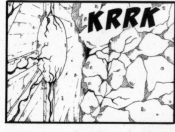

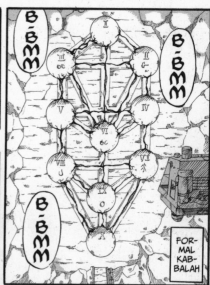

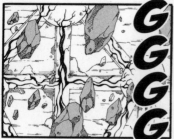

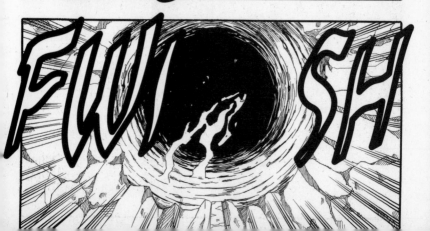

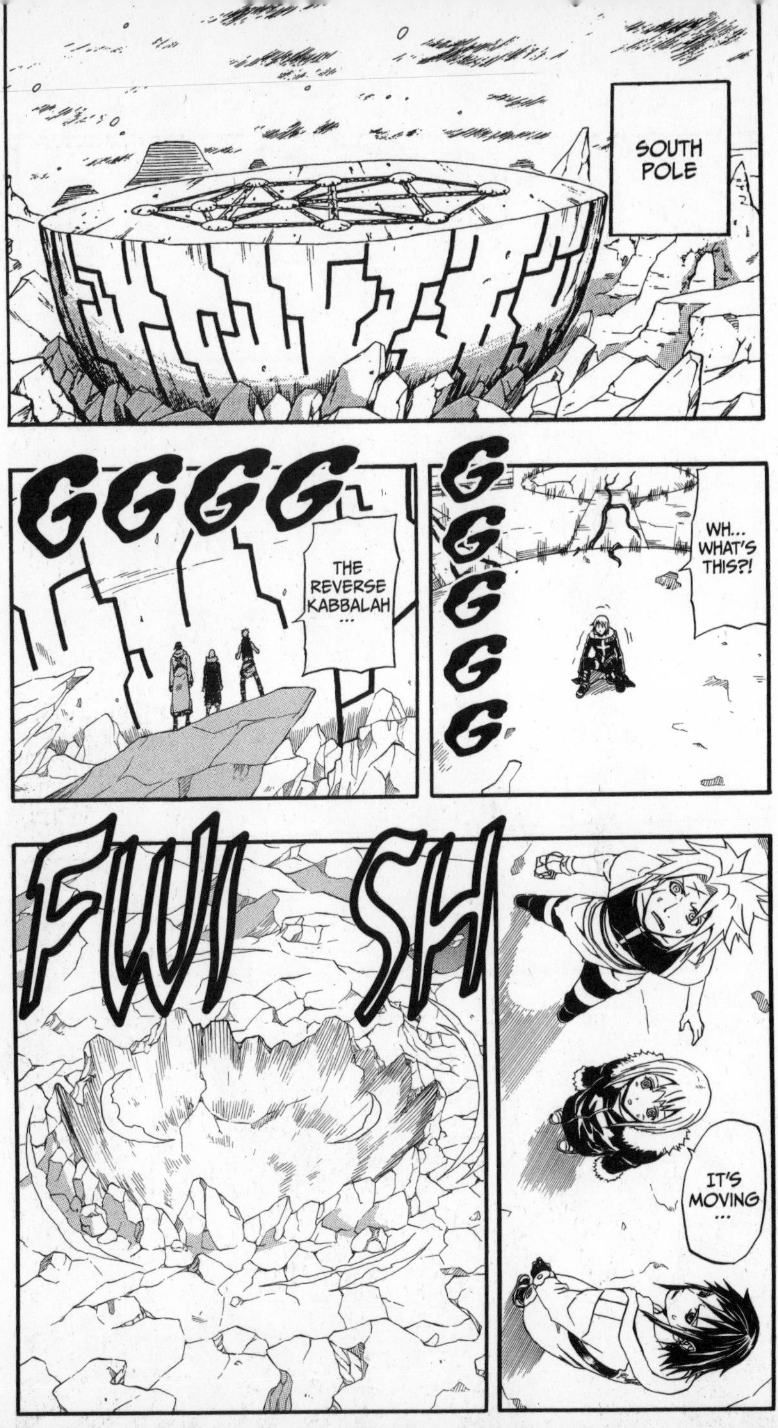
SOUTH POLE
GGGGG
WH... WHAT'S THIS?!
GGGG
THE REVERSE KABBALAH ...
FWI SH
IT'S MOVING ...

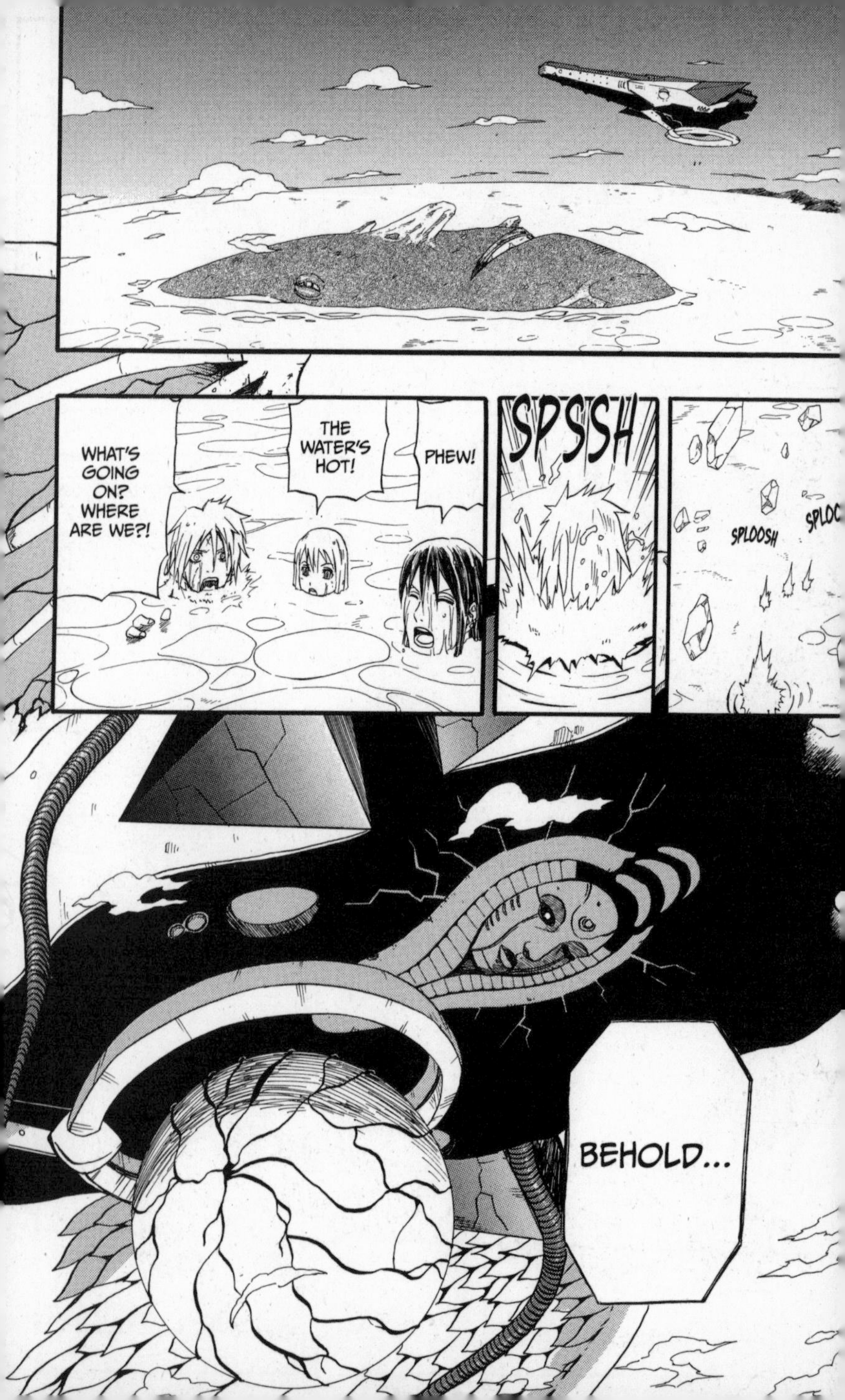

SPLOC
SPLOOSH
SPSSH
PHEW!
THE WATER'S HOT!
WHAT'S GOING ON? WHERE ARE WE?!
BEHOLD...

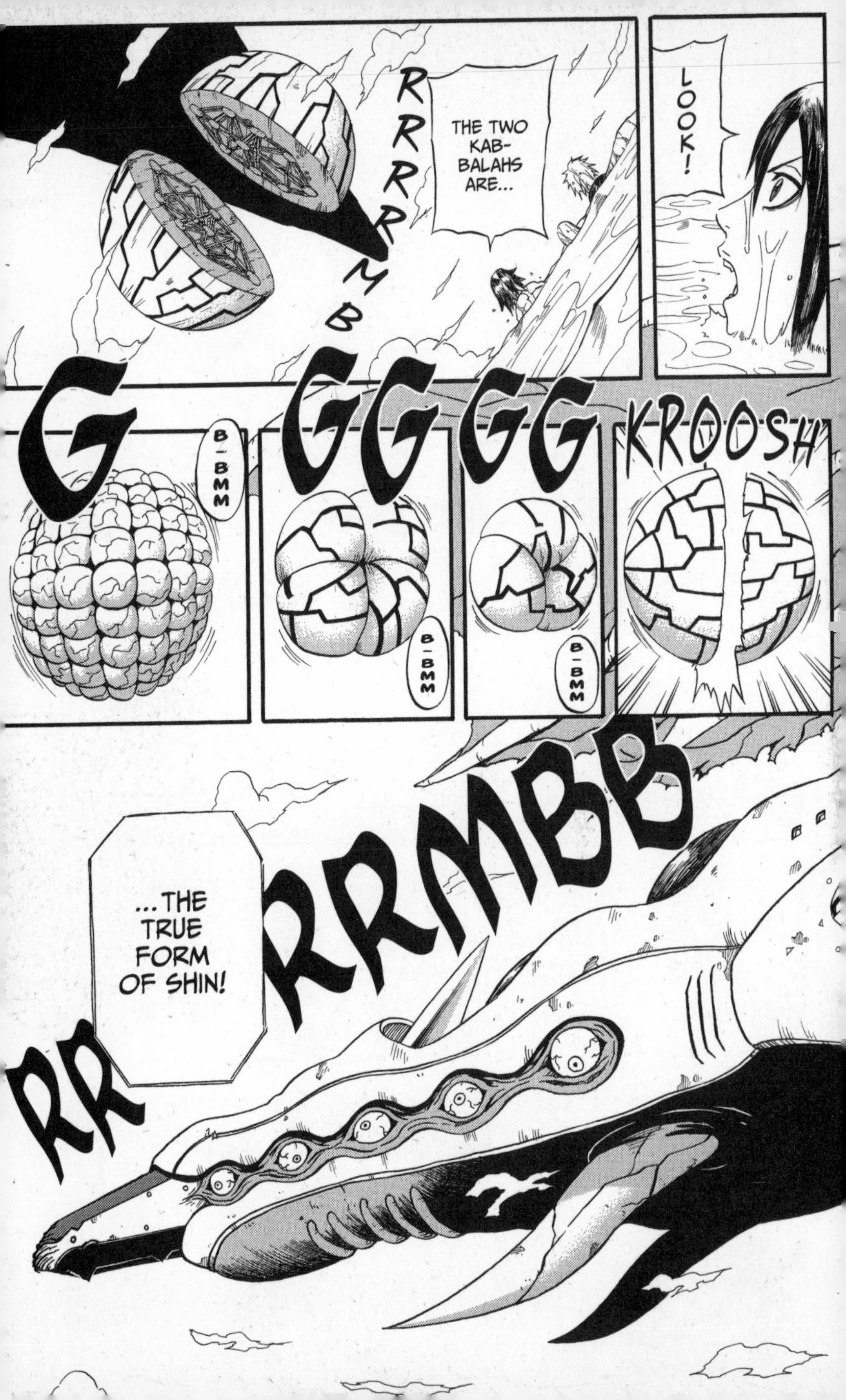

LOOK!
THE TWO KAB-BALAHS ARE...
RRRRRMB
GGGGG
KROOSH
B-BMM
B-BMM
B-BMM
B-BMM
RRRRMBB
...THE TRUE FORM OF SHIN!

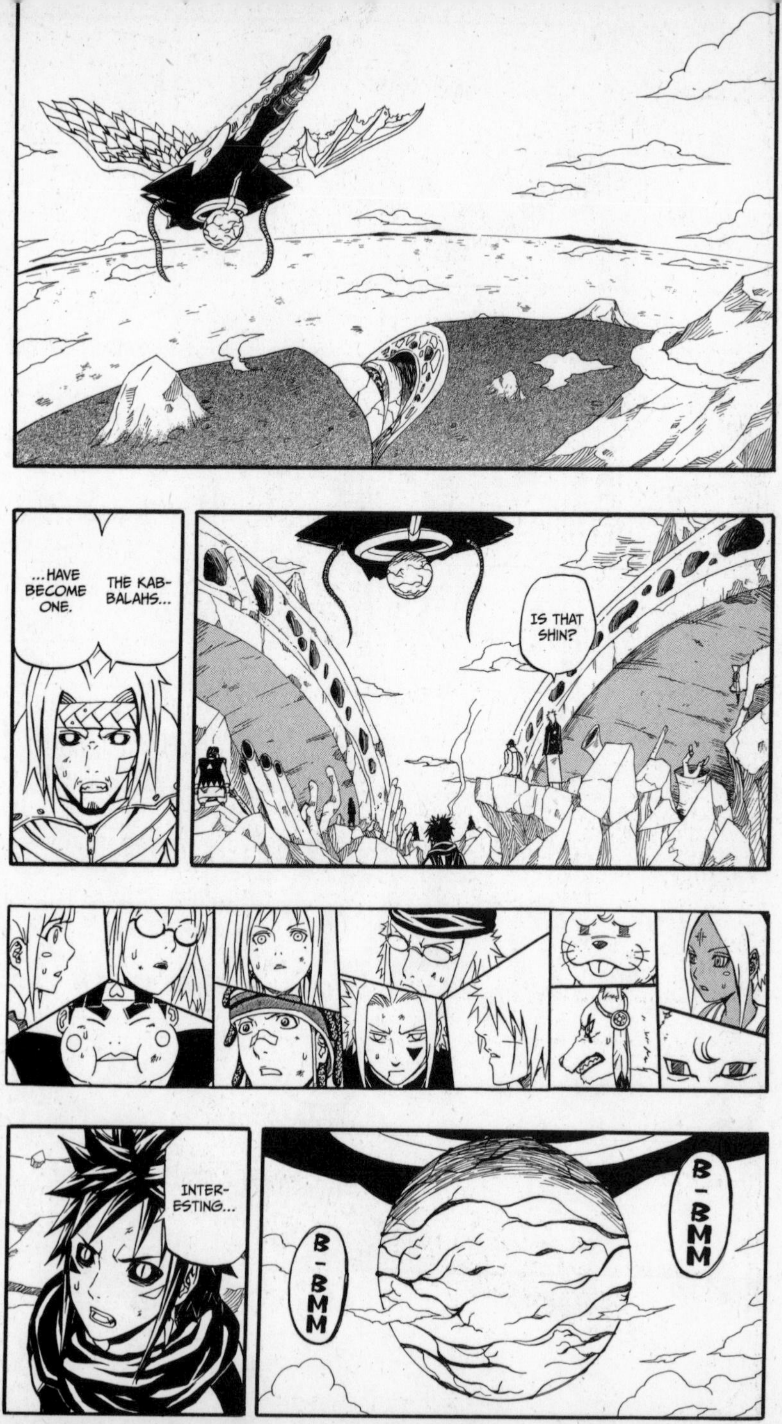
IS THAT SHIN?
THE KAB-BALAHS...
...HAVE BECOME ONE.
B-BMM
B-BMM
INTER-ESTING...

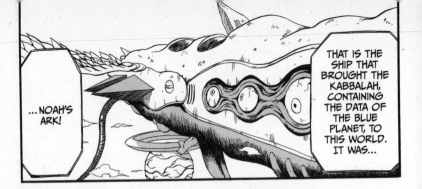

THAT IS THE SHIP THAT BROUGHT THE KABBALAH, CONTAINING THE DATA OF THE BLUE PLANET, TO THIS WORLD. IT WAS...
...NOAH'S ARK!
THE KABBALAH WAS SHIN'S WEAPON...
...A MEMORIZATION DEVICE THAT...
...TRAVELED IN SEARCH OF NEW INFORMATION.
SHIN IS NOT FROM THE BLUE PLANET, HOWEVER, BUT HAS TRAVELED ACROSS SPACE, FROM PLANET TO PLANET...
...ABSORBING INFORMATION, AND WE'RE ONLY A SMALL FRAGMENT OF ITS HISTORY.
DON'T YOU WANT TO FIND OUT...
...
...WHO CREATED SUCH A THING...
...AND SET IT LOOSE?

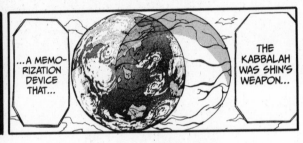

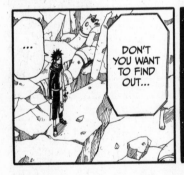

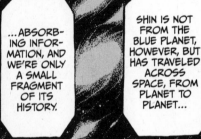

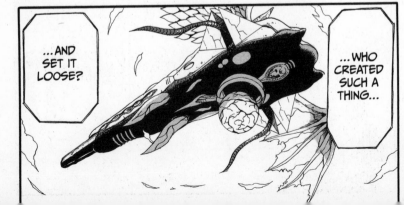

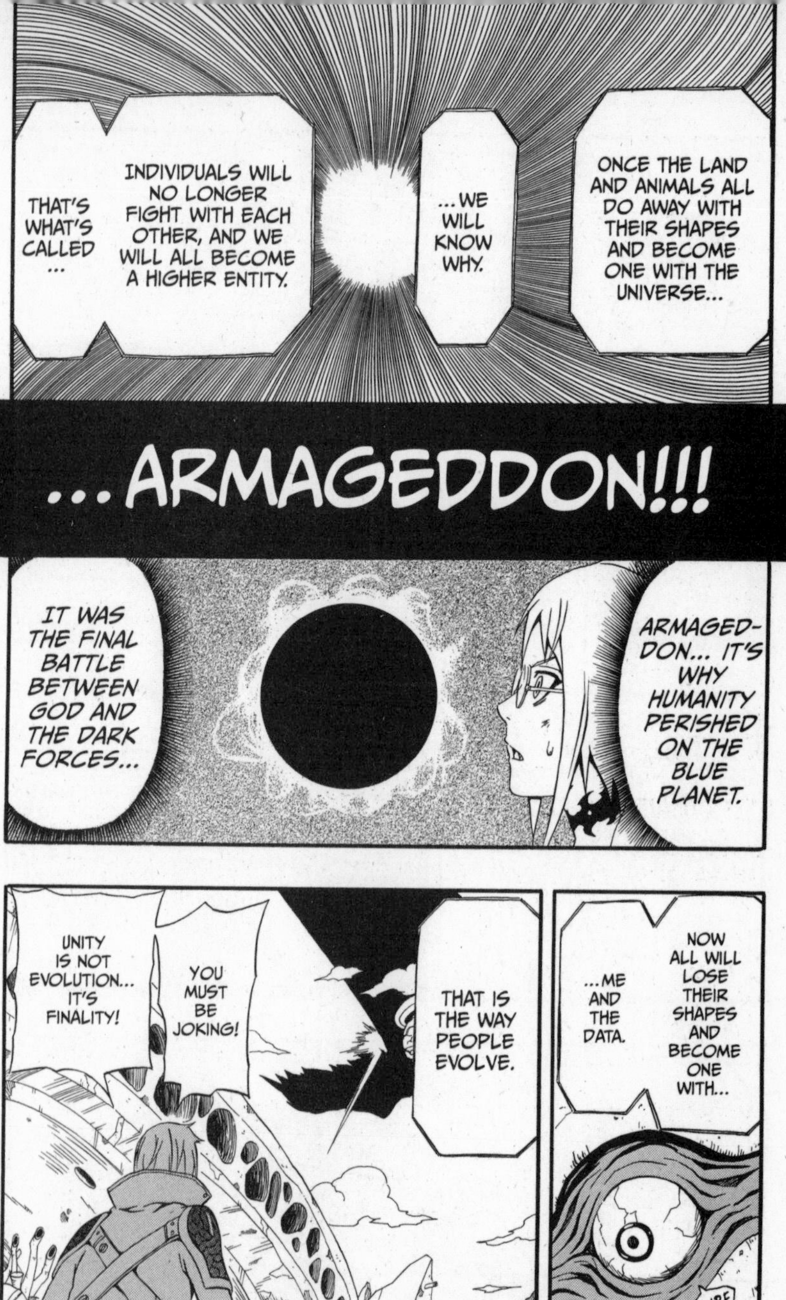
ONCE THE LAND AND ANIMALS ALL DO AWAY WITH THEIR SHAPES AND BECOME ONE WITH THE UNIVERSE...
...WE WILL KNOW WHY.
INDIVIDUALS WILL NO LONGER FIGHT WITH EACH OTHER, AND WE WILL ALL BECOME A HIGHER ENTITY.
THAT'S WHAT'S CALLED ...
...ARMAGEDDON!!!
ARMAGED-DON... IT'S WHY HUMANITY PERISHED ON THE BLUE PLANET.
IT WAS THE FINAL BATTLE BETWEEN GOD AND THE DARK FORCES...
NOW ALL WILL LOSE THEIR SHAPES AND BECOME ONE WITH...
...ME AND THE DATA.
GLARE
THAT IS THE WAY PEOPLE EVOLVE.
YOU MUST BE JOKING!
UNITY IS NOT EVOLUTION... IT'S FINALITY!

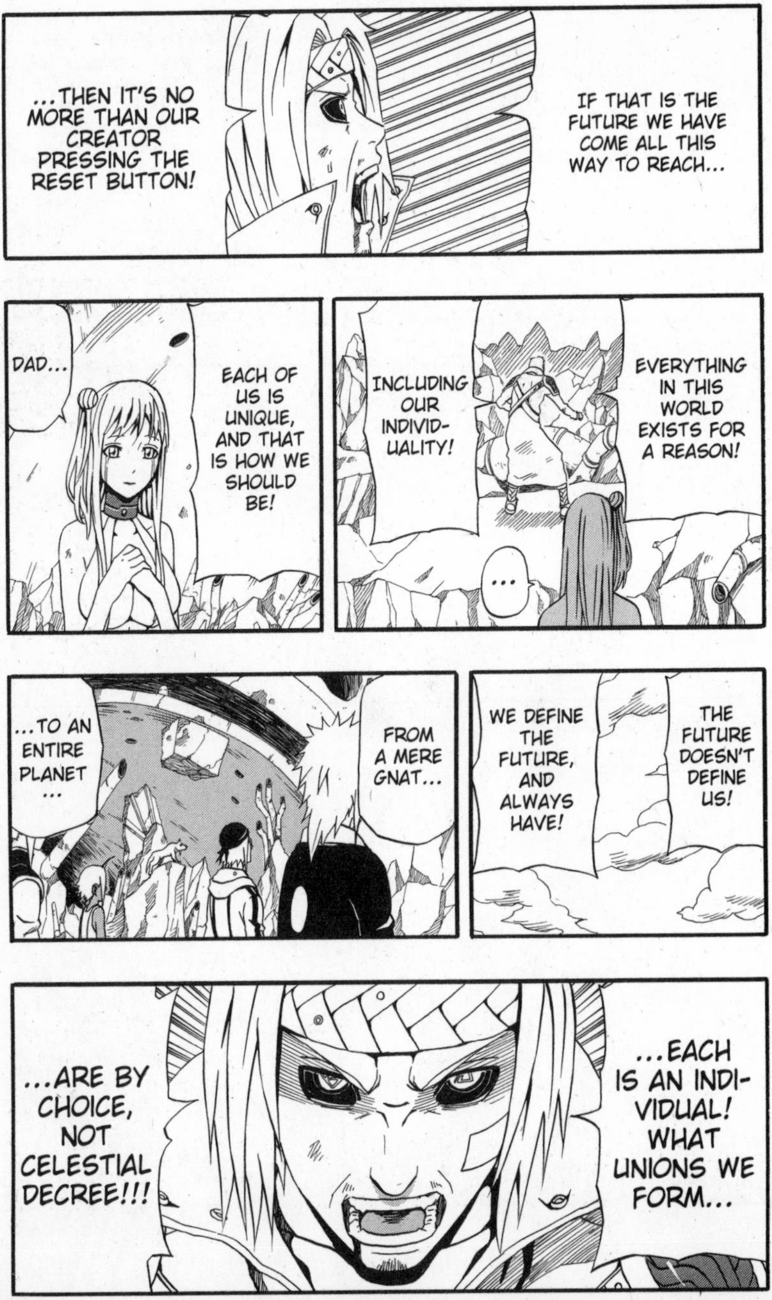
IF THAT IS THE FUTURE WE HAVE COME ALL THIS WAY TO REACH...
...THEN IT'S NO MORE THAN OUR CREATOR PRESSING THE RESET BUTTON!
EVERYTHING IN THIS WORLD EXISTS FOR A REASON!
INCLUDING OUR INDIVIDUALITY!
...
EACH OF US IS UNIQUE, AND THAT IS HOW WE SHOULD BE!
DAD...
THE FUTURE DOESN'T DEFINE US!
WE DEFINE THE FUTURE, AND ALWAYS HAVE!
FROM A MERE GNAT...
...TO AN ENTIRE PLANET...
...EACH IS AN INDIVIDUAL! WHAT UNIONS WE FORM...
...ARE BY CHOICE, NOT CELESTIAL DECREE!!!

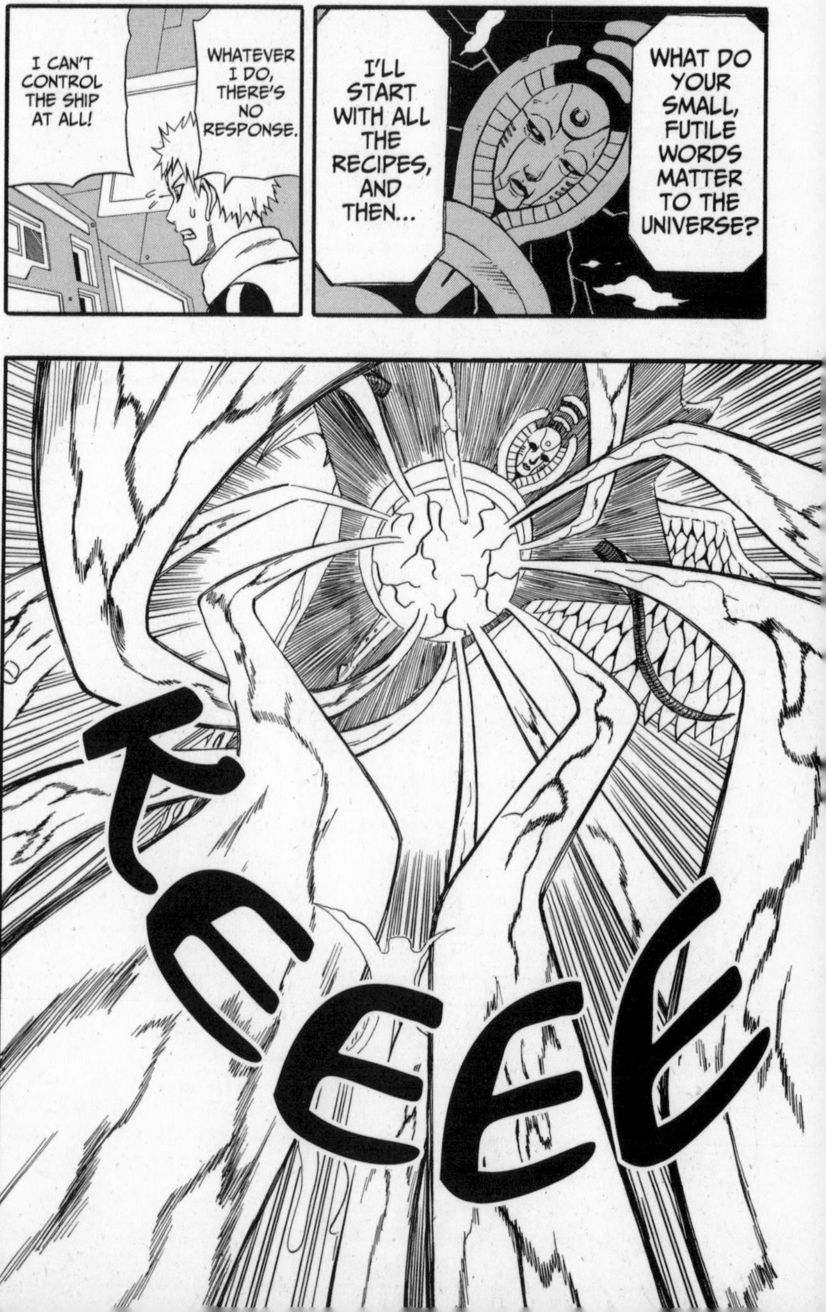
WHAT DO YOUR SMALL, FUTILE WORDS MATTER TO THE UNIVERSE?
I'LL START WITH ALL THE RECIPES, AND THEN...
WHATEVER I DO, THERE'S NO RESPONSE.
I CAN'T CONTROL THE SHIP AT ALL!
KEEEE

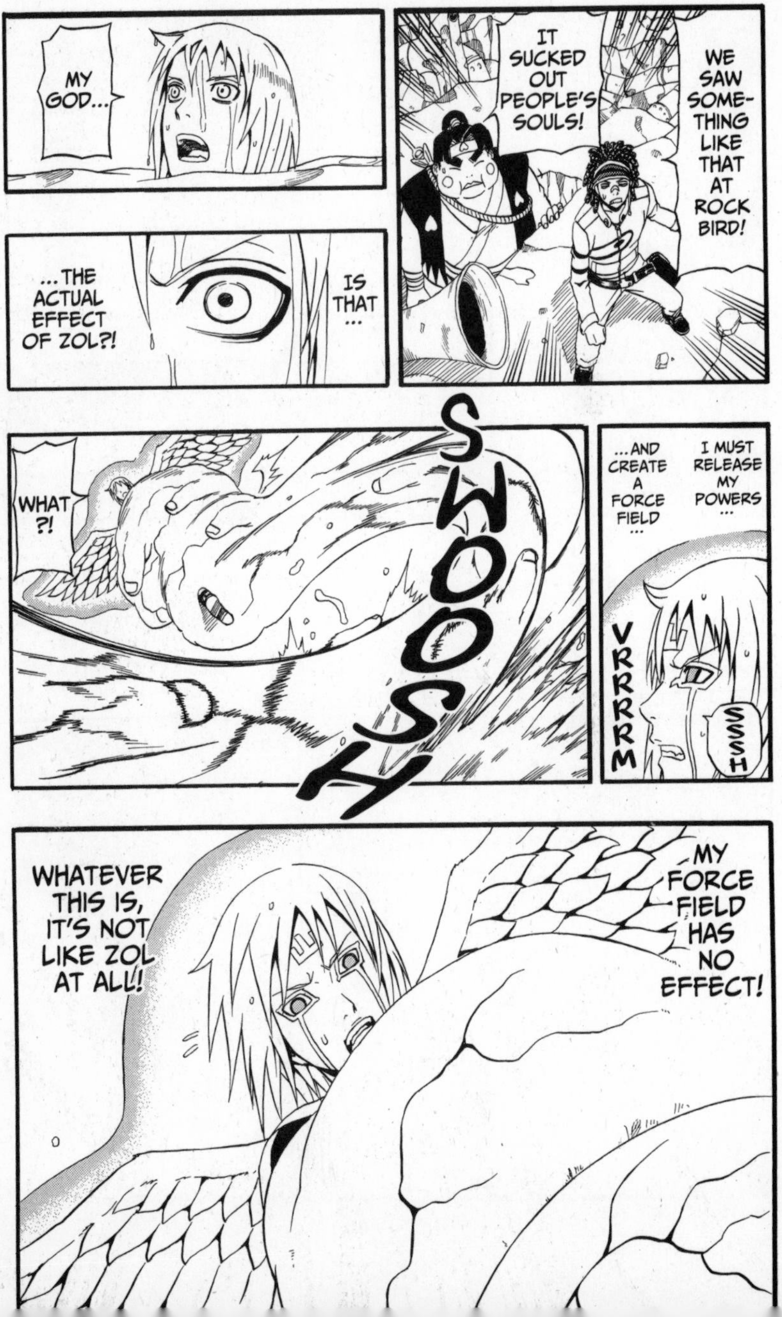
WE SAW SOMETHING LIKE THAT AT ROCK BIRD!
IT SUCKED OUT PEOPLE'S SOULS!
MY GOD...
IS THAT...
...THE ACTUAL EFFECT OF ZOL?!
I MUST RELEASE MY POWERS...
...AND CREATE A FORCE FIELD...
VRRRRM
SSSH
SWOOSH
WHAT?!
MY FORCE FIELD HAS NO EFFECT!
WHATEVER THIS IS, IT'S NOT LIKE ZOL AT ALL!

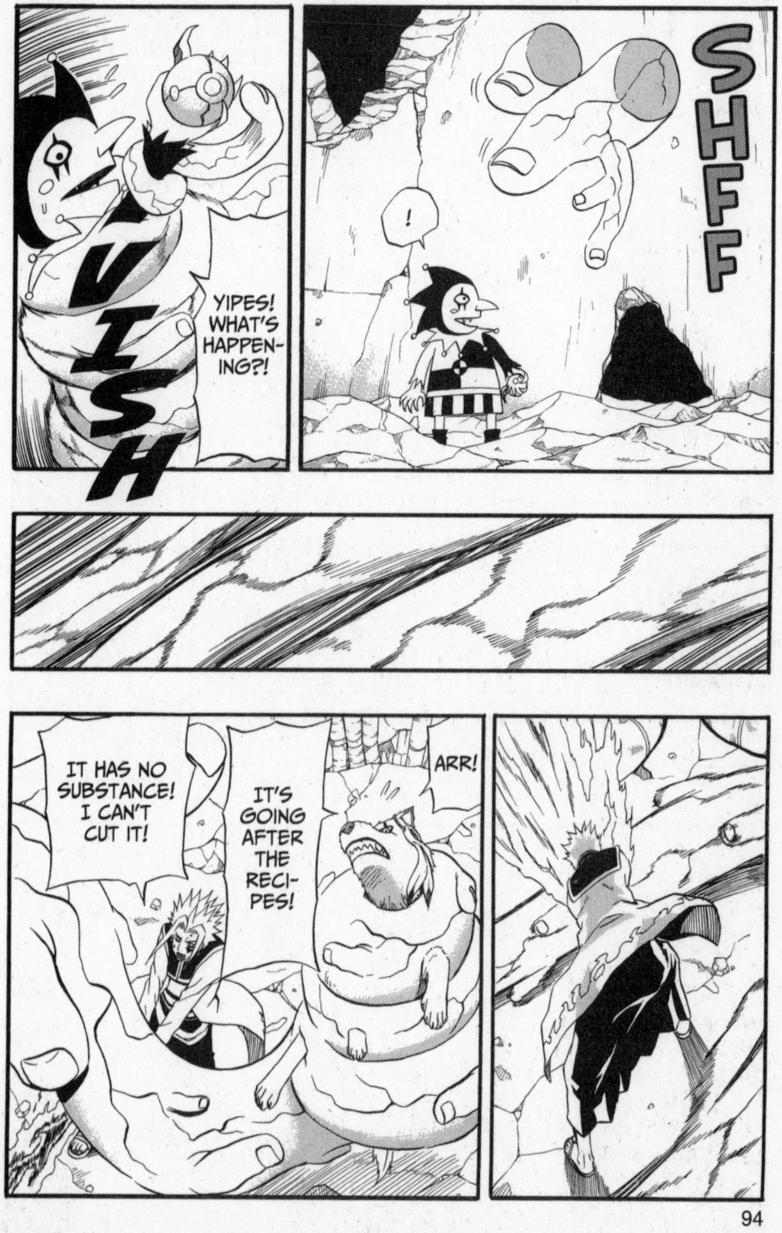
SHFF
!
VUISH
YIPES! WHAT'S HAPPEN-ING?!
ARR!
IT'S GOING AFTER THE RECI-PES!
IT HAS NO SUBSTANCE! I CAN'T CUT IT!

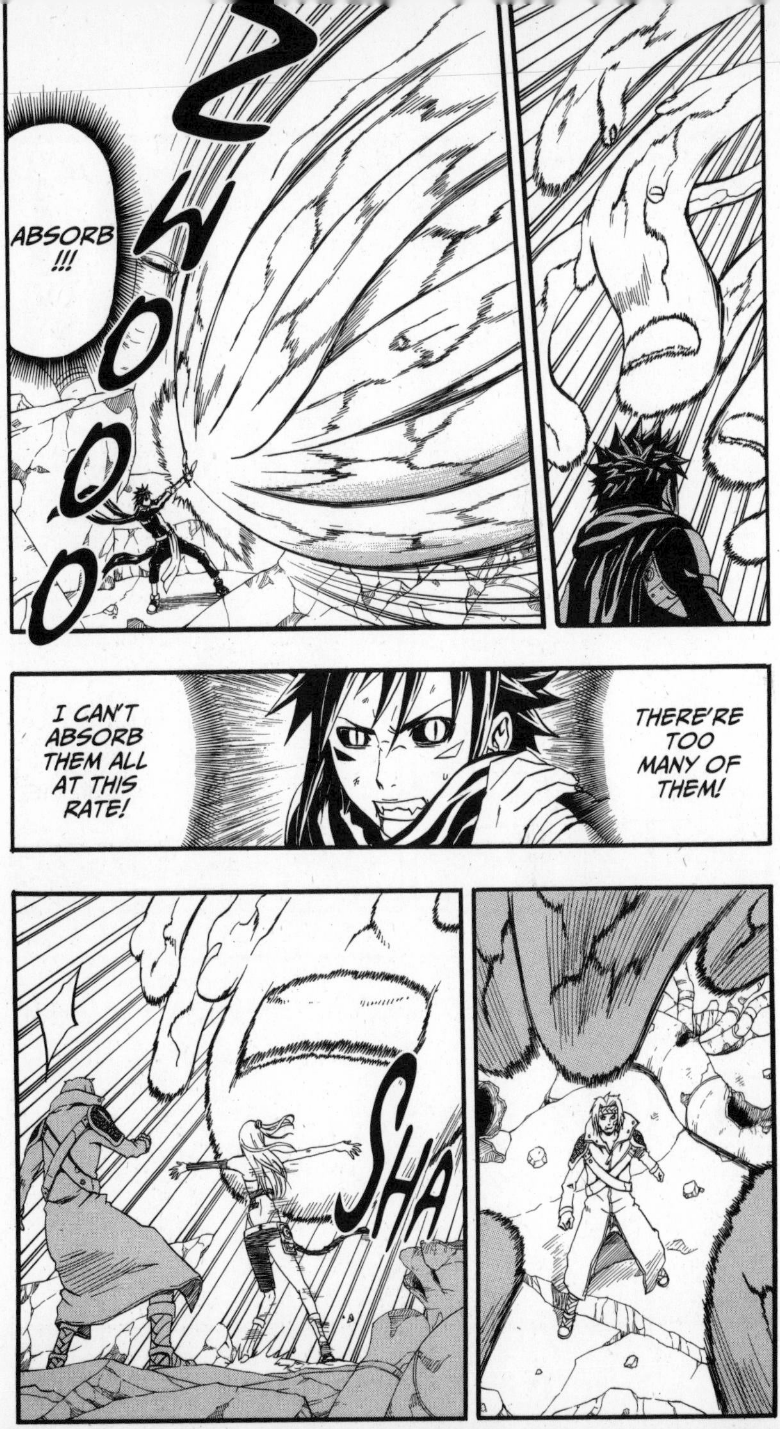
ABSORB !!!
ZWOOOO
THERE'RE TOO MANY OF THEM!
I CAN'T ABSORB THEM ALL AT THIS RATE!
SHA

ZZT

AAAH!

FSSSH

I...

BACK THEN, WHEN YOU LEFT ME...

CLENCH

BACK THEN...

GRRP

....

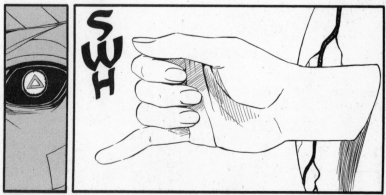

SWH

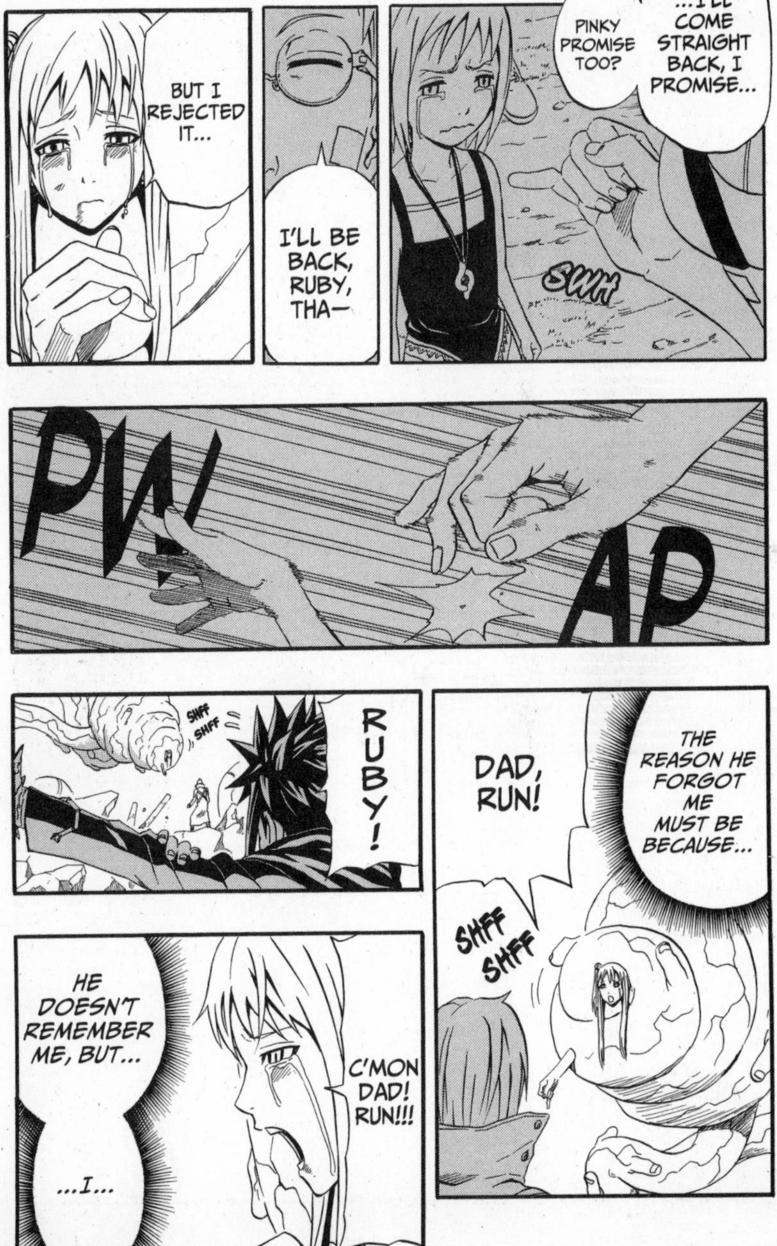
...I'LL COME STRAIGHT BACK, I PROMISE...
PINKY PROMISE TOO?
SWH
I'LL BE BACK, RUBY, THA—
BUT I REJECTED IT...
PW
AP
THE REASON HE FORGOT ME MUST BE BECAUSE...
DAD, RUN!
SHFF SHFF
RUBY!
SHFF SHFF
HE DOESN'T REMEMBER ME, BUT...
C'MON DAD! RUN!!!
...I...

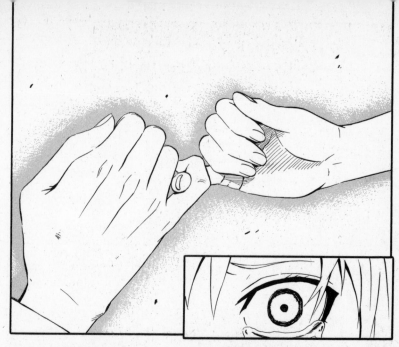

SWUUSH

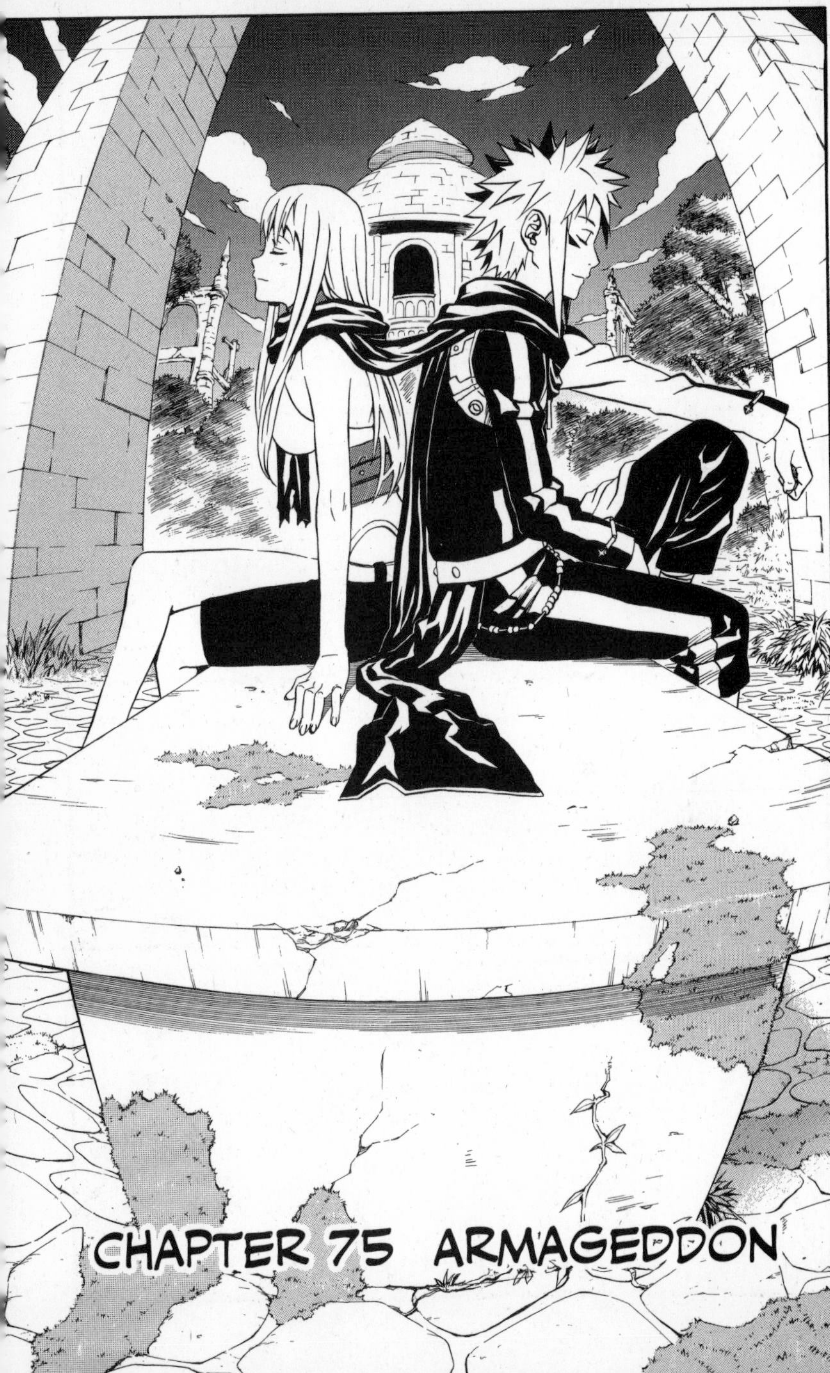
CHAPTER 75 ARMAGEDDON

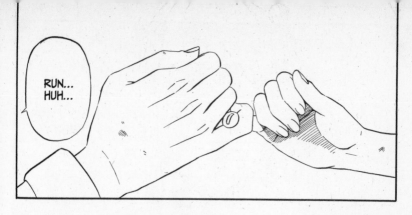

RUN... HUH...
I WON'T RUN AWAY...
TEARS! HAS HE...?
...THIS TIME, NOT FROM MY...
TUG
GRP
...DEAR, WONDERFUL DAUGHTER!

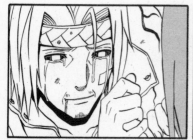

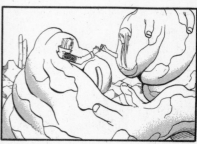

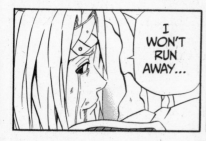

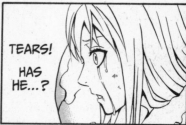

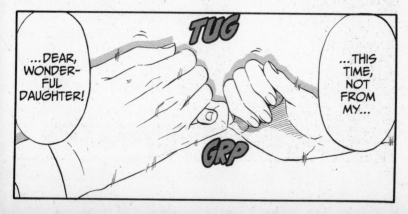

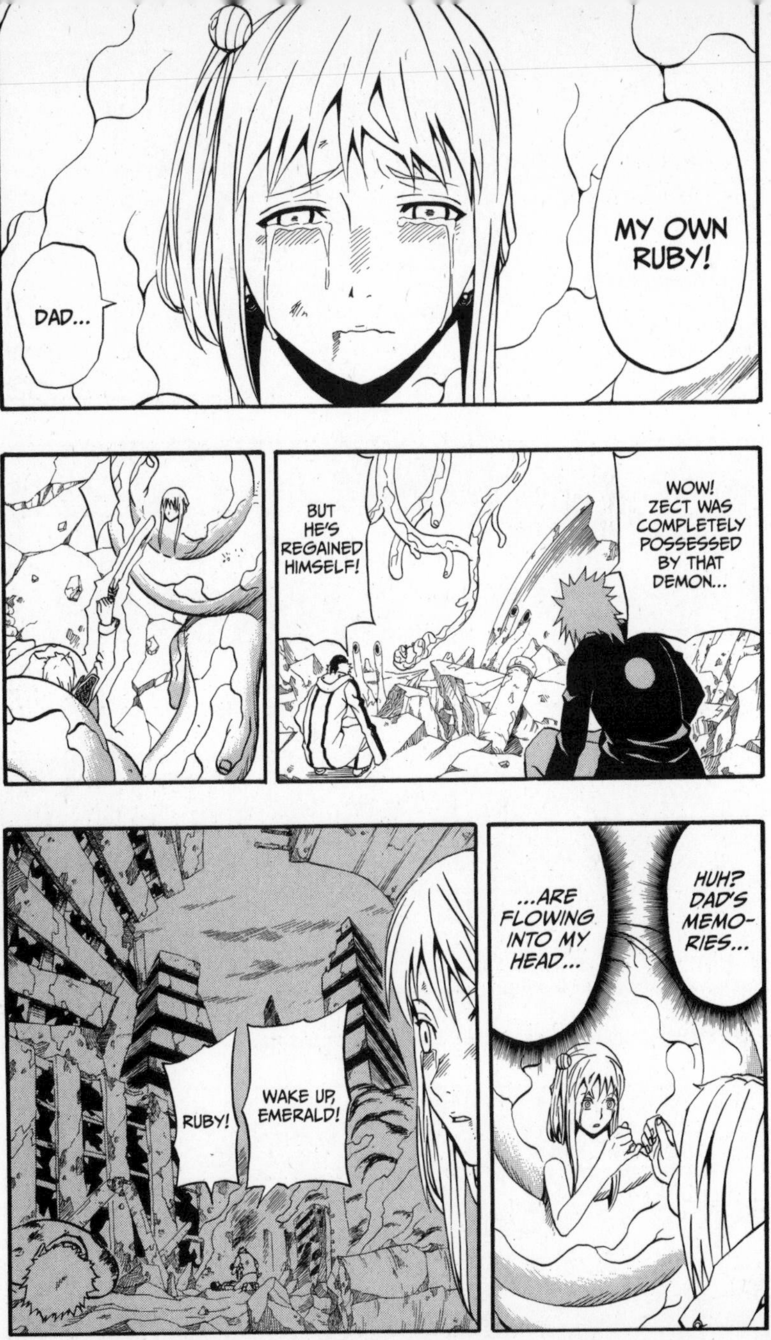
MY OWN RUBY!
DAD...
WOW! ZECT WAS COMPLETELY POSSESSED BY THAT DEMON...
BUT HE'S REGAINED HIMSELF!
HUH? DAD'S MEMO-RIES...
...ARE FLOWING INTO MY HEAD...
WAKE UP, EMERALD!
RUBY!

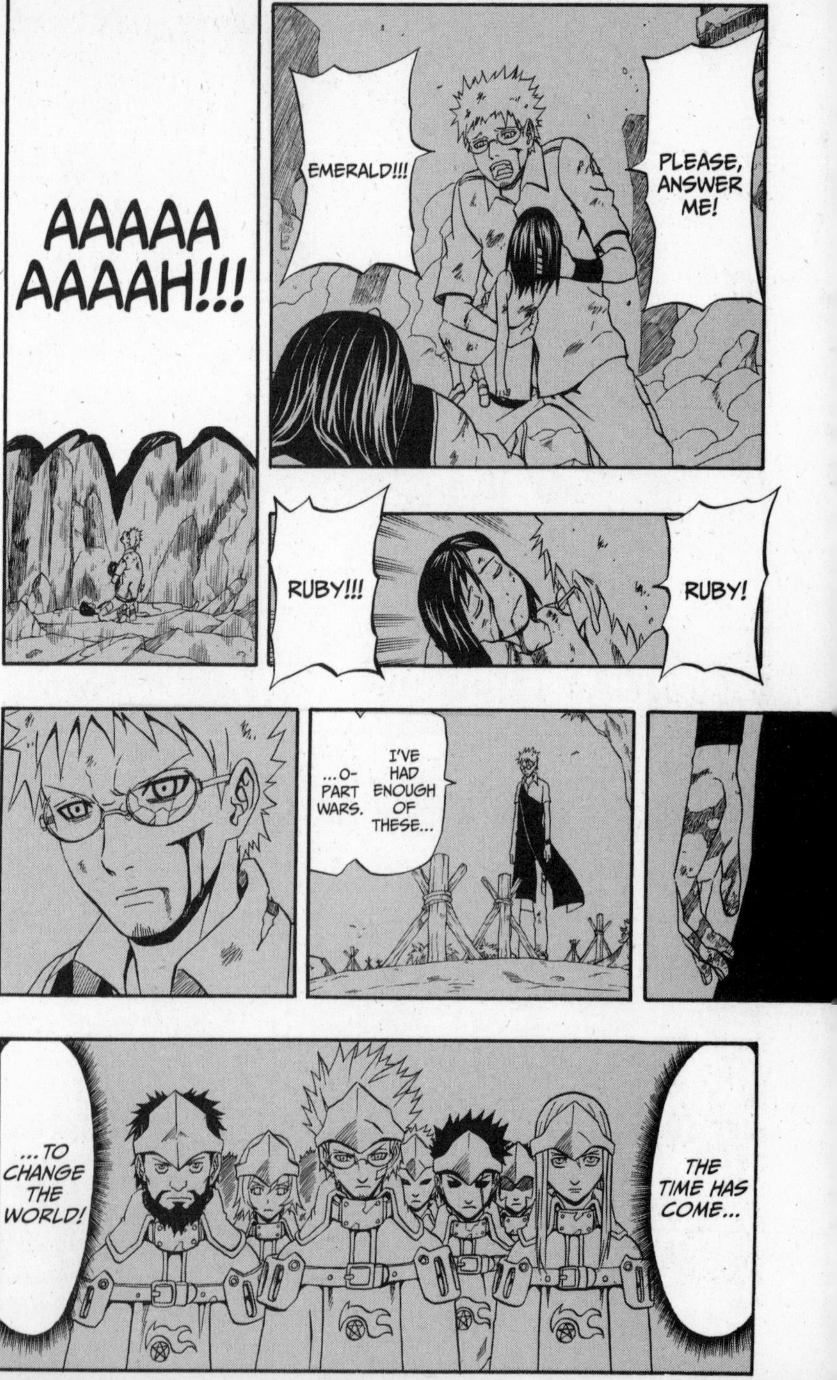
PLEASE, ANSWER ME!
EMERALD!!!
RUBY!
RUBY!!!
AAAAA AAAAH!!!
I'VE HAD ENOUGH OF THESE...
...O-PART WARS.
THE TIME HAS COME...
...TO CHANGE THE WORLD!

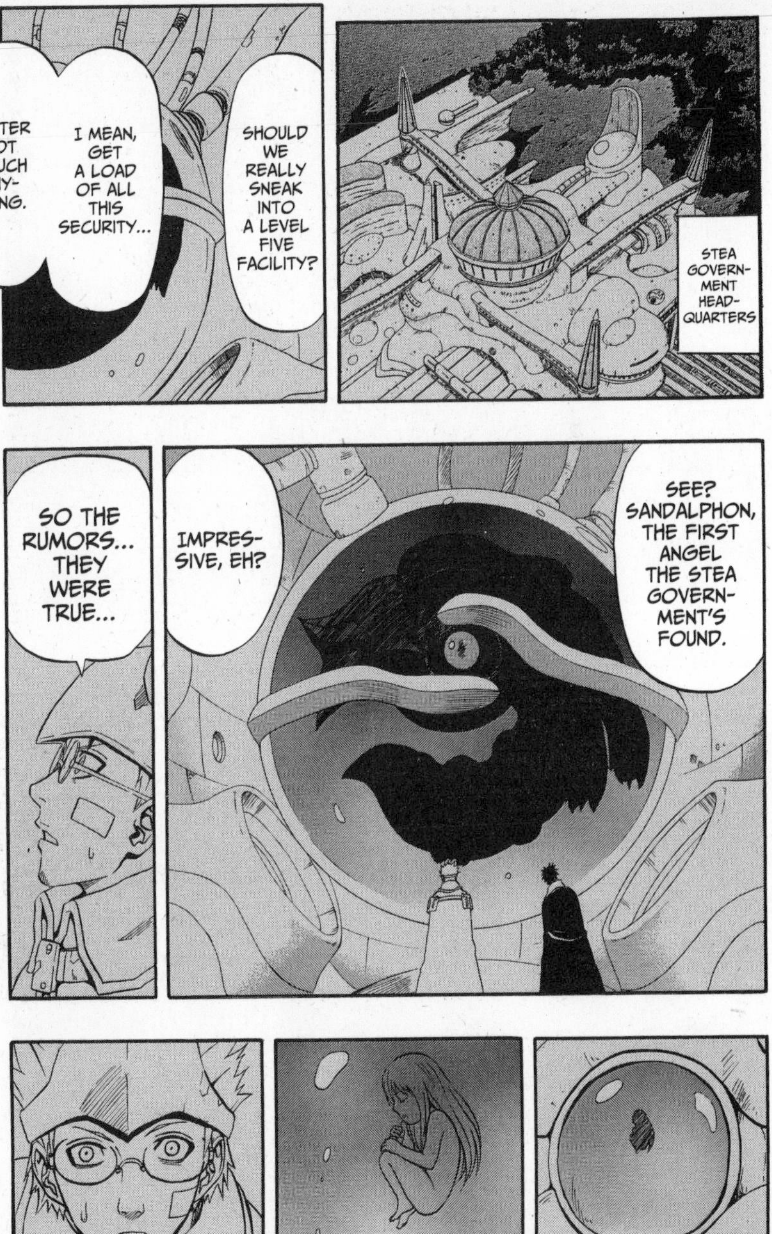
STEA GOVERN-MENT HEAD-QUARTERS
SHOULD WE REALLY SNEAK INTO A LEVEL FIVE FACILITY?
I MEAN, GET A LOAD OF ALL THIS SECURITY...
BETTER NOT TOUCH ANY-THING.
SEE? SANDALPHON, THE FIRST ANGEL THE STEA GOVERN-MENT'S FOUND.
IMPRES-SIVE, EH?
SO THE RUMORS... THEY WERE TRUE...

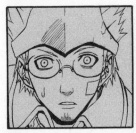

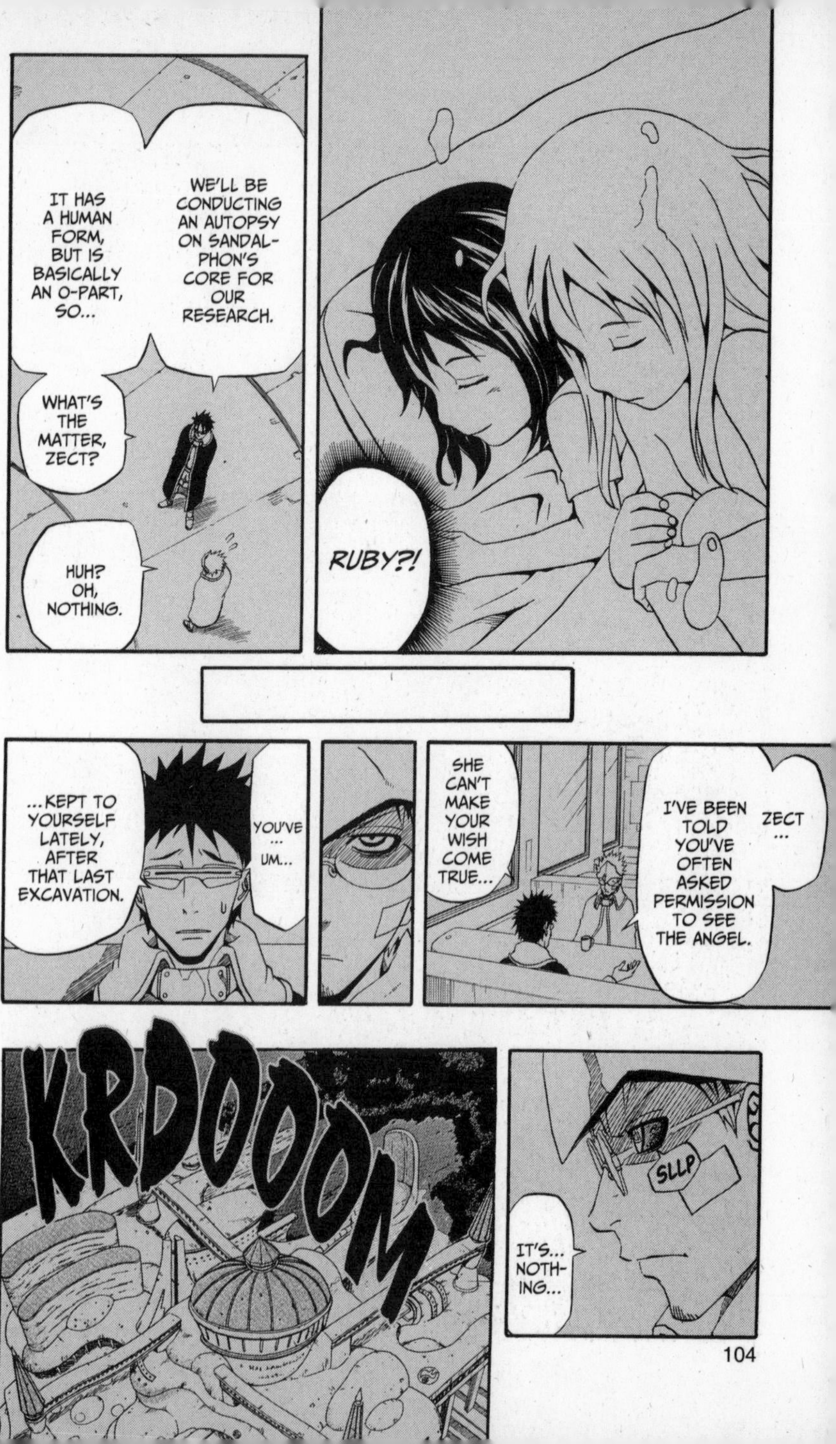
RUBY?!
WE'LL BE CONDUCTING AN AUTOPSY ON SANDAL-PHON'S CORE FOR OUR RESEARCH.
IT HAS A HUMAN FORM, BUT IS BASICALLY AN O-PART, SO...
WHAT'S THE MATTER, ZECT?
HUH? OH, NOTHING.
ZECT...
I'VE BEEN TOLD YOU'VE OFTEN ASKED PERMISSION TO SEE THE ANGEL.
SHE CAN'T MAKE YOUR WISH COME TRUE...
YOU'VE... UM...
...KEPT TO YOURSELF LATELY, AFTER THAT LAST EXCAVATION.
SLLP
IT'S... NOTH-ING...
KRDOOOM

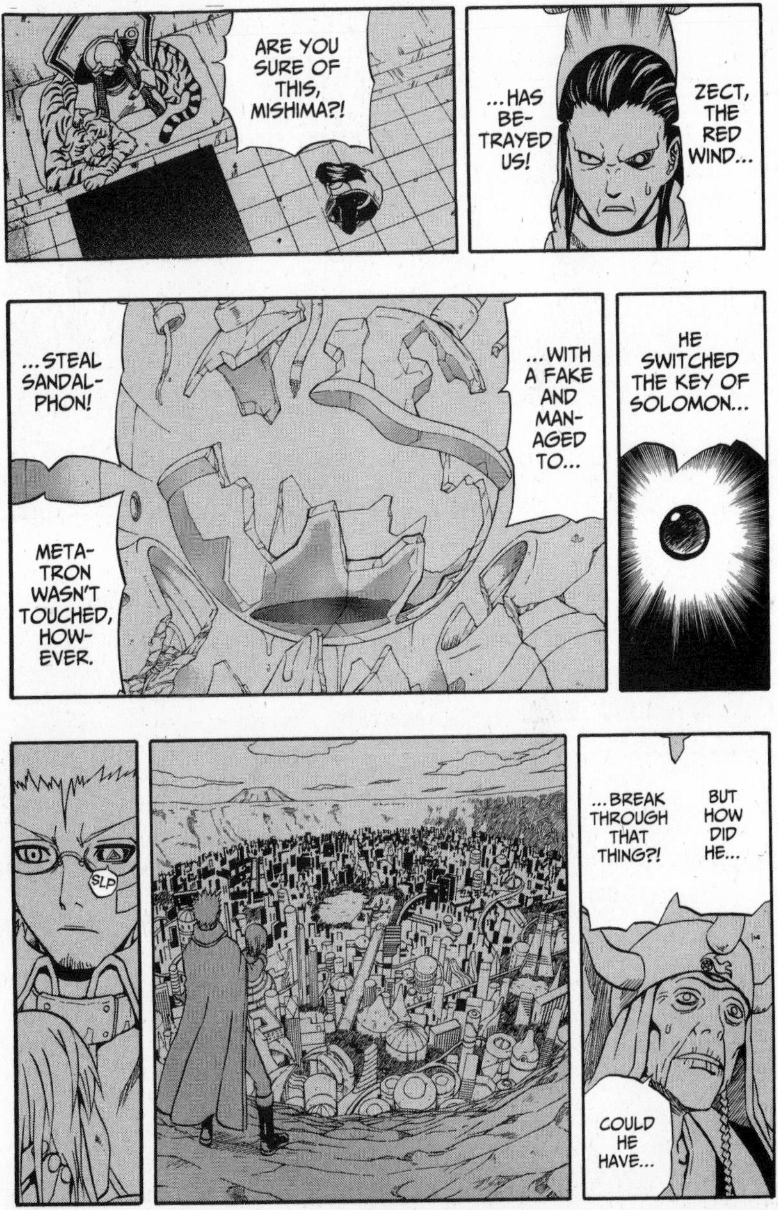
ZECT, THE RED WIND...
...HAS BE-TRAYED US!
ARE YOU SURE OF THIS, MISHIMA?!
HE SWITCHED THE KEY OF SOLOMON...
...WITH A FAKE AND MAN-AGED TO...
...STEAL SANDAL-PHON!
META-TRON WASN'T TOUCHED, HOW-EVER.
BUT HOW DID HE...
...BREAK THROUGH THAT THING?!
COULD HE HAVE...
SLP

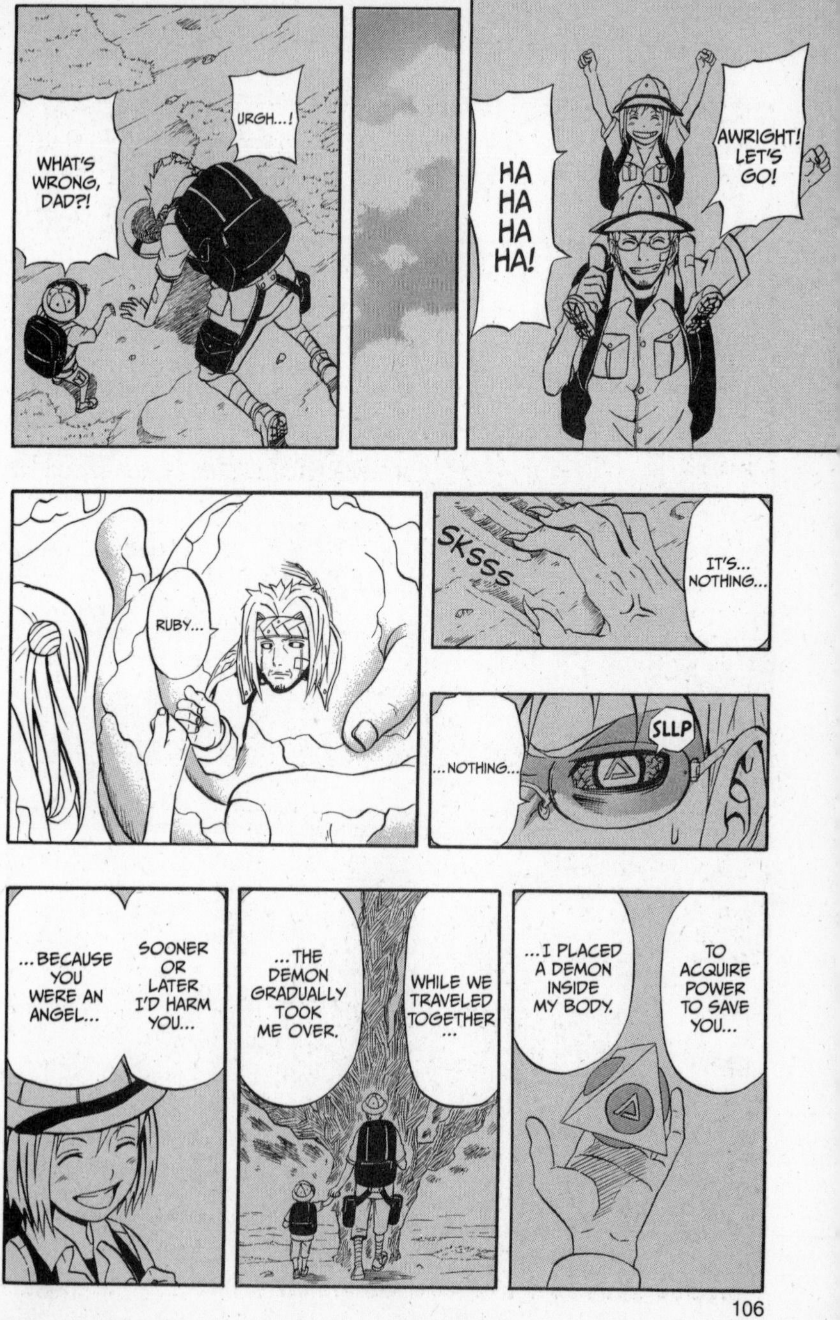
AWRIGHT! LET'S GO!
HA HA HA HA!
URGH...!
WHAT'S WRONG, DAD?!
IT'S... NOTHING...
SKSSS
SLLP
...NOTHING...
RUBY...
TO ACQUIRE POWER TO SAVE YOU...
...I PLACED A DEMON INSIDE MY BODY.
WHILE WE TRAVELED TOGETHER...
...THE DEMON GRADUALLY TOOK ME OVER.
SOONER OR LATER I'D HARM YOU...
...BECAUSE YOU WERE AN ANGEL...

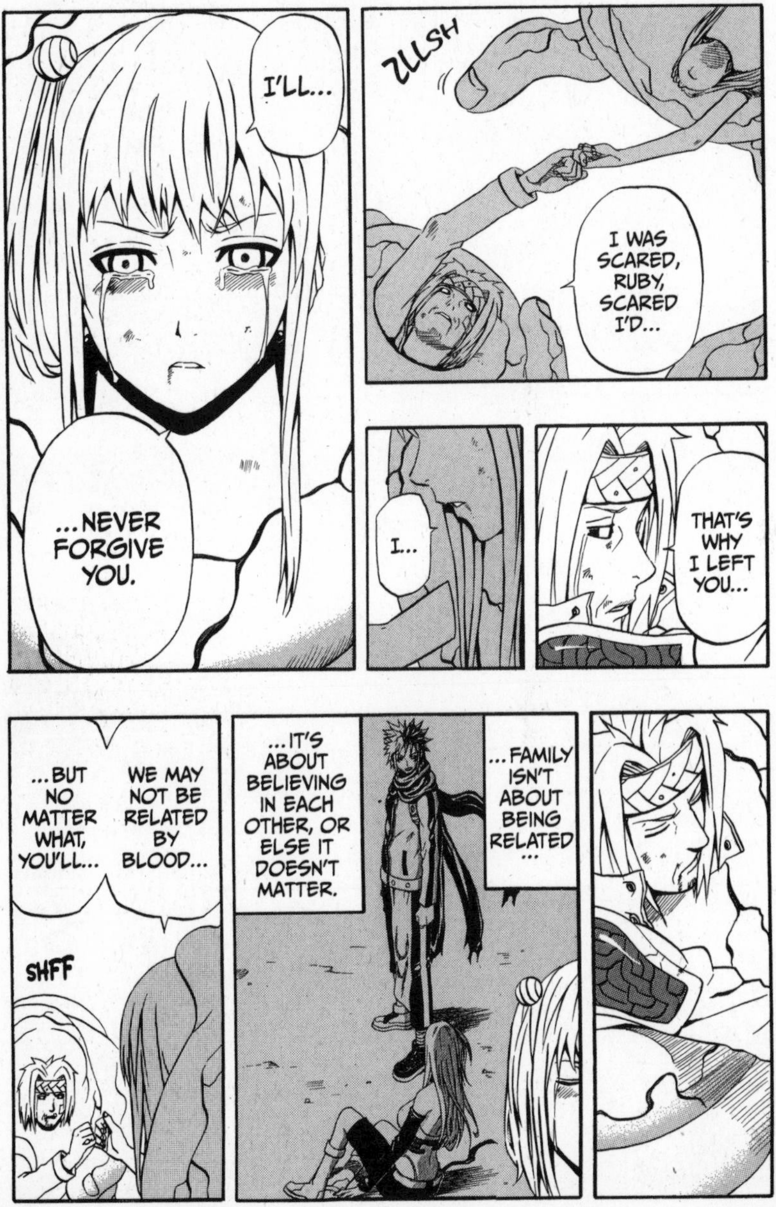
ZLLSH
I WAS SCARED, RUBY, SCARED I'D...
THAT'S WHY I LEFT YOU...
I...
I'LL...
...NEVER FORGIVE YOU.
...FAMILY ISN'T ABOUT BEING RELATED...
...IT'S ABOUT BELIEVING IN EACH OTHER, OR ELSE IT DOESN'T MATTER.
WE MAY NOT BE RELATED BY BLOOD...
...BUT NO MATTER WHAT, YOU'LL...
SHFF

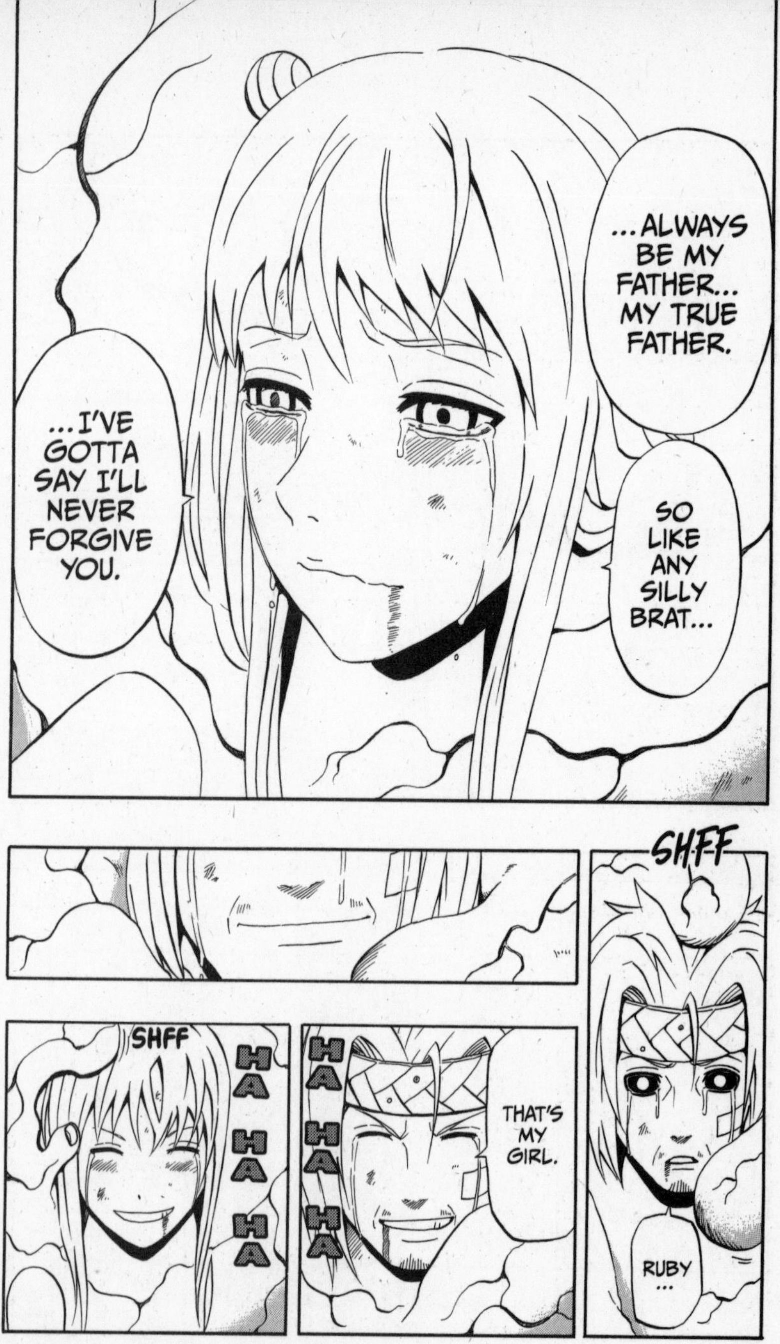
...ALWAYS BE MY FATHER... MY TRUE FATHER.
SO LIKE ANY SILLY BRAT...
...I'VE GOTTA SAY I'LL NEVER FORGIVE YOU.
SHFF
RUBY ...
HA HA HA HA
THAT'S MY GIRL.
HA HA HA
SHFF

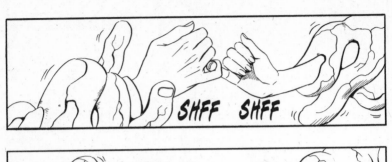

SHFF   SHFF

POIT

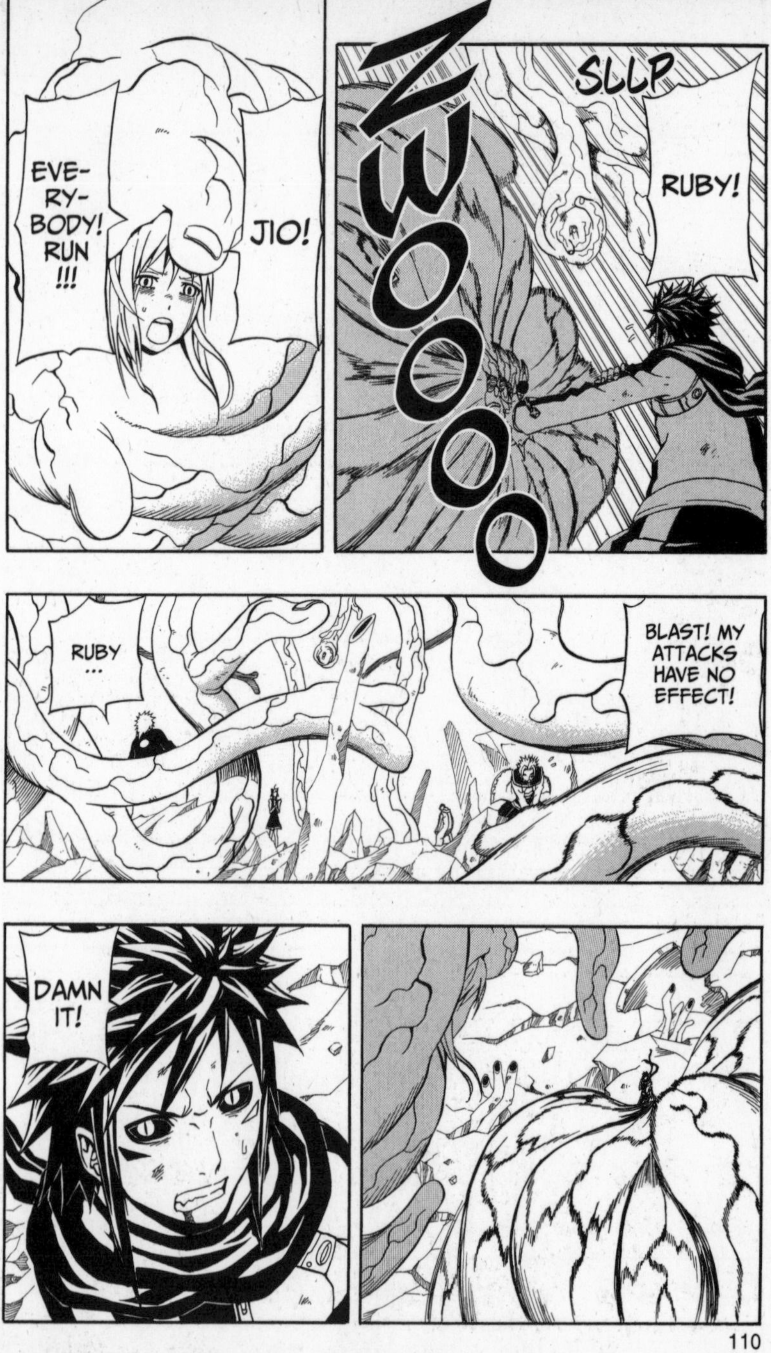
SLLP
NZOOOO
RUBY!
JIO!
EVE-RY-BODY! RUN!!!
BLAST! MY ATTACKS HAVE NO EFFECT!
RUBY...
DAMN IT!

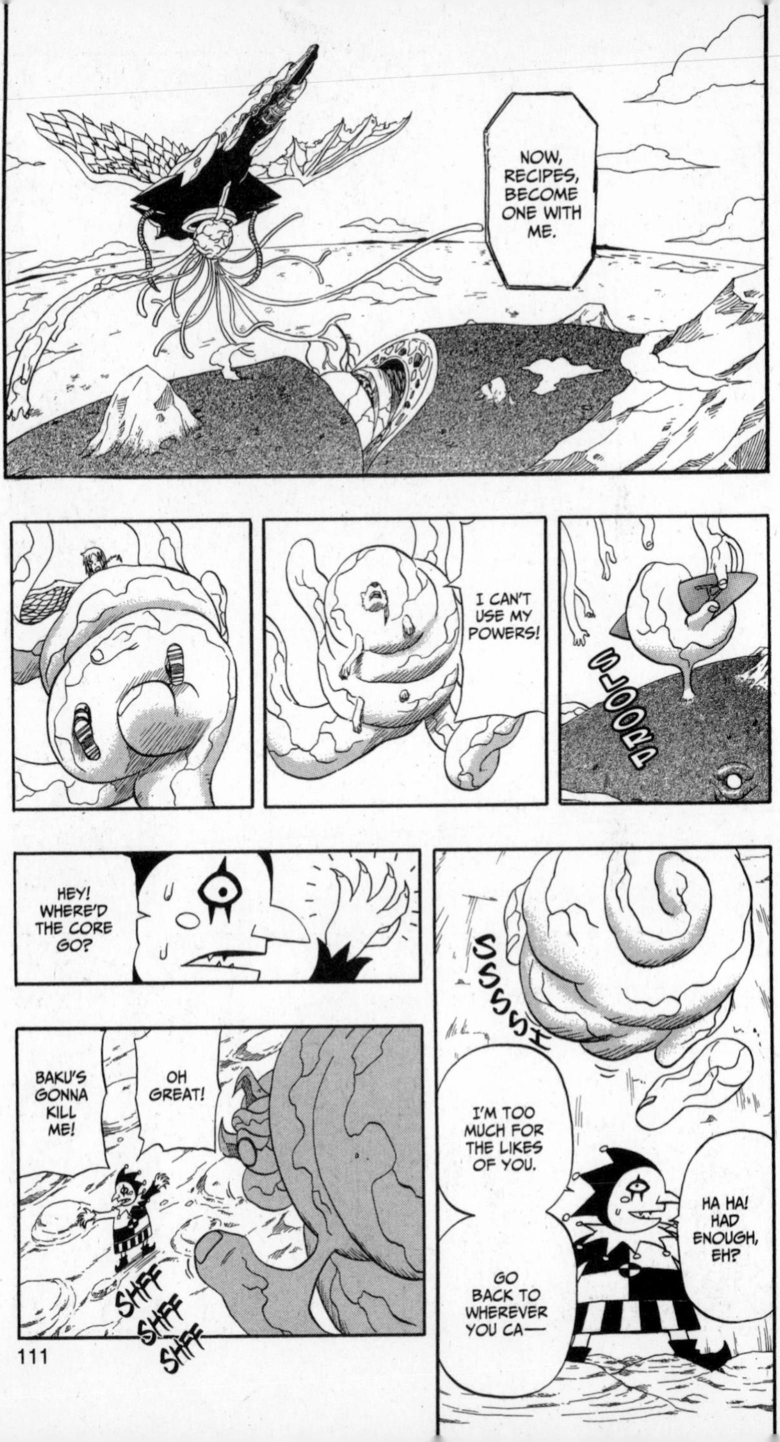
NOW, RECIPES, BECOME ONE WITH ME.
SLOOORP
I CAN'T USE MY POWERS!
SSSSI
HA HA! HAD ENOUGH, EH?
I'M TOO MUCH FOR THE LIKES OF YOU.
GO BACK TO WHEREVER YOU CA—
HEY! WHERE'D THE CORE GO?
OH GREAT!
BAKU'S GONNA KILL ME!
SHFF SHFF SHFF

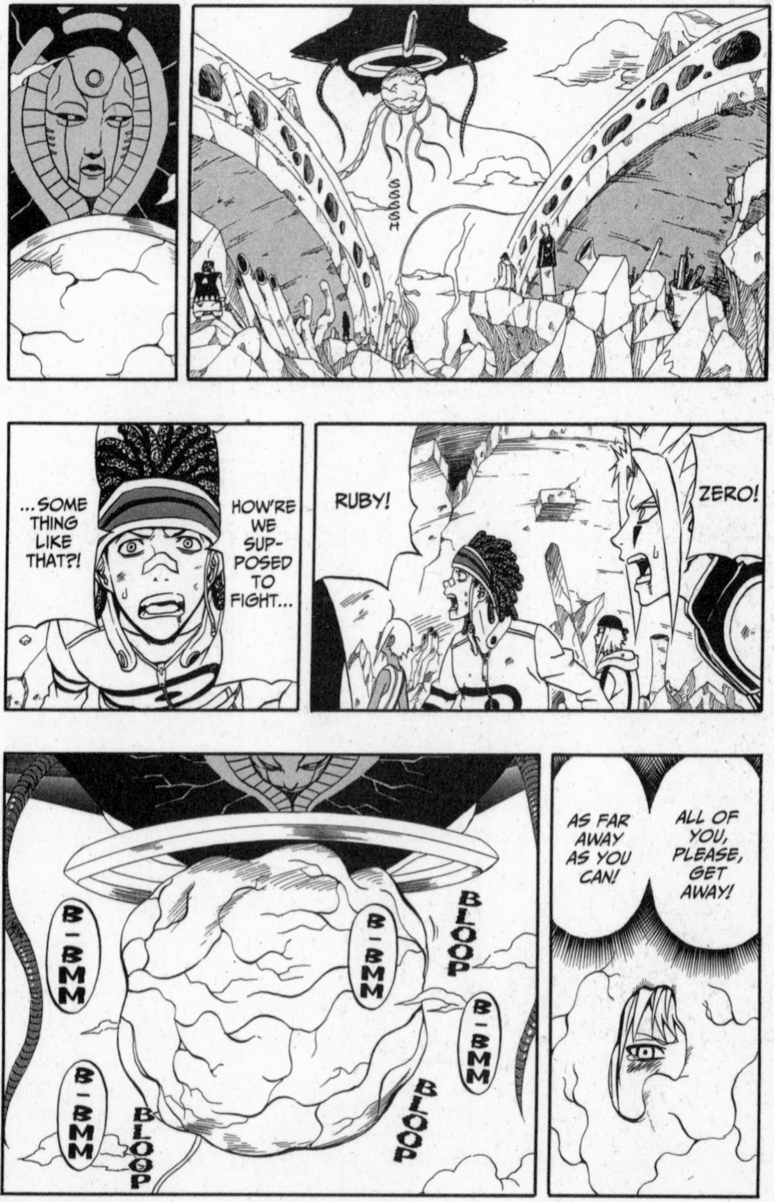
SSSSH
ZERO!
RUBY!
HOW'RE WE SUPPOSED TO FIGHT...
...SOMETHING LIKE THAT?!
ALL OF YOU, PLEASE, GET AWAY!
AS FAR AWAY AS YOU CAN!
BLOOP
B-BMM
B-BMM
BLOOP
B-BMM
B-BMM
BLOOP

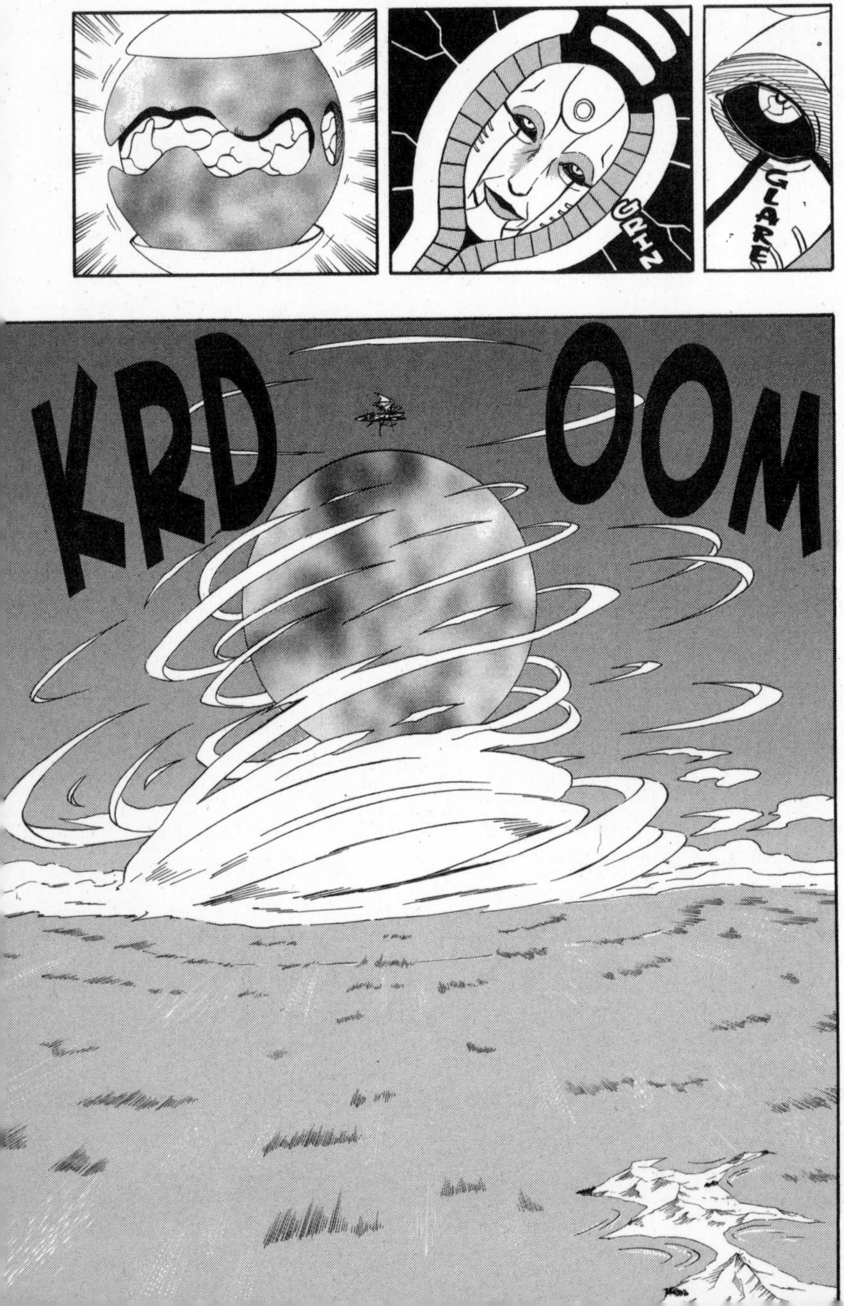
GLARE
GRIN
KRDOOM

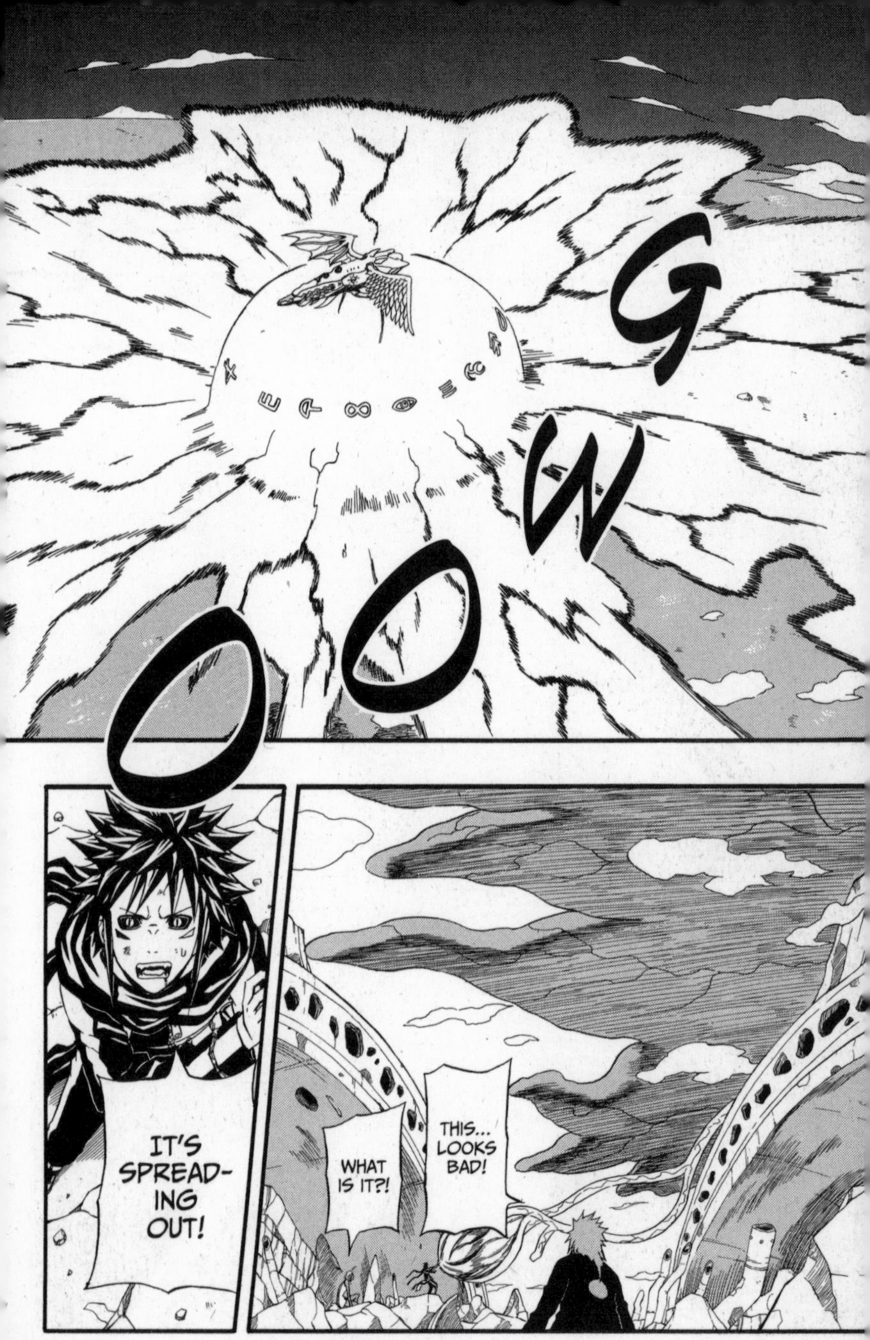
GWOO
THIS... LOOKS BAD!
WHAT IS IT?!
IT'S SPREAD-ING OUT!

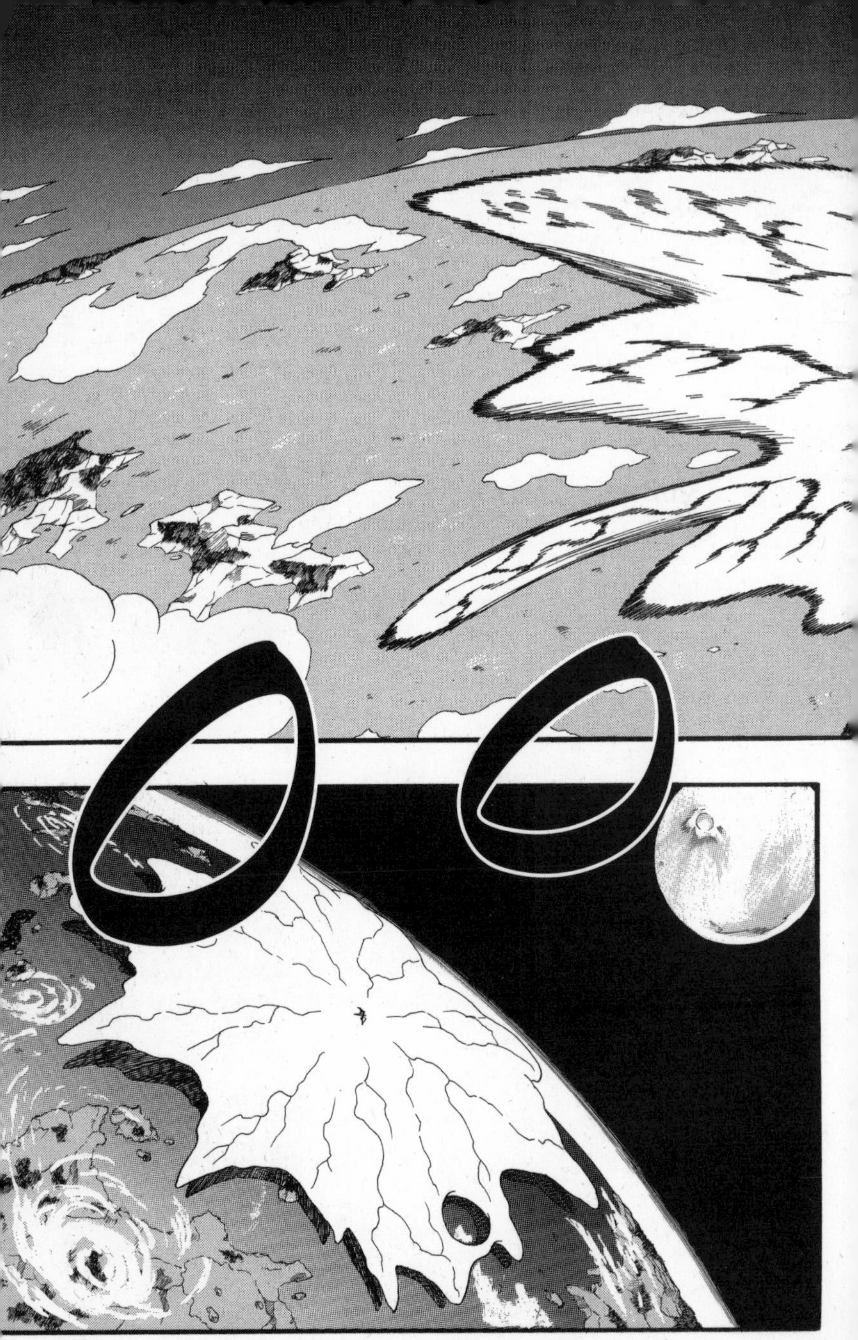

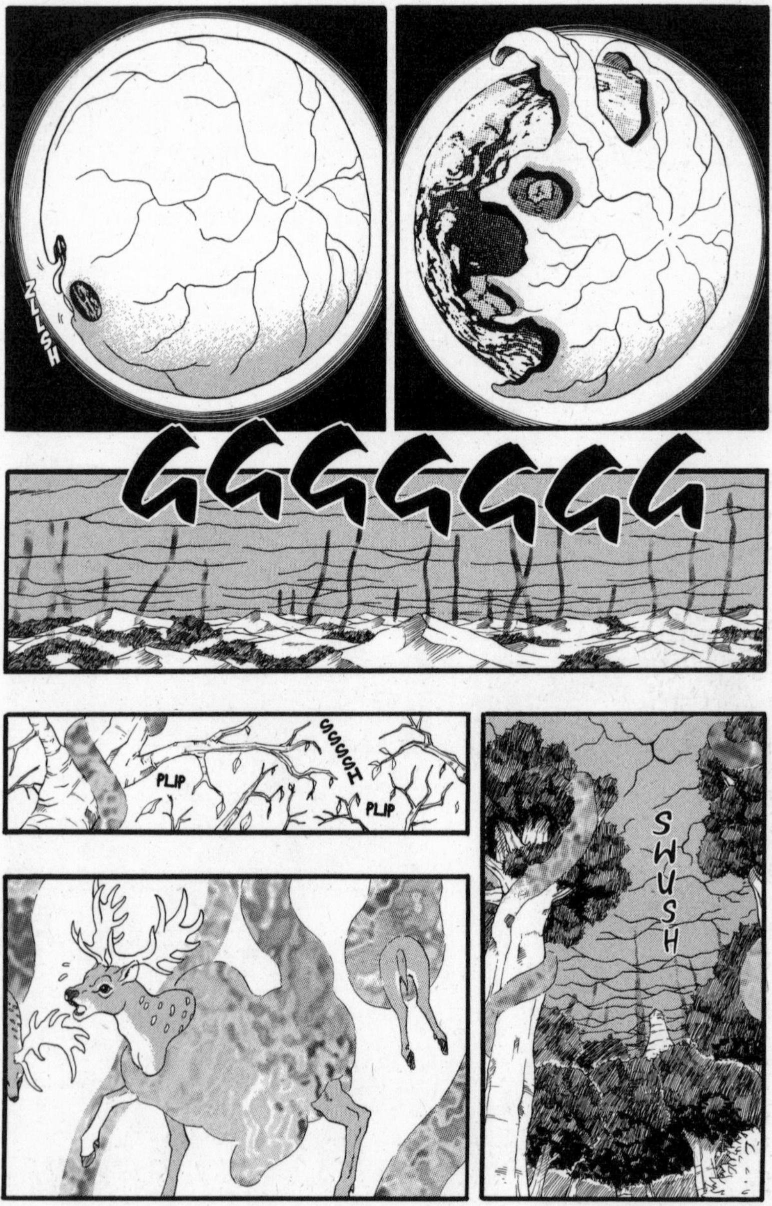
ZLLSH
GGGGGGG
SWUSH
SSSSSH
PLIP
PLIP

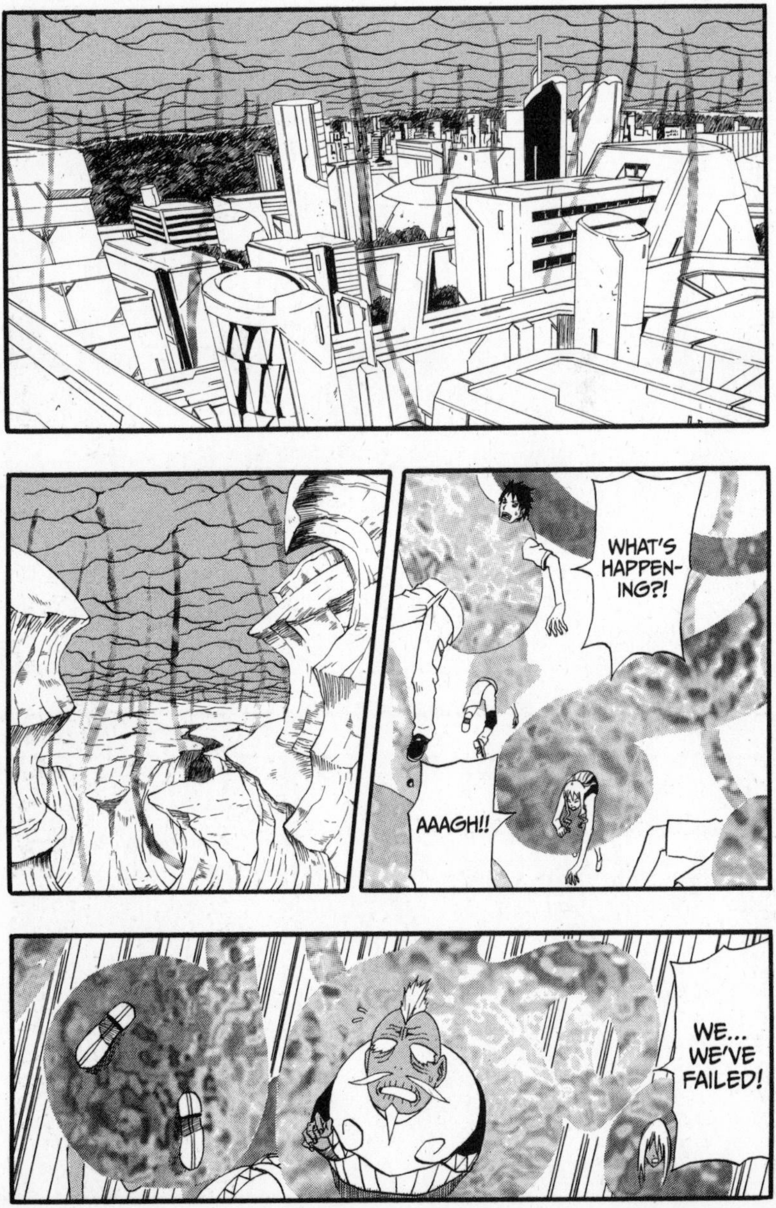
WHAT'S HAPPEN-ING?!
AAAGH!!
WE... WE'VE FAILED!

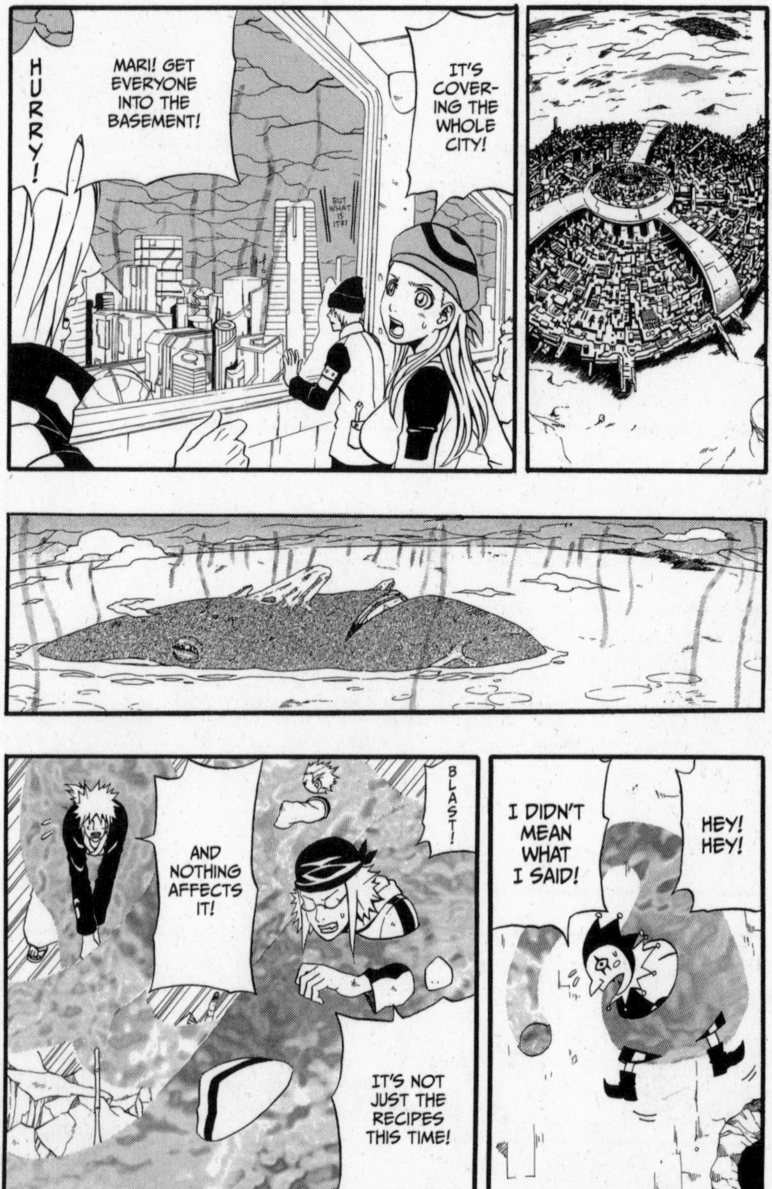
IT'S COVERING THE WHOLE CITY!
BUT WHAT IS IT?!
MARI! GET EVERYONE INTO THE BASEMENT!
HURRY!
HEY! HEY!
I DIDN'T MEAN WHAT I SAID!
BLAST!
AND NOTHING AFFECTS IT!
IT'S NOT JUST THE RECIPES THIS TIME!

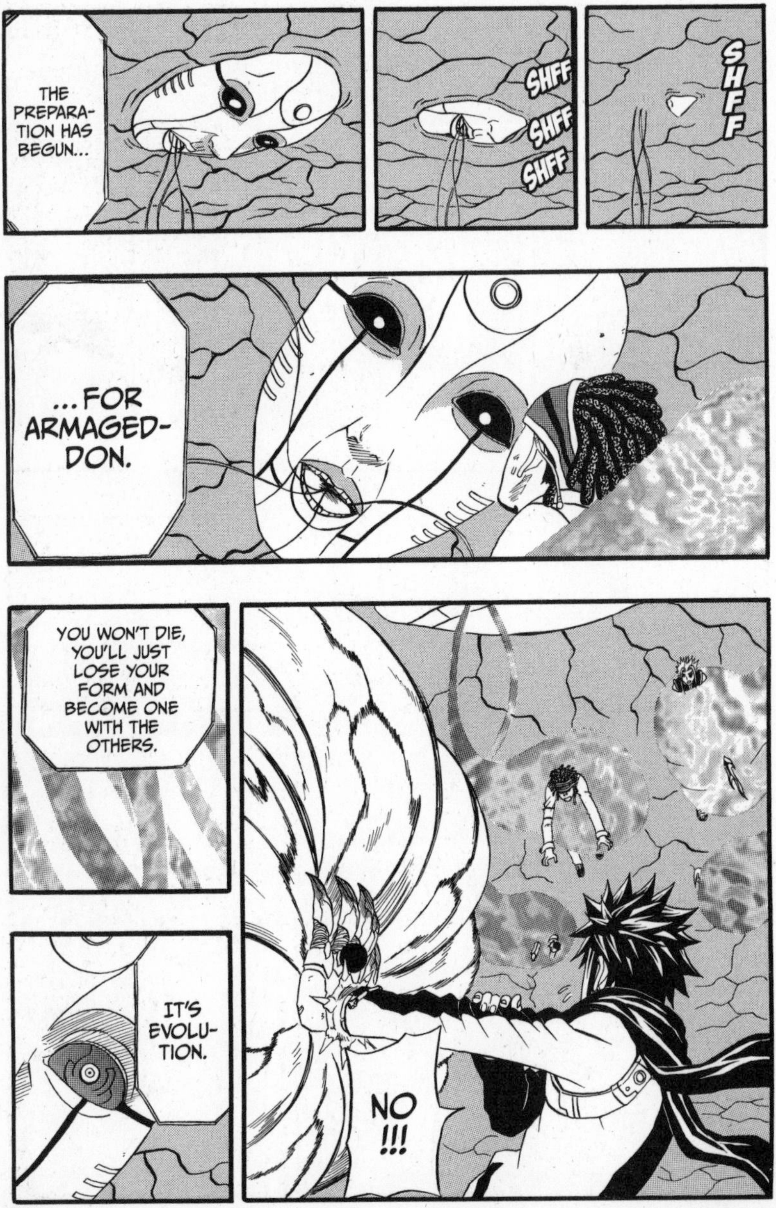
SHFF
SHFF
SHFF
SHFF
THE PREPARATION HAS BEGUN...
...FOR ARMAGEDDON.
NO!!!
YOU WON'T DIE, YOU'LL JUST LOSE YOUR FORM AND BECOME ONE WITH THE OTHERS.
IT'S EVOLUTION.

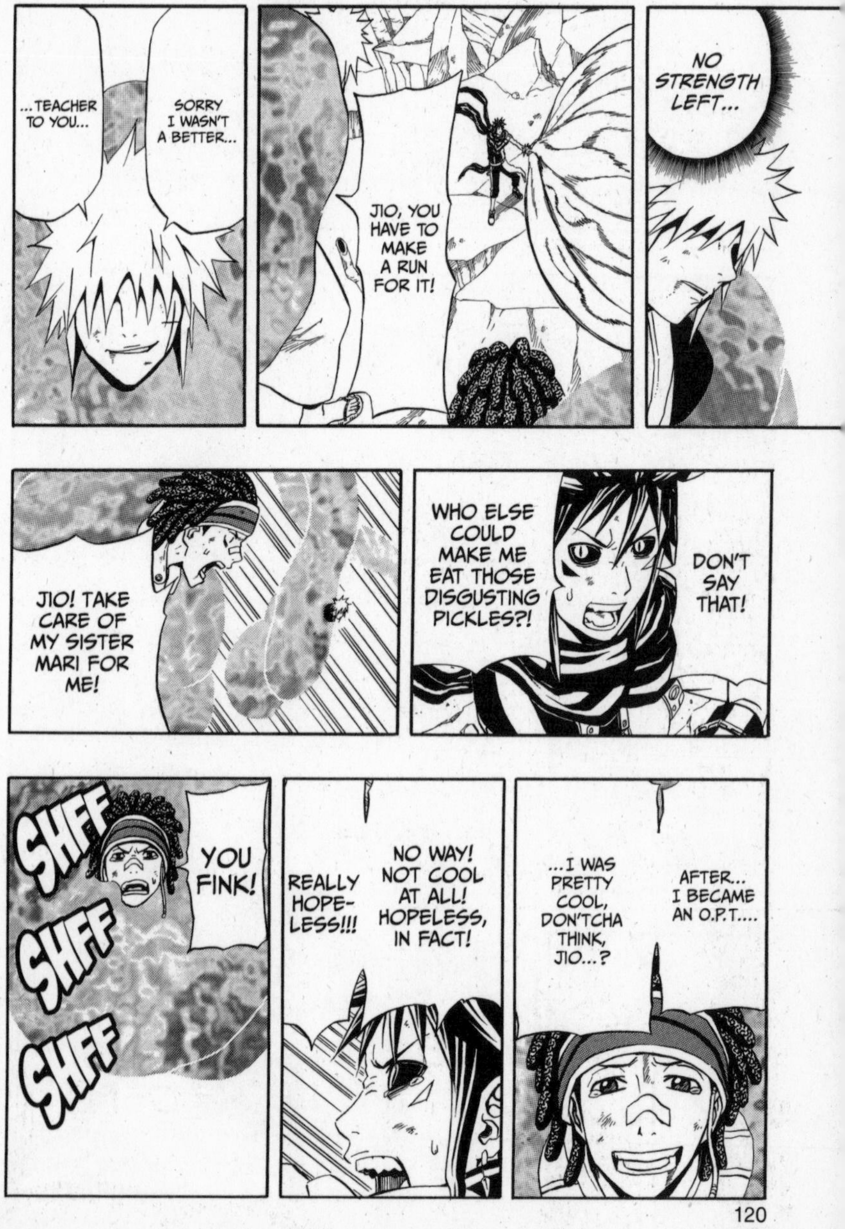
NO STRENGTH LEFT...
JIO, YOU HAVE TO MAKE A RUN FOR IT!
SORRY I WASN'T A BETTER...
...TEACHER TO YOU...
DON'T SAY THAT!
WHO ELSE COULD MAKE ME EAT THOSE DISGUSTING PICKLES?!
JIO! TAKE CARE OF MY SISTER MARI FOR ME!
AFTER... I BECAME AN O.P.T....
...I WAS PRETTY COOL, DON'TCHA THINK, JIO...?
NO WAY! NOT COOL AT ALL! HOPELESS, IN FACT!
REALLY HOPE-LESS!!!
YOU FINK!
SHFF
SHFF
SHFF

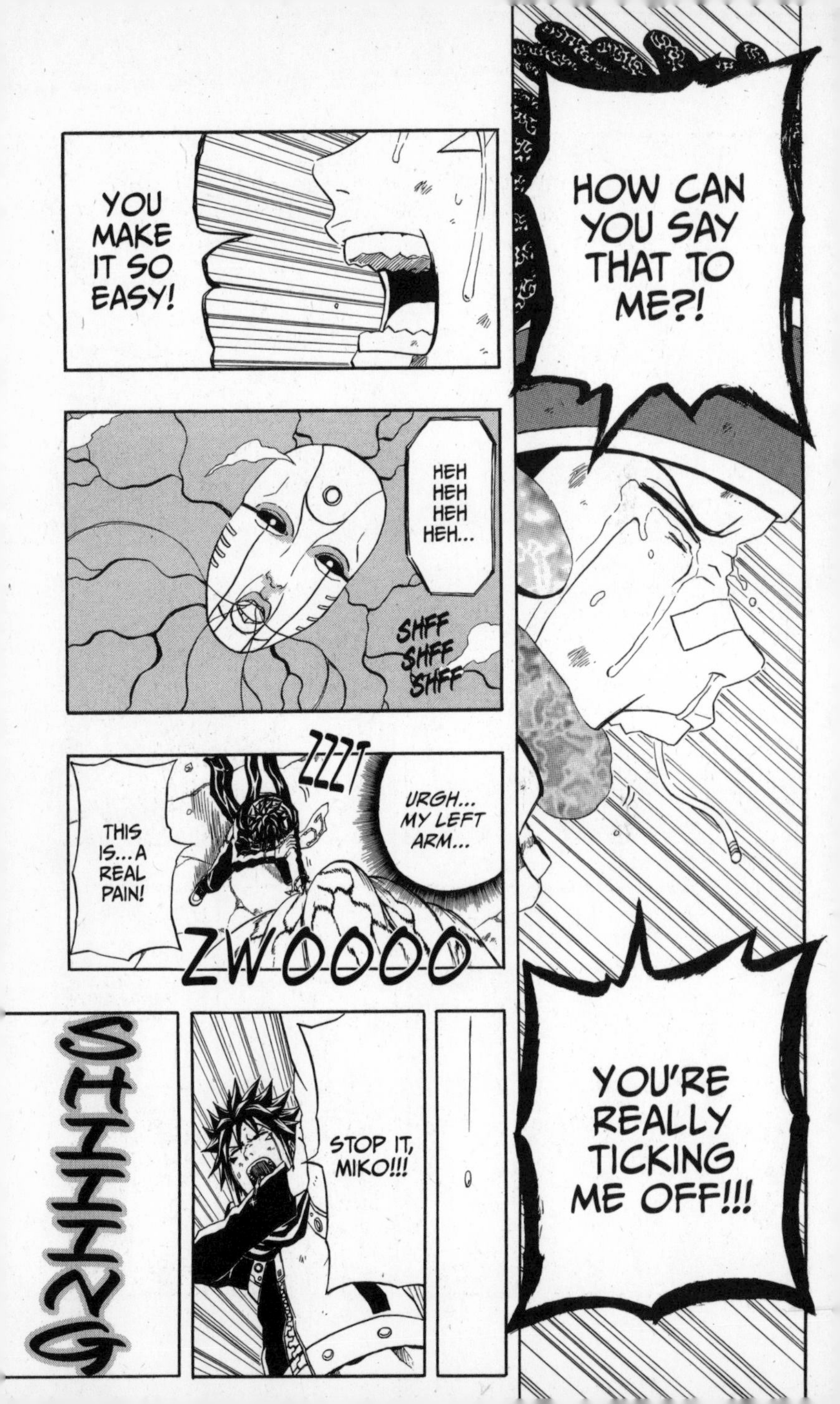

HOW CAN YOU SAY THAT TO ME?!
YOU'RE REALLY TICKING ME OFF!!!
YOU MAKE IT SO EASY!
HEH HEH HEH HEH...
SHFF SHFF SHFF
ZZZT
URGH... MY LEFT ARM...
THIS IS...A REAL PAIN!
ZWOOOO
STOP IT, MIKO!!!
SHIIING

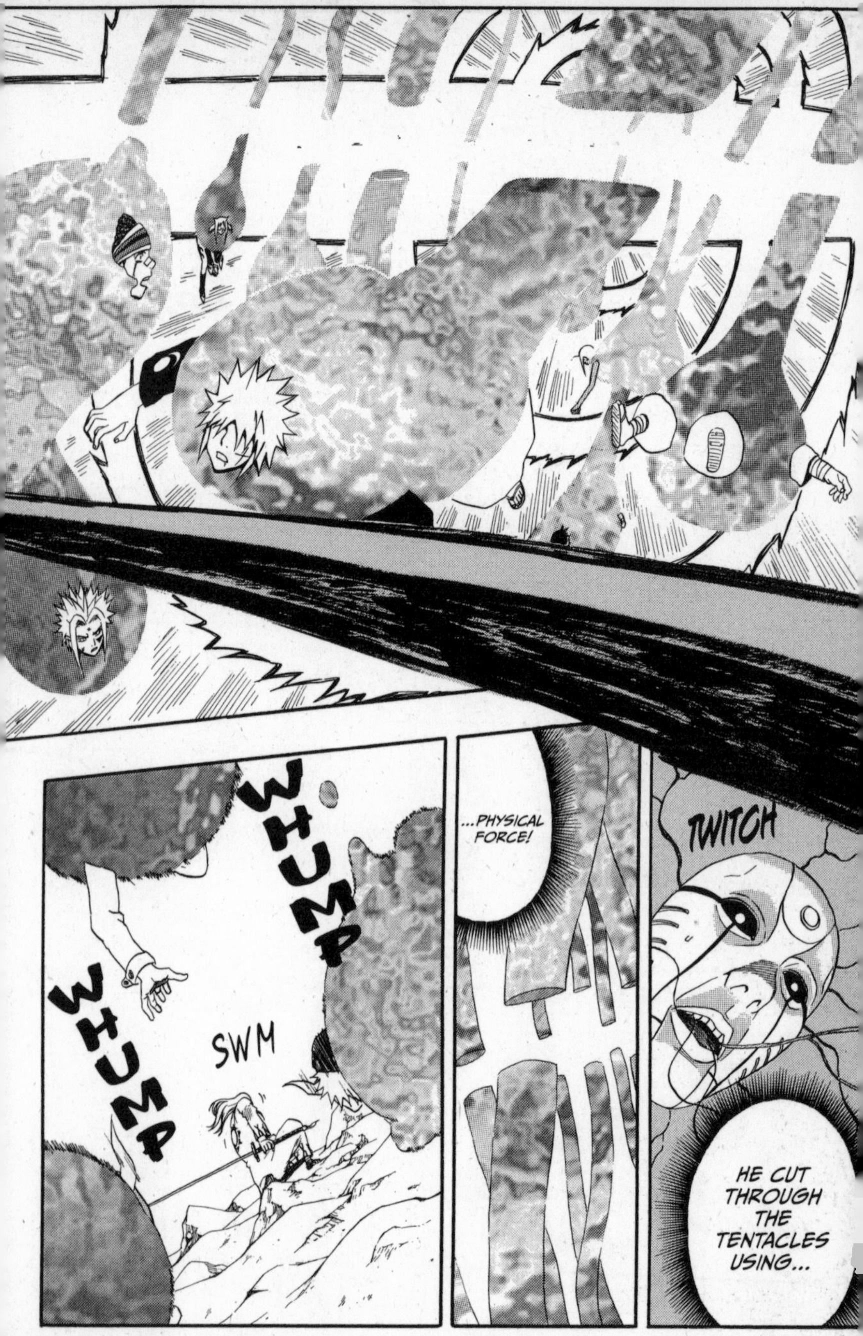
TWITCH
HE CUT THROUGH THE TENTACLES USING...
...PHYSICAL FORCE!
WHUMP
WHUMP
SWM

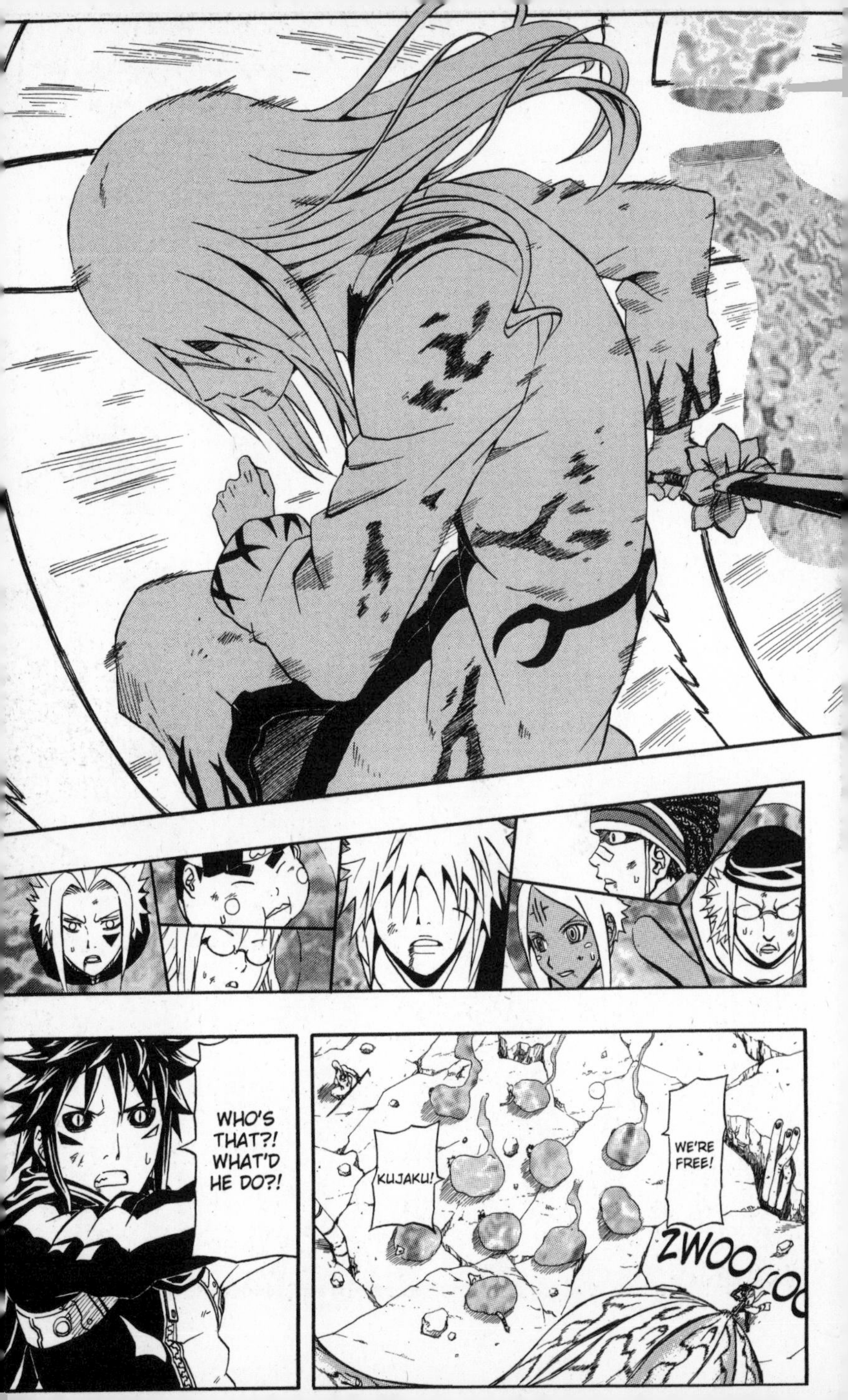
WE'RE FREE!
KUJAKU!
ZWOOSOO
WHO'S THAT?! WHAT'D HE DO?!

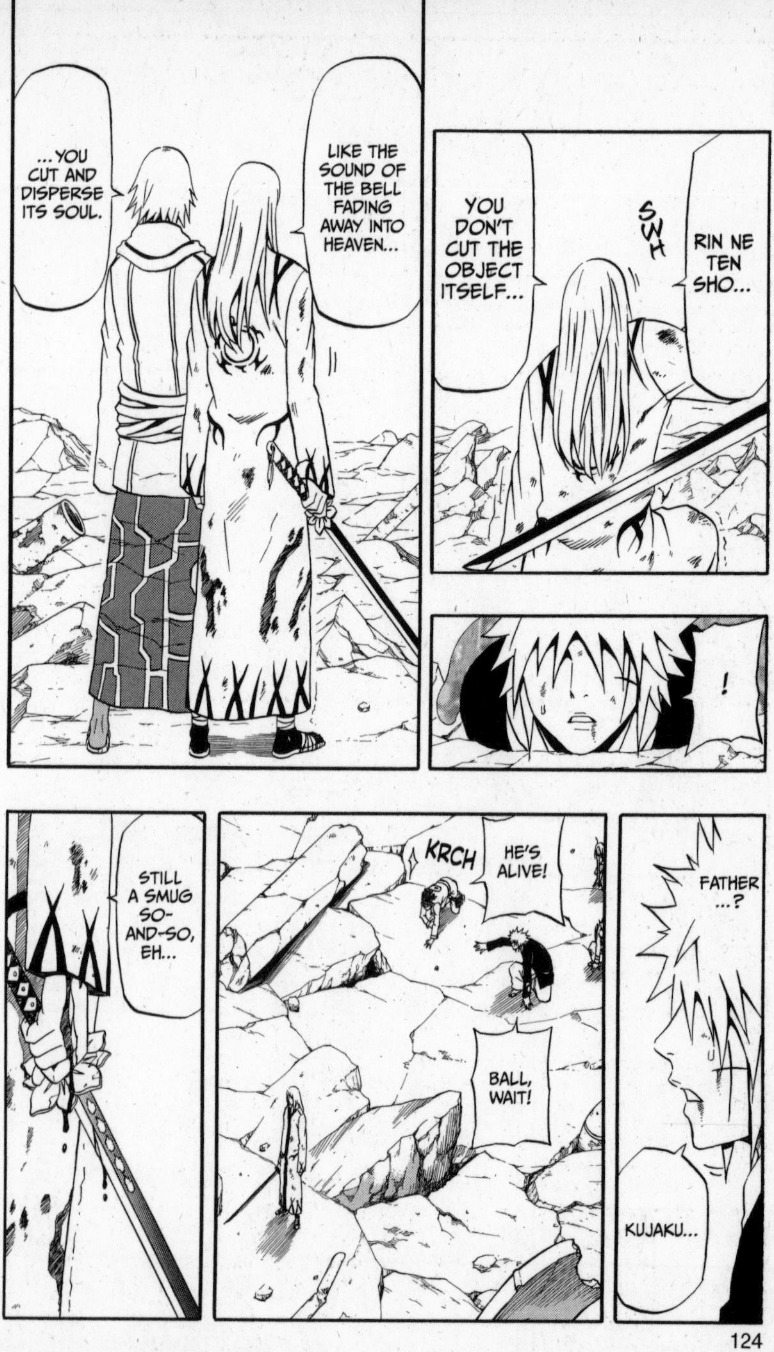
RIN NE TEN SHO...
SWH
YOU DON'T CUT THE OBJECT ITSELF...
!
LIKE THE SOUND OF THE BELL FADING AWAY INTO HEAVEN...
...YOU CUT AND DISPERSE ITS SOUL.
FATHER...?
KUJAKU...
HE'S ALIVE!
KRCH
BALL, WAIT!
STILL A SMUG SO-AND-SO, EH...

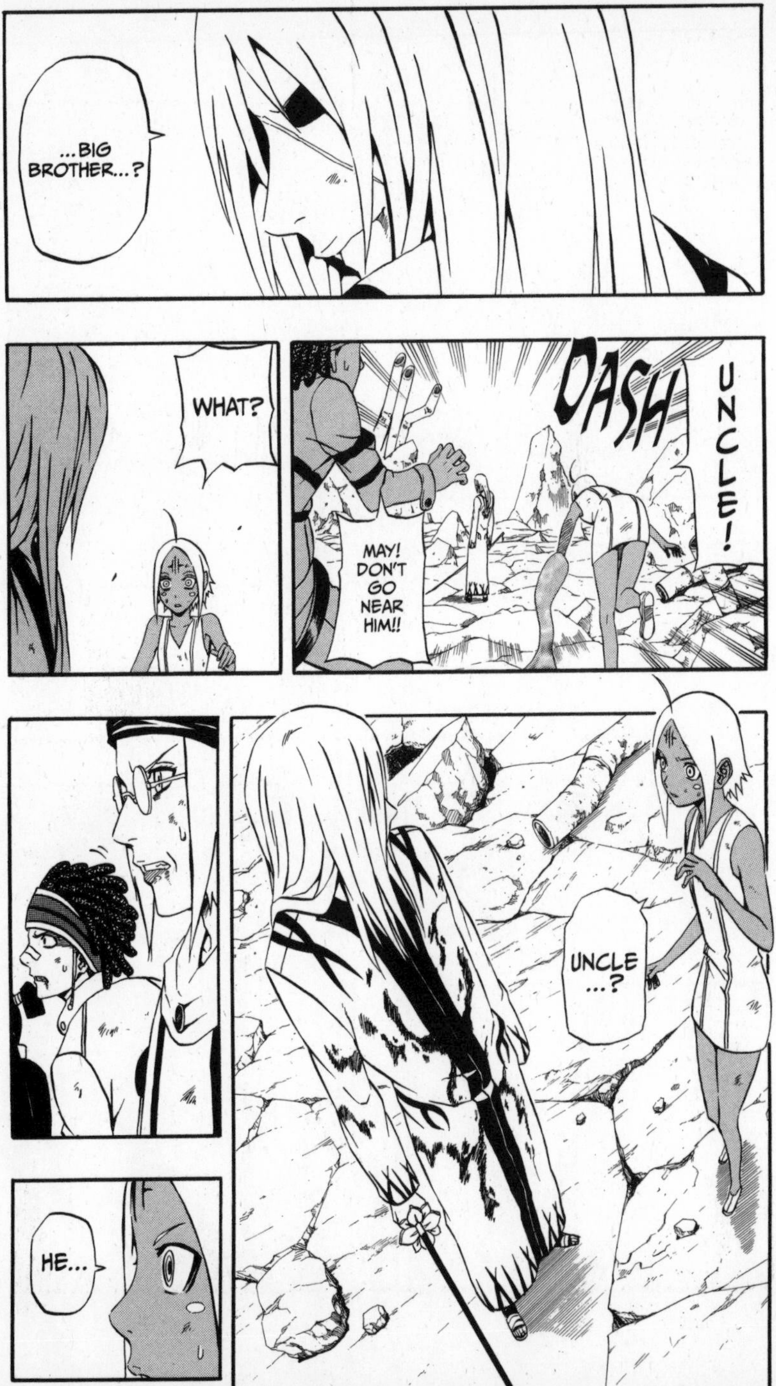
...BIG BROTHER...?
UNCLE!
DASH
MAY! DON'T GO NEAR HIM!!
WHAT?
UNCLE ...?
HE...

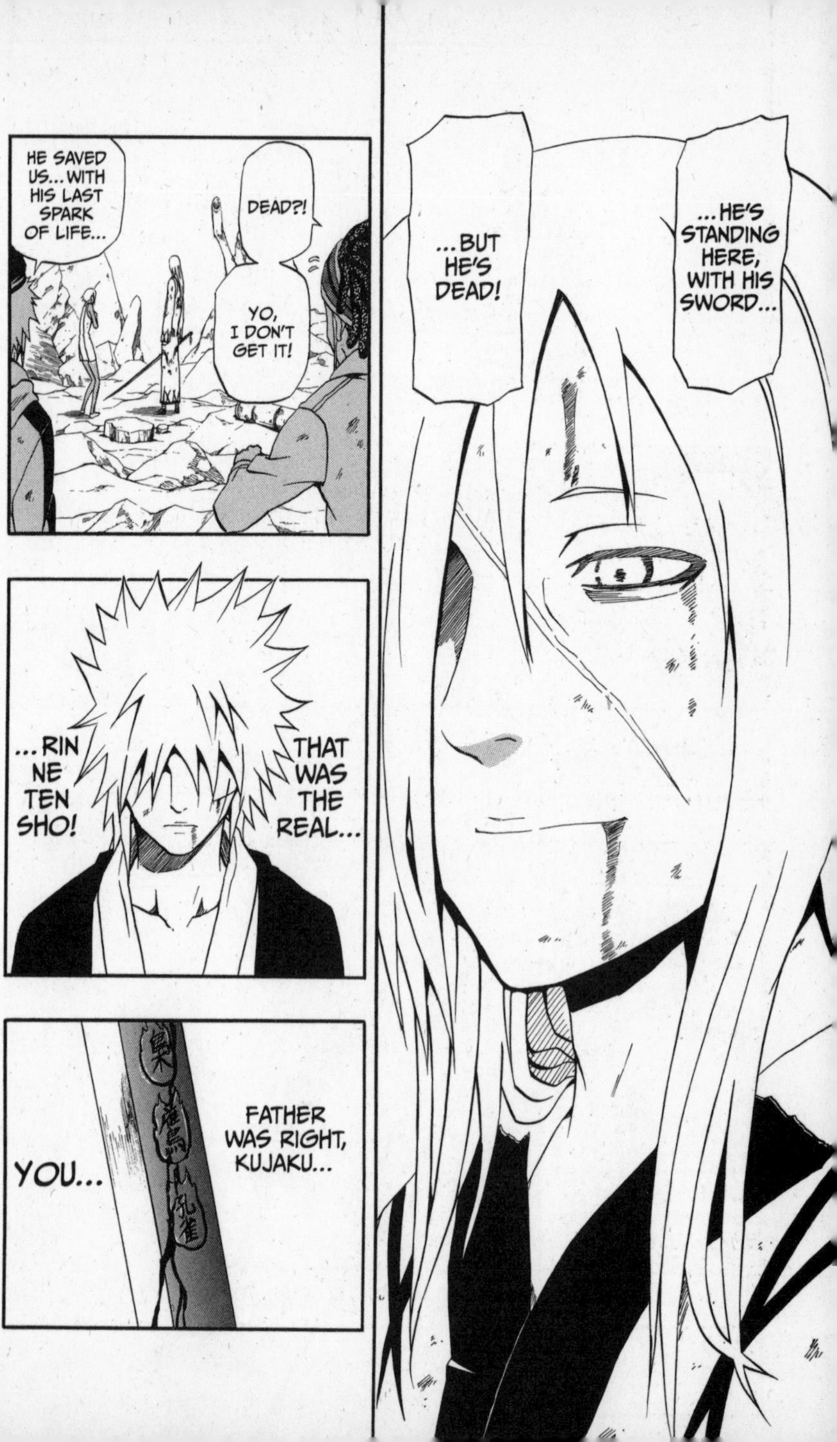
...HE'S STANDING HERE, WITH HIS SWORD...
...BUT HE'S DEAD!
DEAD?!
YO, I DON'T GET IT!
HE SAVED US...WITH HIS LAST SPARK OF LIFE...
THAT WAS THE REAL...
...RIN NE TEN SHO!
FATHER WAS RIGHT, KUJAKU...
YOU...

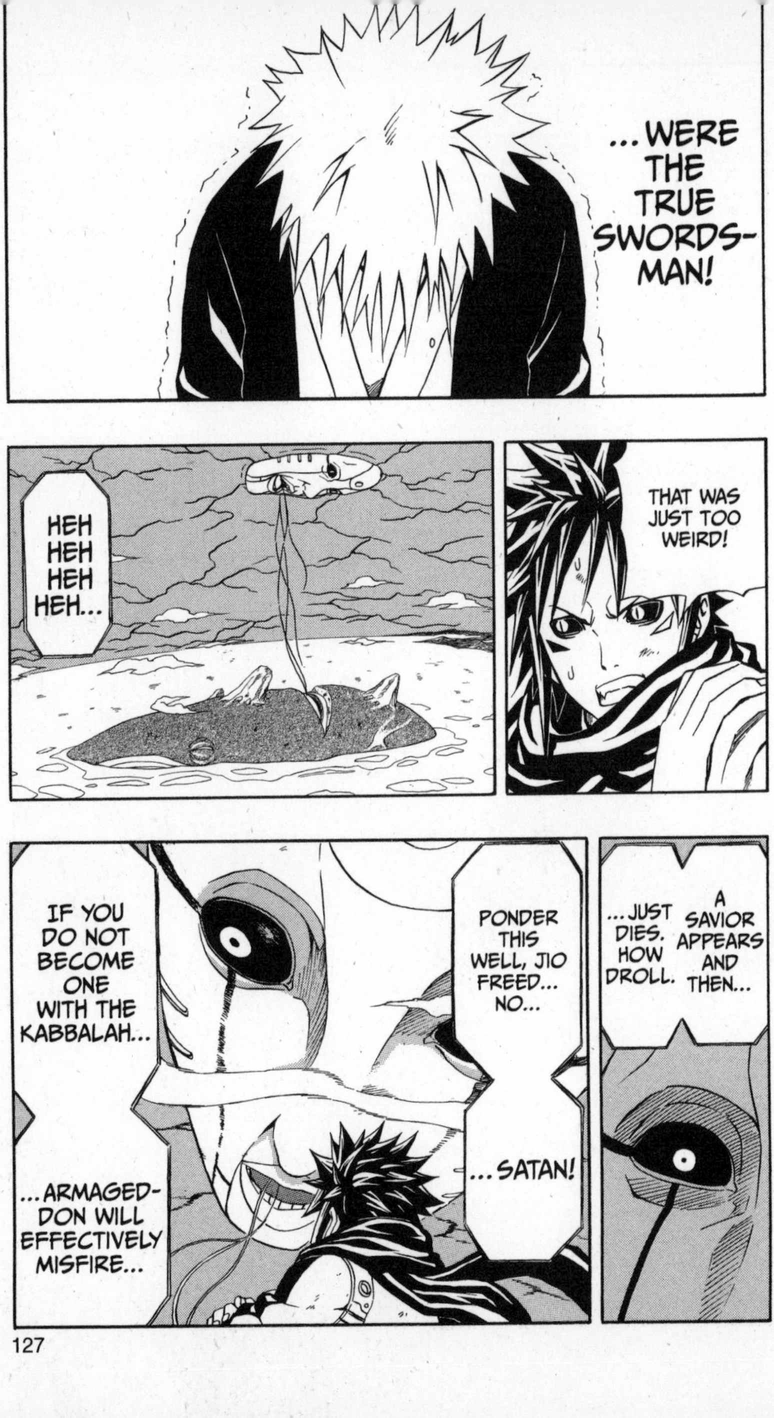
...WERE THE TRUE SWORDSMAN!
THAT WAS JUST TOO WEIRD!
HEH HEH HEH HEH...
A SAVIOR APPEARS AND THEN...
...JUST DIES. HOW DROLL.
PONDER THIS WELL, JIO FREED... NO...
...SATAN!
IF YOU DO NOT BECOME ONE WITH THE KABBALAH...
...ARMAGEDDON WILL EFFECTIVELY MISFIRE...

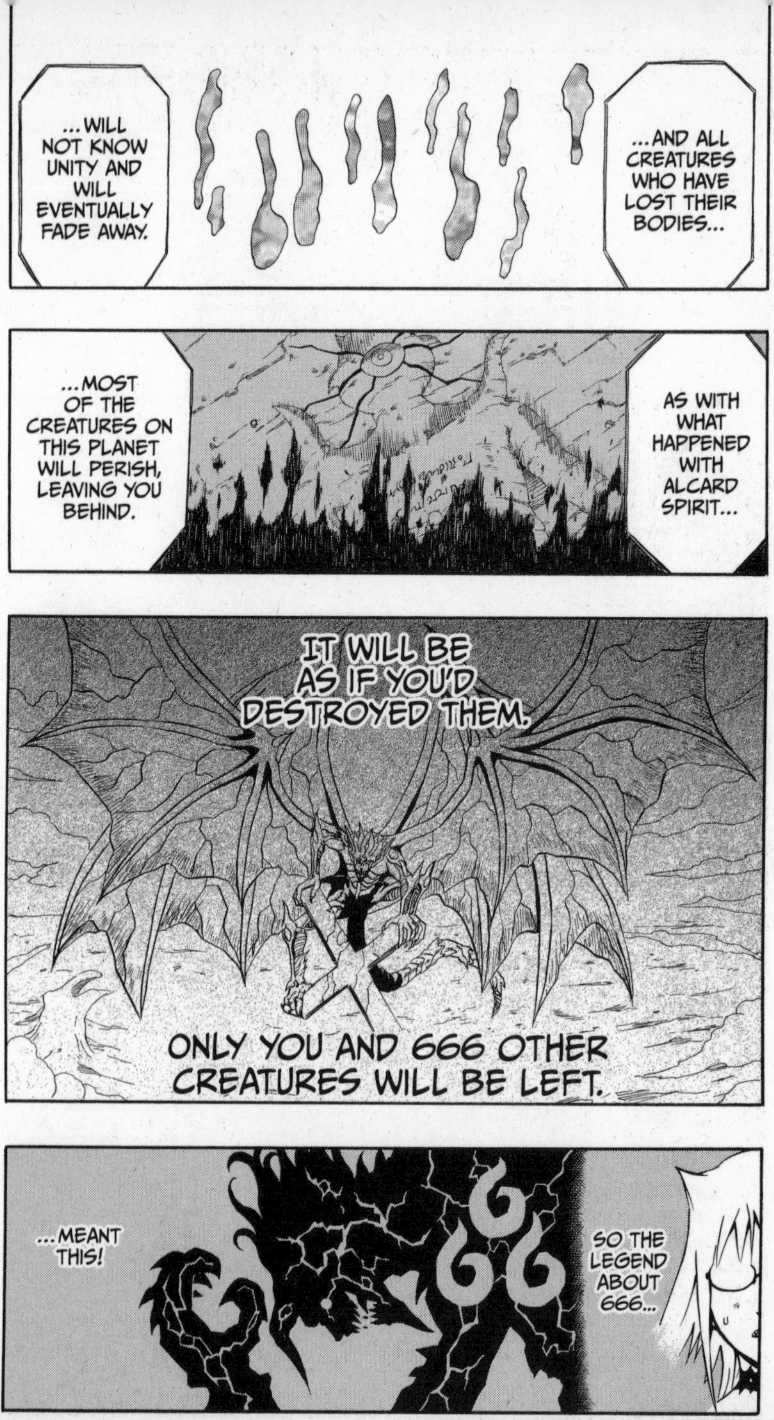
...AND ALL CREATURES WHO HAVE LOST THEIR BODIES...
...WILL NOT KNOW UNITY AND WILL EVENTUALLY FADE AWAY.
AS WITH WHAT HAPPENED WITH ALCARD SPIRIT...
...MOST OF THE CREATURES ON THIS PLANET WILL PERISH, LEAVING YOU BEHIND.
IT WILL BE AS IF YOU'D DESTROYED THEM.
ONLY YOU AND 666 OTHER CREATURES WILL BE LEFT.
SO THE LEGEND ABOUT 666...
...MEANT THIS!
666

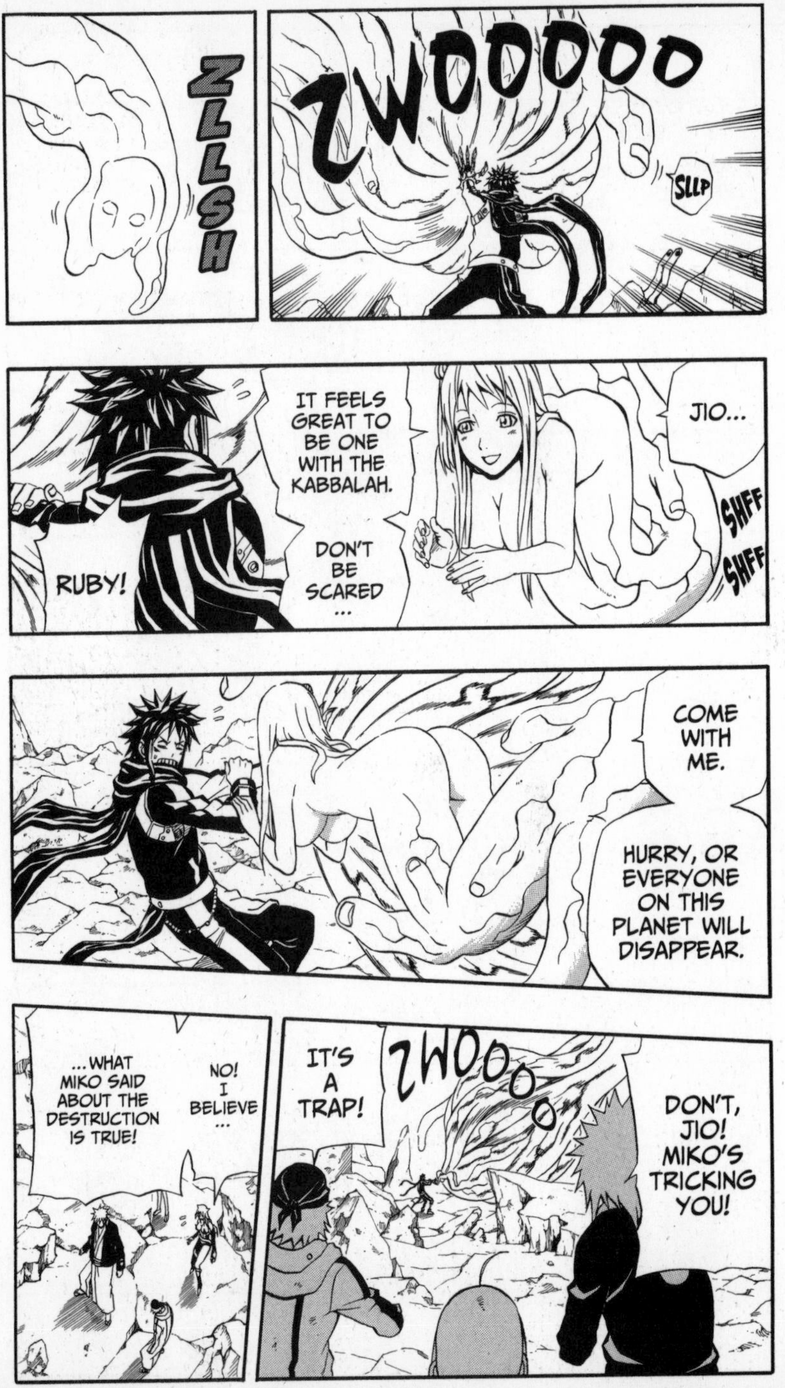
ZWOOOOOO
SLLP
ZLLSH
JIO...
SHFF
SHFF
IT FEELS GREAT TO BE ONE WITH THE KABBALAH.
DON'T BE SCARED ...
RUBY!
COME WITH ME.
HURRY, OR EVERYONE ON THIS PLANET WILL DISAPPEAR.
DON'T, JIO! MIKO'S TRICKING YOU!
ZWOOOOO
IT'S A TRAP!
NO! I BELIEVE ...
...WHAT MIKO SAID ABOUT THE DESTRUCTION IS TRUE!

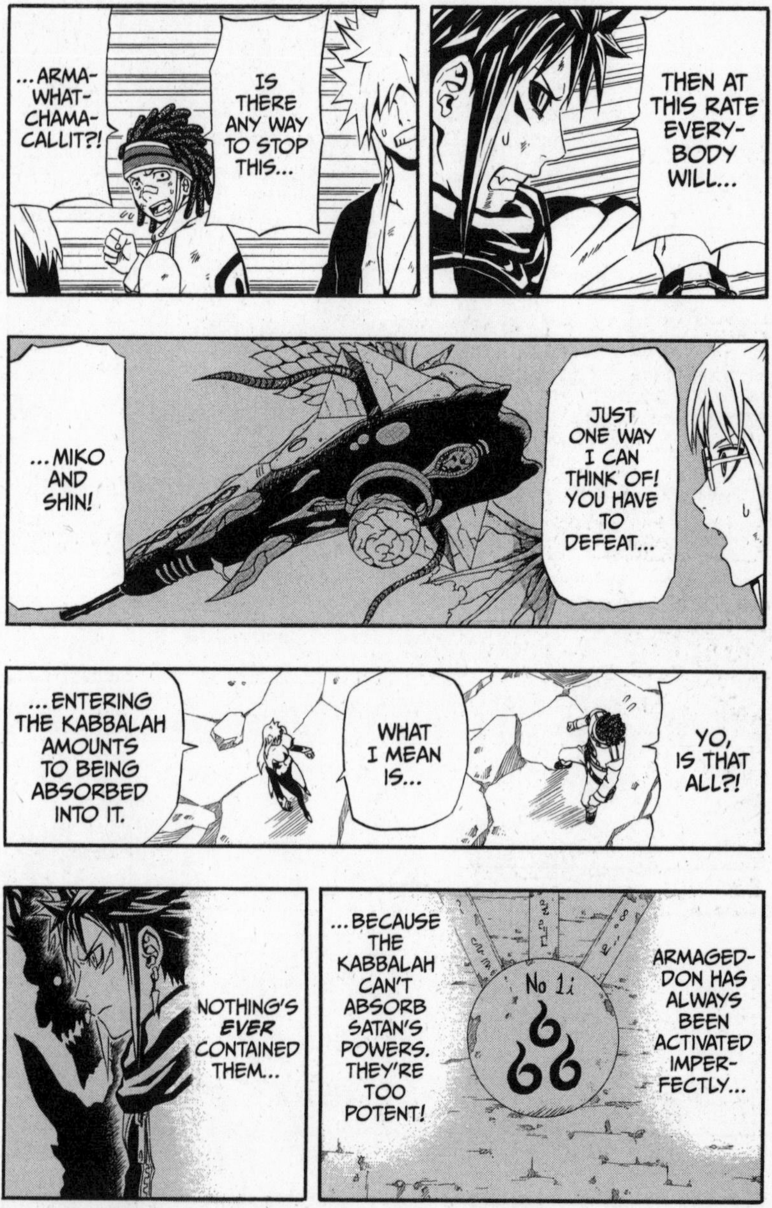
THEN AT THIS RATE EVERYBODY WILL...
IS THERE ANY WAY TO STOP THIS...
...ARMA-WHAT-CHAMA-CALLIT?!
JUST ONE WAY I CAN THINK OF! YOU HAVE TO DEFEAT...
...MIKO AND SHIN!
YO, IS THAT ALL?!
WHAT I MEAN IS...
...ENTERING THE KABBALAH AMOUNTS TO BEING ABSORBED INTO IT.
ARMAGEDDON HAS ALWAYS BEEN ACTIVATED IMPERFECTLY...
No 1i
...BECAUSE THE KABBALAH CAN'T ABSORB SATAN'S POWERS. THEY'RE TOO POTENT!
NOTHING'S *EVER* CONTAINED THEM...

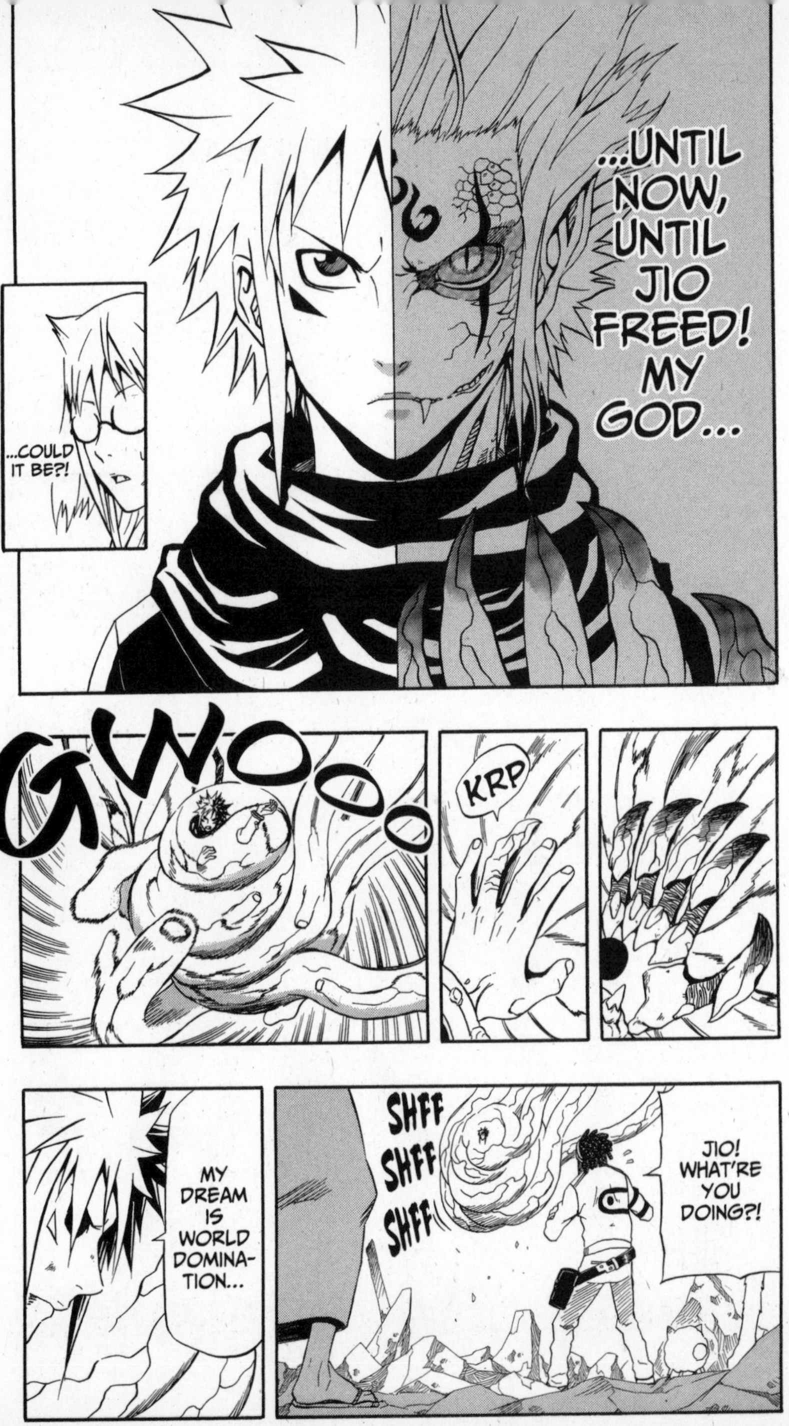
...UNTIL NOW, UNTIL JIO FREED! MY GOD...
...COULD IT BE?!
KRP
GWOOOO
JIO! WHAT'RE YOU DOING?!
SHFF
SHFF
SHFF
MY DREAM IS WORLD DOMINATION...

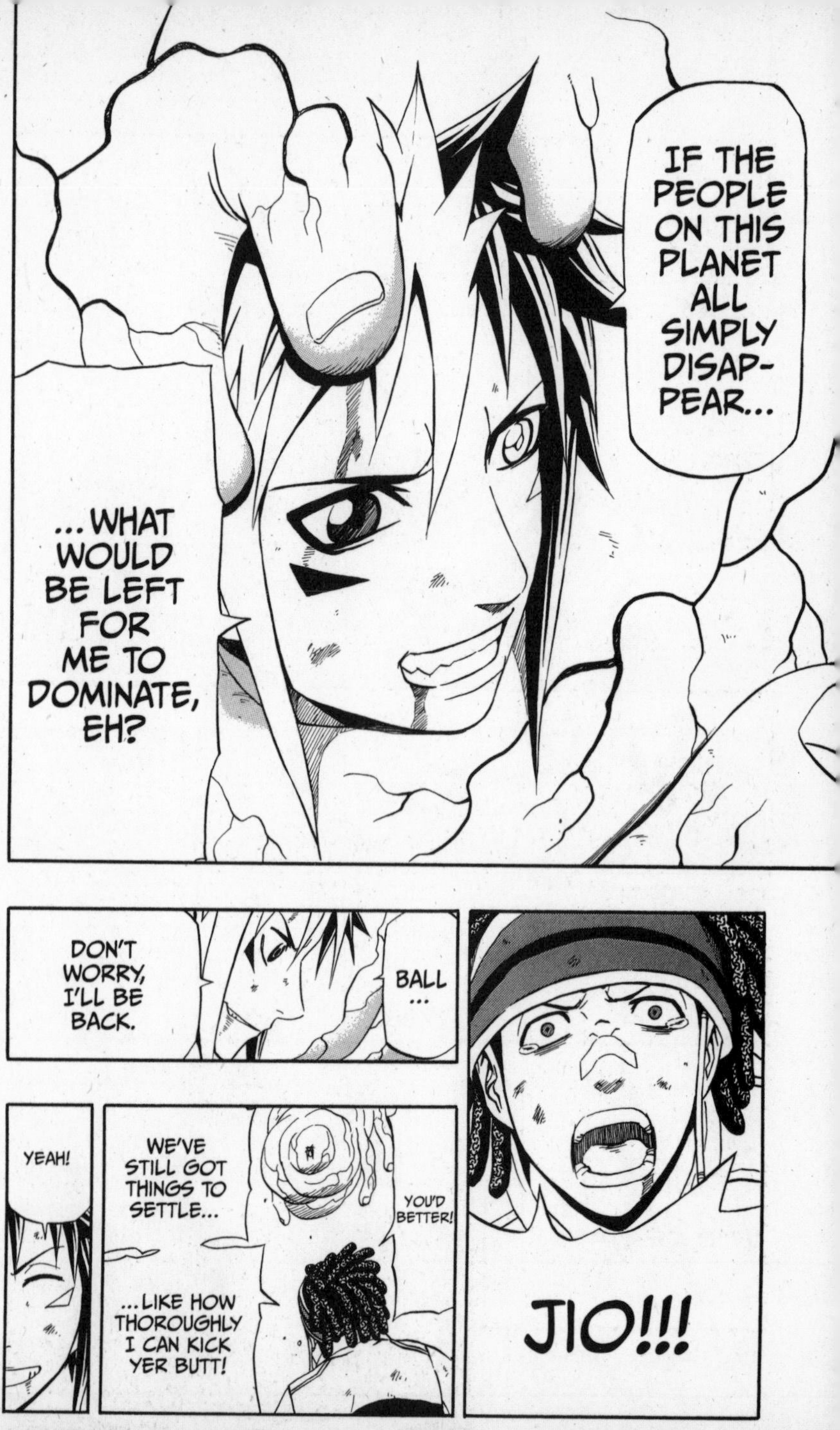
IF THE PEOPLE ON THIS PLANET ALL SIMPLY DISAP-PEAR...
...WHAT WOULD BE LEFT FOR ME TO DOMINATE, EH?
JIO!!!
BALL...
DON'T WORRY, I'LL BE BACK.
YOU'D BETTER!
WE'VE STILL GOT THINGS TO SETTLE...
...LIKE HOW THOROUGHLY I CAN KICK YER BUTT!
YEAH!

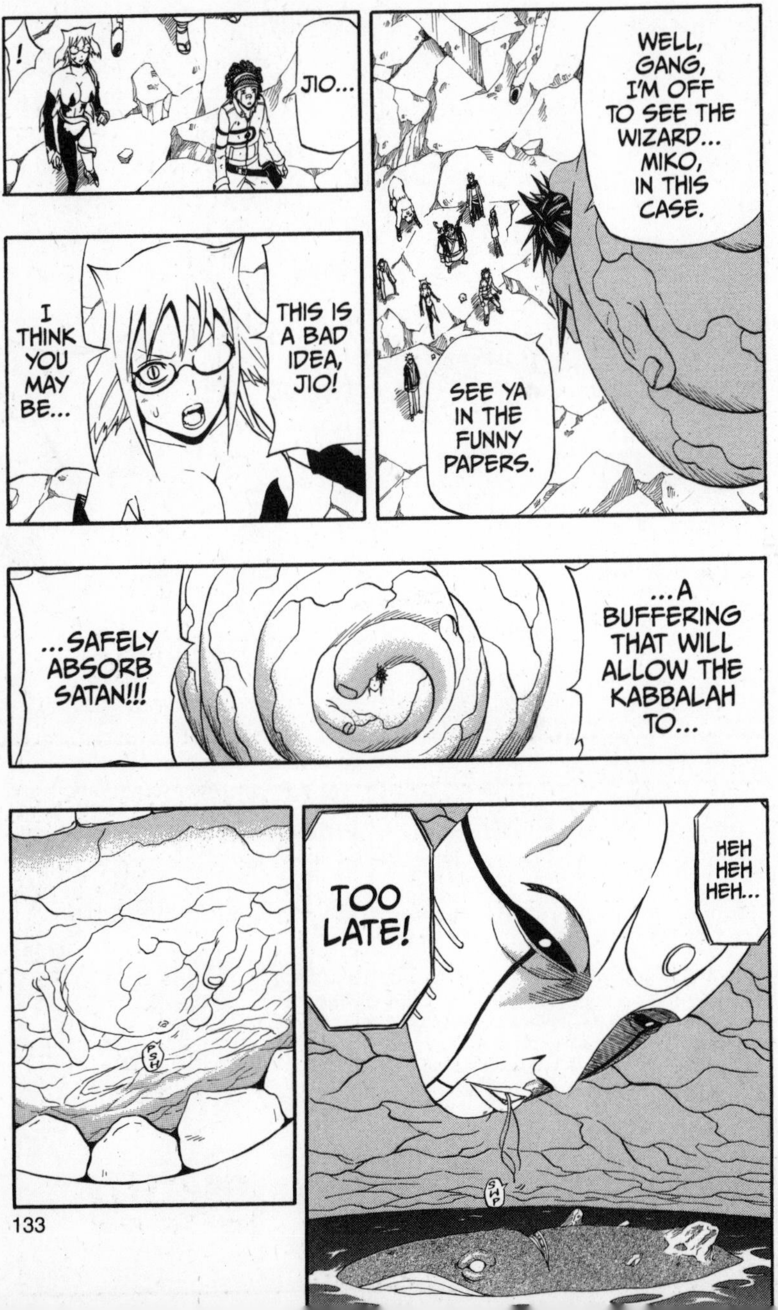
WELL, GANG, I'M OFF TO SEE THE WIZARD... MIKO, IN THIS CASE.
SEE YA IN THE FUNNY PAPERS.
JIO...
!
THIS IS A BAD IDEA, JIO!
I THINK YOU MAY BE...
...A BUFFERING THAT WILL ALLOW THE KABBALAH TO...
...SAFELY ABSORB SATAN!!!
HEH HEH HEH...
TOO LATE!
SHP
PSH

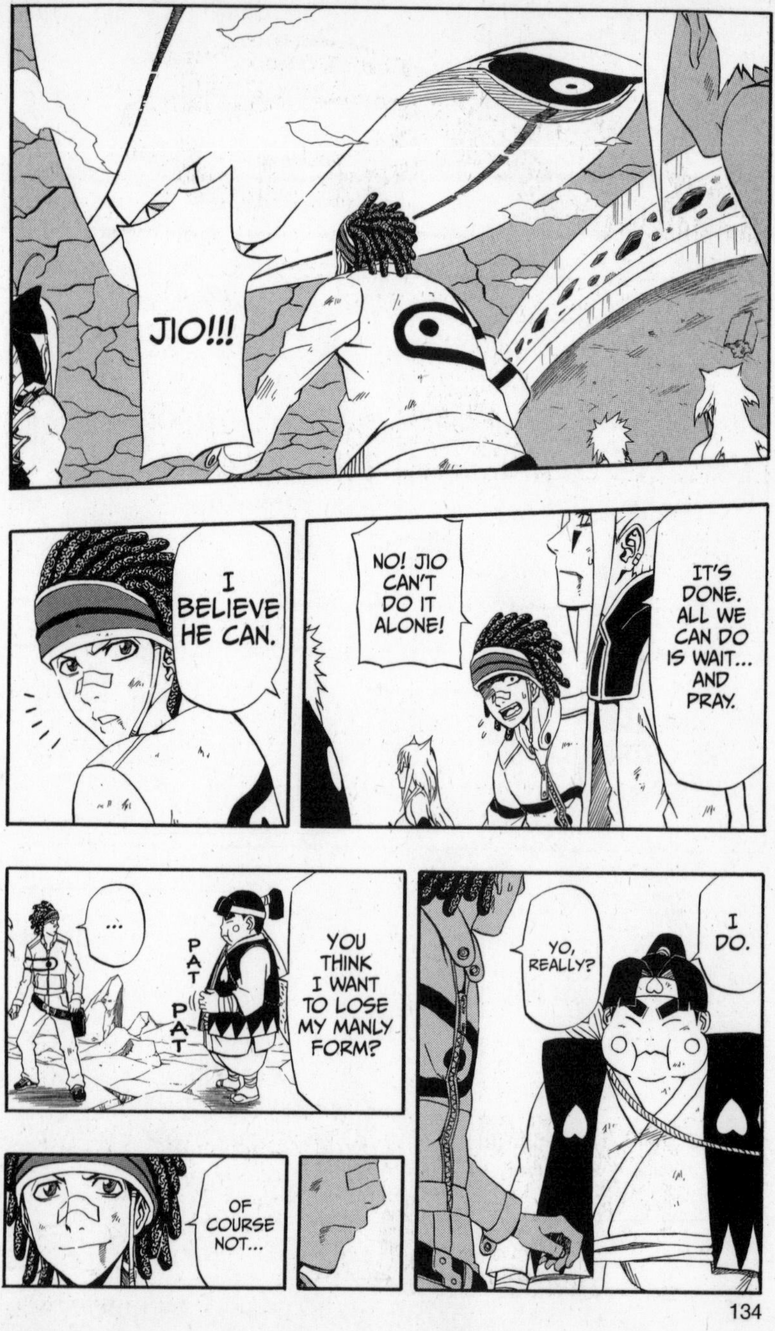
JIO!!!
IT'S DONE. ALL WE CAN DO IS WAIT... AND PRAY.
NO! JIO CAN'T DO IT ALONE!
I BELIEVE HE CAN.
I DO.
YO, REALLY?
YOU THINK I WANT TO LOSE MY MANLY FORM?
PAT PAT
...
OF COURSE NOT...

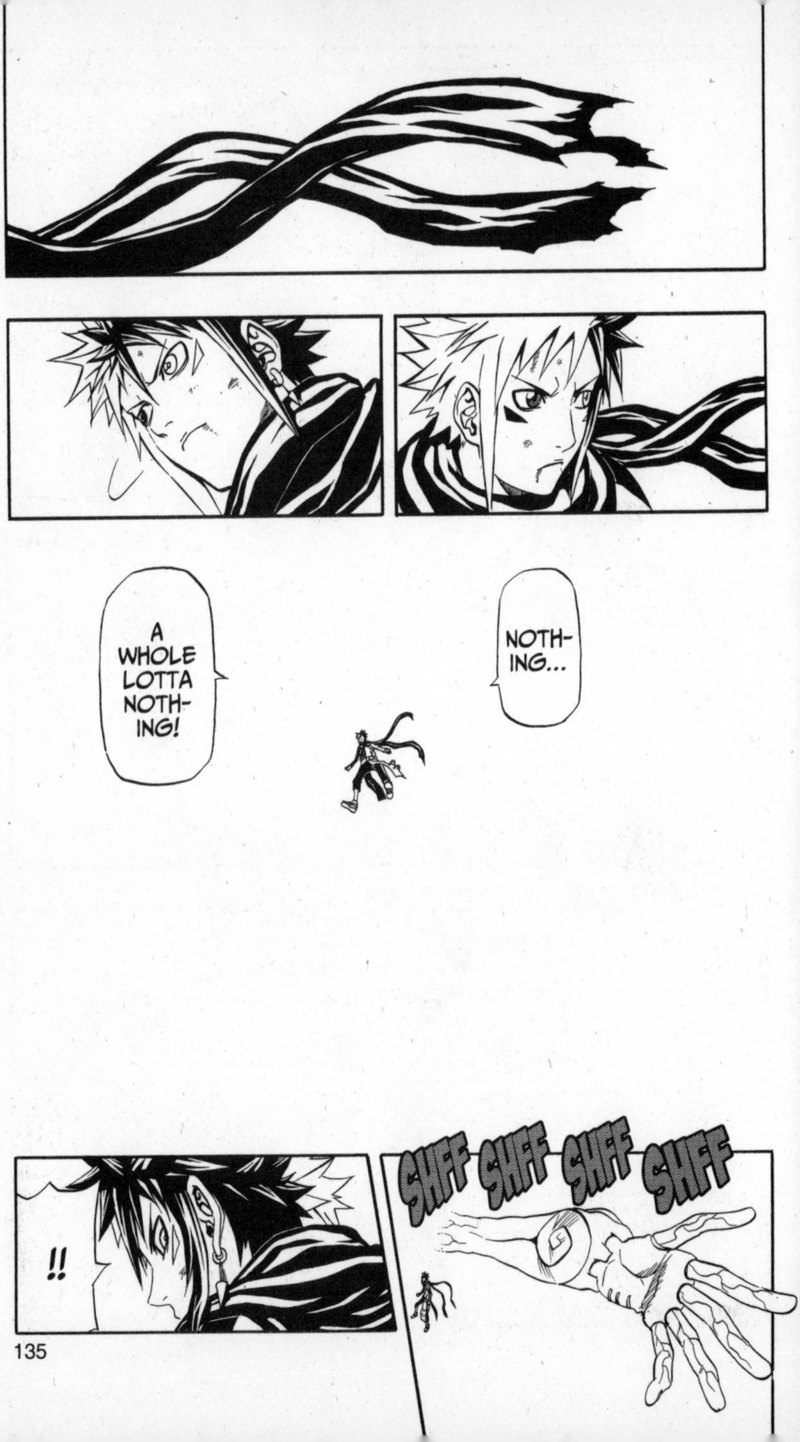
NOTHING...
A WHOLE LOTTA NOTHING!
SHFF SHFF SHFF SHFF
!!

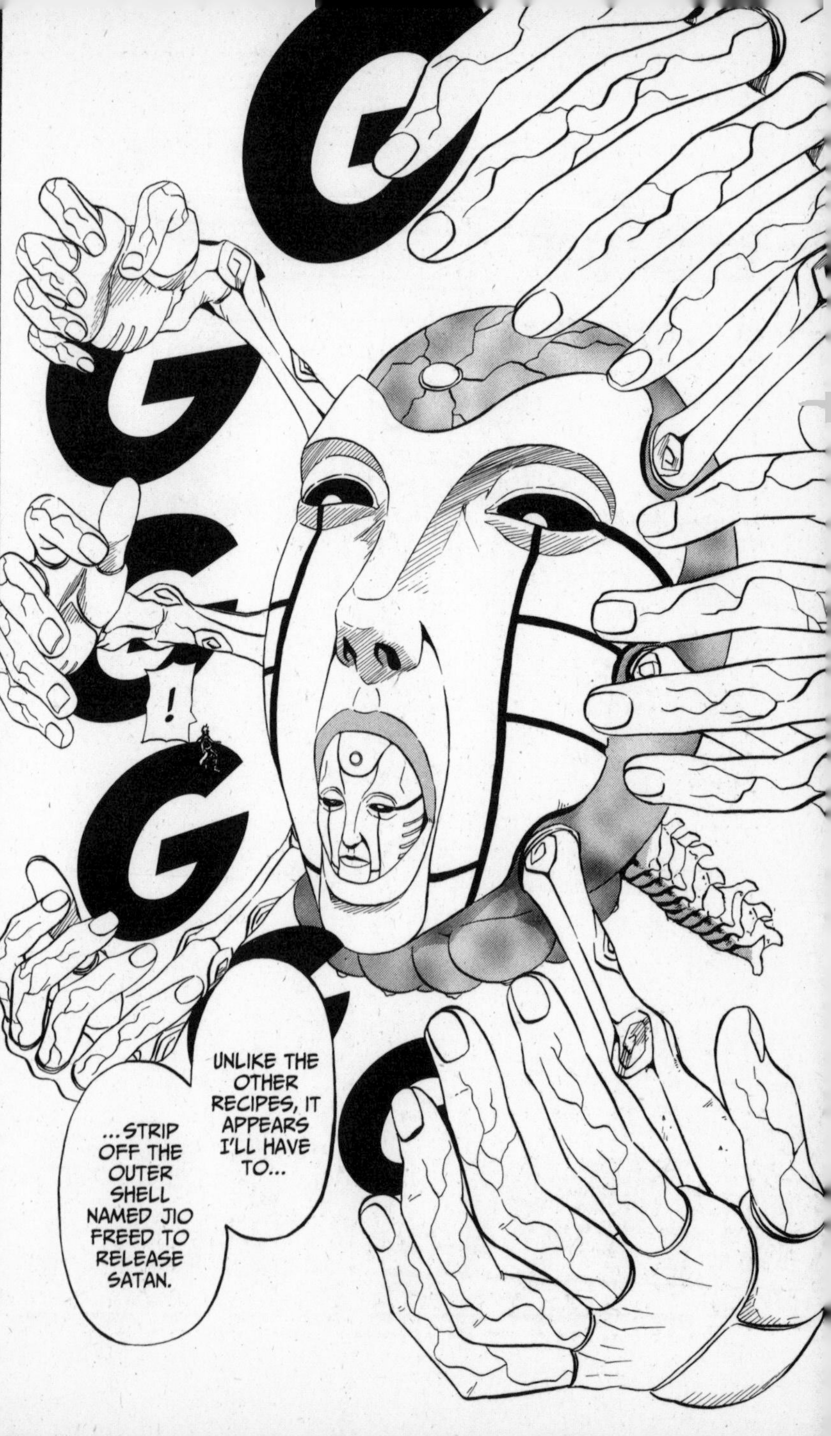
GGGGGG
!
UNLIKE THE OTHER RECIPES, IT APPEARS I'LL HAVE TO...
...STRIP OFF THE OUTER SHELL NAMED JIO FREED TO RELEASE SATAN.

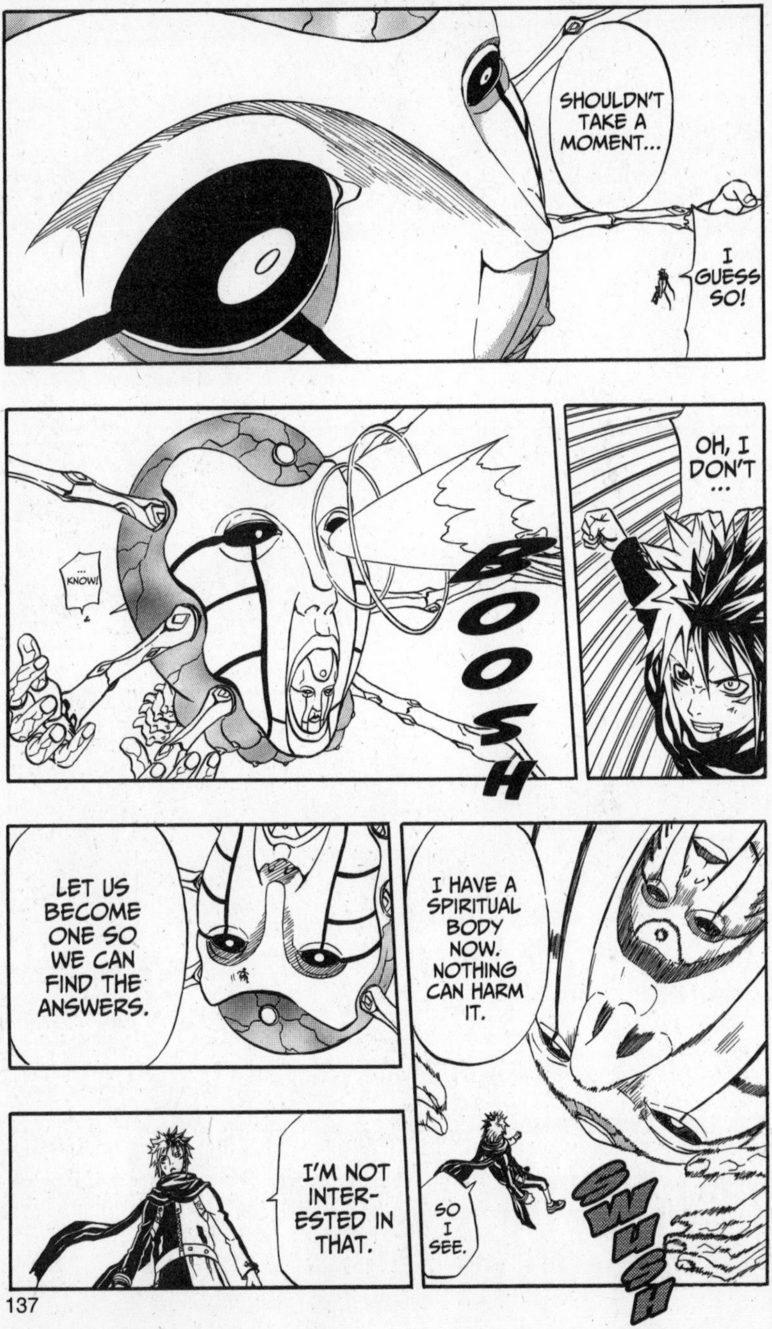
SHOULDN'T TAKE A MOMENT...
I GUESS SO!
OH, I DON'T ...
...KNOW!
BOOSH
I HAVE A SPIRITUAL BODY NOW. NOTHING CAN HARM IT.
SO I SEE.
SWUSH
LET US BECOME ONE SO WE CAN FIND THE ANSWERS.
I'M NOT INTER-ESTED IN THAT.

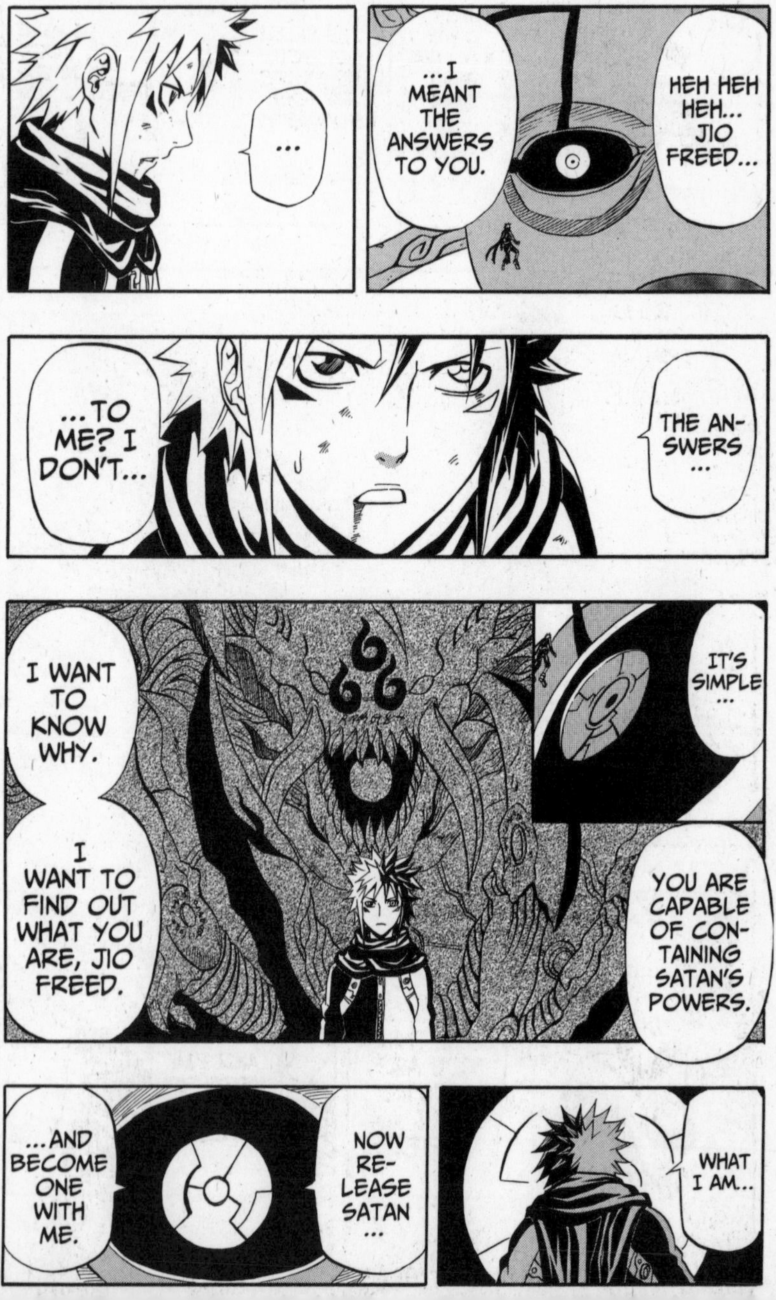
HEH HEH HEH... JIO FREED...
...I MEANT THE ANSWERS TO YOU.
...
THE AN-SWERS...
...TO ME? I DON'T...
IT'S SIMPLE...
I WANT TO KNOW WHY.
I WANT TO FIND OUT WHAT YOU ARE, JIO FREED.
YOU ARE CAPABLE OF CON-TAINING SATAN'S POWERS.
WHAT I AM...
NOW RE-LEASE SATAN...
...AND BECOME ONE WITH ME.

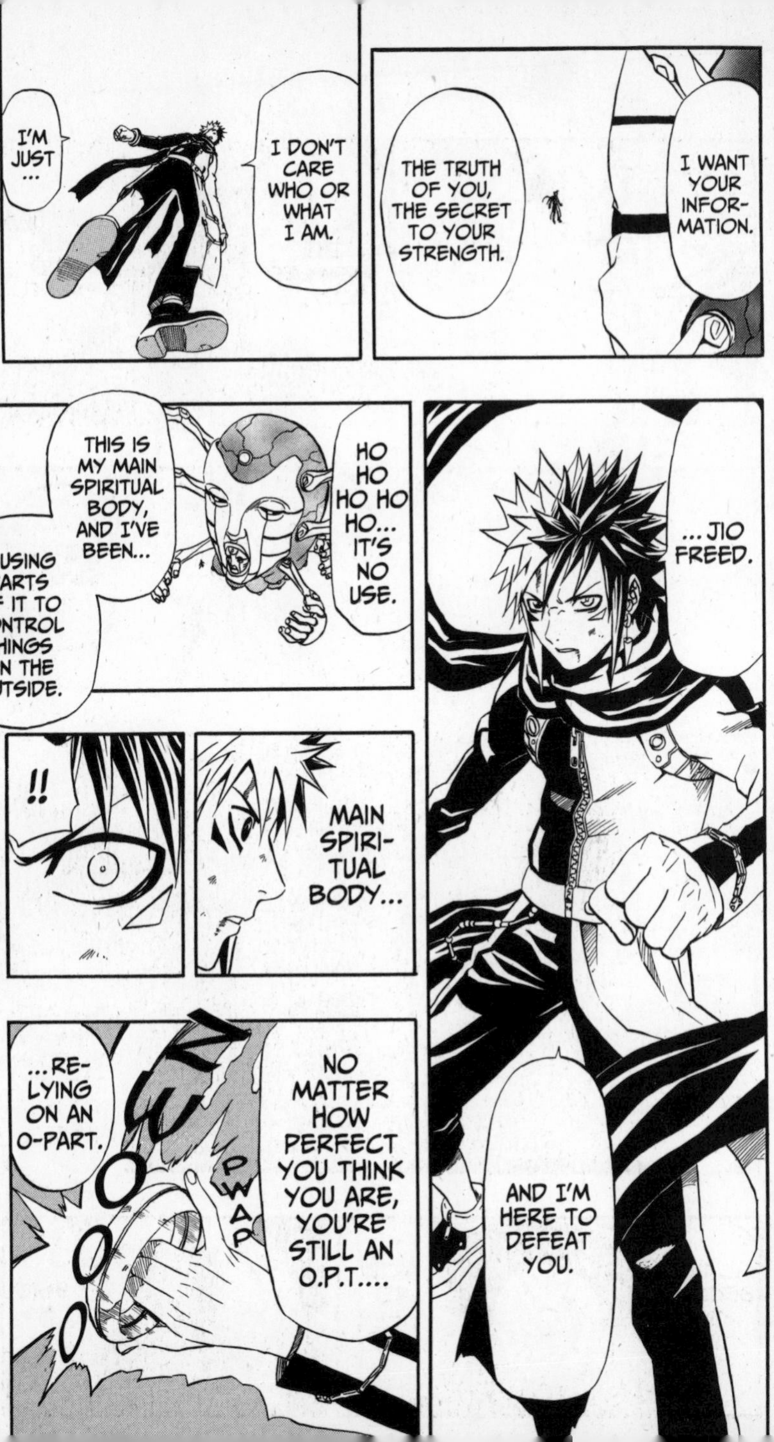
I WANT YOUR INFORMATION.
THE TRUTH OF YOU, THE SECRET TO YOUR STRENGTH.
I DON'T CARE WHO OR WHAT I AM.
I'M JUST ...
...JIO FREED.
AND I'M HERE TO DEFEAT YOU.
HO HO HO HO HO... IT'S NO USE.
THIS IS MY MAIN SPIRITUAL BODY, AND I'VE BEEN...
...USING PARTS OF IT TO CONTROL THINGS ON THE OUTSIDE.
MAIN SPIRI-TUAL BODY...
!!
NO MATTER HOW PERFECT YOU THINK YOU ARE, YOU'RE STILL AN O.P.T....
PWAP
...RE-LYING ON AN O-PART.

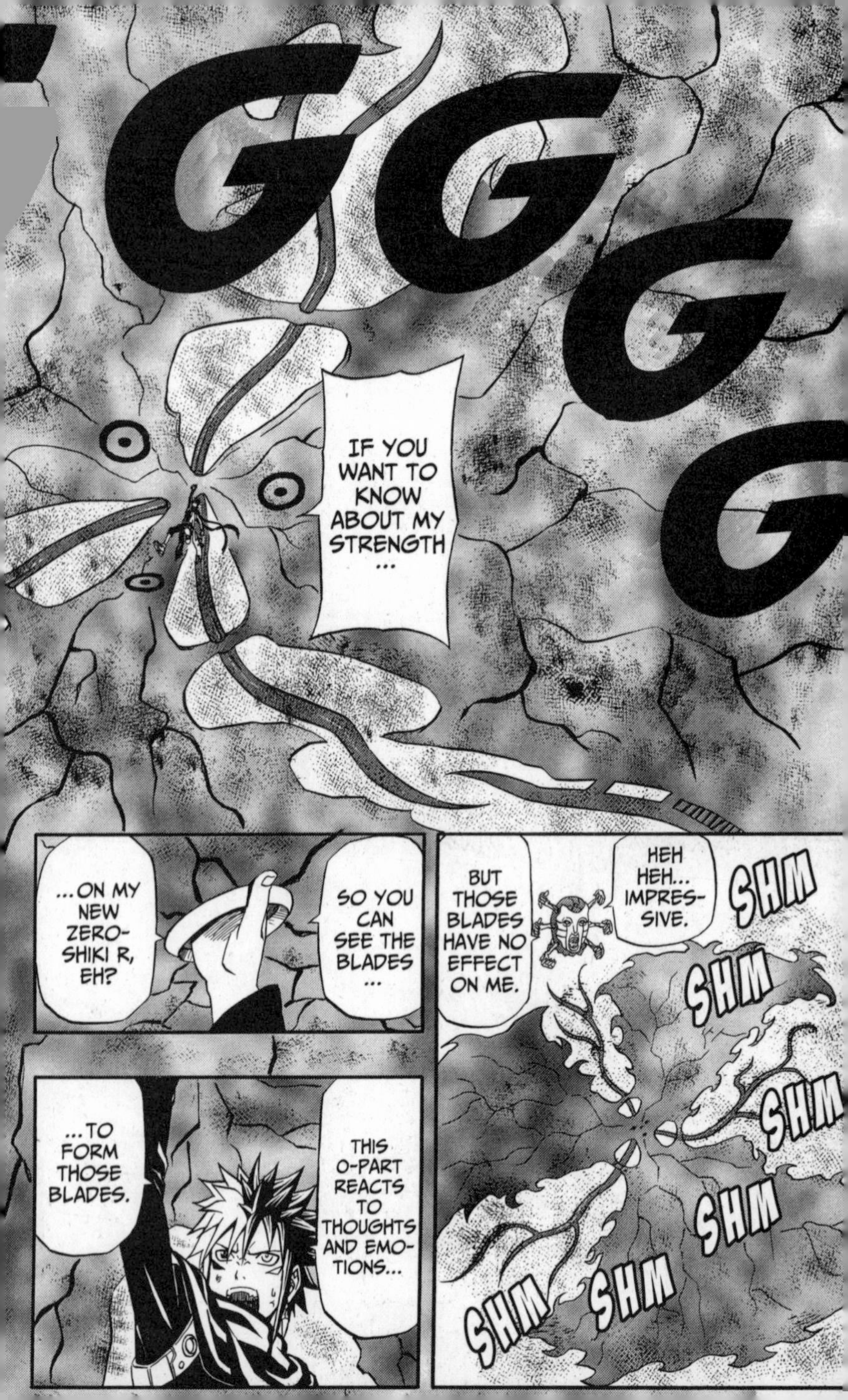
GGGGG
IF YOU WANT TO KNOW ABOUT MY STRENGTH...
HEH HEH... IMPRES-SIVE.
BUT THOSE BLADES HAVE NO EFFECT ON ME.
SHM
SHM
SHM
SHM
SHM
SHM
SO YOU CAN SEE THE BLADES...
...ON MY NEW ZERO-SHIKI R, EH?
THIS O-PART REACTS TO THOUGHTS AND EMO-TIONS...
...TO FORM THOSE BLADES.

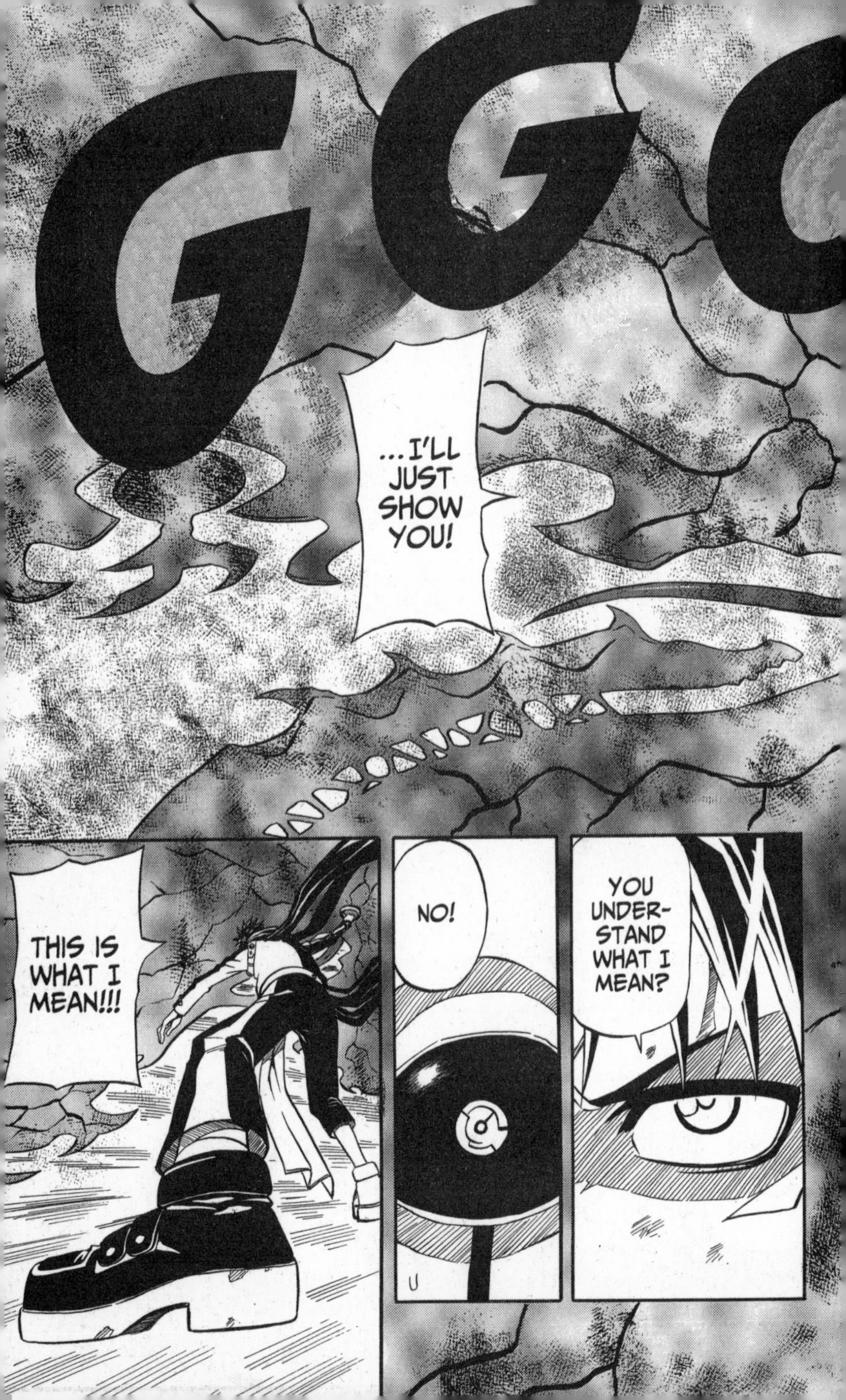
GGG
...I'LL JUST SHOW YOU!
YOU UNDER-STAND WHAT I MEAN?
NO!
THIS IS WHAT I MEAN!!!

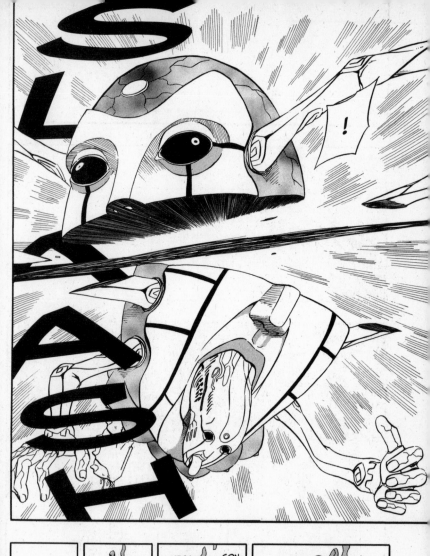

...DING...

...FA-... NO... I'M...

...NESS... ...CON-SCIOUS...

...I'M LOSING... WHAT...?

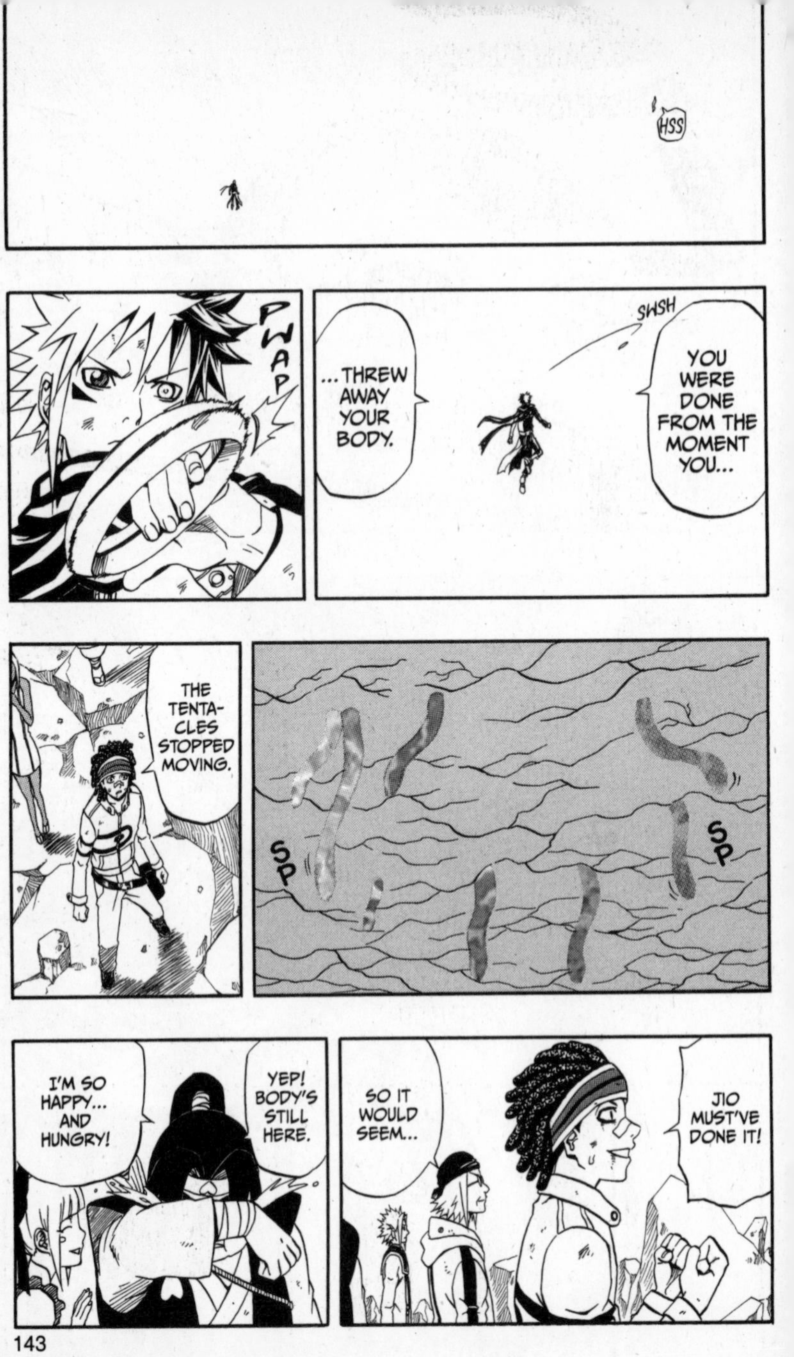
HSS
SWSH
YOU WERE DONE FROM THE MOMENT YOU...
...THREW AWAY YOUR BODY.
PWAP
SP
SP
THE TENTA-CLES STOPPED MOVING.
JIO MUST'VE DONE IT!
SO IT WOULD SEEM...
YEP! BODY'S STILL HERE.
I'M SO HAPPY... AND HUNGRY!

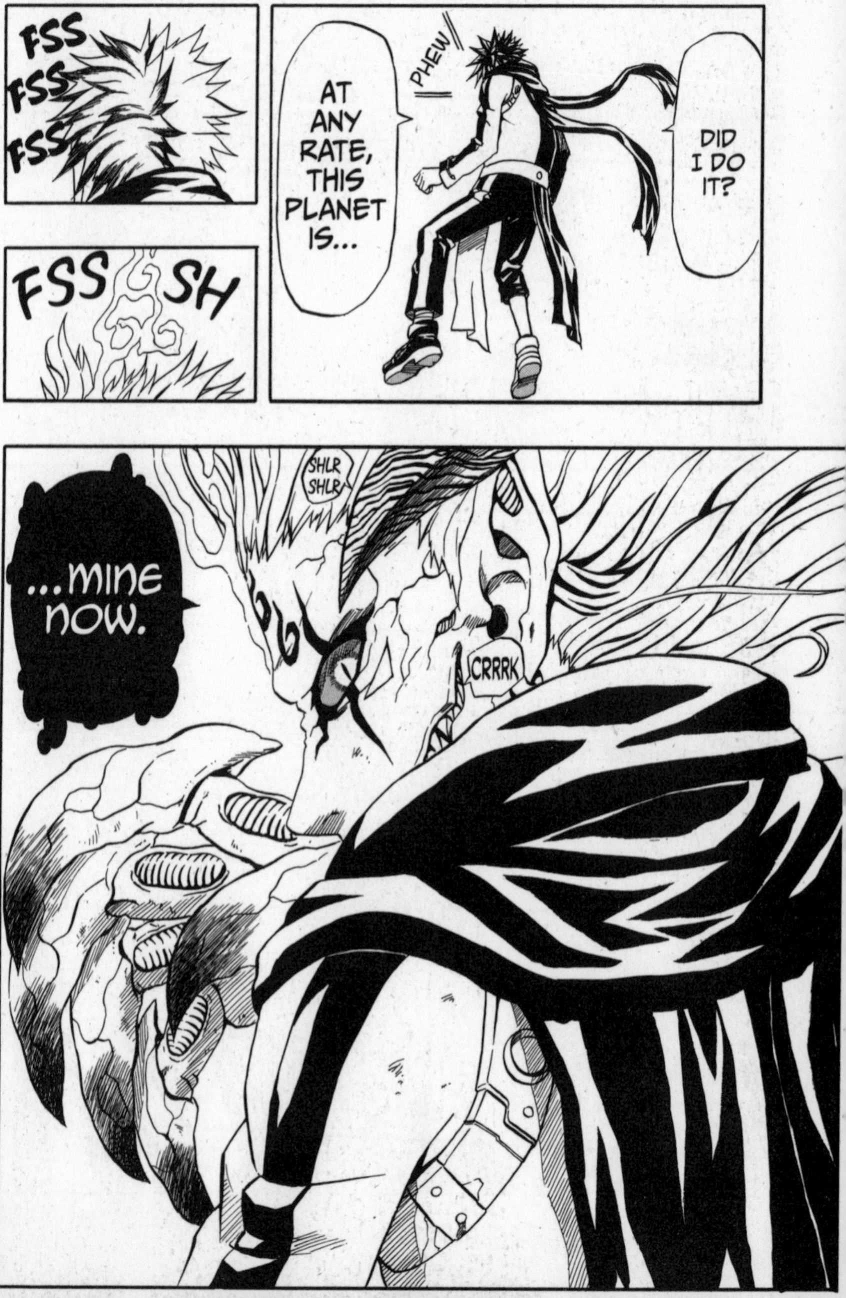
DID I DO IT?
PHEW
AT ANY RATE, THIS PLANET IS...
FSS FSS FSS
FSSSH
SHLR SHLR
...mine now.
CRRRK

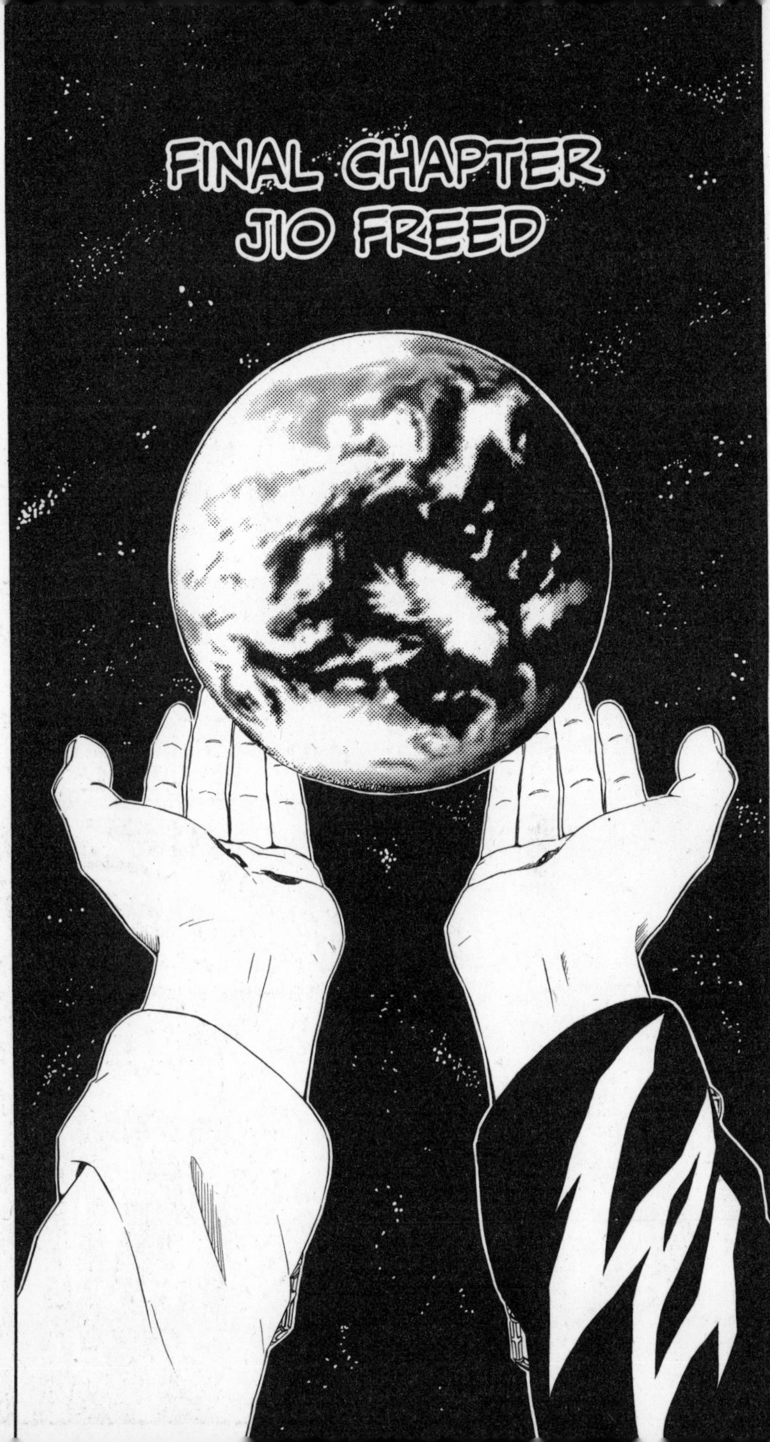
FINAL CHAPTER
JIO FREED

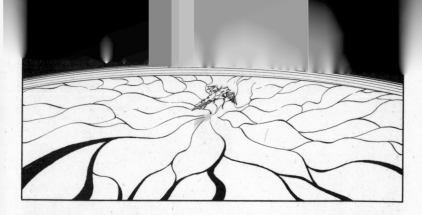

ADJUSTING MAIN PROGRAM.

SWITCHING TO FREEDOM PROGRAM, RECALIBRATING AND RESTORING.

PROGRAM REVERTING TO ORIGINAL STATE.

FREEDOM

PROGRAM AMATERASU MIKO DELETED.

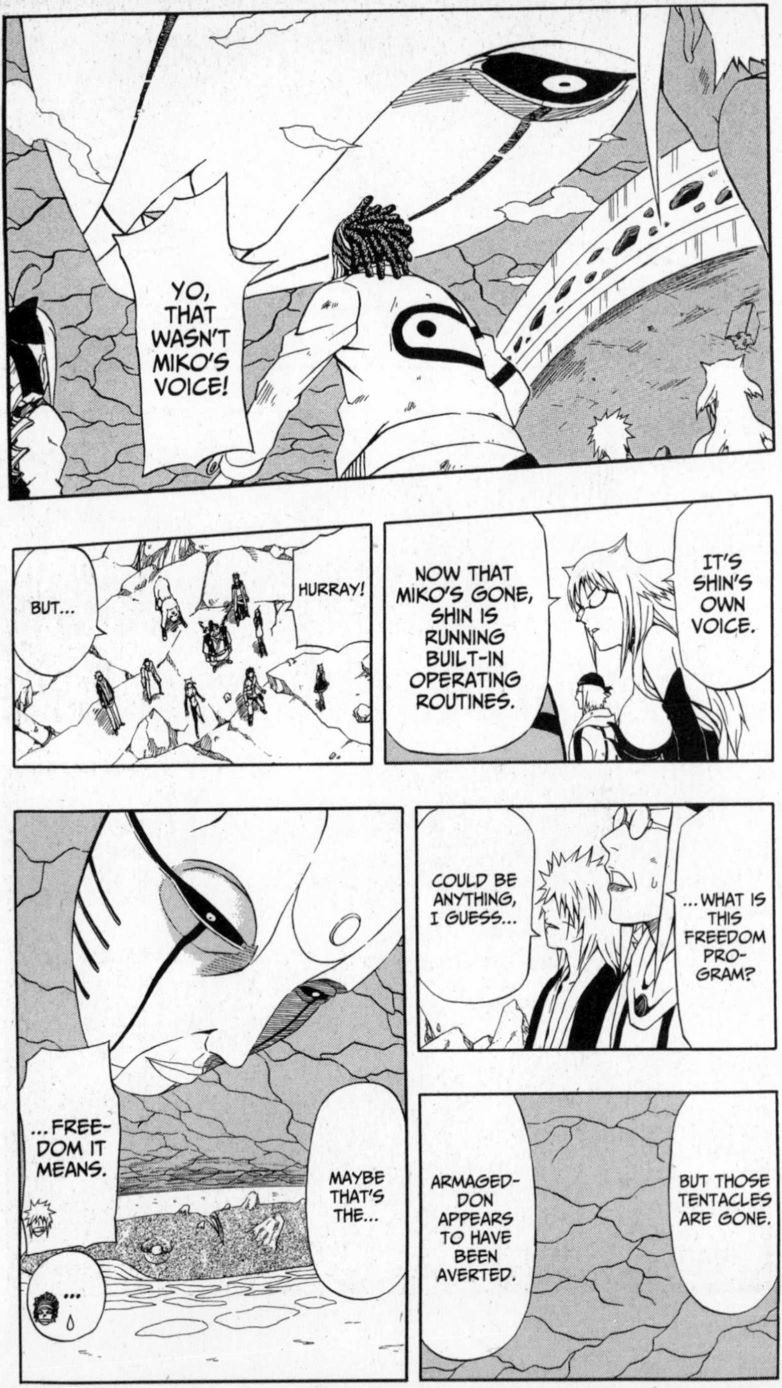

YO, THAT WASN'T MIKO'S VOICE!
IT'S SHIN'S OWN VOICE.
NOW THAT MIKO'S GONE, SHIN IS RUNNING BUILT-IN OPERATING ROUTINES.
HURRAY!
BUT...
...WHAT IS THIS FREEDOM PRO-GRAM?
COULD BE ANYTHING, I GUESS...
BUT THOSE TENTACLES ARE GONE.
ARMAGED-DON APPEARS TO HAVE BEEN AVERTED.
MAYBE THAT'S THE...
...FREE-DOM IT MEANS.
...

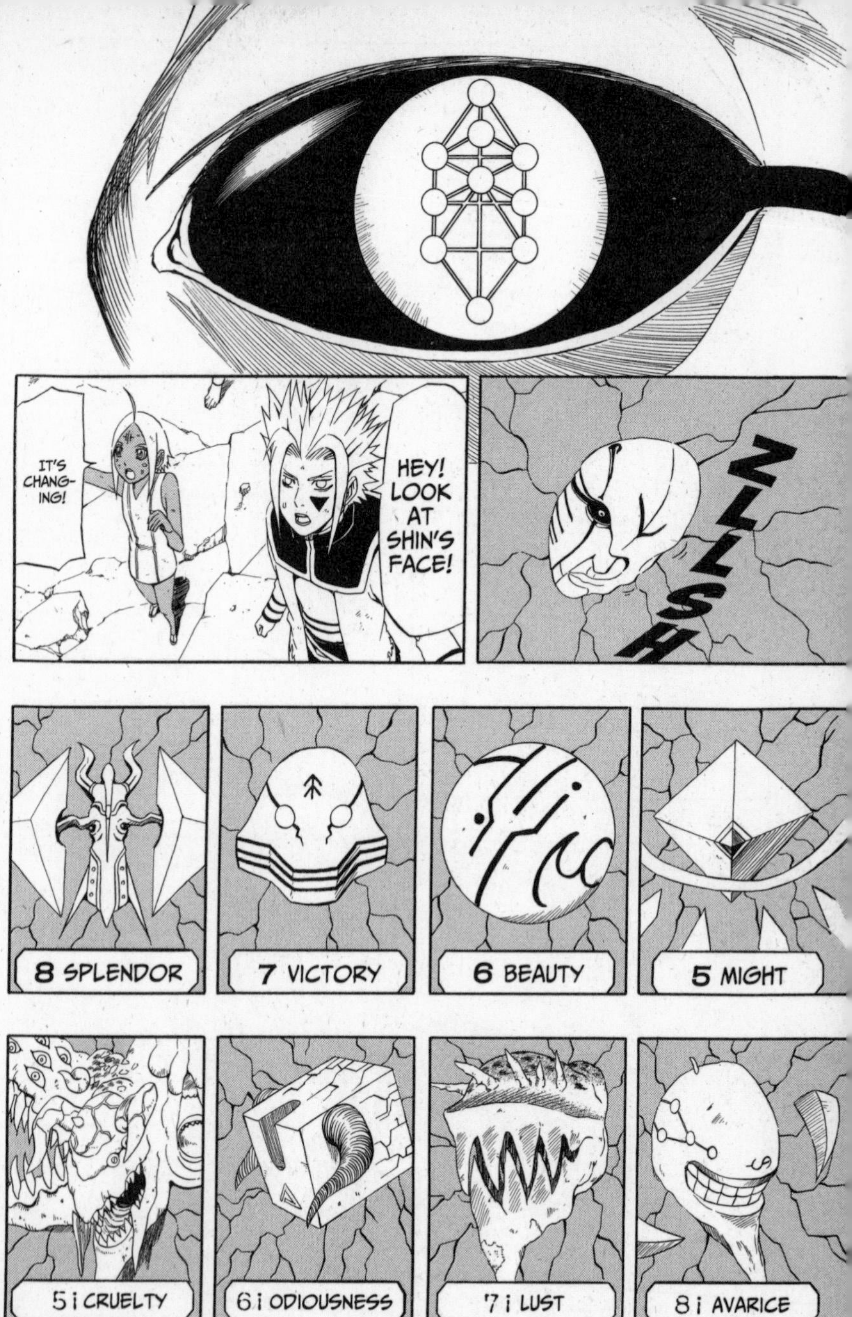

ZLLSH
HEY! LOOK AT SHIN'S FACE!
IT'S CHANG-ING!
5 MIGHT
6 BEAUTY
7 VICTORY
8 SPLENDOR
8 i AVARICE
7 i LUST
6 i ODIOUSNESS
5 i CRUELTY

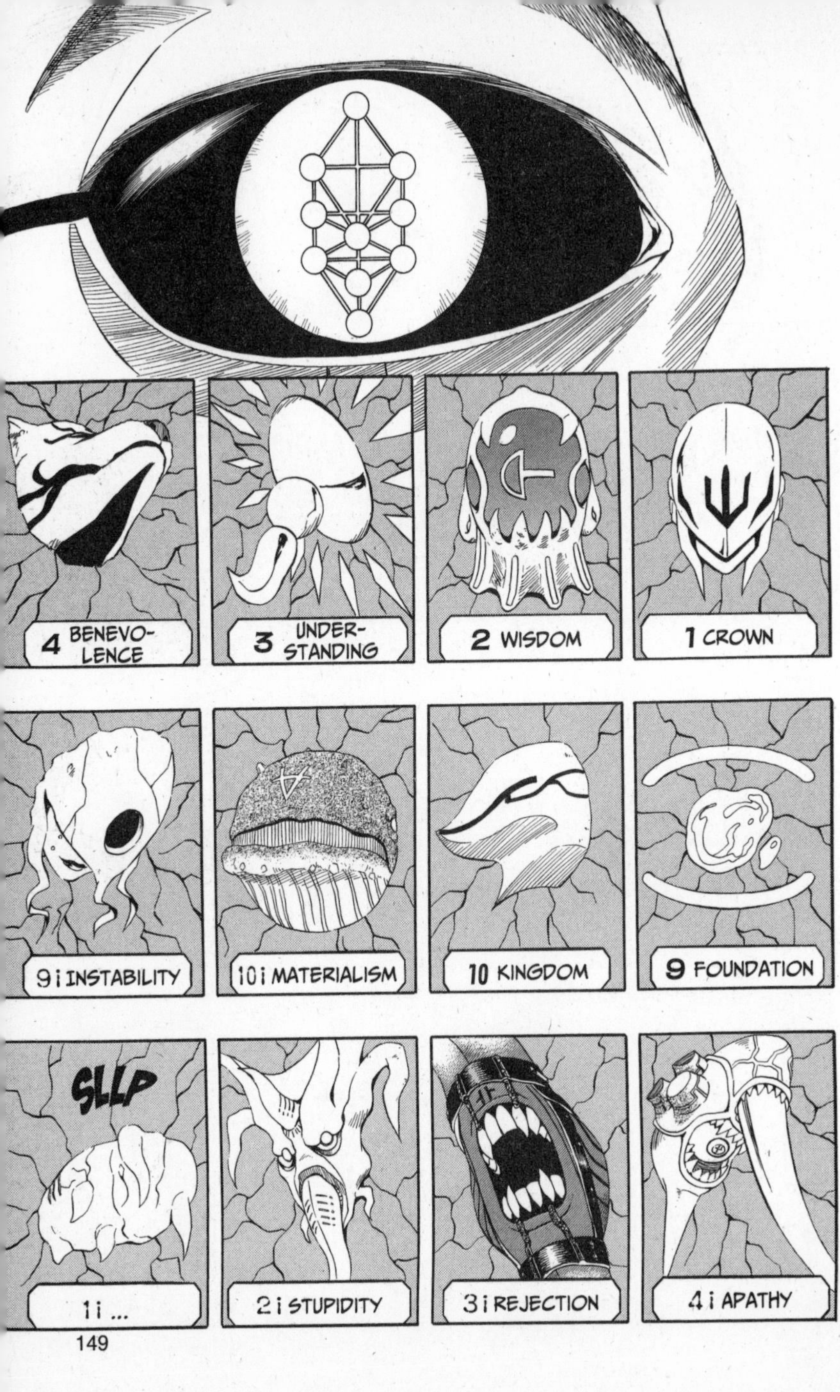
1 CROWN
2 WISDOM
3 UNDER-STANDING
4 BENEVO-LENCE
9 FOUNDATION
10 KINGDOM
10i MATERIALISM
9i INSTABILITY
4i APATHY
3i REJECTION
2i STUPIDITY
SLLP
1i ...

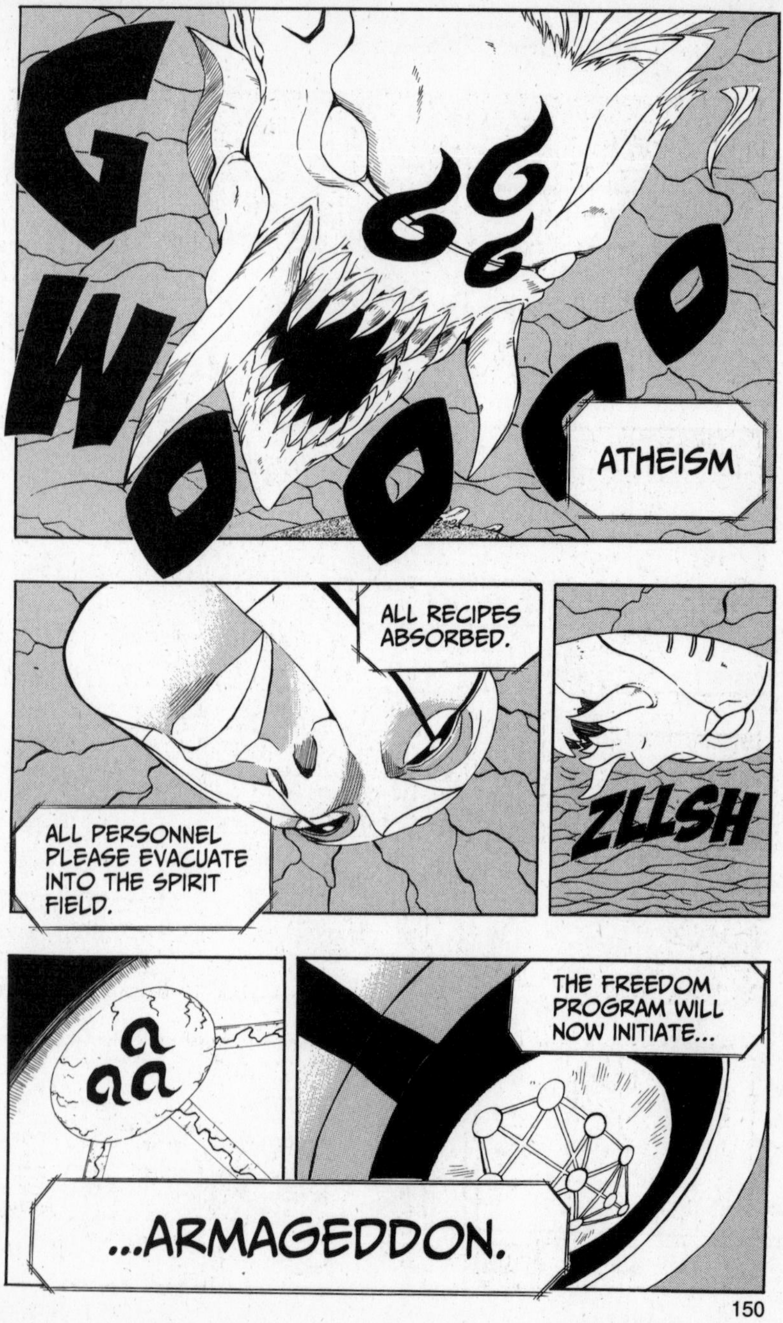
GWOOOO
ATHEISM
ZLLSH
ALL RECIPES ABSORBED.
ALL PERSONNEL PLEASE EVACUATE INTO THE SPIRIT FIELD.
THE FREEDOM PROGRAM WILL NOW INITIATE...
aaa
...ARMAGEDDON.

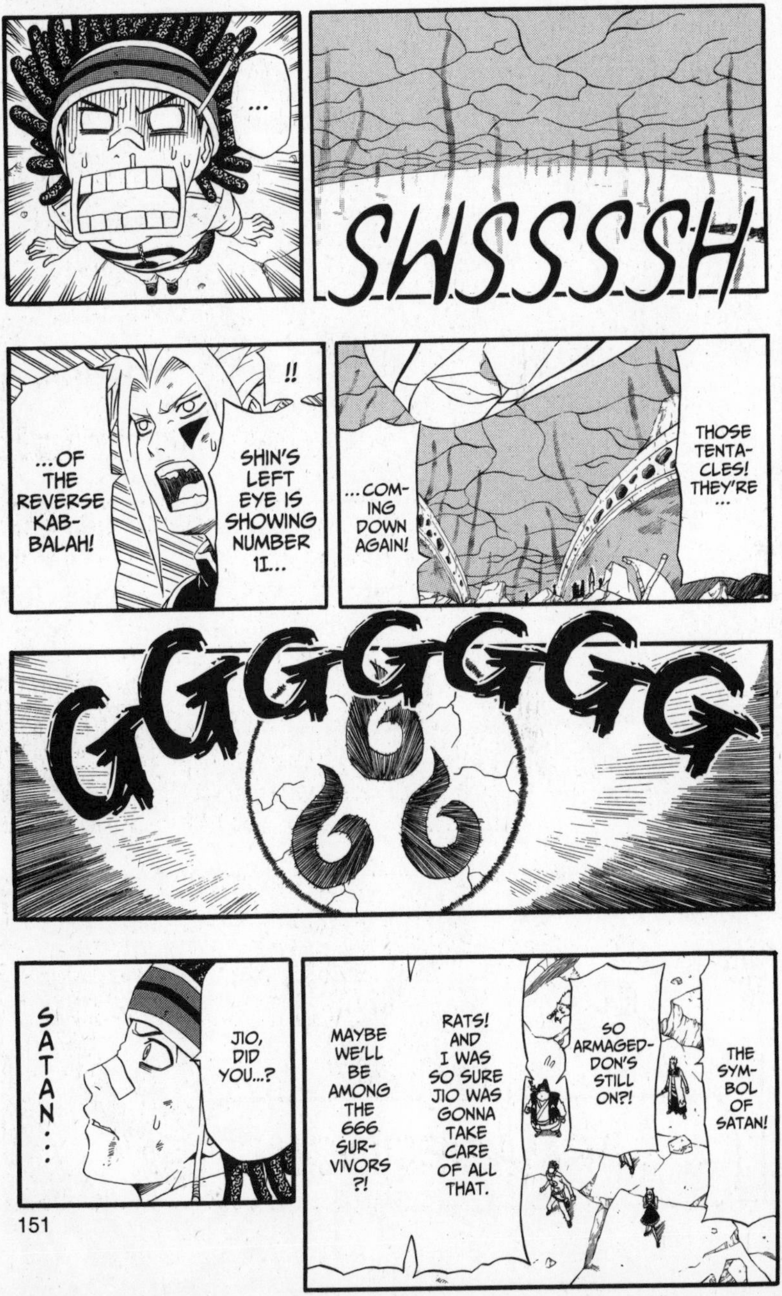
SWSSSSH
...
!!
THOSE TENTA-CLES! THEY'RE ...
...COM-ING DOWN AGAIN!
SHIN'S LEFT EYE IS SHOWING NUMBER 11...
...OF THE REVERSE KAB-BALAH!
GGGGGGG
THE SYM-BOL OF SATAN!
SO ARMAGED-DON'S STILL ON?!
RATS! AND I WAS SO SURE JIO WAS GONNA TAKE CARE OF ALL THAT.
MAYBE WE'LL BE AMONG THE 666 SUR-VIVORS?!
JIO, DID YOU...?
SATAN...

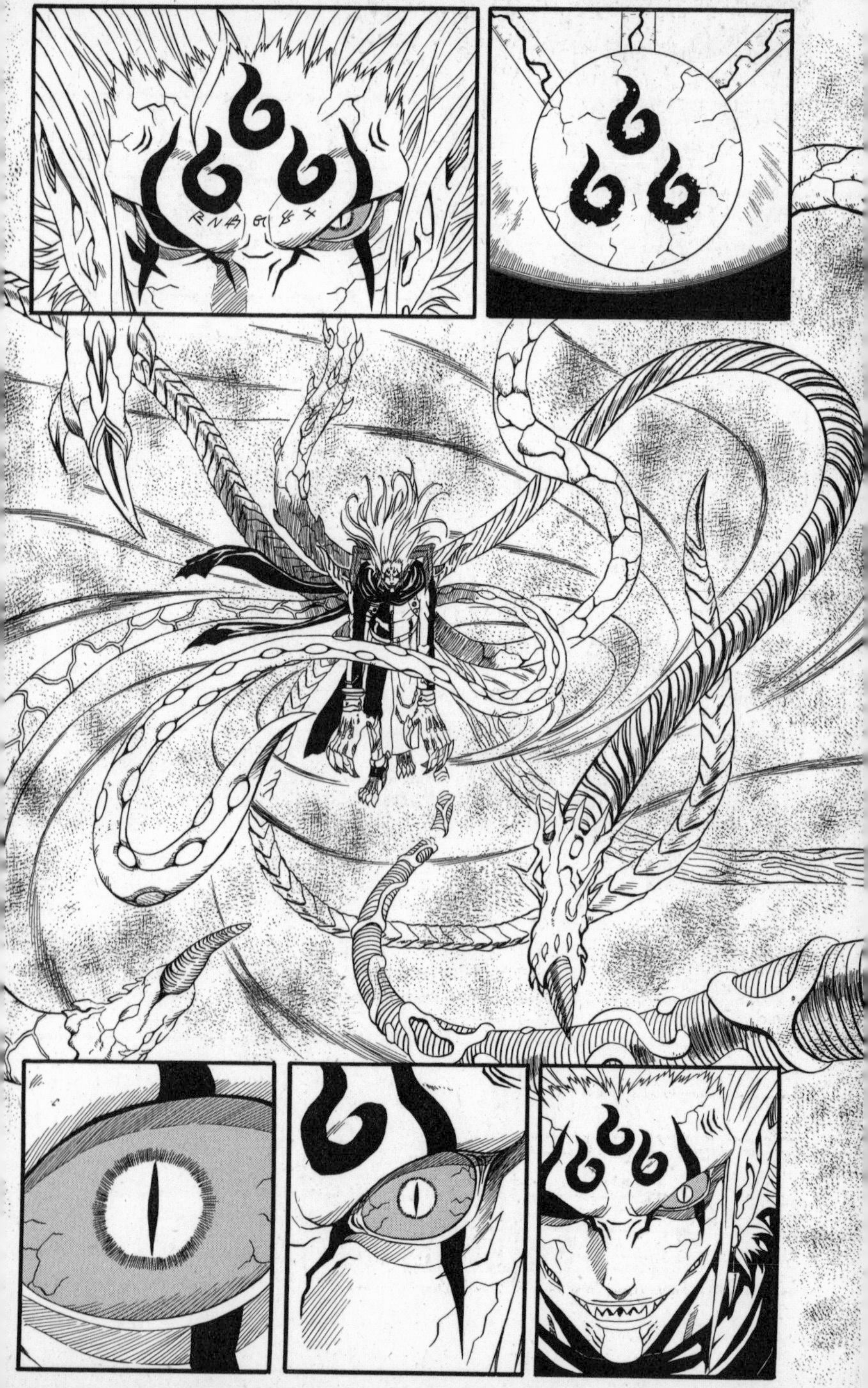

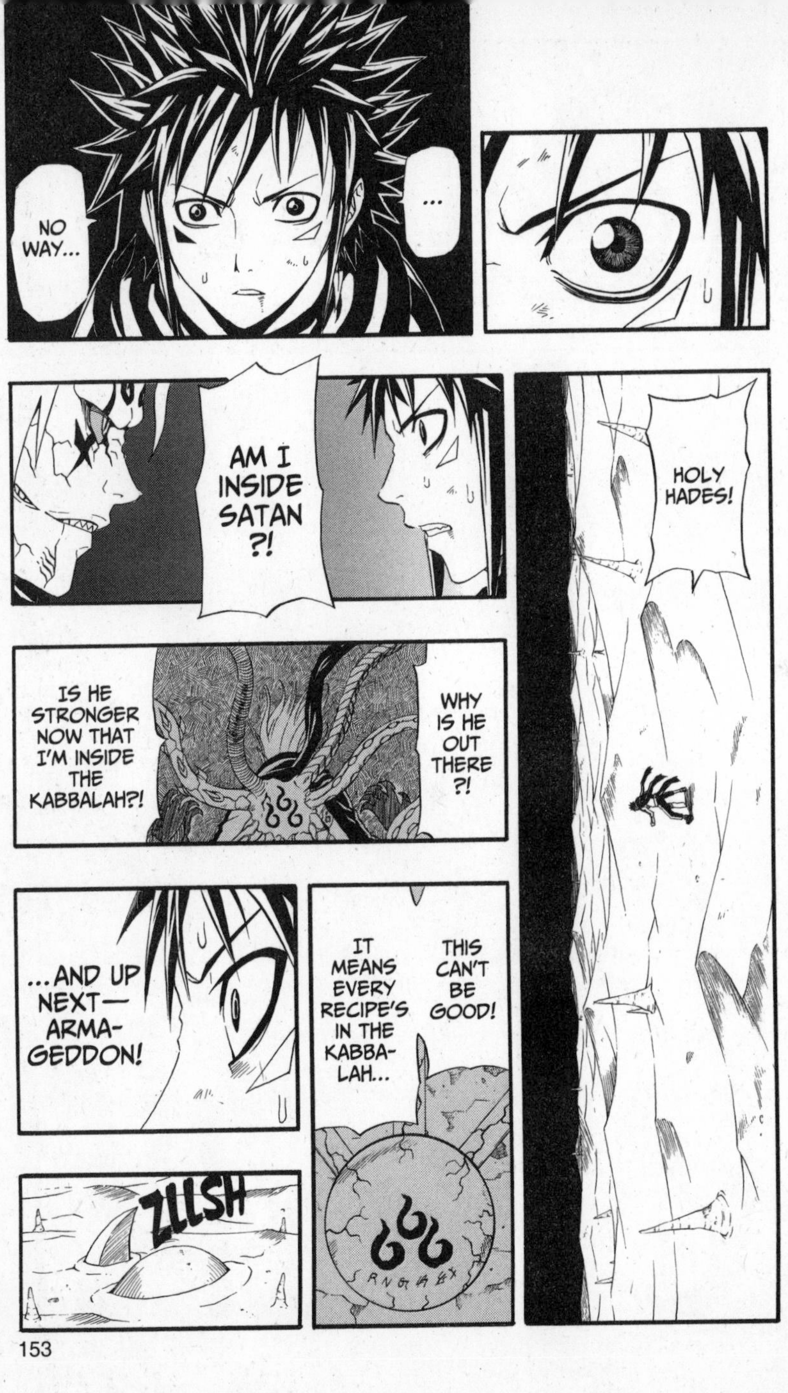
...
NO WAY...
HOLY HADES!
AM I INSIDE SATAN?!
WHY IS HE OUT THERE?!
IS HE STRONGER NOW THAT I'M INSIDE THE KABBALAH?!
THIS CAN'T BE GOOD!
IT MEANS EVERY RECIPE'S IN THE KABBALAH...
...AND UP NEXT—ARMAGEDDON!
ZILSH

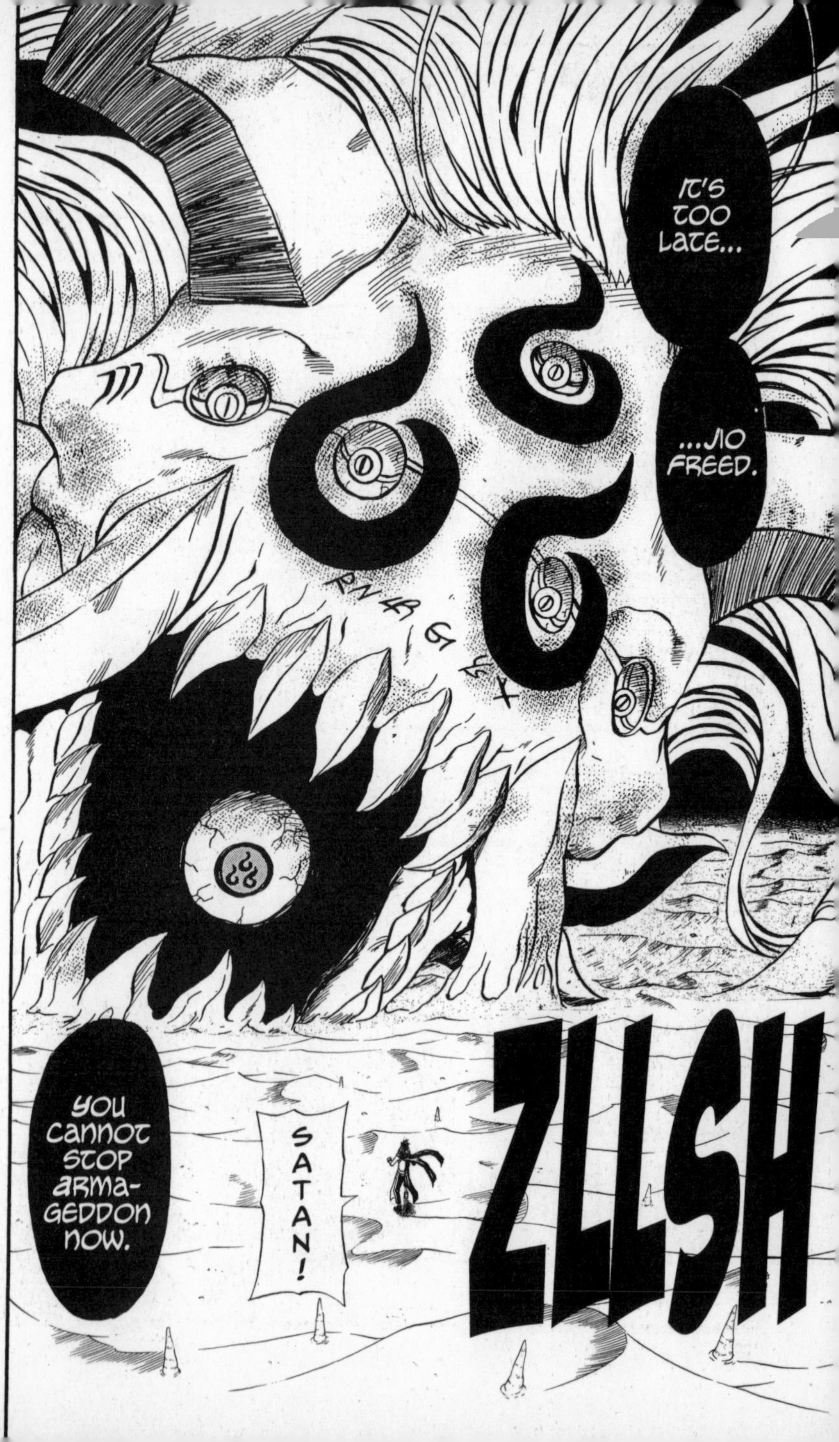
IT'S TOO LATE...
...NO FREED.
ZLLSH
SATAN!
YOU CANNOT STOP ARMA-GEDDON NOW.

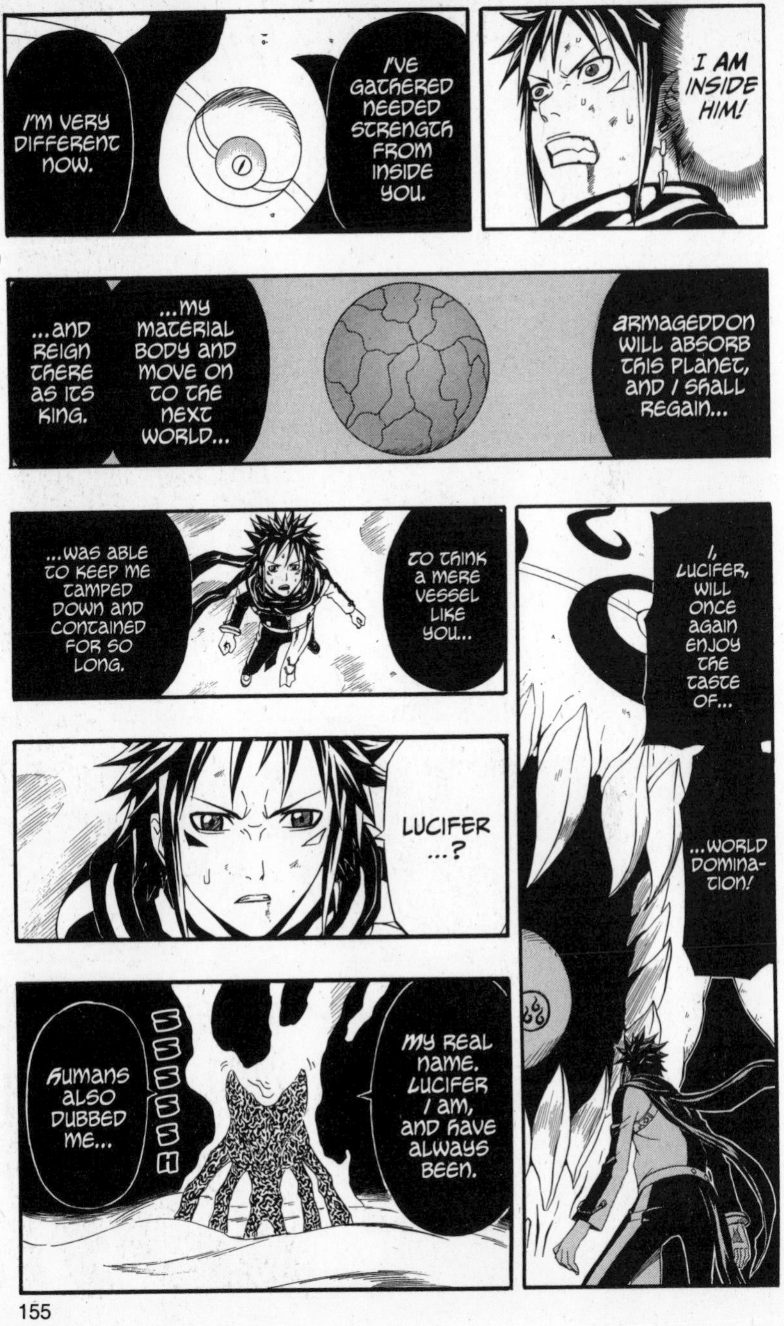
I AM INSIDE HIM!
I'VE GATHERED NEEDED STRENGTH FROM INSIDE YOU.
I'M VERY DIFFERENT NOW.
ARMAGEDDON WILL ABSORB THIS PLANET, AND I SHALL REGAIN...
...MY MATERIAL BODY AND MOVE ON TO THE NEXT WORLD...
...AND REIGN THERE AS ITS KING.
I, LUCIFER, WILL ONCE AGAIN ENJOY THE TASTE OF...
...WORLD DOMINATION!
TO THINK A MERE VESSEL LIKE YOU...
...WAS ABLE TO KEEP ME TAMPED DOWN AND CONTAINED FOR SO LONG.
LUCIFER ...?
MY REAL NAME. LUCIFER I AM, AND HAVE ALWAYS BEEN.
SSSSSH
HUMANS ALSO DUBBED ME...

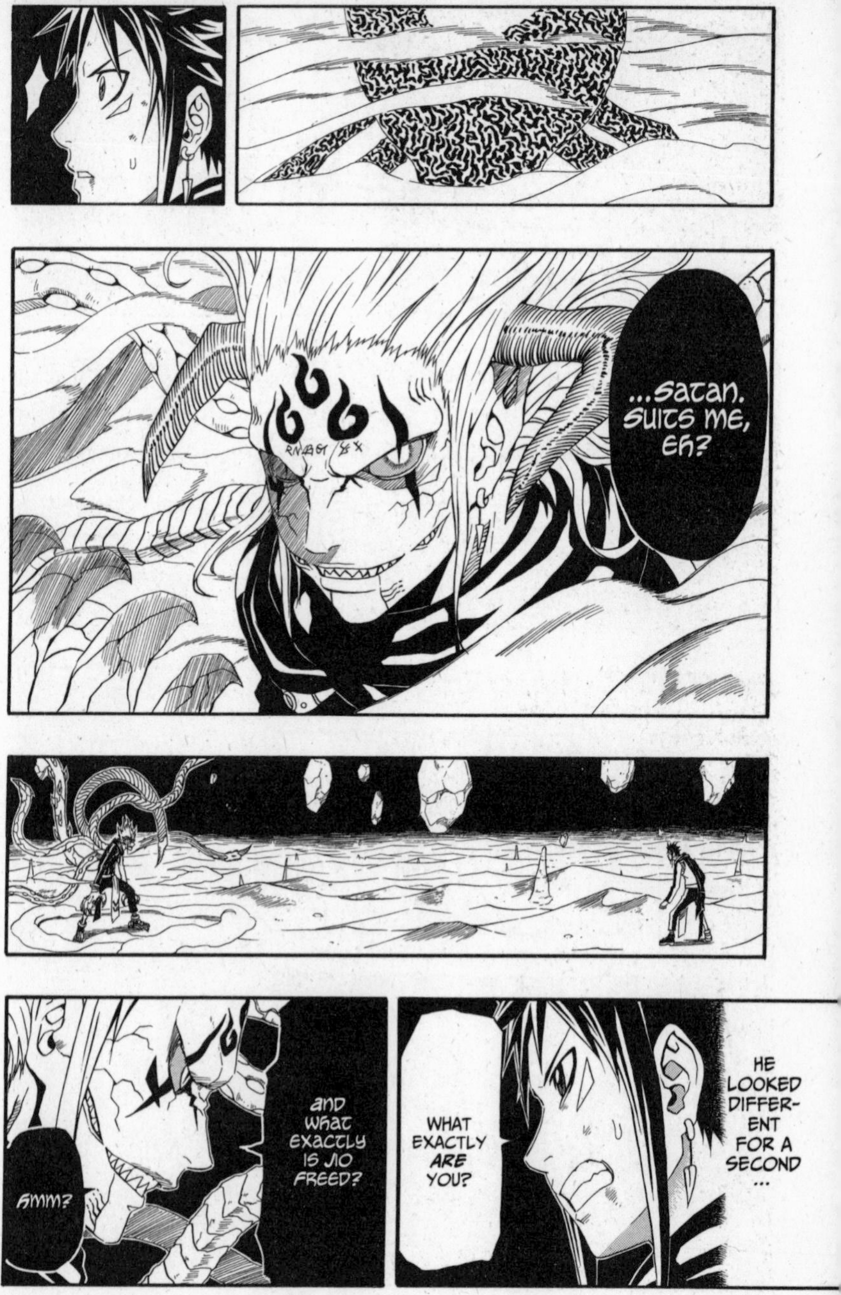
...SATAN. SUITS ME, EH?
HE LOOKED DIFFER-ENT FOR A SECOND ...
WHAT EXACTLY ARE YOU?
AND WHAT EXACTLY IS JIO FREED?
HMM?

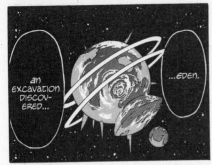

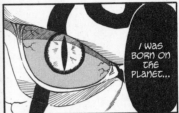

I WAS BORN ON THE PLANET...
...EDEN.
AN EXCAVATION DISCOVERED...
...SHIN...
...IN THE EARTH.
AN ARTIFACT...
...POSSESSED OF PERPETUAL ENERGY.
I WAS A MEMBER OF...

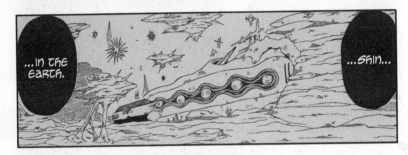

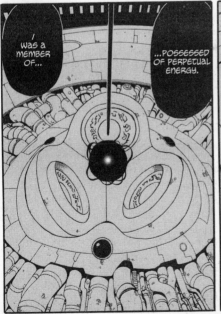

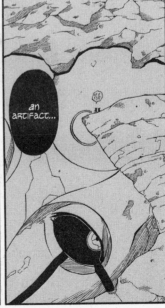

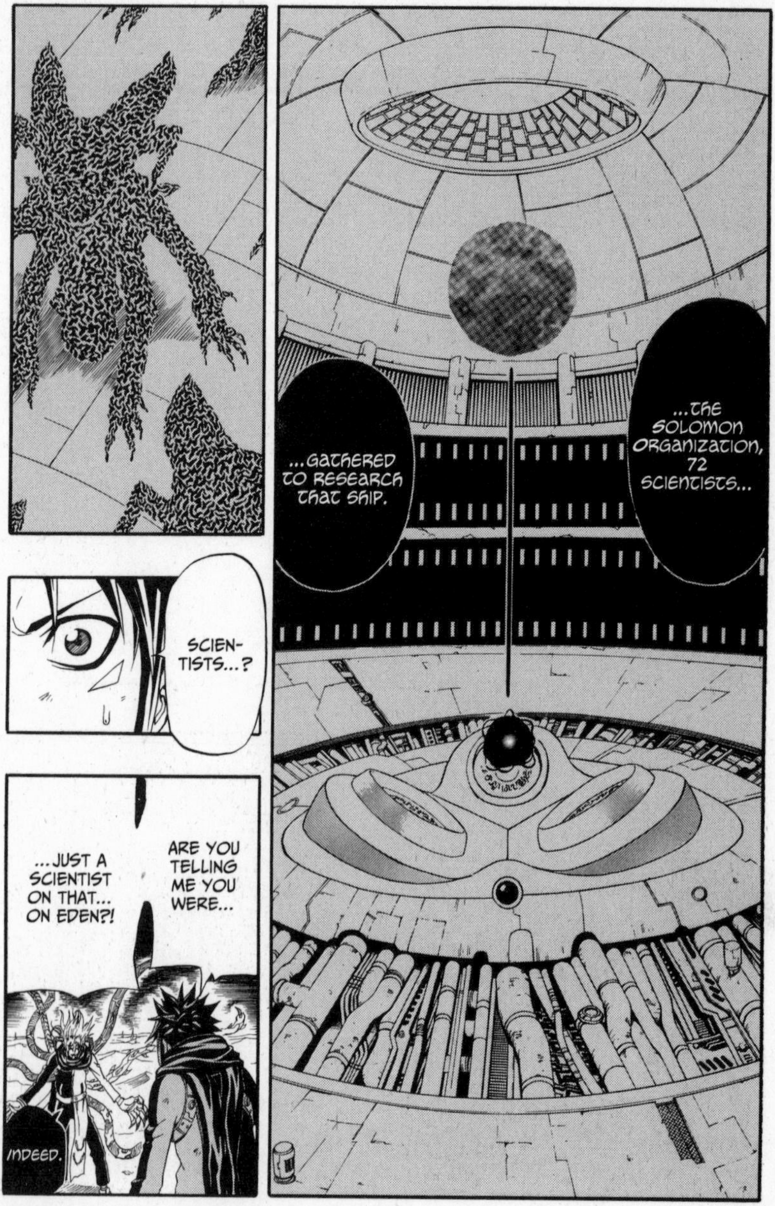
...THE SOLOMON ORGANIZATION, 72 SCIENTISTS...
...GATHERED TO RESEARCH THAT SHIP.
SCIEN-TISTS...?
ARE YOU TELLING ME YOU WERE...
...JUST A SCIENTIST ON THAT... ON EDEN?!
INDEED.

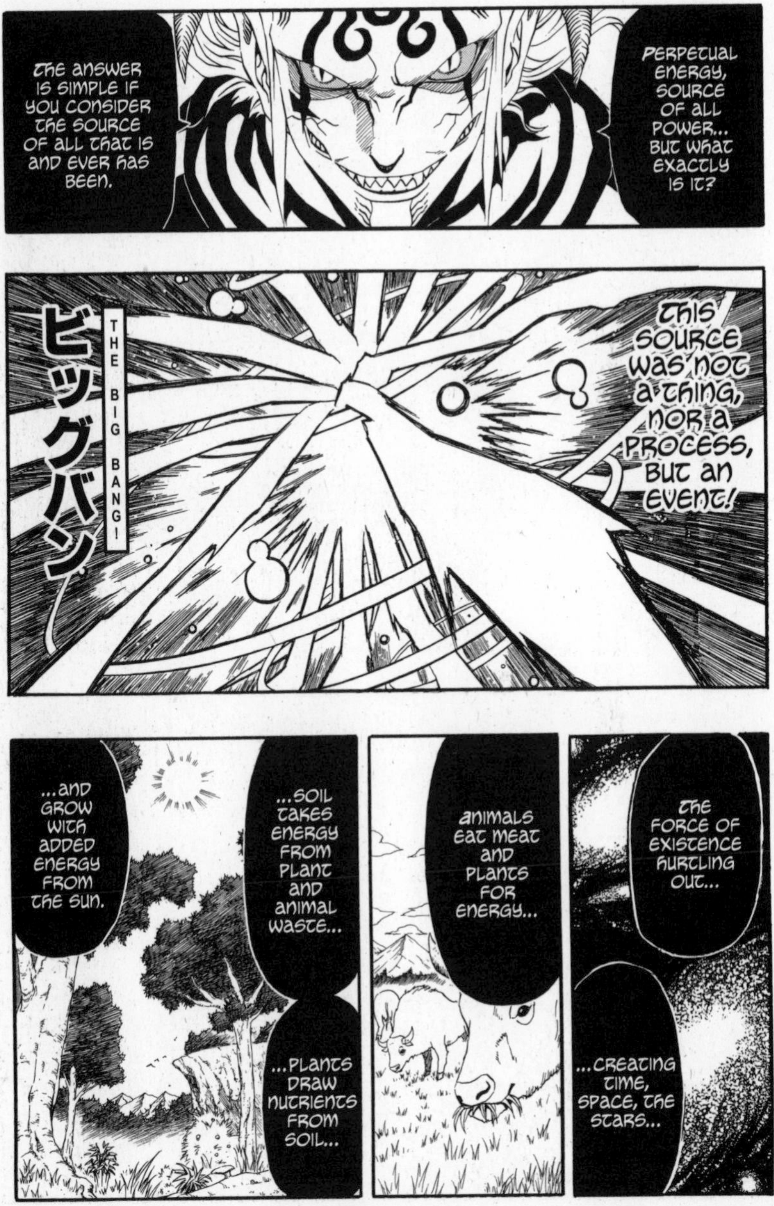
Perpetual energy, source of all power... but what exactly is it?
The answer is simple if you consider the source of all that is and ever has been.
This source was not a thing, nor a process, but an event!
ビッグバン
THE BIG BANG!
The force of existence hurtling out...
...creating time, space, the stars...
Animals eat meat and plants for energy...
...soil takes energy from plant and animal waste...
...plants draw nutrients from soil...
...and grow with added energy from the sun.

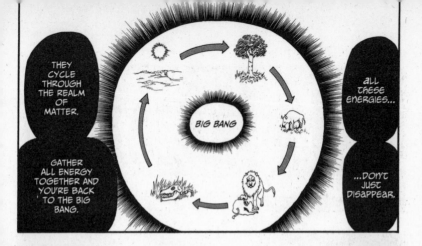

ALL THESE ENERGIES...
...DON'T JUST DISAPPEAR.
THEY CYCLE THROUGH THE REALM OF MATTER.
BIG BANG
GATHER ALL ENERGY TOGETHER AND YOU'RE BACK TO THE BIG BANG.
BUT ALL THAT ENERGY HAS...
...SPREAD OUT AND WEAK-ENED.
AND THIS SOLOMON ORGANIZATION DECIDED TO DO SOMETHING ABOUT IT?
THAT'S RIGHT.
OUT OF OUR RESEARCH ON SHIN, WE CREATED...
...THE DATA MEMORI-ZATION DEVICE.
THE KABBALAH.

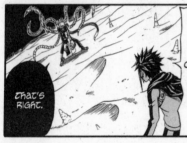

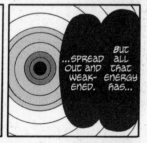

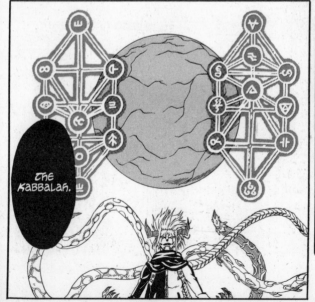

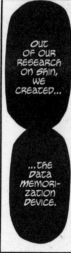

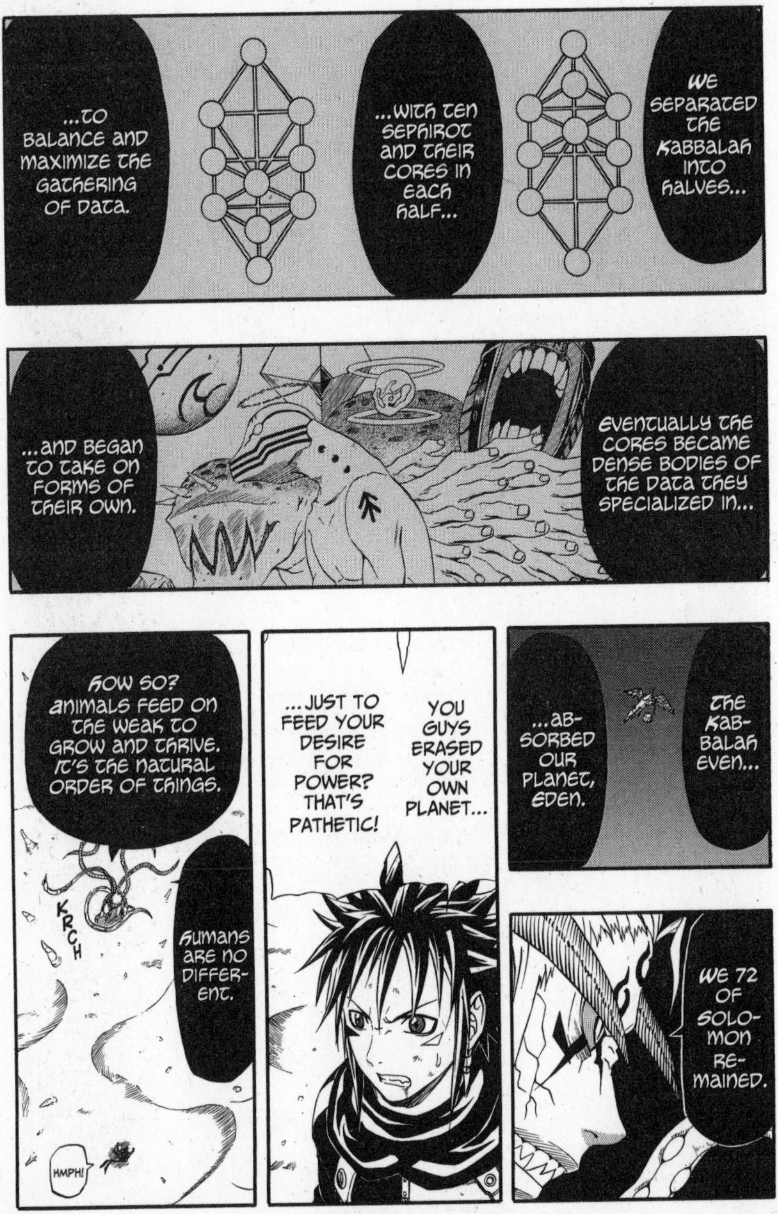
WE SEPARATED THE KABBALAH INTO HALVES...
...WITH TEN SEPHIROT AND THEIR CORES IN EACH HALF...
...TO BALANCE AND MAXIMIZE THE GATHERING OF DATA.
EVENTUALLY THE CORES BECAME DENSE BODIES OF THE DATA THEY SPECIALIZED IN...
...AND BEGAN TO TAKE ON FORMS OF THEIR OWN.
THE KABBALAH EVEN...
...ABSORBED OUR PLANET, EDEN.
WE 72 OF SOLOMON REMAINED.
YOU GUYS ERASED YOUR OWN PLANET...
...JUST TO FEED YOUR DESIRE FOR POWER? THAT'S PATHETIC!
HOW SO? ANIMALS FEED ON THE WEAK TO GROW AND THRIVE. IT'S THE NATURAL ORDER OF THINGS.
KRCH
HUMANS ARE NO DIFFERENT.
HMPH!

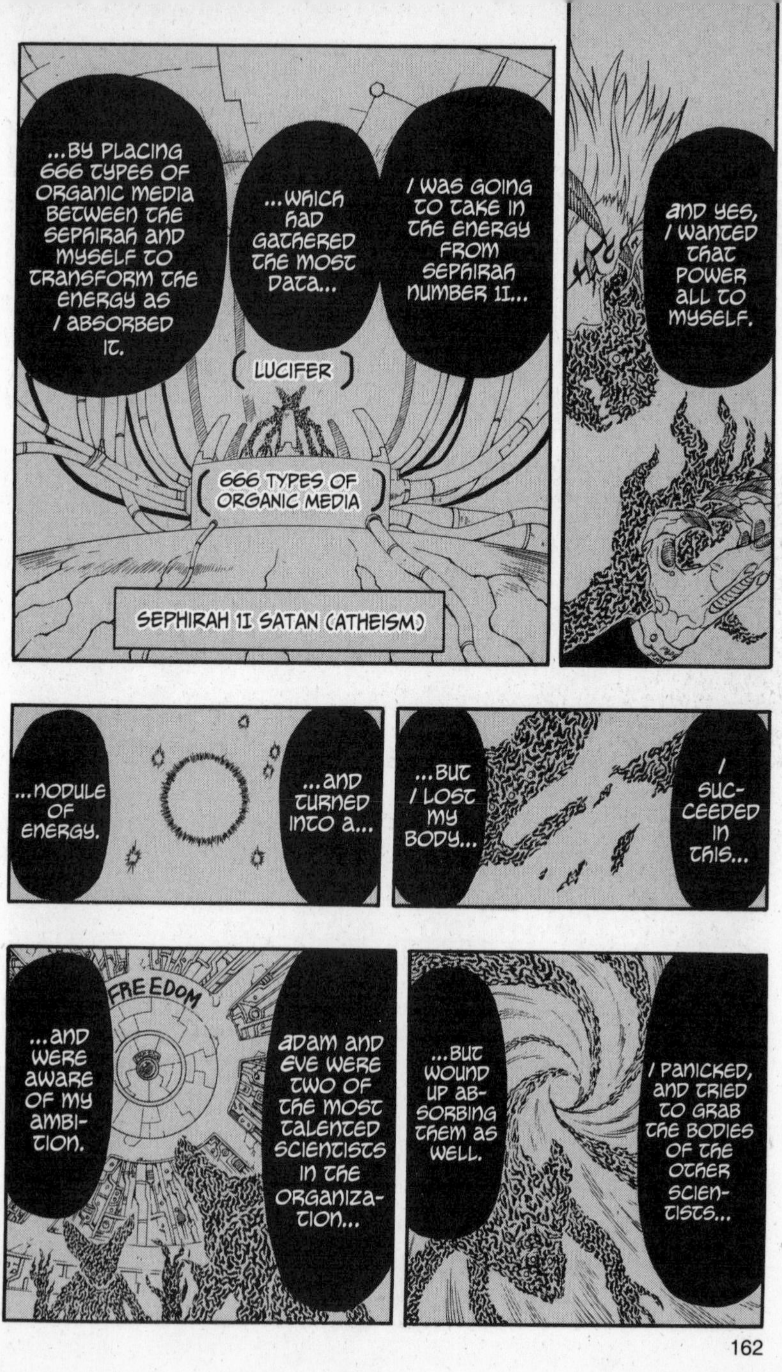
AND YES, I WANTED THAT POWER ALL TO MYSELF.
I WAS GOING TO TAKE IN THE ENERGY FROM SEPHIRAH NUMBER 11...
...WHICH HAD GATHERED THE MOST DATA...
...BY PLACING 666 TYPES OF ORGANIC MEDIA BETWEEN THE SEPHIRAH AND MYSELF TO TRANSFORM THE ENERGY AS I ABSORBED IT.
LUCIFER
666 TYPES OF ORGANIC MEDIA
SEPHIRAH 11 SATAN (ATHEISM)
I SUC-CEEDED IN THIS...
...BUT I LOST MY BODY...
...AND TURNED INTO A...
...NODULE OF ENERGY.
I PANICKED, AND TRIED TO GRAB THE BODIES OF THE OTHER SCIEN-TISTS...
...BUT WOUND UP AB-SORBING THEM AS WELL.
ADAM AND EVE WERE TWO OF THE MOST TALENTED SCIENTISTS IN THE ORGANIZA-TION...
FREEDOM
...AND WERE AWARE OF MY AMBI-TION.

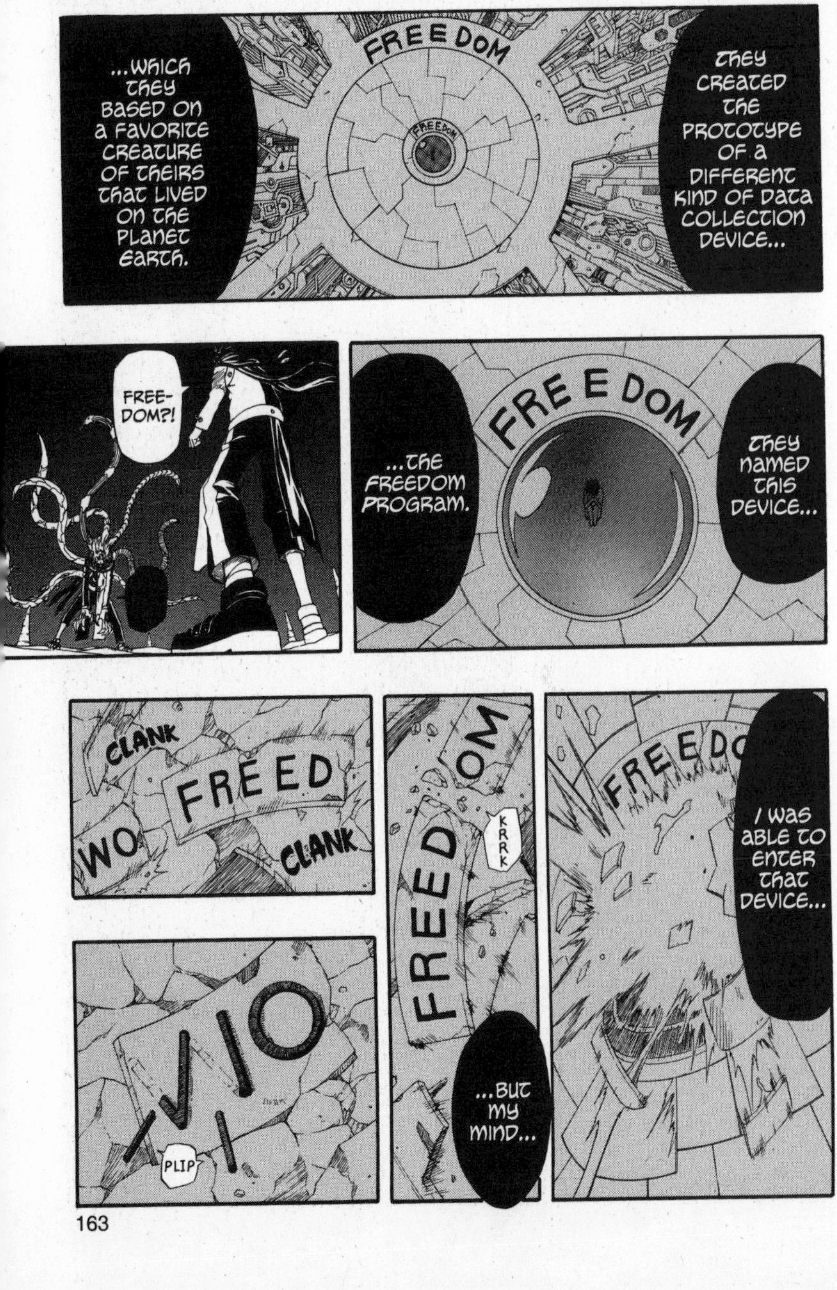

THEY CREATED THE PROTOTYPE OF A DIFFERENT KIND OF DATA COLLECTION DEVICE...
FREEDOM
FREEDOM
...WHICH THEY BASED ON A FAVORITE CREATURE OF THEIRS THAT LIVED ON THE PLANET EARTH.
THEY NAMED THIS DEVICE...
FREEDOM
...THE FREEDOM PROGRAM.
FREE-DOM?!
I WAS ABLE TO ENTER THAT DEVICE...
FREEDO
OM
KRRK
FREEDOM
...BUT MY MIND...
CLANK
FREED
WO
CLANK
VIO
PLIP

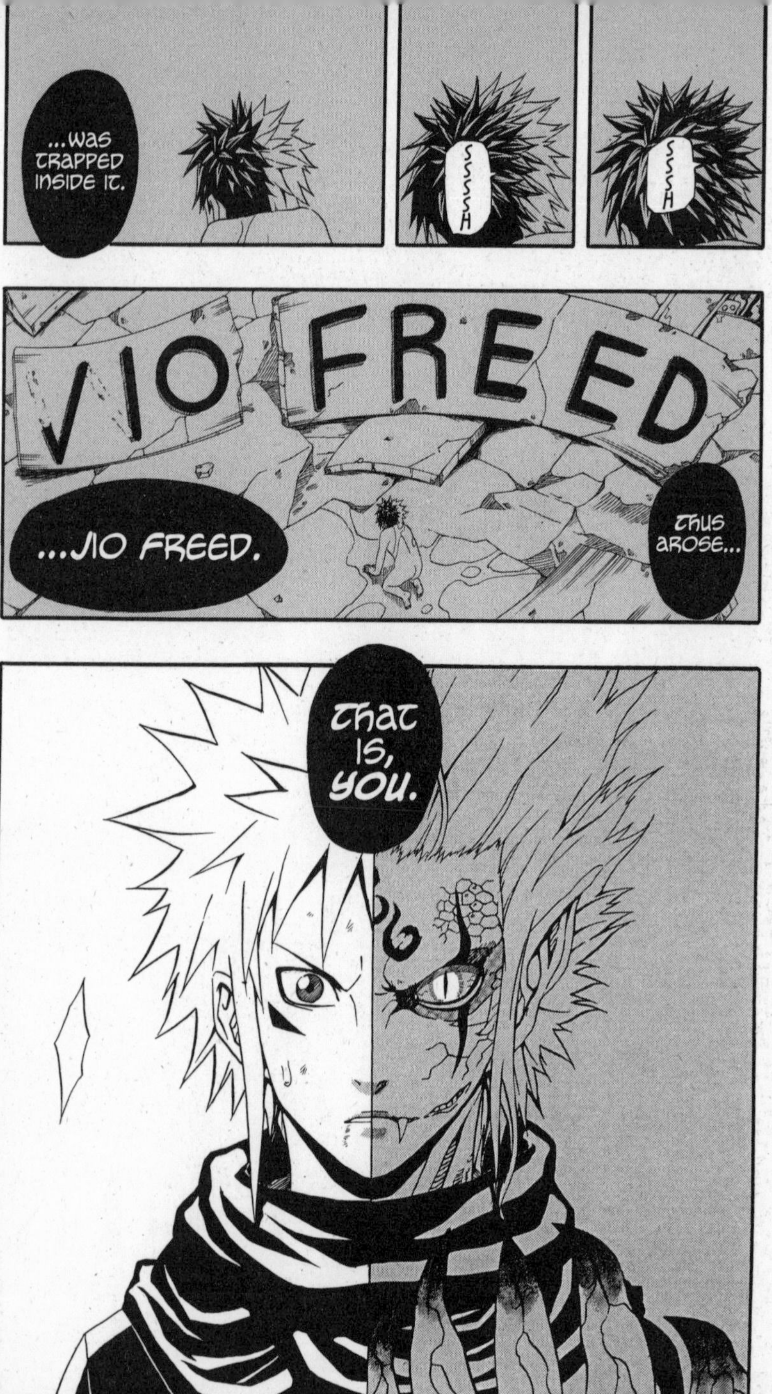
SSSH
SSSSH
...WAS TRAPPED INSIDE IT.
VIO FREED
THUS AROSE...
...VIO FREED.
THAT IS, YOU.

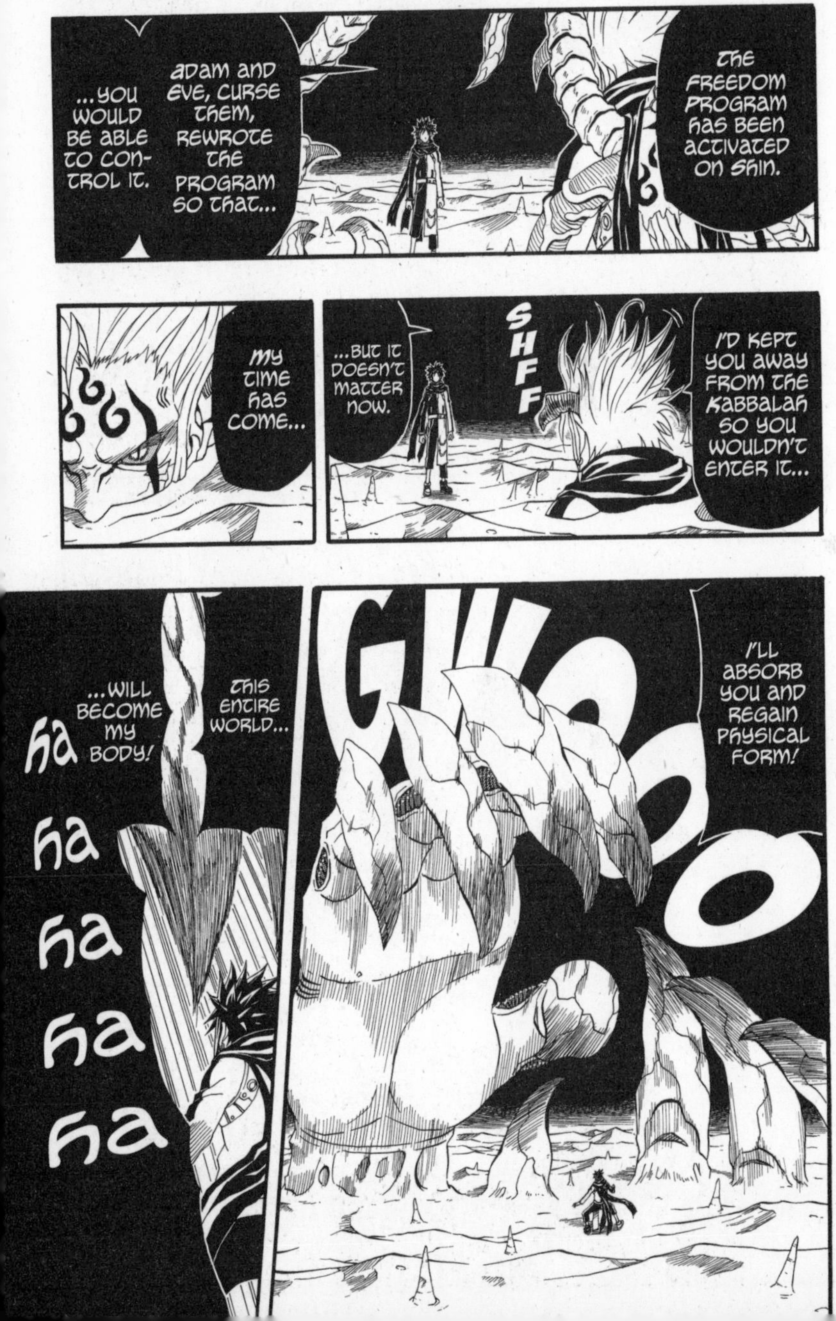
THE FREEDOM PROGRAM HAS BEEN ACTIVATED ON SHIN.
ADAM AND EVE, CURSE THEM, REWROTE THE PROGRAM SO THAT...
...YOU WOULD BE ABLE TO CONTROL IT.
I'D KEPT YOU AWAY FROM THE KABBALAH SO YOU WOULDN'T ENTER IT...
SHFF
...BUT IT DOESN'T MATTER NOW.
MY TIME HAS COME...
I'LL ABSORB YOU AND REGAIN PHYSICAL FORM!
GWOOOO
THIS ENTIRE WORLD...
...WILL BECOME MY BODY!
HA HA HA HA HA

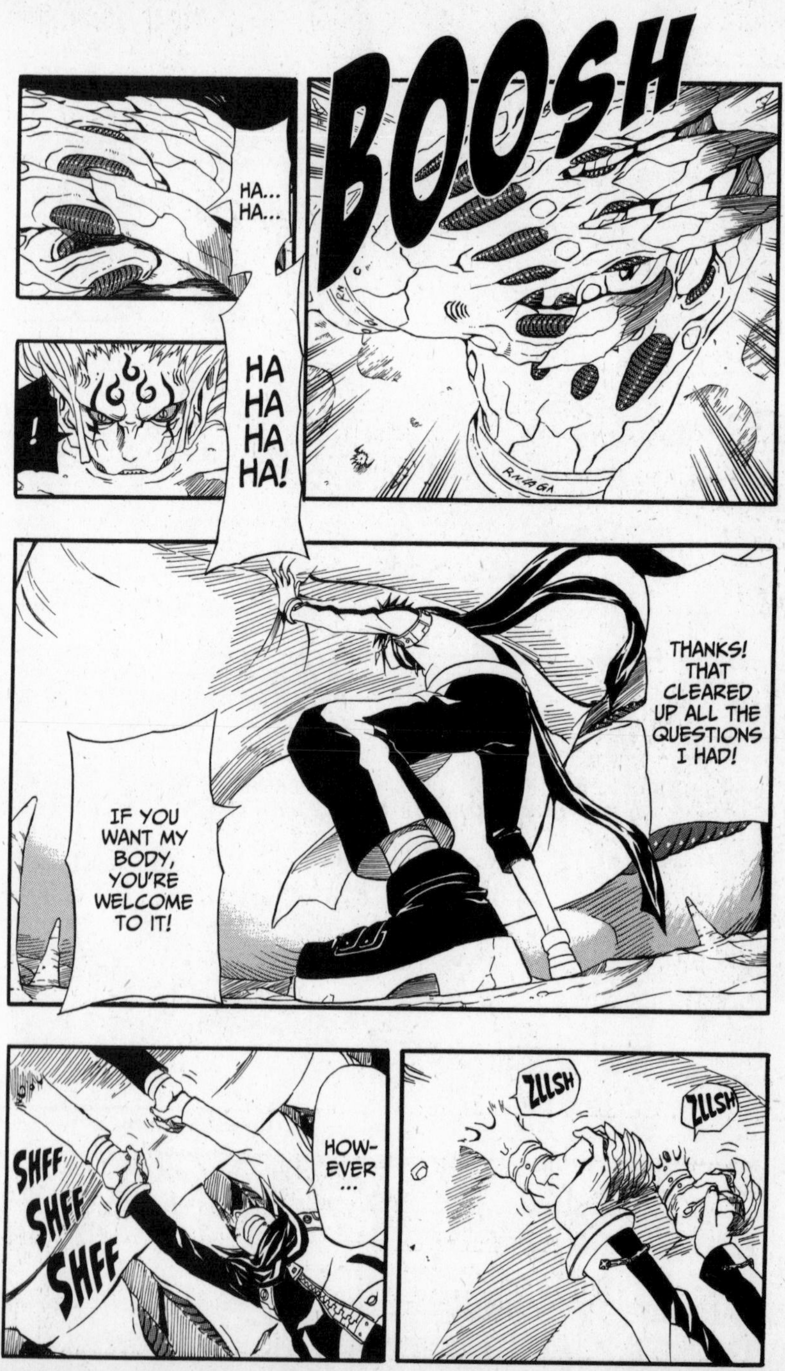
BOOSH
HA... HA...
!
HA HA HA HA!
THANKS! THAT CLEARED UP ALL THE QUESTIONS I HAD!
IF YOU WANT MY BODY, YOU'RE WELCOME TO IT!
ZLLSH
ZLLSH
HOW-EVER...
SHFF
SHFF
SHFF

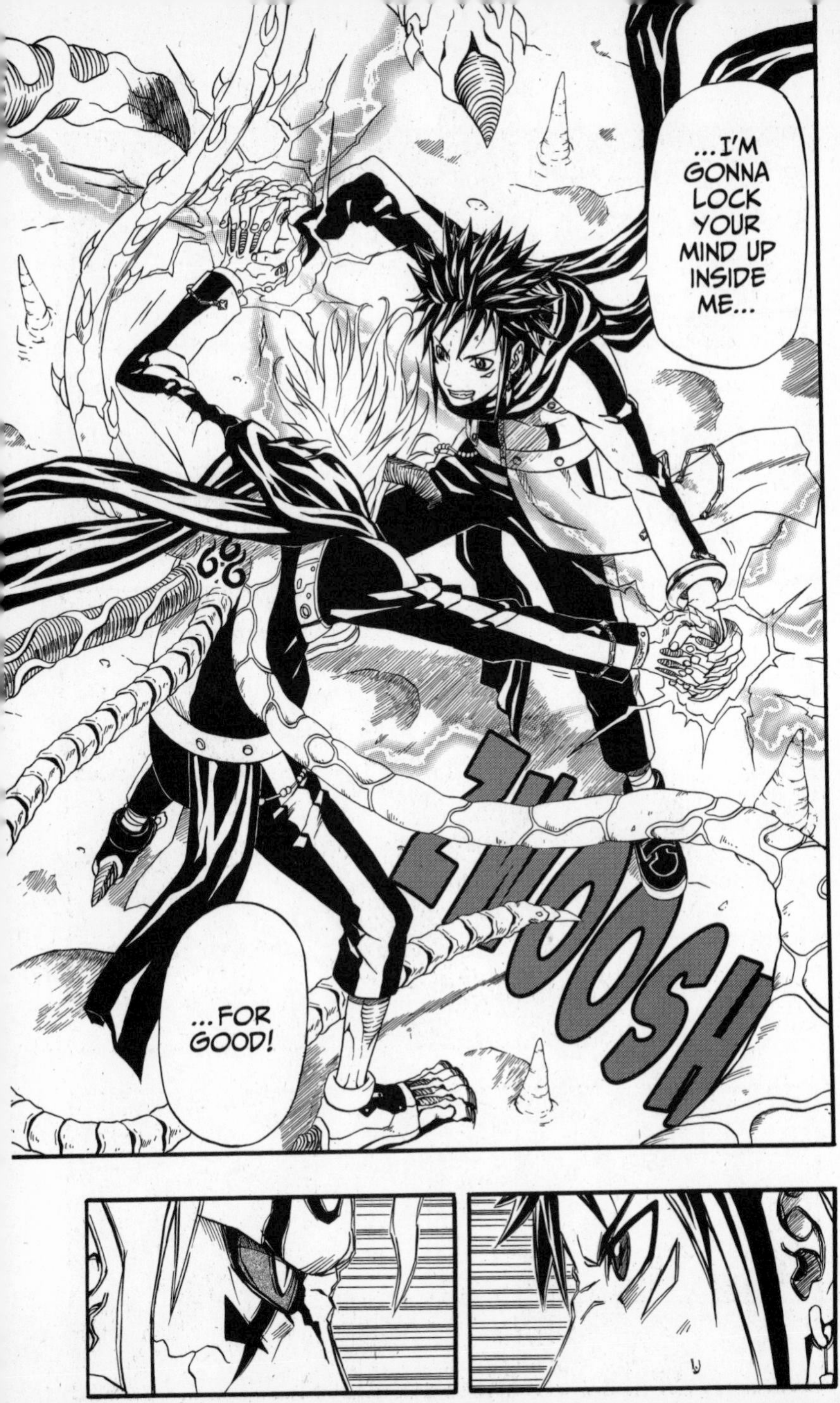
...I'M GONNA LOCK YOUR MIND UP INSIDE ME...
WHOOSH
...FOR GOOD!

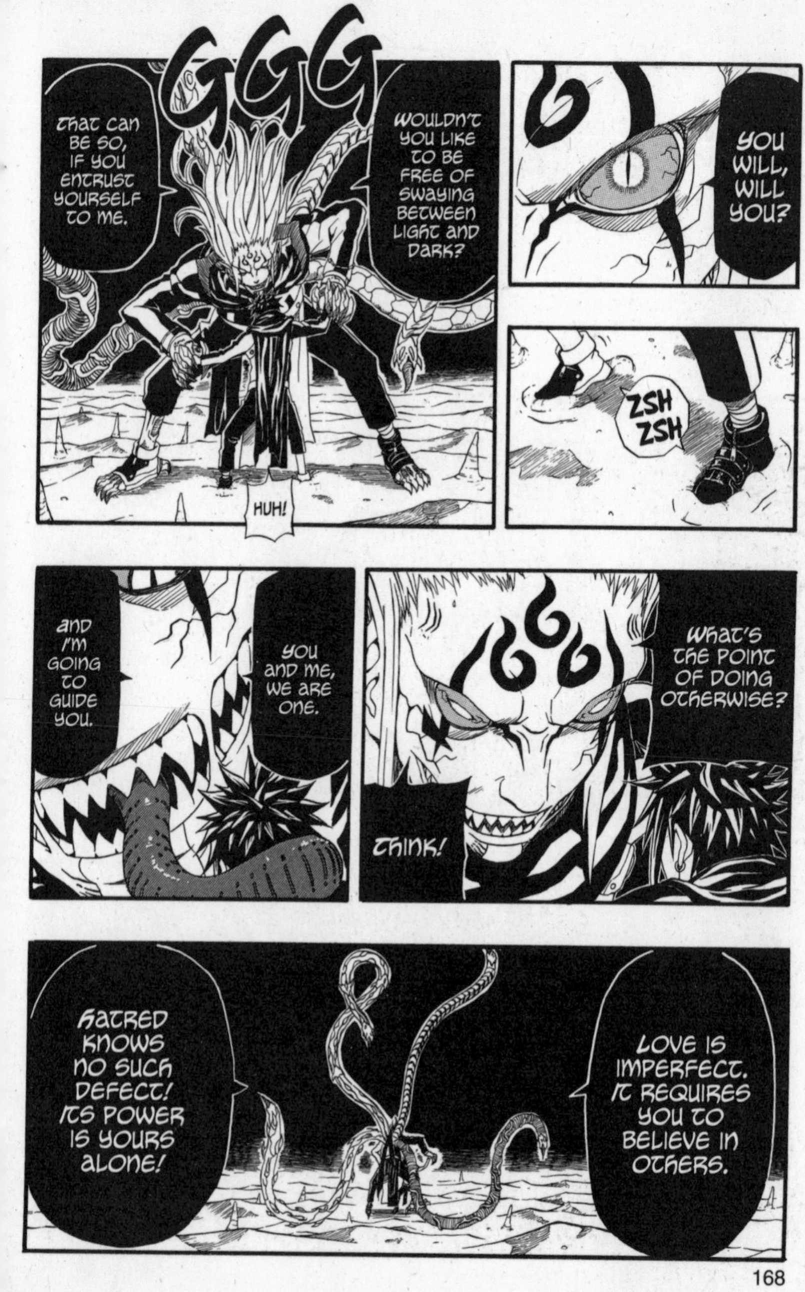
YOU WILL, WILL YOU?
ZSH ZSH
WOULDN'T YOU LIKE TO BE FREE OF SWAYING BETWEEN LIGHT AND DARK?
GGG
THAT CAN BE SO, IF YOU ENTRUST YOURSELF TO ME.
HUH!
WHAT'S THE POINT OF DOING OTHERWISE?
THINK!
YOU AND ME, WE ARE ONE.
AND I'M GOING TO GUIDE YOU.
LOVE IS IMPERFECT. IT REQUIRES YOU TO BELIEVE IN OTHERS.
HATRED KNOWS NO SUCH DEFECT! ITS POWER IS YOURS ALONE!

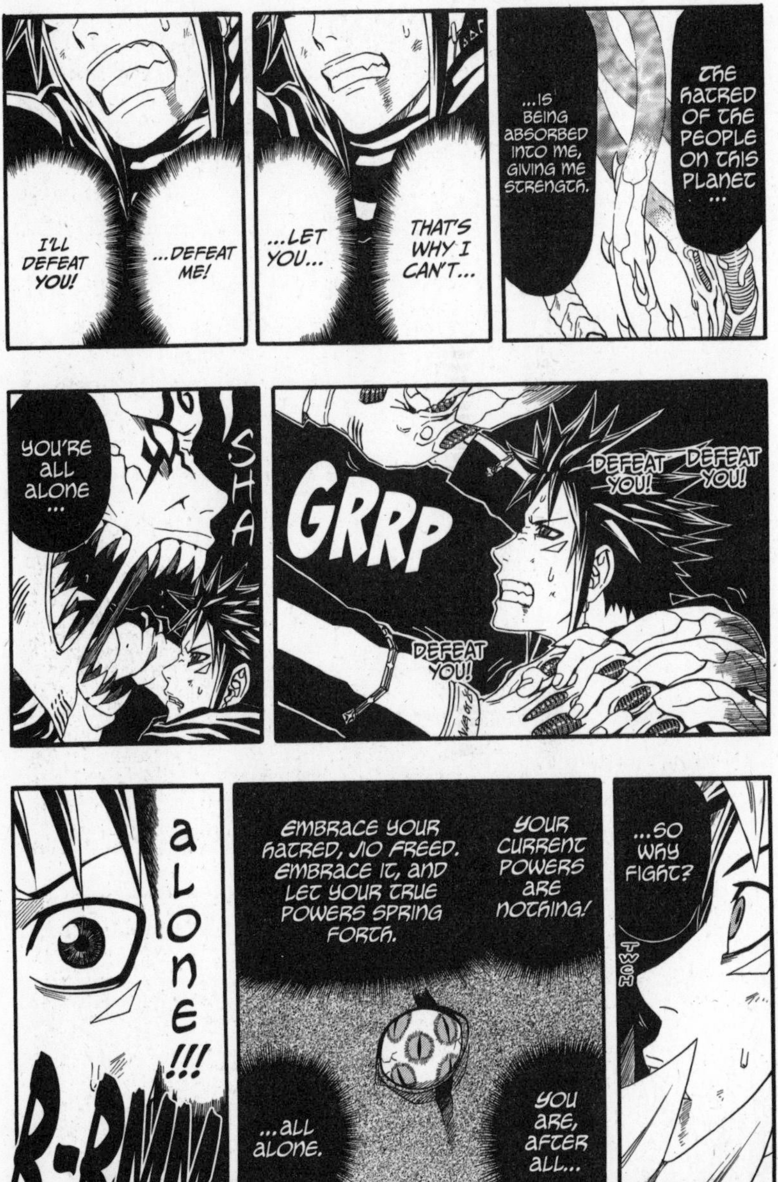
THE HATRED OF THE PEOPLE ON THIS PLANET ...
...IS BEING ABSORBED INTO ME, GIVING ME STRENGTH.
THAT'S WHY I CAN'T...
...LET YOU...
...DEFEAT ME!
I'LL DEFEAT YOU!
DEFEAT YOU!
DEFEAT YOU!
GRRP
DEFEAT YOU!
SHA
YOU'RE ALL ALONE ...
...SO WHY FIGHT?
TWCH
YOUR CURRENT POWERS ARE NOTHING!
EMBRACE YOUR HATRED, JIO FREED. EMBRACE IT, AND LET YOUR TRUE POWERS SPRING FORTH.
YOU ARE, AFTER ALL...
...ALL ALONE.
ALONE!!!
B-BMM

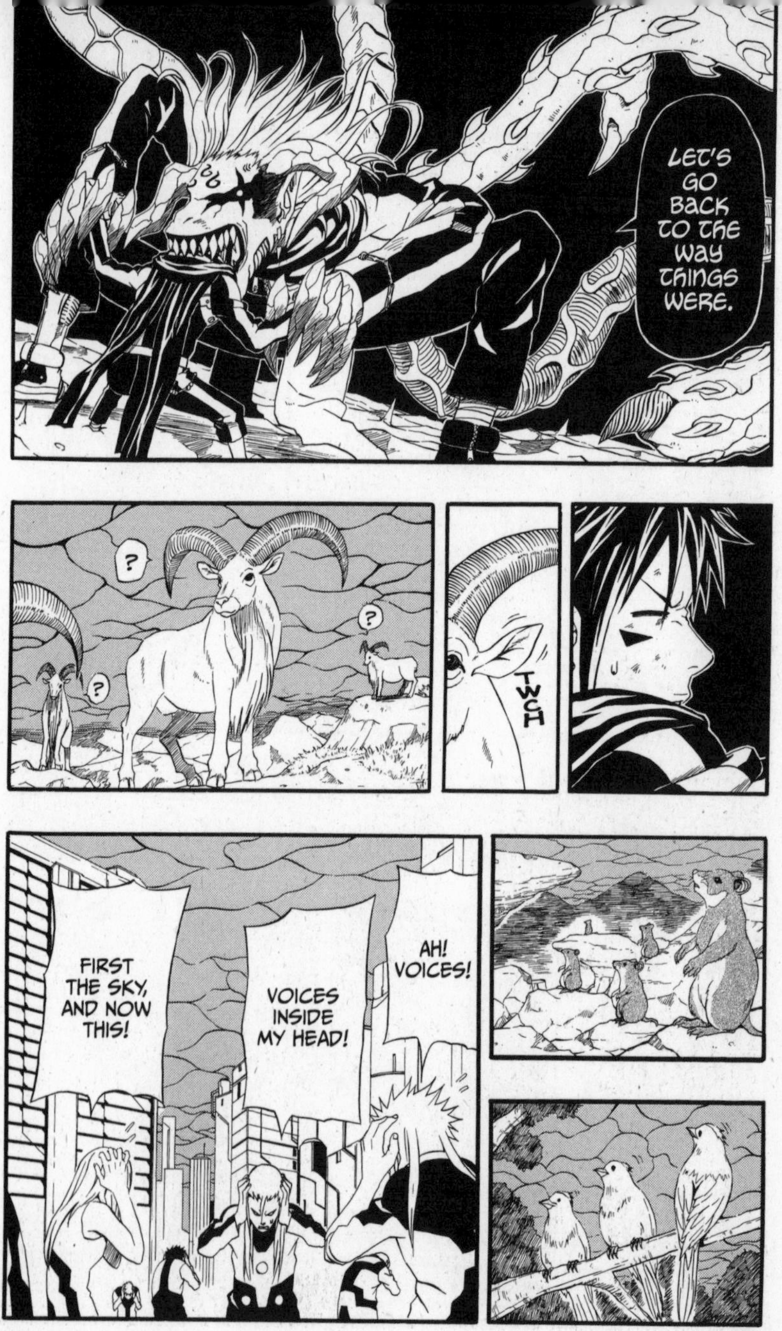
LET'S GO BACK TO THE WAY THINGS WERE.
?
?
?
TWCH
AH! VOICES!
VOICES INSIDE MY HEAD!
FIRST THE SKY, AND NOW THIS!

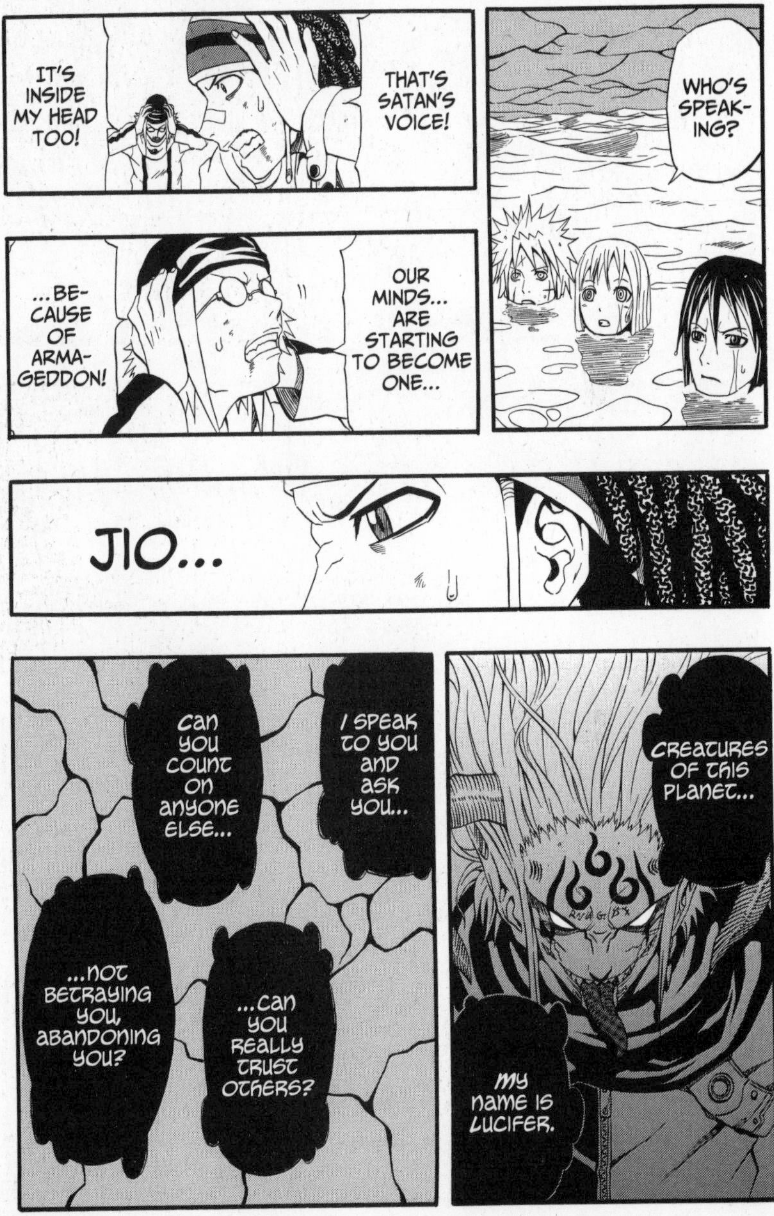
WHO'S SPEAK-ING?
THAT'S SATAN'S VOICE!
IT'S INSIDE MY HEAD TOO!
OUR MINDS... ARE STARTING TO BECOME ONE...
...BE-CAUSE OF ARMA-GEDDON!
JIO...
CREATURES OF THIS PLANET...
MY NAME IS LUCIFER.
I SPEAK TO YOU AND ASK YOU...
CAN YOU COUNT ON ANYONE ELSE...
...CAN YOU REALLY TRUST OTHERS?
...NOT BETRAYING YOU, ABANDONING YOU?

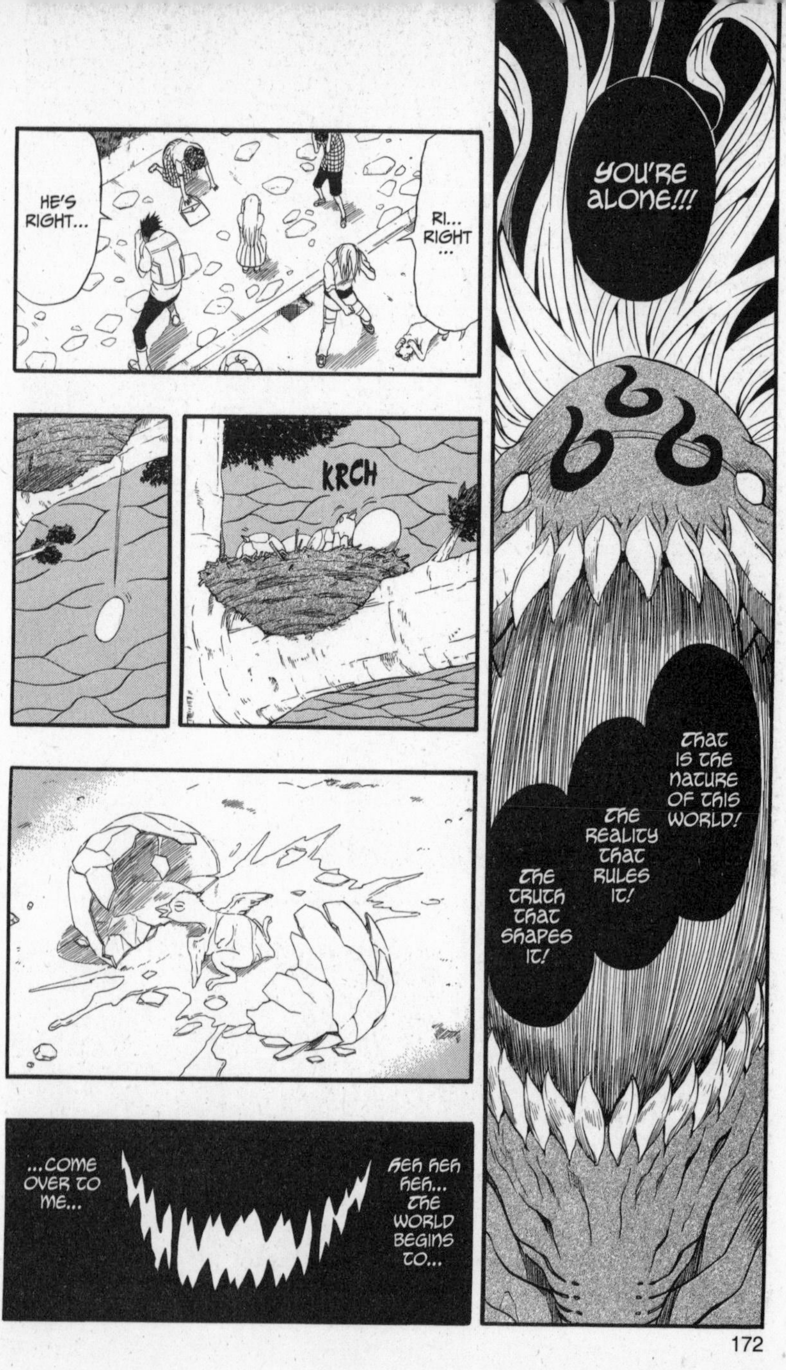
YOU'RE ALONE!!!
THAT IS THE NATURE OF THIS WORLD!
THE REALITY THAT RULES IT!
THE TRUTH THAT SHAPES IT!
RI... RIGHT ...
HE'S RIGHT...
KRCH
HEH HEH HEH... THE WORLD BEGINS TO...
...COME OVER TO ME...

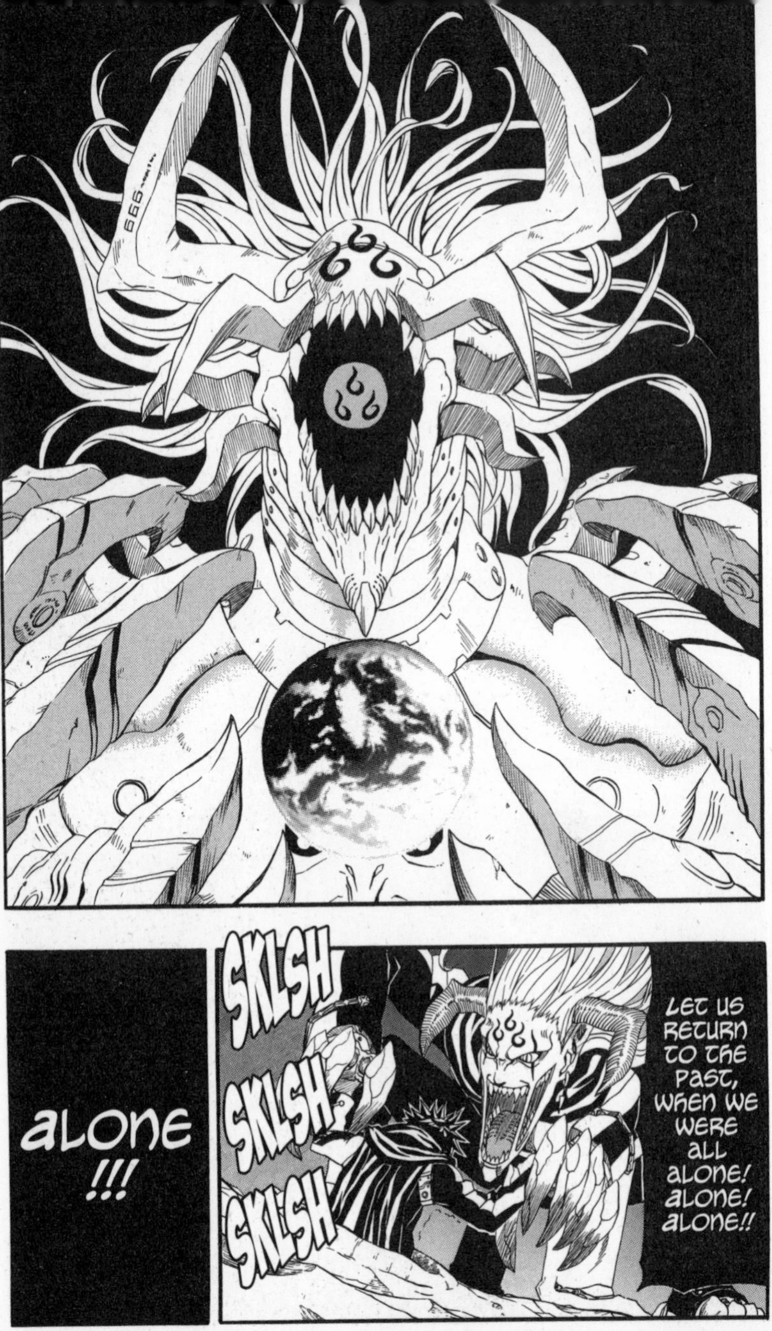
LET US RETURN TO THE PAST, WHEN WE WERE ALL ALONE! ALONE! ALONE!!
SKLSH
SKLSH
SKLSH
ALONE !!!

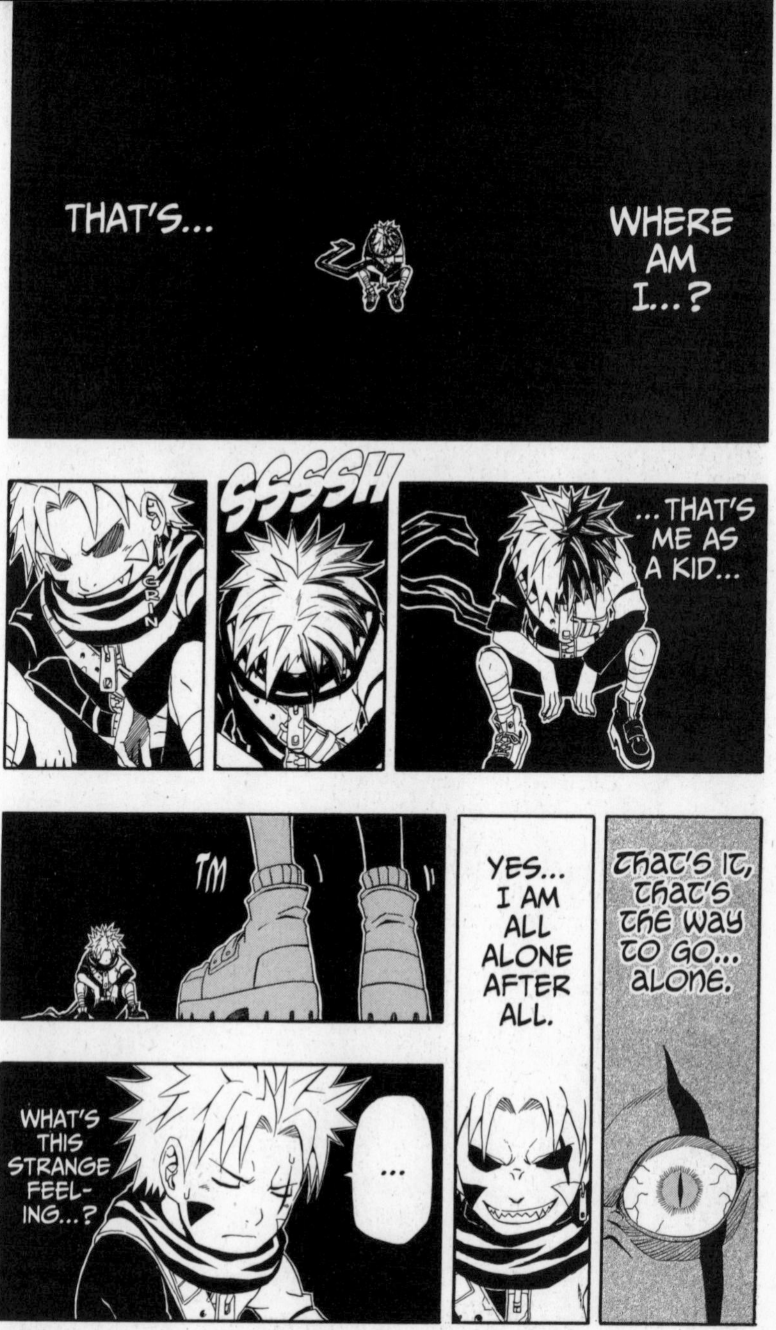
WHERE AM I...?
THAT'S...
...THAT'S ME AS A KID...
SSSSH
GRIN
THAT'S IT, THAT'S THE WAY TO GO... ALONE.
YES... I AM ALL ALONE AFTER ALL.
TM
...
WHAT'S THIS STRANGE FEEL-ING...?

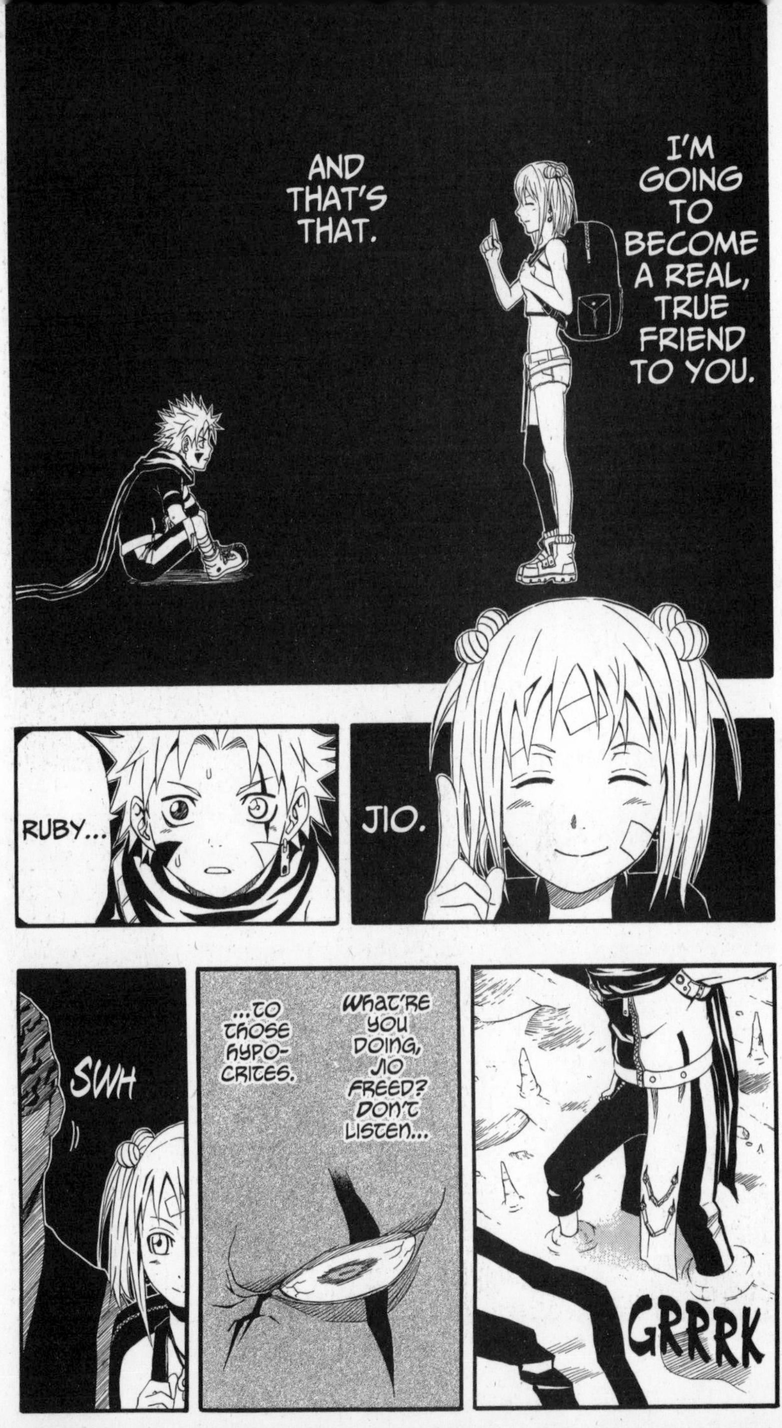
I'M GOING TO BECOME A REAL, TRUE FRIEND TO YOU.
AND THAT'S THAT.
JIO.
RUBY...
GRRRK
WHAT'RE YOU DOING, JIO FREED? DON'T LISTEN...
...TO THOSE HYPOCRITES.
SWH

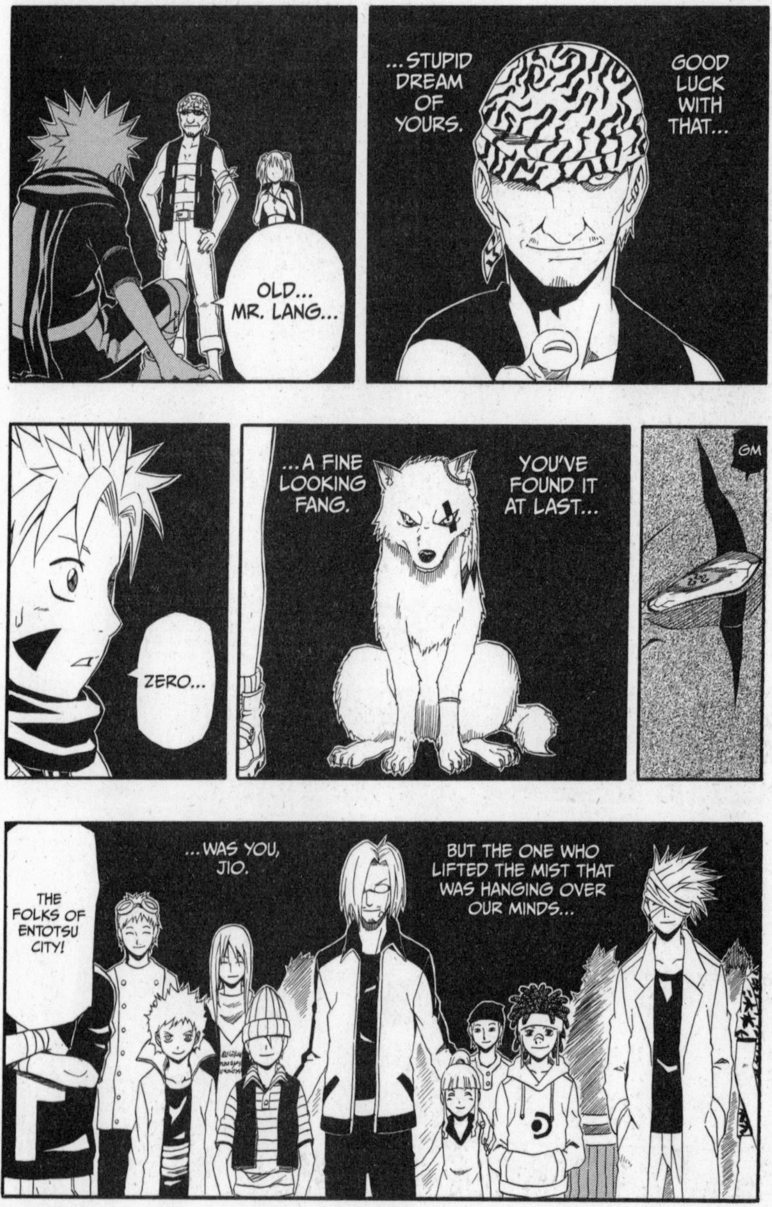
GOOD LUCK WITH THAT...
...STUPID DREAM OF YOURS.
OLD... MR. LANG...
GM
YOU'VE FOUND IT AT LAST...
...A FINE LOOKING FANG.
ZERO...
BUT THE ONE WHO LIFTED THE MIST THAT WAS HANGING OVER OUR MINDS...
...WAS YOU, JIO.
THE FOLKS OF ENTOTSU CITY!

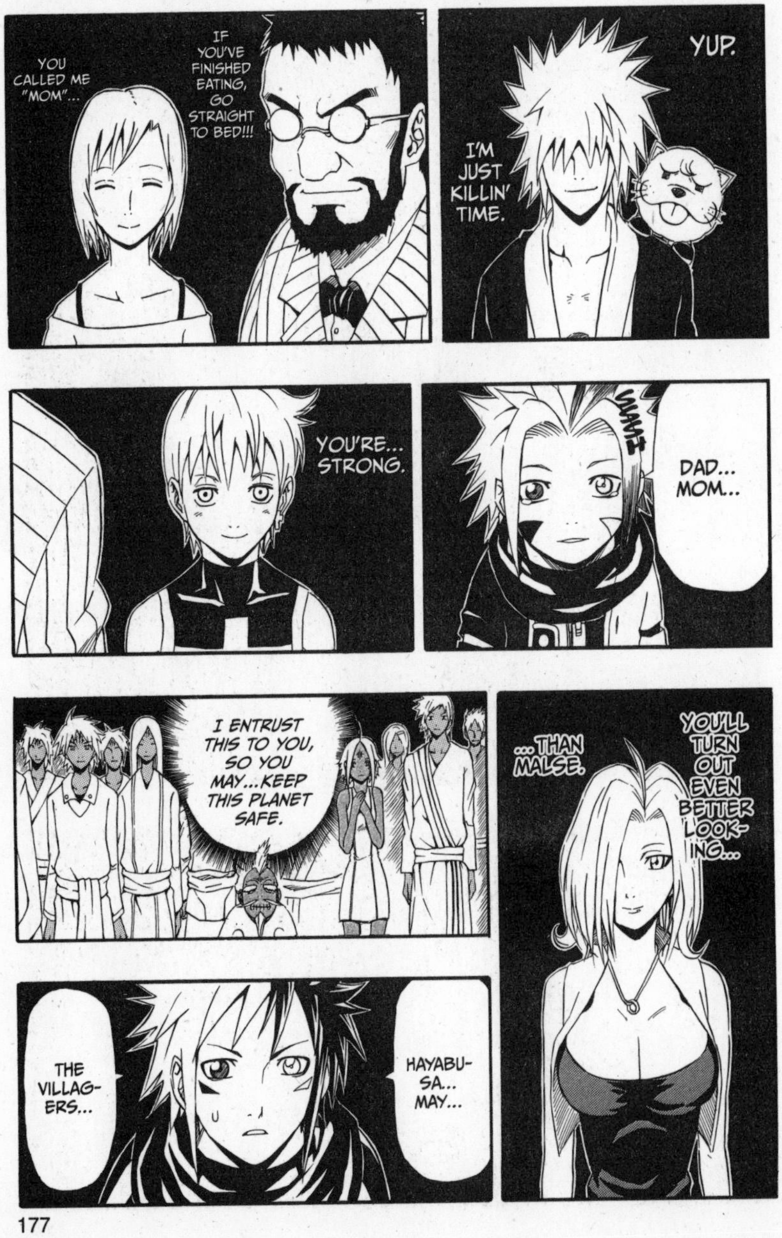
YUP.
I'M JUST KILLIN' TIME.
IF YOU'VE FINISHED EATING, GO STRAIGHT TO BED!!!
YOU CALLED ME "MOM"...
DAD... MOM...
YOU'RE... STRONG.
YOU'LL TURN OUT EVEN BETTER LOOKING...
...THAN MALSE.
I ENTRUST THIS TO YOU, SO YOU MAY...KEEP THIS PLANET SAFE.
HAYABUSA... MAY...
THE VILLAGERS...

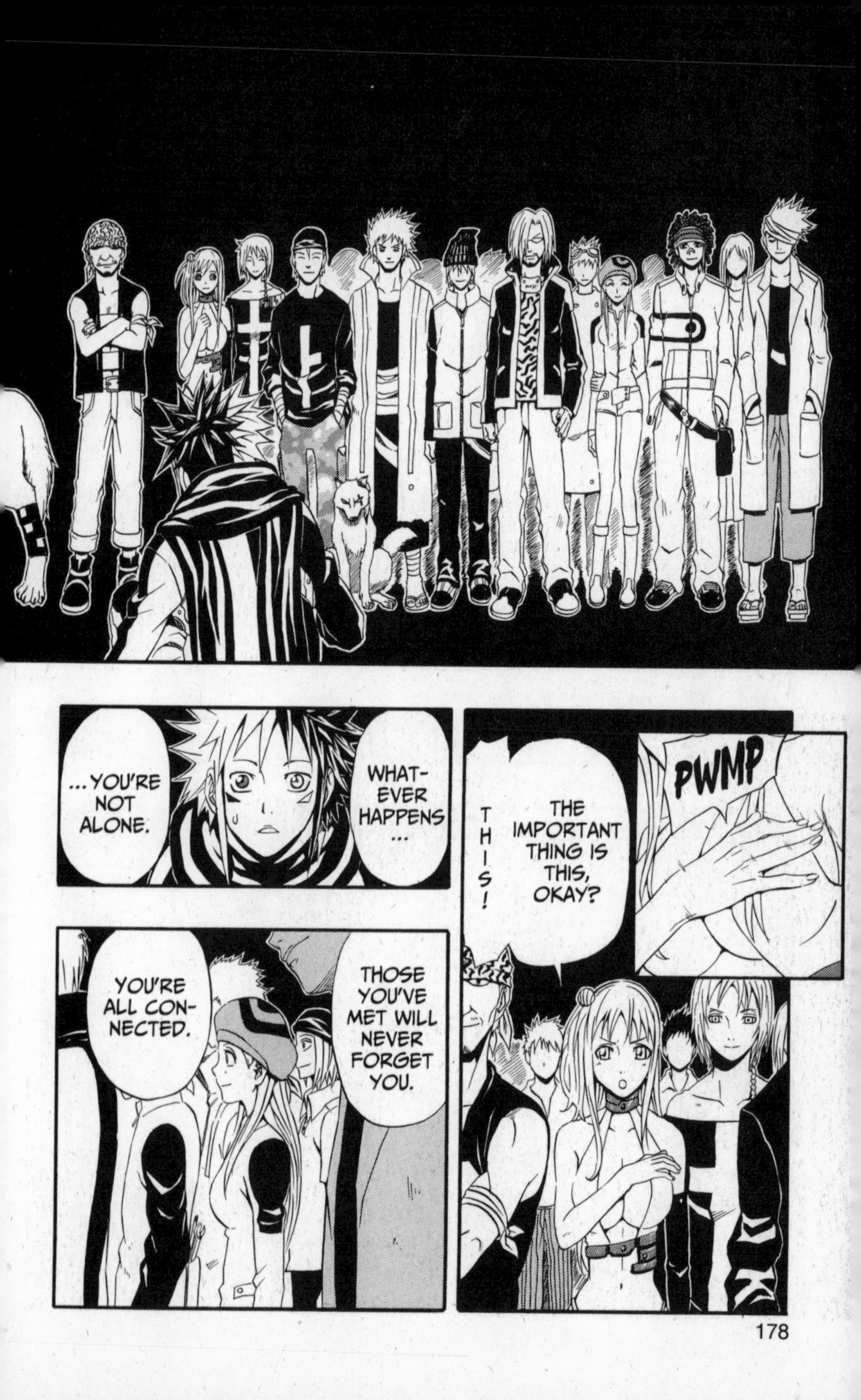
PWMP
THE IMPORTANT THING IS THIS, OKAY?
THIS!
WHAT-EVER HAPPENS...
...YOU'RE NOT ALONE.
THOSE YOU'VE MET WILL NEVER FORGET YOU.
YOU'RE ALL CON-NECTED.

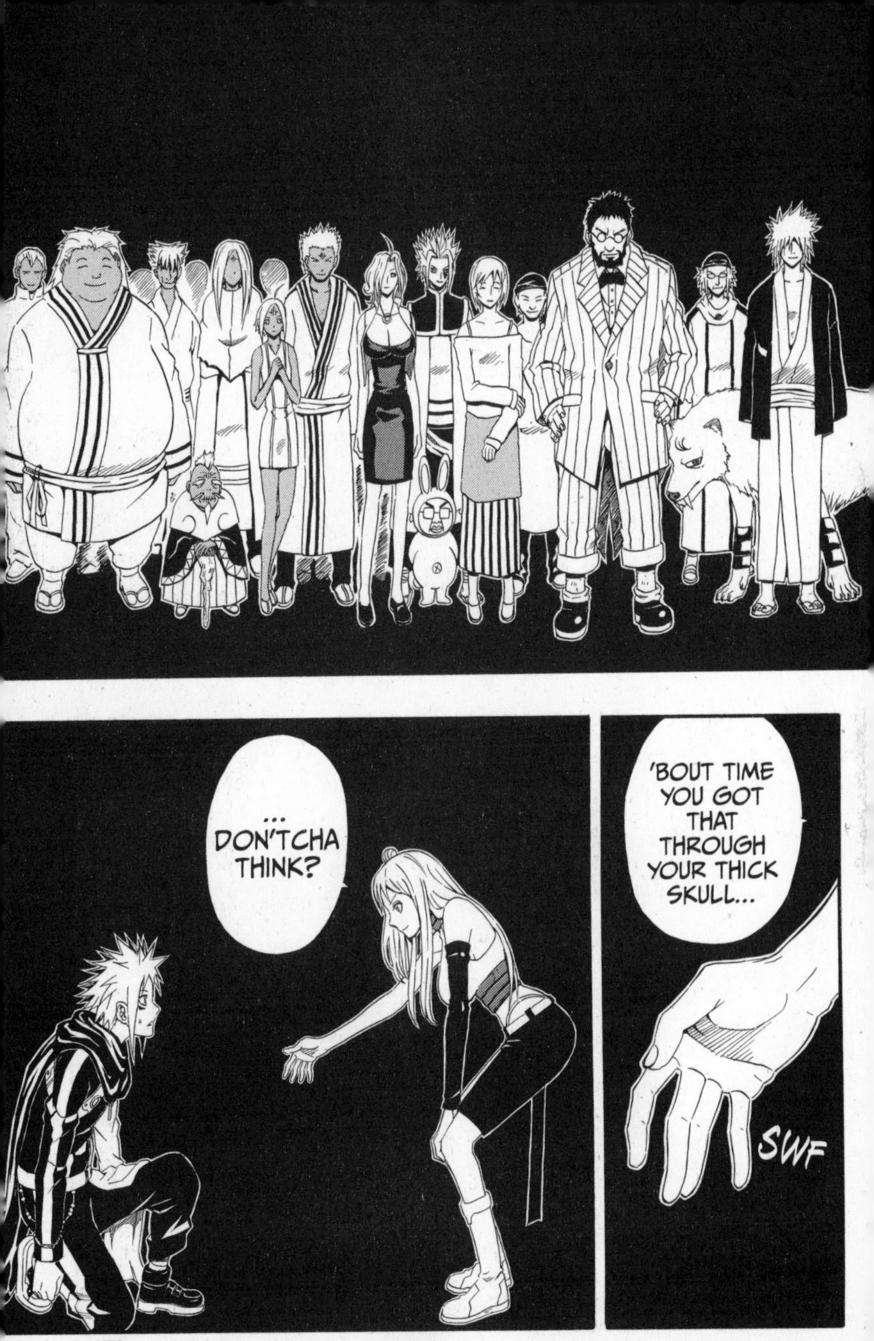
'BOUT TIME YOU GOT THAT THROUGH YOUR THICK SKULL...
SWF
... DON'TCHA THINK?

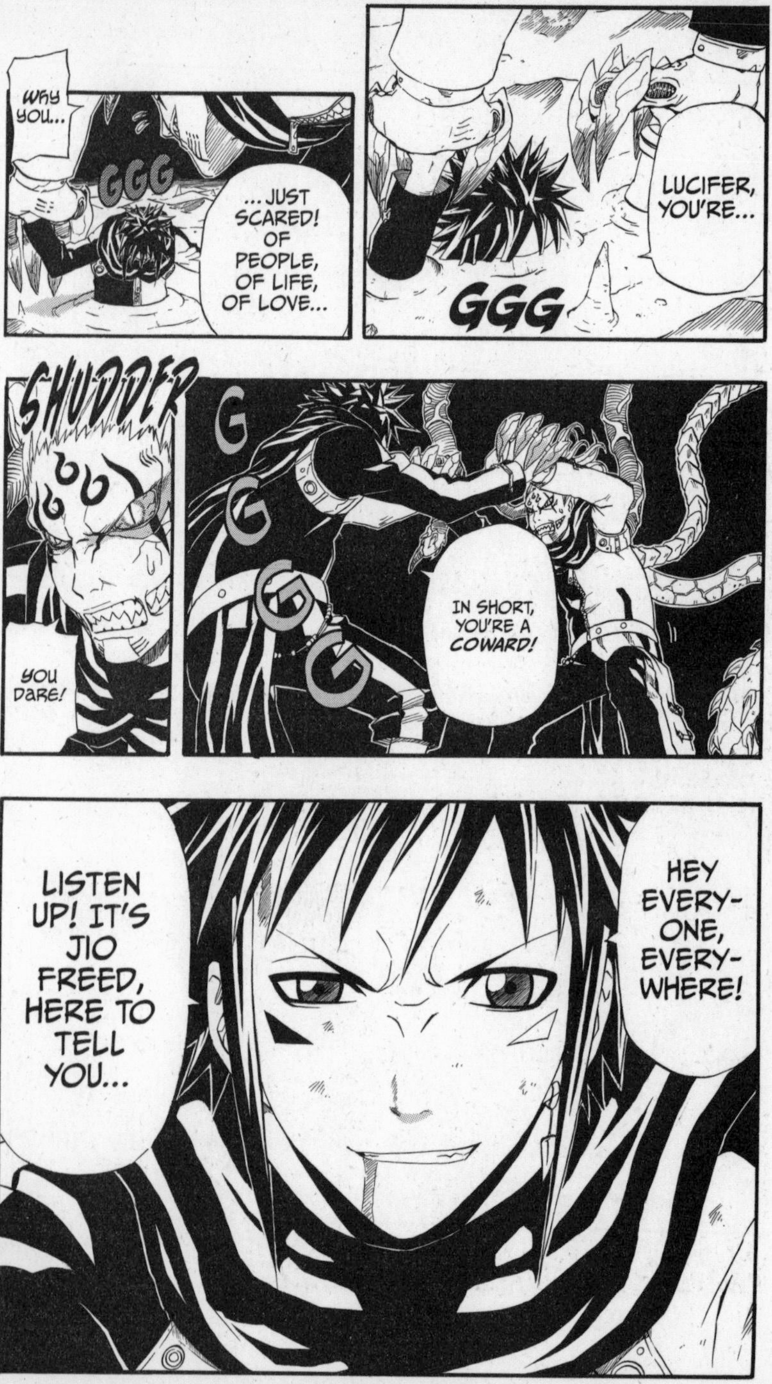
LUCIFER, YOU'RE...
GGG
...JUST SCARED! OF PEOPLE, OF LIFE, OF LOVE...
WHY YOU...
GGG
G G G G
IN SHORT, YOU'RE A COWARD!
SHUDDER
YOU DARE!
HEY EVERY-ONE, EVERY-WHERE!
LISTEN UP! IT'S JIO FREED, HERE TO TELL YOU...

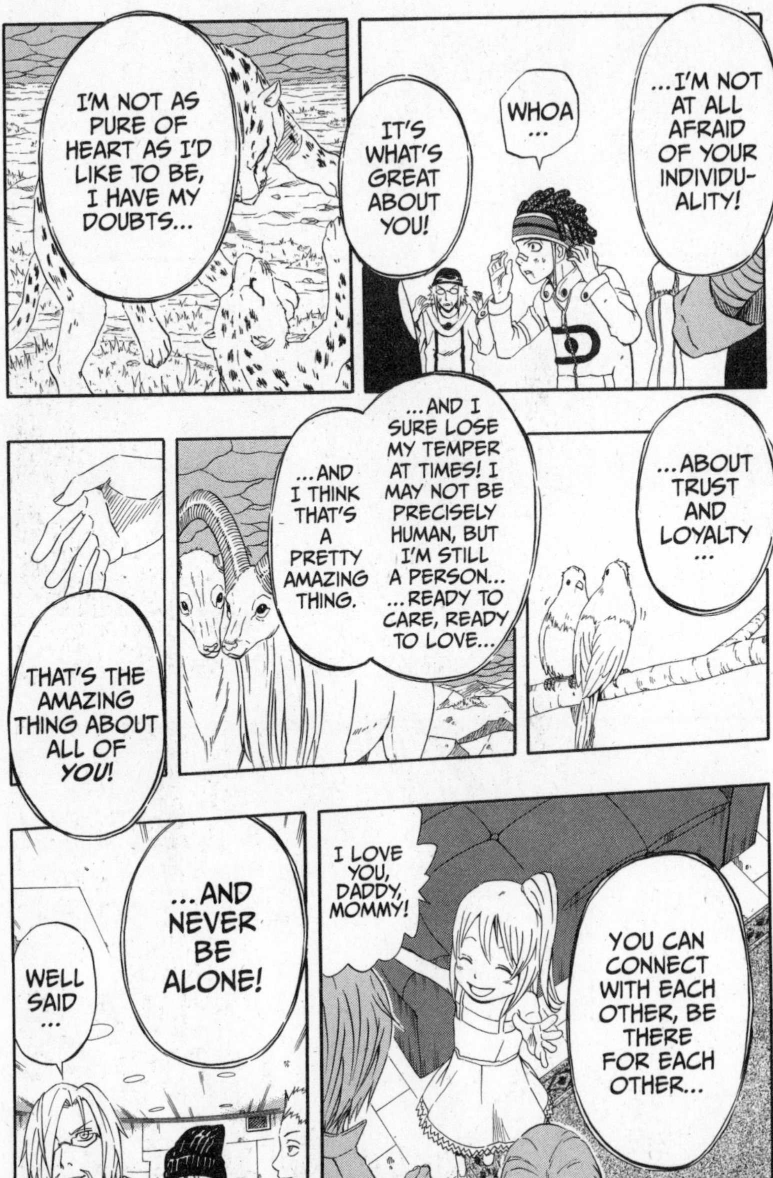
...I'M NOT AT ALL AFRAID OF YOUR INDIVIDU-ALITY!
WHOA ...
IT'S WHAT'S GREAT ABOUT YOU!
I'M NOT AS PURE OF HEART AS I'D LIKE TO BE, I HAVE MY DOUBTS...
...ABOUT TRUST AND LOYALTY ...
...AND I SURE LOSE MY TEMPER AT TIMES! I MAY NOT BE PRECISELY HUMAN, BUT I'M STILL A PERSON... ...READY TO CARE, READY TO LOVE...
...AND I THINK THAT'S A PRETTY AMAZING THING.
THAT'S THE AMAZING THING ABOUT ALL OF *YOU*!
YOU CAN CONNECT WITH EACH OTHER, BE THERE FOR EACH OTHER...
I LOVE YOU, DADDY, MOMMY!
...AND NEVER BE ALONE!
WELL SAID ...

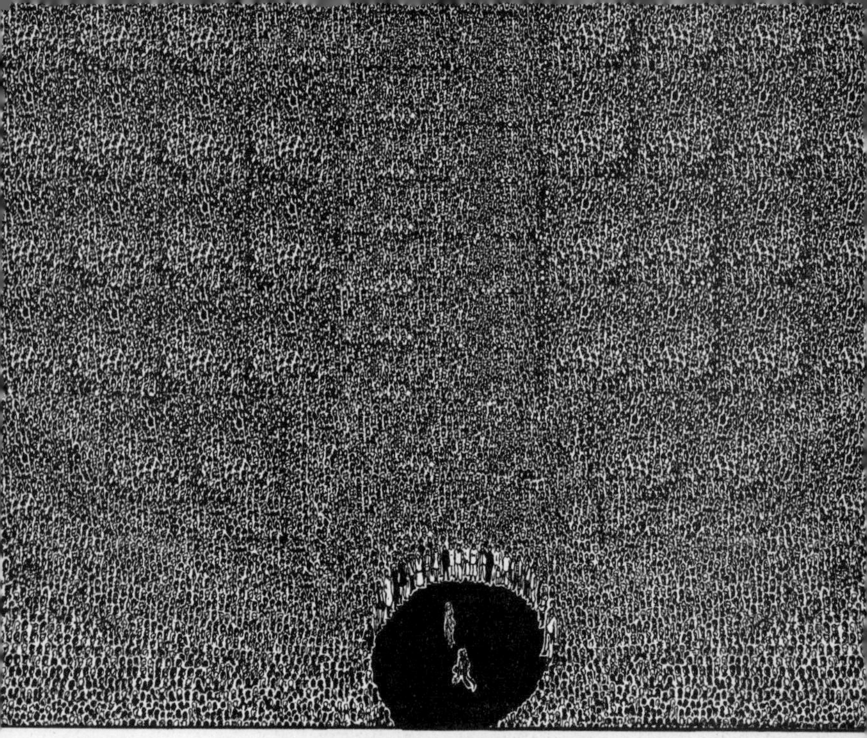

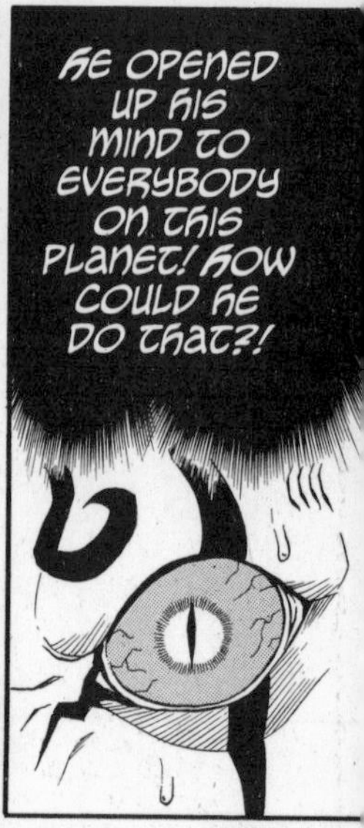
HE OPENED UP HIS MIND TO EVERYBODY ON THIS PLANET! HOW COULD HE DO THAT?!

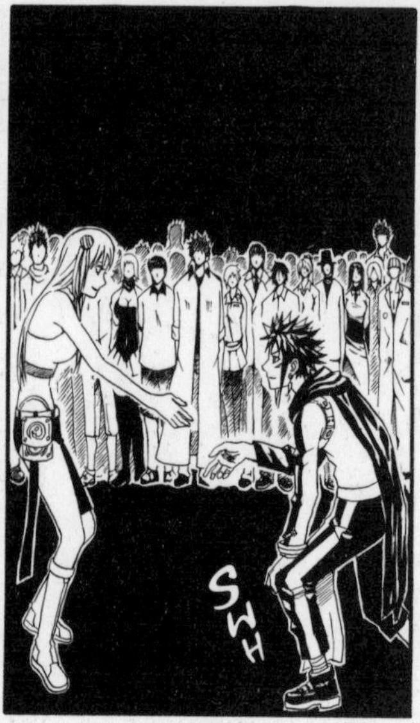
SWH

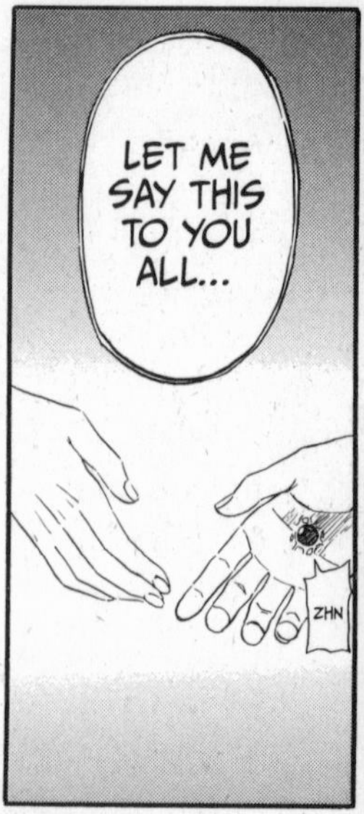
LET ME SAY THIS TO YOU ALL...
ZHN

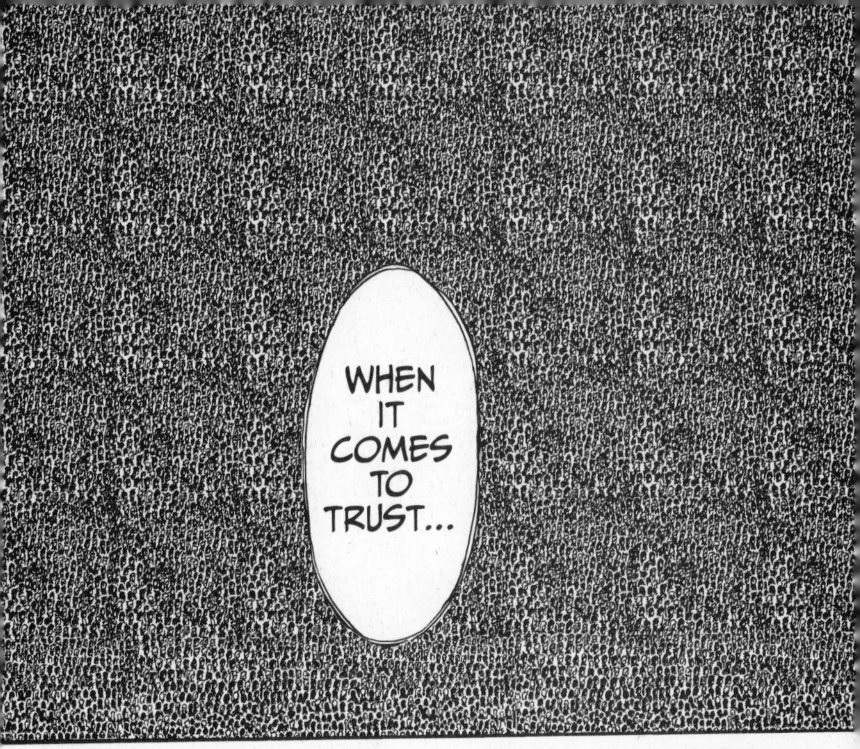
WHEN IT COMES TO TRUST...

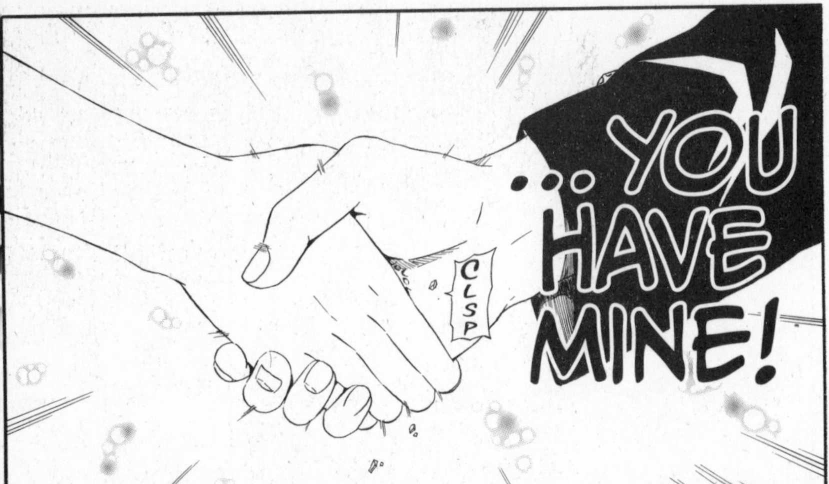
CLSP
...YOU HAVE MINE!

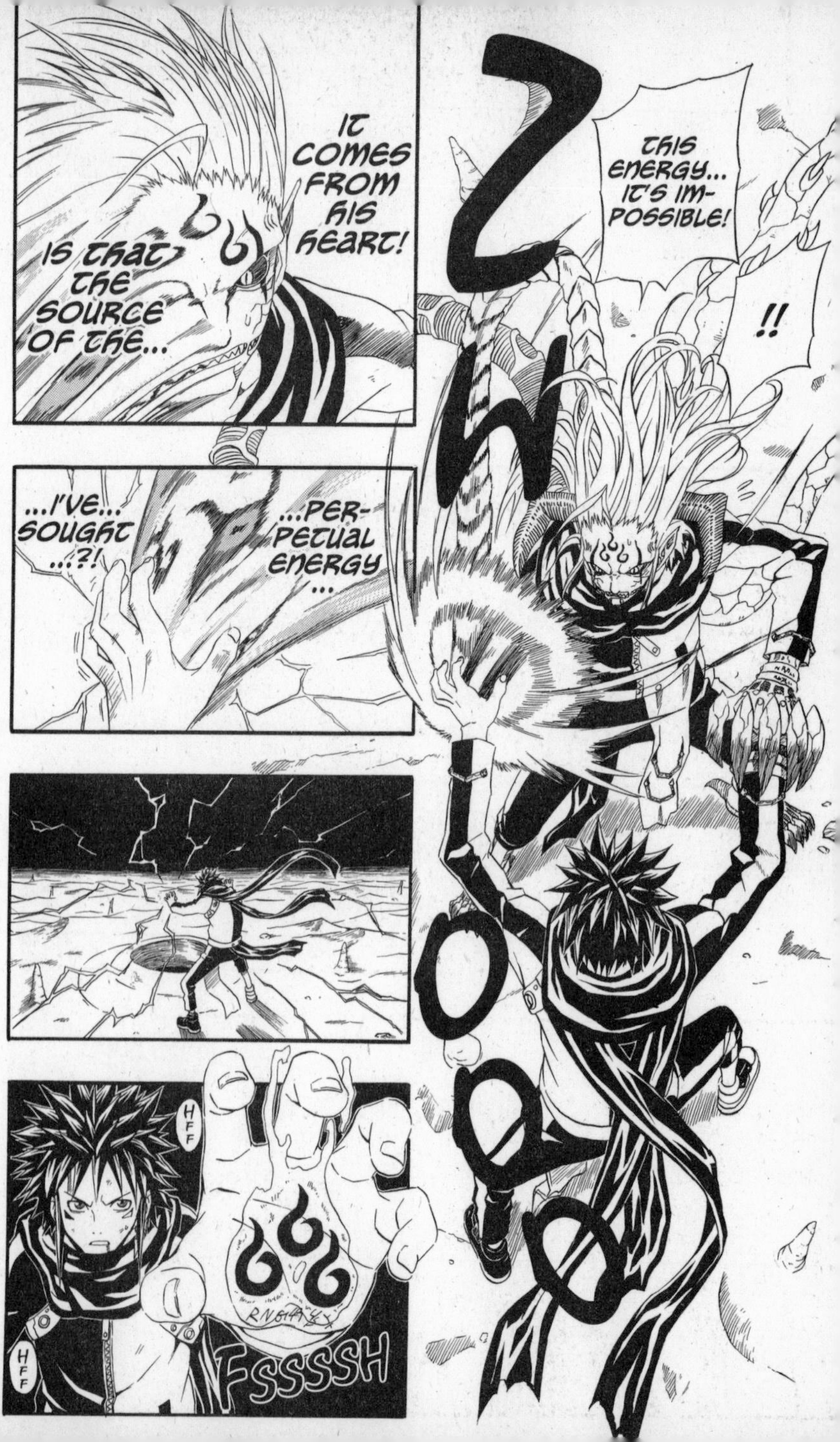
THIS ENERGY... IT'S IM-POSSIBLE!
!!
IT COMES FROM HIS HEART!
IS THAT THE SOURCE OF THE...
...PER-PETUAL ENERGY...
...I'VE... SOUGHT ...?!
HFF
HFF
FSSSSH

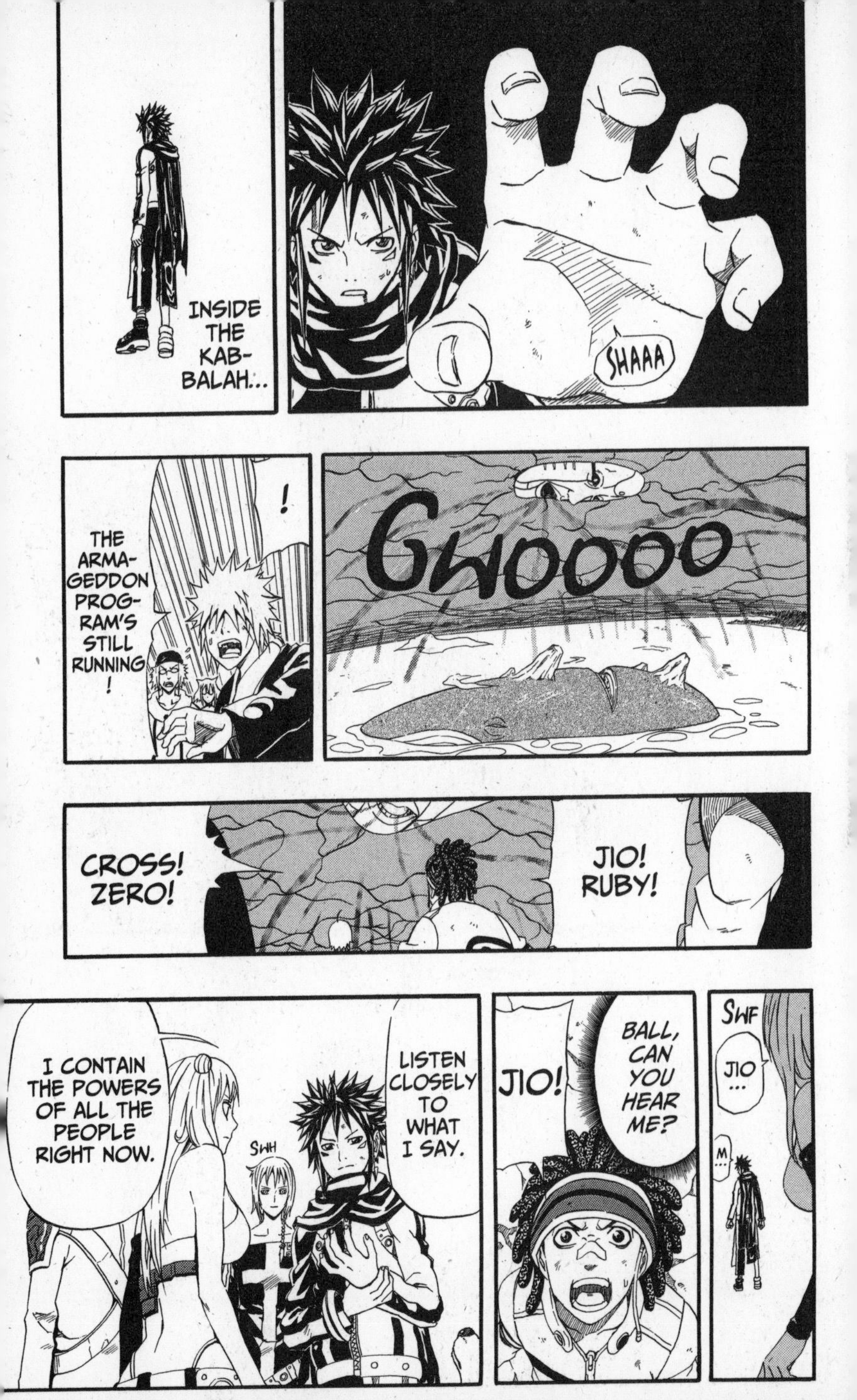
SHAAA
INSIDE THE KABBALAH...
GWOOOO
!
THE ARMAGEDDON PROGRAM'S STILL RUNNING!
JIO! RUBY!
CROSS! ZERO!
SWF
JIO...
M...
BALL, CAN YOU HEAR ME?
JIO!
LISTEN CLOSELY TO WHAT I SAY.
SWH
I CONTAIN THE POWERS OF ALL THE PEOPLE RIGHT NOW.

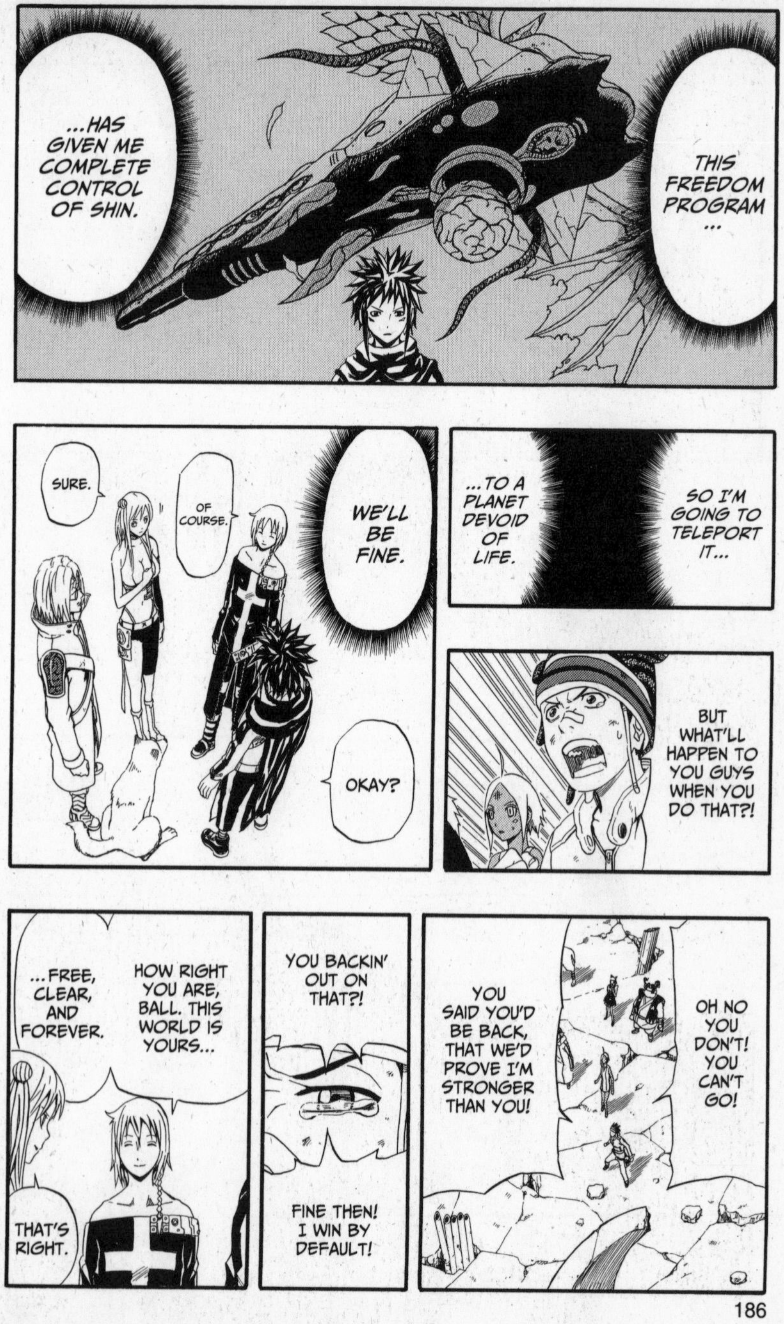
THIS FREEDOM PROGRAM ...
...HAS GIVEN ME COMPLETE CONTROL OF SHIN.
SO I'M GOING TO TELEPORT IT...
...TO A PLANET DEVOID OF LIFE.
BUT WHAT'LL HAPPEN TO YOU GUYS WHEN YOU DO THAT?!
WE'LL BE FINE.
OKAY?
OF COURSE.
SURE.
OH NO YOU DON'T! YOU CAN'T GO!
YOU SAID YOU'D BE BACK, THAT WE'D PROVE I'M STRONGER THAN YOU!
YOU BACKIN' OUT ON THAT?!
FINE THEN! I WIN BY DEFAULT!
HOW RIGHT YOU ARE, BALL. THIS WORLD IS YOURS...
...FREE, CLEAR, AND FOREVER.
THAT'S RIGHT.

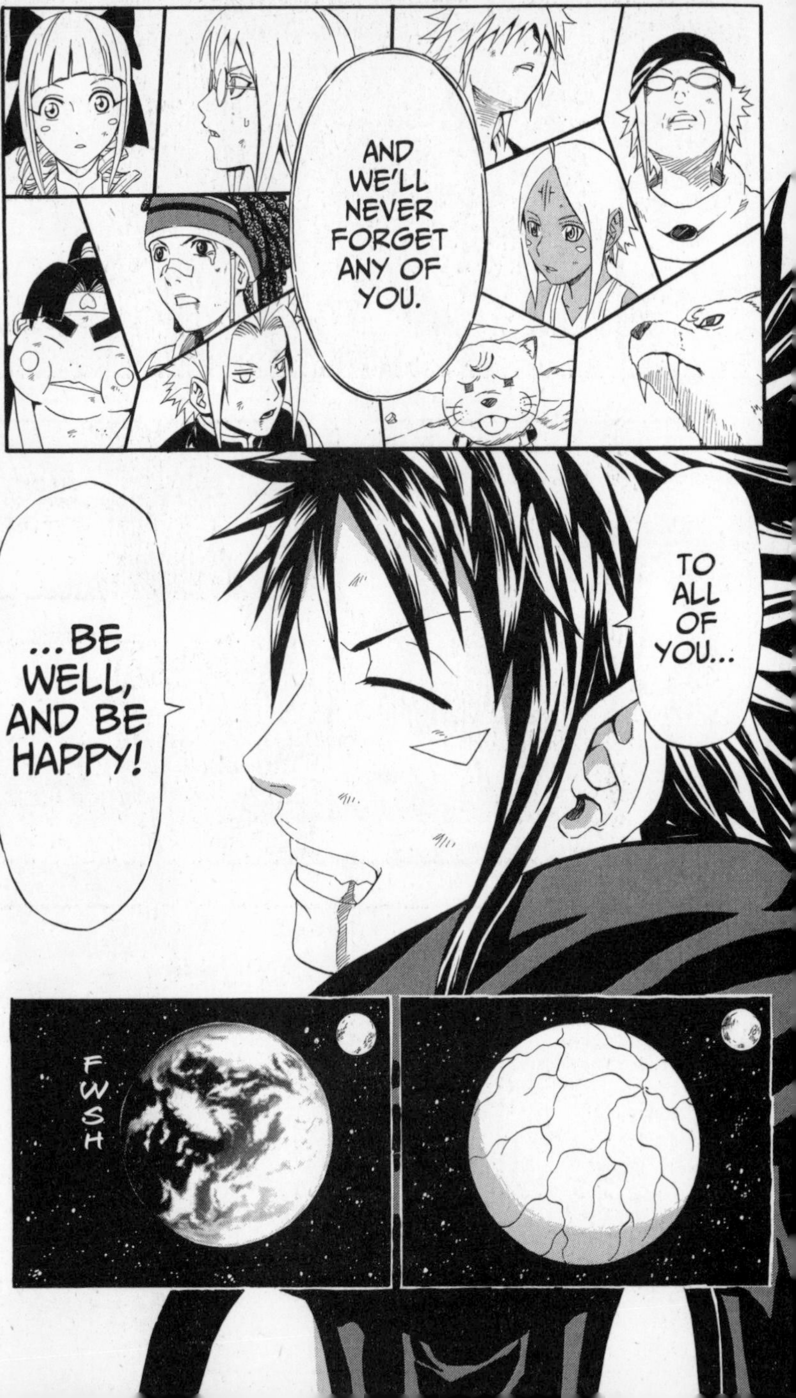
AND WE'LL NEVER FORGET ANY OF YOU.
TO ALL OF YOU...
...BE WELL, AND BE HAPPY!
FWSH

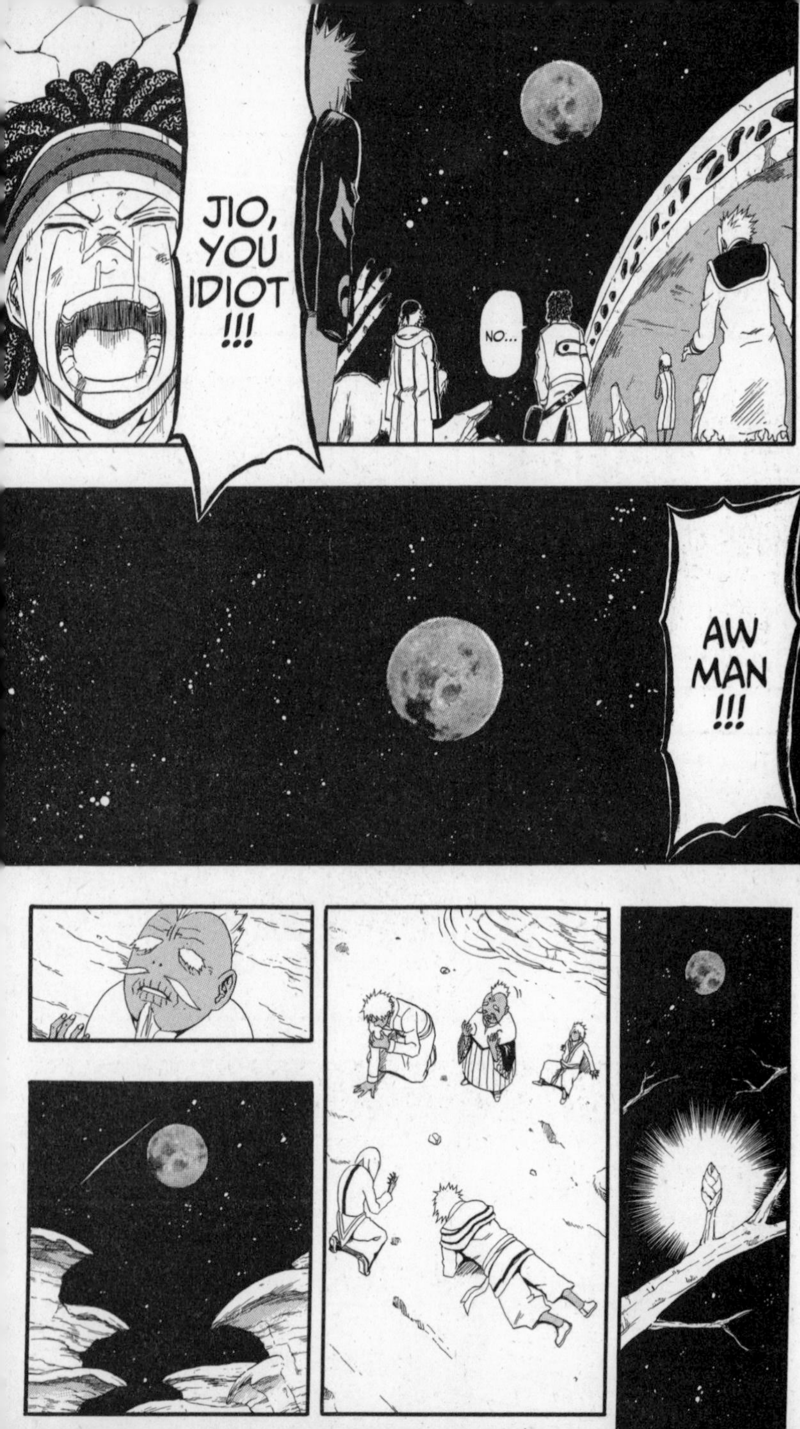
NO...
JIO, YOU IDIOT!!!
AW MAN!!!

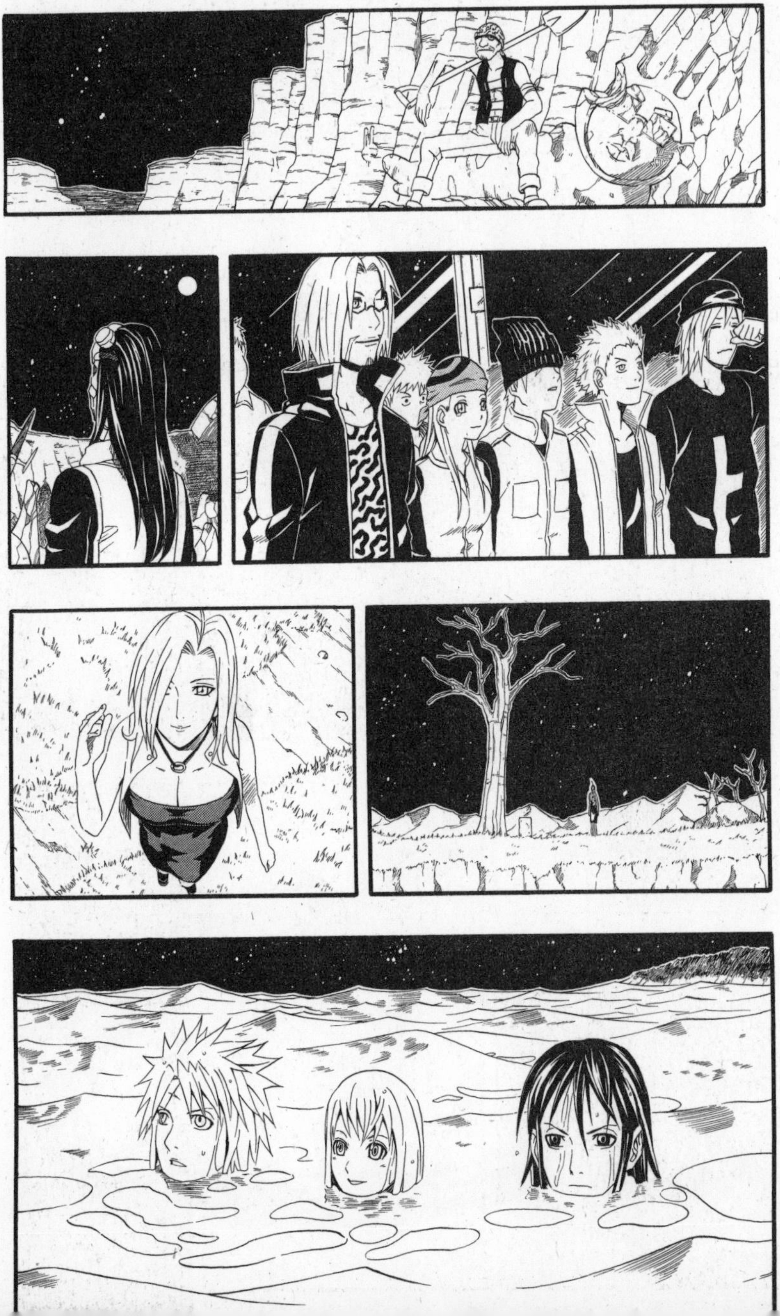

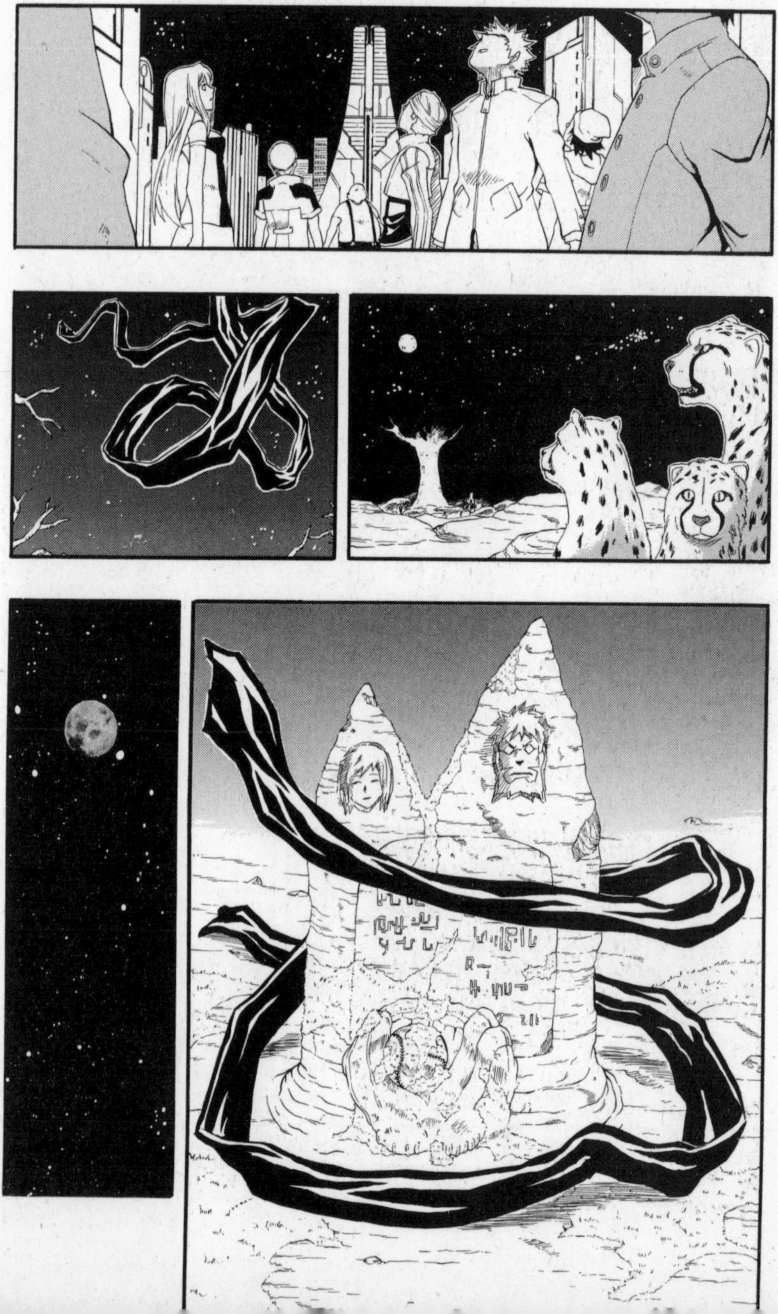

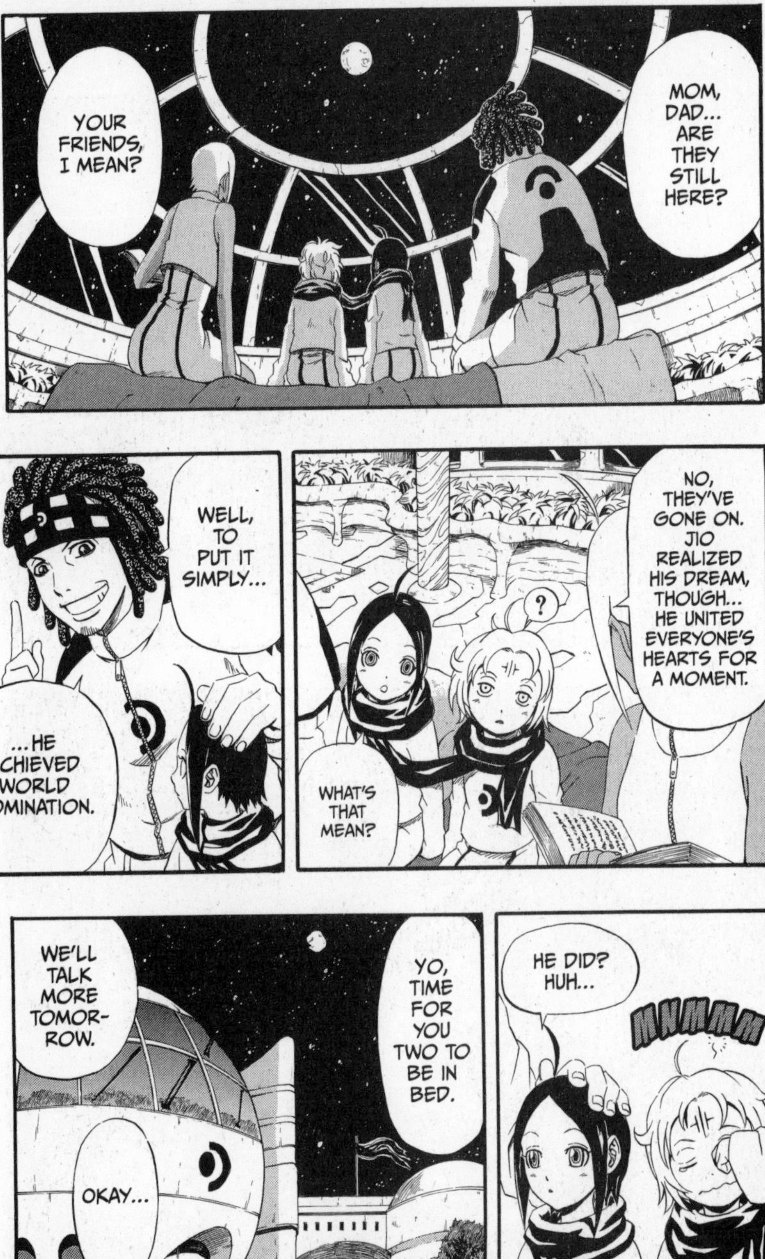
MOM, DAD... ARE THEY STILL HERE?
YOUR FRIENDS, I MEAN?
NO, THEY'VE GONE ON. JIO REALIZED HIS DREAM, THOUGH... HE UNITED EVERYONE'S HEARTS FOR A MOMENT.
?
WHAT'S THAT MEAN?
WELL, TO PUT IT SIMPLY...
...HE ACHIEVED WORLD DOMINATION.
HE DID? HUH...
MNMMM
YO, TIME FOR YOU TWO TO BE IN BED.
WE'LL TALK MORE TOMOR-ROW.
OKAY...

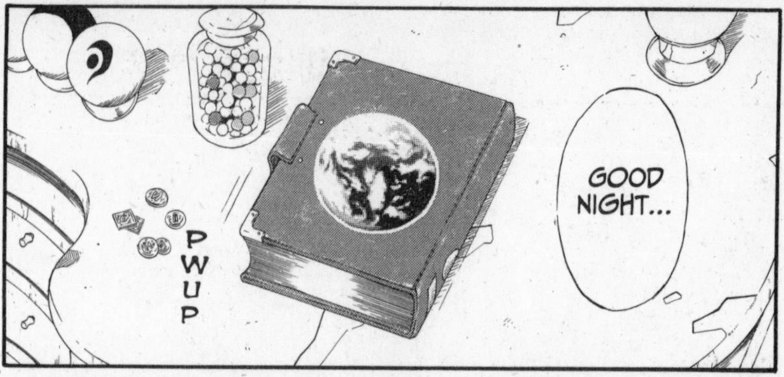
GOOD NIGHT...
PWUP

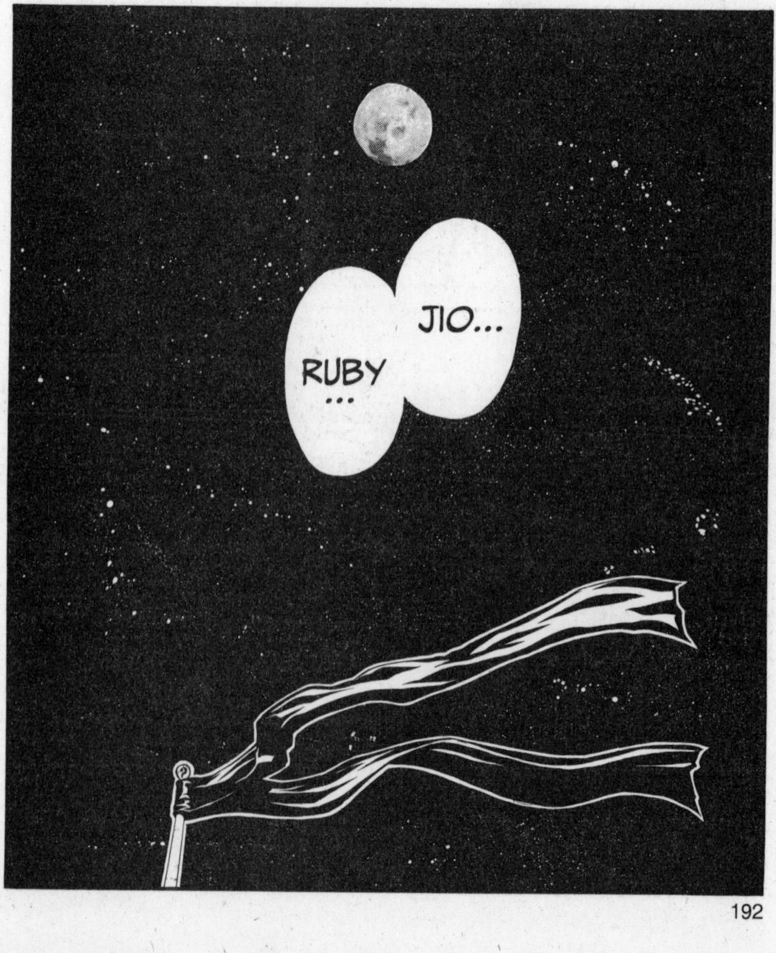
JIO...
RUBY...

SEISHI AND THANKS

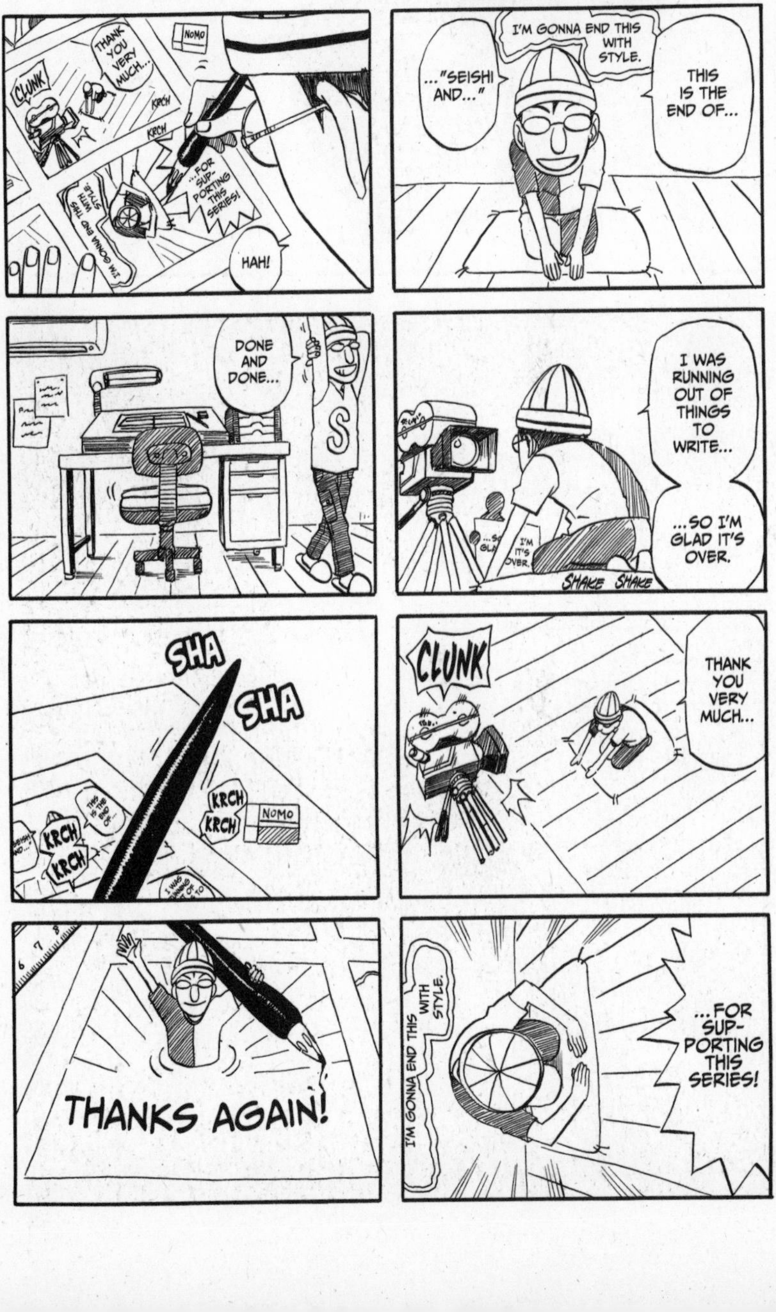
I'M GONNA END THIS WITH STYLE.
THIS IS THE END OF...
..."SEISHI AND..."
NOMO
THANK YOU VERY MUCH...
CLUNK
KRCH
KRCH
...FOR SUP-PORTING THIS SERIES!
I'M GONNA END THIS WITH STYLE.
HAH!
I WAS RUNNING OUT OF THINGS TO WRITE...
...SO I'M GLAD IT'S OVER.
I'M IT'S OVER.
SHAKE SHAKE
DONE AND DONE...
S
CLUNK
THANK YOU VERY MUCH...
SHA
SHA
KRCH
KRCH
NOMO
THIS IS THE END OF...
KRCH
KRCH
...FOR SUP-PORTING THIS SERIES!
I'M GONNA END THIS WITH STYLE.
THANKS AGAIN!

O-PARTS HUNTER - ASSISTANTS

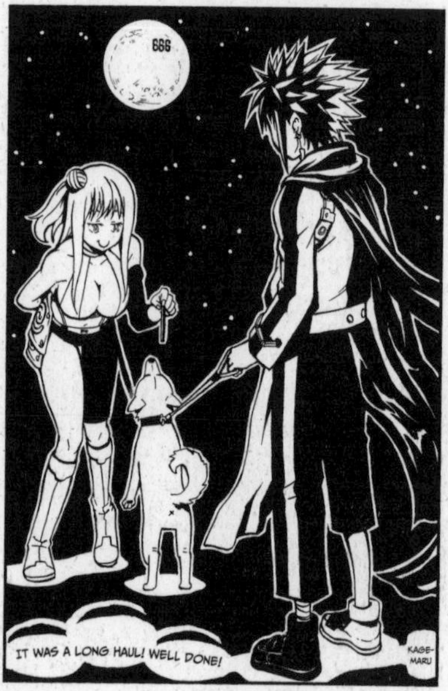
666
IT WAS A LONG HAUL! WELL DONE!
KAGE-MARU

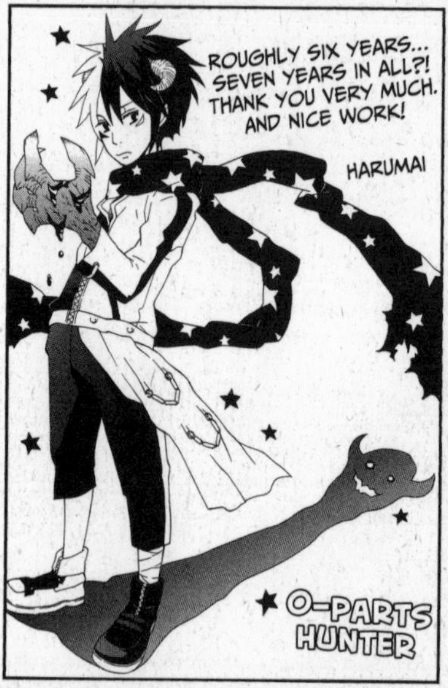
ROUGHLY SIX YEARS... SEVEN YEARS IN ALL?! THANK YOU VERY MUCH. AND NICE WORK!
HARUMAI
O-PARTS HUNTER

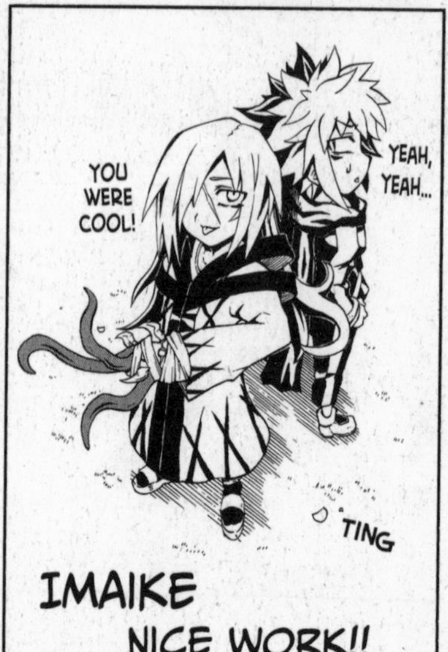
YEAH, YEAH...
YOU WERE COOL!
TING
IMAIKE
NICE WORK!!

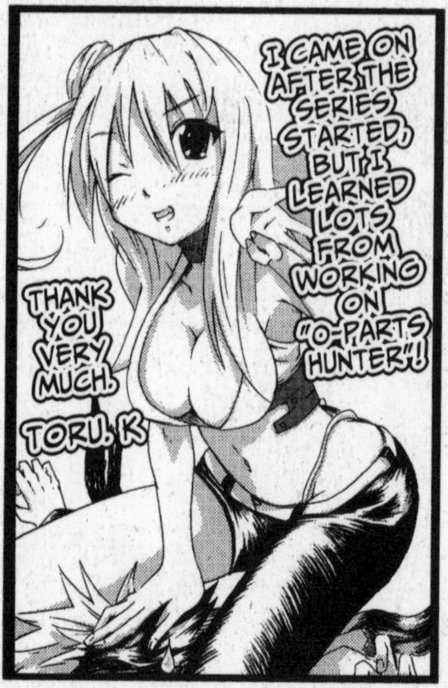
I CAME ON AFTER THE SERIES STARTED, BUT I LEARNED LOTS FROM WORKING ON "O-PARTS HUNTER"!
THANK YOU VERY MUCH.
TORU. K

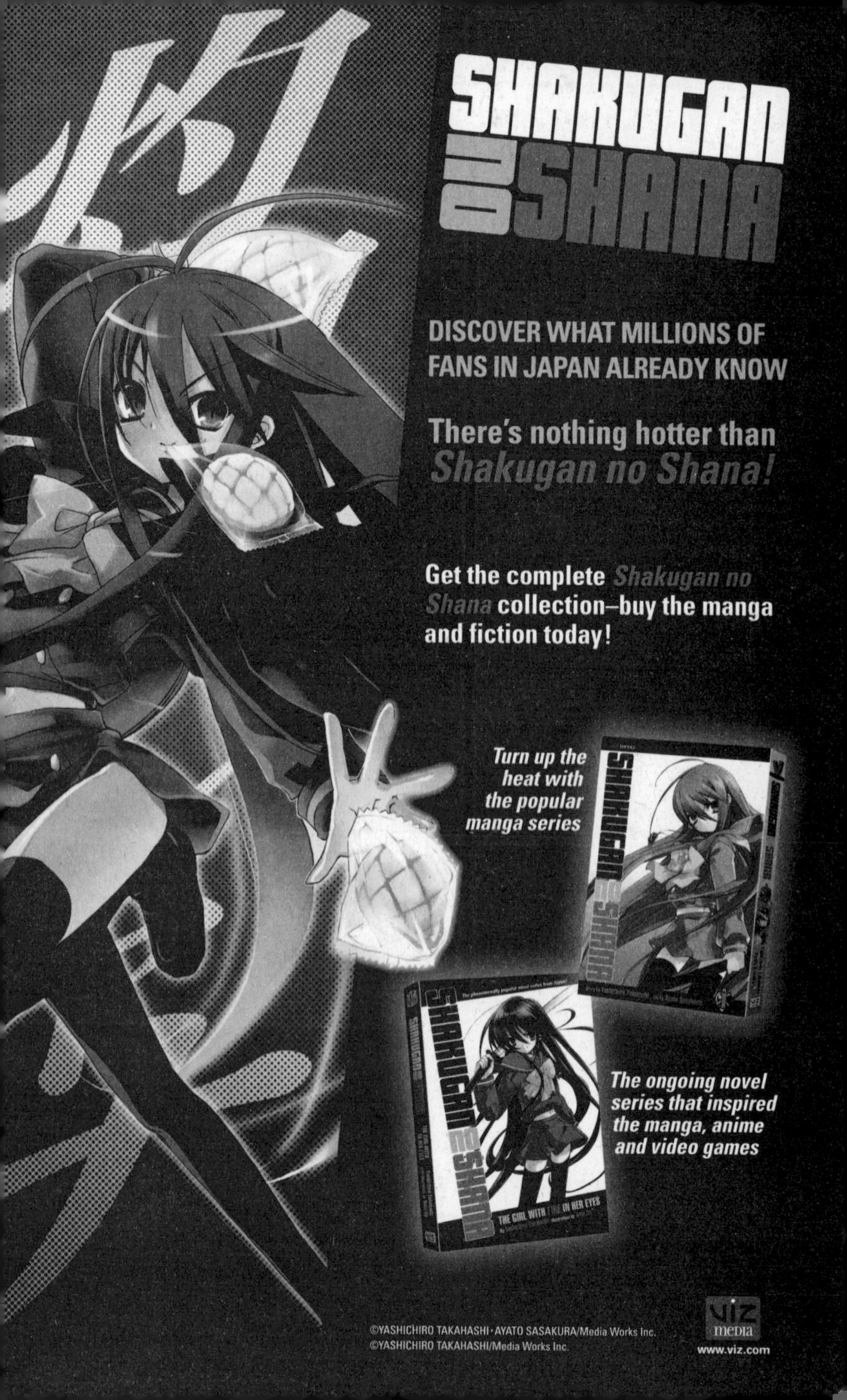
SHAKUGAN NO SHANA
DISCOVER WHAT MILLIONS OF FANS IN JAPAN ALREADY KNOW
There's nothing hotter than Shakugan no Shana!
Get the complete Shakugan no Shana collection–buy the manga and fiction today!
Turn up the heat with the popular manga series
The ongoing novel series that inspired the manga, anime and video games
THE GIRL WITH FIRE IN HER EYES
©YASHICHIRO TAKAHASHI · AYATO SASAKURA/Media Works Inc.
©YASHICHIRO TAKAHASHI/Media Works Inc.
viz media
www.viz.com

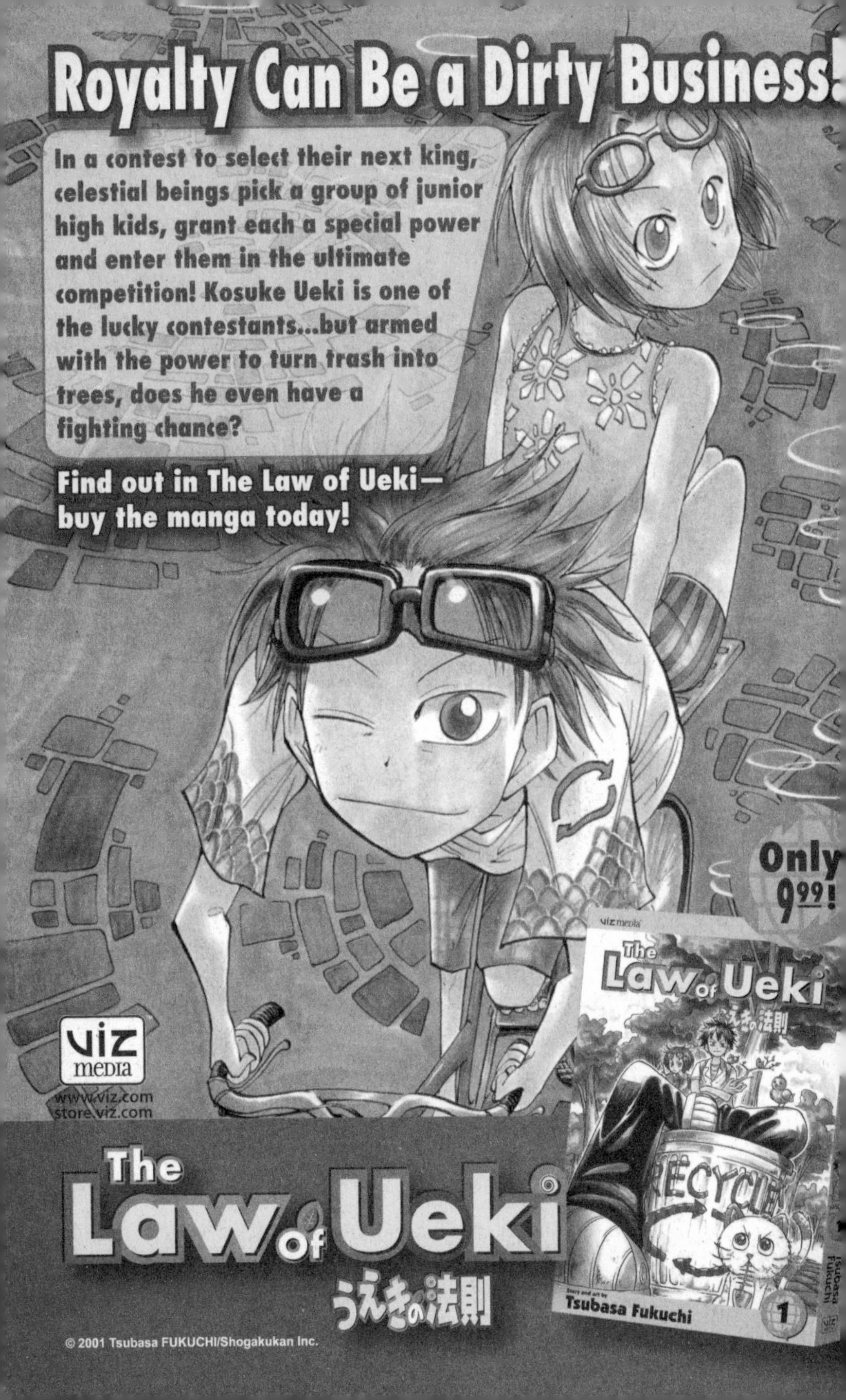
Royalty Can Be a Dirty Business!
In a contest to select their next king, celestial beings pick a group of junior high kids, grant each a special power and enter them in the ultimate competition! Kosuke Ueki is one of the lucky contestants...but armed with the power to turn trash into trees, does he even have a fighting chance?
Find out in The Law of Ueki—buy the manga today!
Only 9.99!
viz media
The Law of Ueki
うえきの法則
RECYCLE
Tsubasa Fukuchi
1
viz media
www.viz.com
store.viz.com
The Law of Ueki
うえきの法則
© 2001 Tsubasa FUKUCHI/Shogakukan Inc.

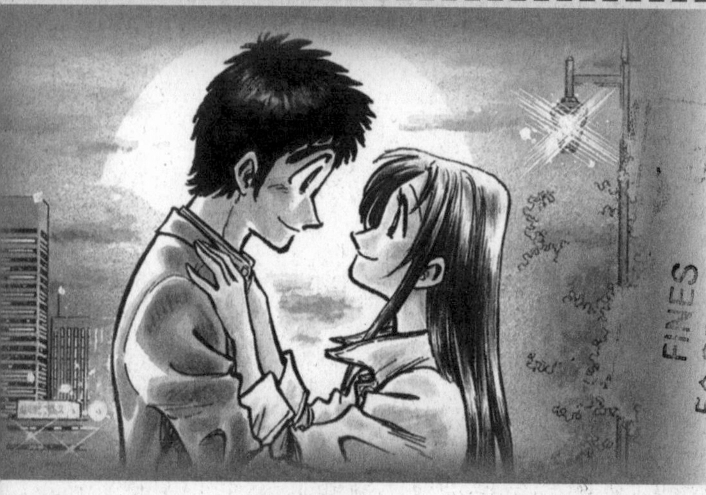

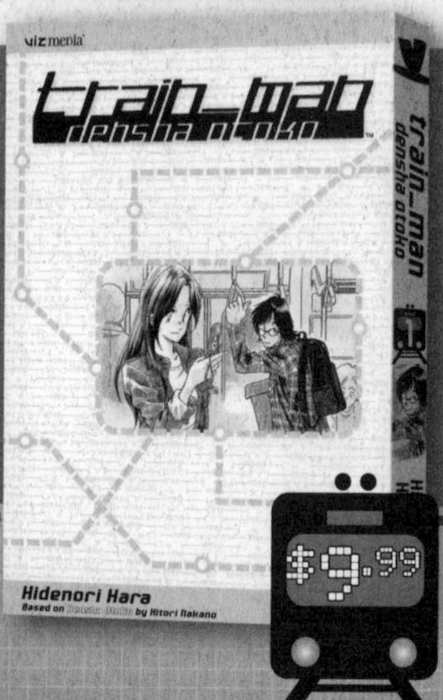

viz media
train_man densha otoko
Hidenori Hara
$9.99

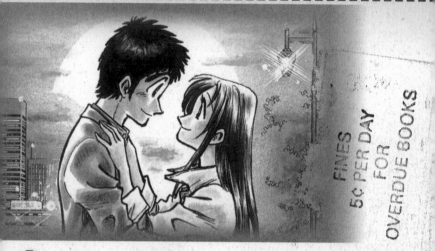

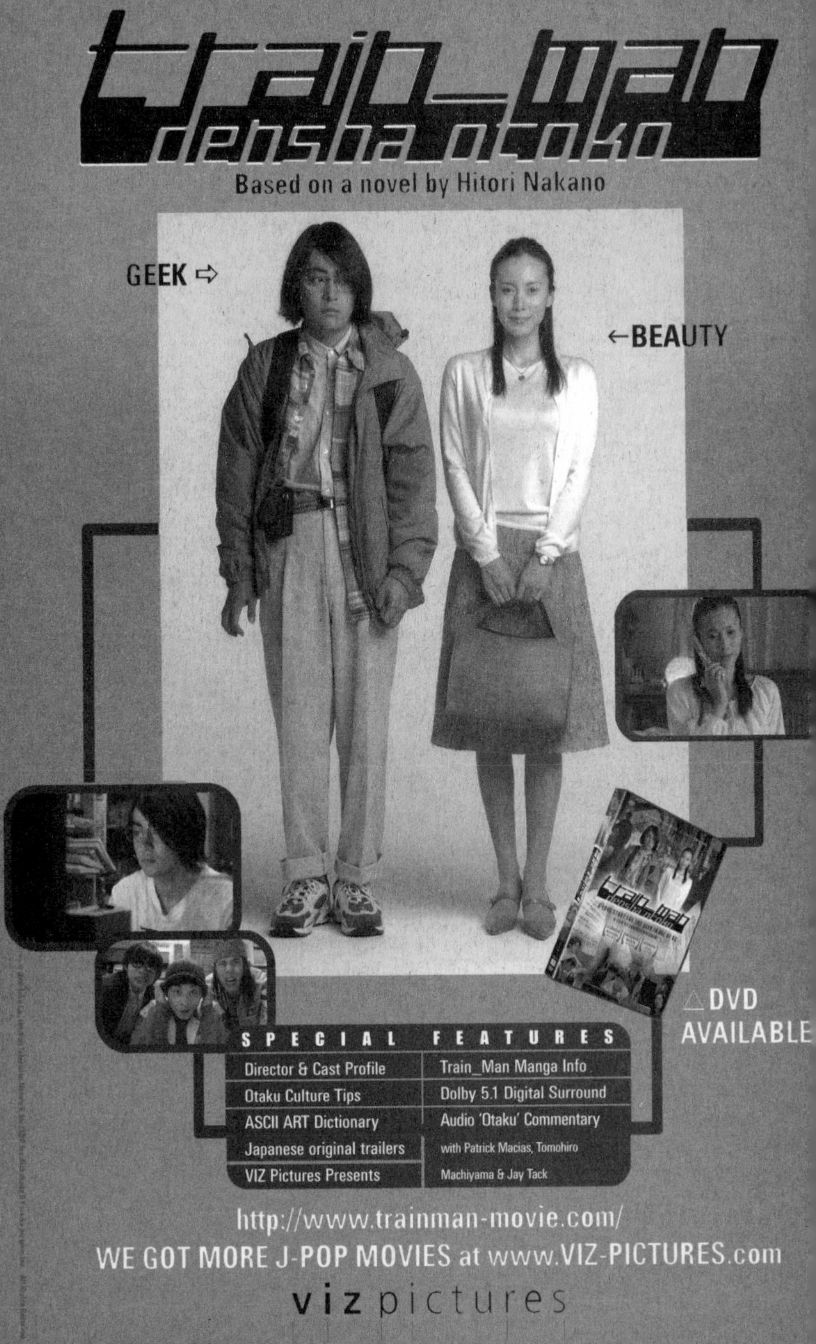
train_man
densha otoko
Based on a novel by Hitori Nakano
GEEK ⇨
←BEAUTY
△DVD
AVAILABLE
SPECIAL FEATURES
Director & Cast Profile
Otaku Culture Tips
ASCII ART Dictionary
Japanese original trailers
VIZ Pictures Presents
Train_Man Manga Info
Dolby 5.1 Digital Surround
Audio 'Otaku' Commentary
with Patrick Macias, Tomohiro Machiyama & Jay Tack
http://www.trainman-movie.com/
WE GOT MORE J-POP MOVIES at www.VIZ-PICTURES.com
viz pictures